KT-367-275

A Dictionary of Contemporary France

by

Richard Aplin
University of Leicester

with the collaboration of

Joseph Montchamp
Agrégé de l'Université

Hodder & Stoughton
LONDON SYDNEY AUCKLAND

British Library Cataloguing in Publication Data

Aplin, Richard
  Dictionary of Contemporary France
  I. Title
  944

  ISBN 0-340-55753-2

First published 1993
Impression number   10 9 8 7 6 5 4 3 2 1
Year   1998 1997 1996 1995 1994 1993

© 1993 Richard Aplin

All rights reserved. No part of this publication may be reproduced or
transmitted in any form or by any means, electronic or mechanical, including
photocopy, recording, or any information storage and retrieval system, without
permission in writing from the publisher or under licence from the Copyright
Licensing Agency Limited. Further details of such licences (for reprographic
reproduction) may be obtained from the Copyright Licensing Agency Limited,
of 90 Tottenham Court Road, London W1P 9HE.

Typeset by Rowland Phototypesetting Limited, Bury St Edmunds, Suffolk.
Printed in Great Britain for the educational publishing division of Hodder and
Stoughton Limited, Mill Road, Dunton Green, Sevenoaks, Kent TN13 2YA by
Clays Ltd, St Ives plc.

To the memory of my father,
Thomas James Aplin (1918–1992)

Foreword

This dictionary is intended for readers of French who wish to have an explanation of the terms and acronyms they meet in the course of their study of the contemporary French press, where a bilingual dictionary does not provide an adequate reference. It is, therefore, addressed to all students of French beyond elementary level, as well as those readers whose knowledge of the language is advanced but who are unfamiliar with some of the detail of the contemporary French situation.

I have made no attempt to include tourist gazeteer or culinary references, as there already exists a large range of specialist works which meet those needs. Instead, I have concentrated on those terms which arise in material such as *Le Point*, *Le Monde* or *L'Express* which are unexplained in the original text because the writer assumes that no further explanation is necessary. These terms tend to relate to institutions, public figures and recent historical events. The final selection is necessarily personal, but I have attempted to apply some criteria which will explain why, for instance, some famous names seem to be missing. Generally speaking, I have interpreted 'contemporary' as being post-1970. The reader will, however, find examples of events and personalities which pre-date this time, as there are some which simply cannot be excluded on grounds of date alone, as their influence on the contemporary scene is still of major significance.

The arrangement of the entries is on strict alphabetical lines, regardless of the spaces between words. Acronyms are provided in the main body of the text with their full form, and their explanation will be found under the full reference. Each word found in capital letters refers the reader to another keyword, and the intention is to indicate as wide a range of entries relating to the original keyword as possible so that as full a picture of the general area can be seen, without entries repeating the content of others.

I have taken the *Quid 1992* interpretation of *agglomération* as the standard, and populations of *départements* and *communes*

are also taken from that edition. Under entries for the
départements, urban areas with populations of over 10,000 are
listed, except in the Paris area, in which the minimum
population for a *commune* to qualify is higher, the exact figure
depending on the level of urbanisation of the area.

I have been immensely encouraged in the task of preparing this
book by family, friends and colleagues. Joseph Montchamp
has been an inspiration of many of the entries, and has also
been invaluable in checking the accuracy of much of the rest.
His comments have kept me amused as well as informed.
Adrian Stokes and Tom Whiteside have encouraged me to
keep going when problems arose, generously providing between
them technological and moral support. My wife, Sheilah, has
taken on board the detailed checking of the text, an unenviable
task carried out under very tight deadlines. She and my
daughters, Elizabeth and Caroline, have stoically tolerated my
appropriation of their time and space in order to complete this
project. If the book has any worth at all, it is due to the
combined efforts of all who have been involved.

Richard Aplin
Leicester

About the author

Richard Aplin taught French in comprehensive schools in Wiltshire and Oxfordshire for 16 years before taking up posts in teacher education. He is currently Modern Languages Tutor and Head of the Secondary Postgraduate Certificate of Education course at the University of Leicester.

He has written and co-written a number of language course materials published by Hodder & Stoughton, amongst which *Introduction to Language* and *Orientations*, and has written scripts for BBC Schools Radio.

AB See: *ALLOCATION DE BASE*

ACADÉMICIEN
A member of one of the learned ACADÉMIES. The phrase
'*Membre de l'Académie*', if not otherwise specified, normally
refers to membership of the ACADÉMIE FRANÇAISE.

ACADÉMICIENNE See: *YOURCENAR, MARGUERITE*

ACADÉMIE
The administrative area for the organisation of the public
education service, an *académie* is presided over by a RECTEUR
who has overall responsibility for educational affairs in the area.
A corps of INSPECTEURS, responsible to the recteur, maintains
a monitoring and evaluation role over the LYCÉES. There are 26
académies in metropolitan France and two overseas (ANTILLES-
GUYANNE, RÉUNION).
   The term *académie* is also used for the learned bodies
composed of distinguished elected members, five of which
form the INSTITUT DE FRANCE. '*L'Académie*' usually refers to the
ACADÉMIE FRANÇAISE. See also: INSPECTEUR D'ACADÉMIE

ACADÉMIE DES BEAUX-ARTS
Tracing its foundation back to 1648 when Le Brun founded the
Académie royale de peinture et sculpture, and Colbert's
foundation of the *Académie royale d'architecture* in 1671, the
Académie des beaux-arts now includes members from the fields
of sculpture, painting, architecture, engraving, musical
composition, cinema and television. There are also 15
distinguished foreign associates. The *Académie des beaux-arts*
is affiliated to the INSTITUT DE FRANCE.

ACADÉMIE DES INSCRIPTIONS ET BELLES-LETTRES
Originally known at the time of its inception in 1663 as the

Petite Académie, it now has a role in supporting studies of antiquity and sponsors archaeological investigations. There are 45 full members. The *Académie des inscriptions et belles-lettres* is affiliated to the INSTITUT DE FRANCE.

ACADÉMIE DES SCIENCES
Founded in 1666, the *Académie des sciences* has 130 full members drawn from all the principal branches of science. It is divided into two major divisions – mathematical and physical sciences, and chemical, natural and medical sciences – each division being further sub-divided into sections. It maintains international links with similar national bodies. The *Académie des sciences* is affiliated to the INSTITUT DE FRANCE.

ACADÉMIE DES SCIENCES MORALES ET POLITIQUES
The most recently founded (1795) of the five ACADÉMIES in the INSTITUT DE FRANCE, it has 50 members, drawn largely from the fields of philosophy, ethics, sociology, law, economics, history and geography.

ACADÉMIE FRANÇAISE
Founded in 1635 by Louis XIII, at the behest of Cardinal Richelieu, with the role of affirming the French language as the national language of administration and culture, and of providing the standard model for national and international use. It is composed of 40 elected members, one of whom takes the role of permanent secretary. Each ACADÉMICIEN, who must be of French nationality, occupies a numbered FAUTEUIL until his or her death. The members are drawn largely from the ranks of eminent scholars or creative writers.

In its role of approving the standard form of the French language, it has produced a number of editions of the *Dictionnaire de l'Académie française*. The first volume of the ninth edition appeared in 1986, and the entire edition has, at the time of writing, reached letter E. In addition, the *Académie* makes periodic pronouncements about acceptable and unacceptable usage of French, and although this creates much public interest, its deliberations are not always taken entirely seriously.

It also grants a number of literary prizes, the award of which guarantees critical interest and respectable sales figures to an author.

The *Académie française* is affiliated to the INSTITUT DE FRANCE.

ACADÉMIE GONCOURT
A group of 10 authors whose decision each November, delivered theatrically at the Drouant restaurant in Paris, on the award of a literary prize of 50 francs to a writer of prose, creates avid interest and speculation each year. The award was created by Edmond de Goncourt's will in memory of his brother Jules, who had died 26 years earlier in 1870. It was first awarded in 1903.

The restaurant traditionally pays for the meal, and the members offer a tip. The event is surrounded by mystique and excitement. Some of the winners have become international successes, the highest sales having been achieved by André MALRAUX's *La Condition humaine*, winner in 1933.

Since 1977, the *secrétaire général* has been François NOURRISSIER.

ACADÉMIE NATIONALE DE MÉDECINE
Often referred to as the *Académie de médecine*, its history dates back to a foundation by Louis XVIII in 1820. It is composed of 130 eminent specialists, divided into a number of sections, including general and specialised medicine, general and specialised surgery, epidemiology and public health, biological science, veterinary science and pharmacology. It has associations with similar national bodies in over 100 countries.

ACCOR
The controlling company which owns hotel chains such as MERCURE, NOVOTEL and IBIS/URBIS.

ACCUSÉ DE RÉCEPTION
A formal receipt or acknowledgement certifying that a document has been received.

ACO See: *ACTION CATHOLIQUE OUVRIÈRE*

ACTE AUTHENTIQUE
A deed which has been authenticated by a NOTAIRE or a law

officer with appropriate competence. An *acte* is drawn up on special forms which carry stamp duty (PAPIER TIMBRÉ). Perhaps the most common deed is that relating to property sale and purchase.

ACTE DE NOTORIÉTÉ
A document which can be provided in emergency by the JUGE of the TRIBUNAL D'INSTANCE of the place of birth or residence, which certifies the details normally included in a birth or marriage certificate.

ACTION CATHOLIQUE OUVRIÈRE (ACO)
A militant lay catholic organisation, with an evangelical mission among workers. It tends to be critical of conservative catholicism.

ACTION DIRECTE
A left-wing terrorist group which carried out a number of bomb attacks against establishment and government targets, as well as American and Jewish interests in France during the 1980s.

ACTION HUMANITAIRE
Within the MITTERRAND government, a SECRÉTAIRE D'ÉTAT has responsibility for monitoring and encouraging humanitarian attitudes.

ACTION OUVRIÈRE ET PROFESSIONNELLE (AOP)
A political pressure group within the RASSEMBLEMENT POUR LA RÉPUBLIQUE, set up in 1977 to promote the party's influence in the workplace.

ACTUEL
A monthly current affairs magazine with a readership of about 200,000.

ADAMOV, ARTHUR (1908–1970)
A dramatist of Armenian origin, who lived in France from the age of 16. He was prominent in the post-war theatre, and his work is characterised by demonstrations of people's loneliness and inability to communicate.

ADIDAS
An international producer of sports and leisure clothing and accessories, particularly known for footwear, formerly under German control but now owned by Bernard TAPIE.

ADMINISTRATION
This is the generic term for the French government bureaucracy. Reference to '*l'Administration*', unqualified by the name of a particular administrative branch, is an acknowledgement of the highly centralised machine of the civil service.

AÉROPORT DE PARIS
The state-owned company which operates the three civil airports for Paris, Charles-de-Gaulle at ROISSY, ORLY and Le BOURGET, and a number of minor aerodromes within a 50 kilometre radius of the capital.

AÉROSPATIALE
Also known as SNIAS (*Société nationale des industries aéronautiques et spatiales*), this state-owned company employs about 12,000 in the area of Toulouse, and has other plants near Marseille and Nantes. The firm was a partner in the Anglo-French CONCORDE project, and is the major French participant in the construction of the European Airbus.
    Three-fifths of its turnover is accounted for by its construction of arms.

AÉROTRAIN
An experimental train, riding on, and guided by, horizontal and vertical cushions of air, was placed in experimental service on a special 18 kilometre track near Orléans in 1969. Various feasibility studies have been developed since then, including a proposal for a system in the Marseille area.

AFARS See: *DJIBOUTI*

AFD See: *ALLOCATION DE FIN DE DROITS*

AFFAIRES ÉTRANGÈRES, MINISTÈRE DES
The foreign ministry of France, based in offices on the Quai d'Orsay in Paris. As well as the MINISTRE D'ÉTAT, there are two

MINISTRES DÉLÉGUÉS, one of whom deals with the FRANCOPHONIE, and a SECRÉTAIRE D'ÉTAT with responsibility for international cultural relations.

AFFICHAGE

Throughout France, one often sees on walls the defiant words '*Défense d'afficher – loi du 29 juillet 1881*'. This law which mainly concerns the freedom of the press, in fact gives protection only to publicly owned buildings. There are, however, restrictions on advertising hoardings and bill-posting, dating from 1979 and 1980. This particularly relates to environmentally sensitive sites, residential property and rural areas. Damaging monuments with graffiti or other marks carries a penalty of up to two months' imprisonment.

During elections there are different regulations. The paper used for election posters must not be white or in the national *tricolore* colours. There are strict rules about the timing of appearance of posters and the number of sites used.

AFME See: *AGENCE DE L'ENVIRONNEMENT ET DE LA MAÎTRISE DE L'ÉNERGIE*

AFP See: *AGENCE FRANCE-PRESSE*

AGENCE DE L'ENVIRONNEMENT ET DE LA MAÎTRISE DE L'ÉNERGIE (ADEME)

Founded in 1982 as a replacement for a number of bodies aimed at effecting fuel economies, formerly known as the *Agence française pour la maîtrise de l'énergie* (AFME). Its role is to encourage industry, agriculture and domestic users to make improved use of energy supplies, and in particular to explore ways of making better use of energy recycling .

AGENCE FRANCE-PRESSE (AFP)

An autonomous, government sponsored and international news media agency, operating throughout the world. In addition to its press activities, it acts as an information gathering organisation for about 2,000 clients, including major ministries.

AGENCE NATIONALE POUR L'AMÉLIORATION DE L'HABITAT (ANAH)

This body distributes grants to owners of residential property built before 1975 in order to finance improvements in energy saving or insulation. Homes built before 1948 qualify for grants to bring the property up to contemporary standards of construction, sanitation, etc.

AGENCE NATIONALE POUR L'EMPLOI (ANPE)
This is an agency operating on behalf of the MINISTÈRE DU TRAVAIL, which acts as a support for those seeking employment, training or career advice and provides a service to employers seeking employees. In the early 1990s its aims are to improve its local accessibility, and to develop co-operative programmes with other agencies. For unemployed people claiming the ALLOCATION DE CHÔMAGE, it acts as the first stage in the process. Claimants have to register with ANPE in order to prove their entitlement to benefit. Certain unemployed people qualify for financial support from ANPE for expenses incurred in their search for work.

AGENT IMMOBILIER
An estate agent, usually self-employed or working as a member of a small firm, and locally based. The profession is self-regulating, and bona fide agents are members of the national professional associations, and register their businesses at the local PRÉFECTURE. Each agency sets its own fees, and these have by law to be displayed on the business's premises.

AGENT TITULAIRE
Civil servants in France, once they have been recruited to a permanent post by CONCOURS, have tenure of employment and, except in case of gross misdeeds, cannot be dismissed from government service until compulsory retirement age.

AGF See: *ASSURANCES GÉNÉRALES DE FRANCE*

AGGLOMÉRATION
An urban area comprising a number of administrative districts or COMMUNES. It can be a relatively small town area with a suburb attached, or a group of neighbouring towns and villages, provided at least two *communes* are involved.

AGRÉGATION
The most highly sought after CONCOURS in the field of secondary

education. A fixed number of PROFESSEUR AGRÉGÉ posts are available in specific subjects each year, and the number of candidates usually outnumbers the places available by an enormous margin. Thus, in English in 1990, 195 posts were available, and 178 appointments were made, from 922 candidates. In philosophy all 87 posts available were filled, but from 737 candidates. There are separate conditions for promotions to the *Agrégation interne* from within the teaching force.

AGRICULTURE ET DE LA FORÊT, MINISTÈRE DE L'
This ministry has played a significant part in representing the interests of French farmers in shaping the Common Agricultural Policy of the European Community. It has also had a major influence on coping with the effects of the substantial demographic change in rural areas since the Second World War. See also: EXODE RURAL

AIDE AU RETOUR
Since the mid 1970s there has been a general policy to discourage immigration into France, except from member-states of the European Community. *Aide au retour* is one of the tactics used to put the policy into effect. It aims to provide support for those of foreign nationality who decide to return to their country of origin, and is linked to cases where the people concerned are victims of long-term unemployment. The policy was suspended when the Socialist government took office in 1981, but was resumed in 1983. It is a controversial issue, as those involved are not usually white Europeans, and the policy has been criticised as racist.

Nevertheless, France maintains its tradition of harbouring refugees. See also: IMMIGRATION; OFFICE FRANÇAIS DE PROTECTION DES RÉFUGIÉS ET APATRIDES

AIDE FRANÇAISE
International aid provided by the French Government comprising technical and cultural co-operation programmes, grants and loans, food aid and financial support. About 1.5 per cent of the gross national product is committed to this programme annually.

Countries most indebted to France are those in the FRANCOPHONIE community in Africa. Similarly, the bulk of the technical co-operation programmes are carried out there. The cultural co-operation programme is more widely disseminated throughout the world. See also: SERVICE NATIONAL

AIDE JUDICIAIRE
Legal aid, partial or full, is available to those who satisfy certain conditions of income. The claimant is able to nominate legal representatives, but they are not obliged to act on his or her behalf. If no lawyer can be found, the BÂTONNIER, or the equivalent official, will designate a lawyer who is bound to take the case. About 85 per cent of legal aid applications are accepted. If the claimant loses the case, the legal aid will cover only his or her costs.

Limited free legal consultations are available at the MAIRIE for those who do not have the resources to pay for legal advice.

AIDE MÉNAGÈRE
Old people may qualify for home help of up to 60 hours per month, financed by one of the social agencies. The local CENTRE COMMUNAL D'ACTION SOCIALE is the normal body which organises home help.

AIDE PERSONNALISÉE AU LOGEMENT (APL)
A payment made to those who satisfy certain conditions of taxable income to support rental payments, property loan repayments and improvement works to property. After 1993 the APL will merge with the ALLOCATION LOGEMENT. Payments are made direct to the landlord or loan company by the CAISSE D'ALLOCATIONS FAMILIALES or CAISSE DE MUTUALITÉ SOCIALE AGRICOLE.

AIDE SOCIALE
These comprise social payments to those whose income is low, especially the sick and the elderly, but also to children who are otherwise not beneficiaries of the SÉCURITÉ SOCIALE system. The *Aide sociale* payments are administered by the DIRECTION DÉPARTEMENTALE DE L'ACTION SANITAIRE ET SOCIALE (DDASS).

Refund of social payments made to the elderly can be demanded
from the estate after their death.

AIN
A DÉPARTEMENT in the RHÔNE-ALPES region, named after a
tributary of the Rhône, with a 1990 population of 471,016. The
CHEF-LIEU is Bourg-en-Bresse (urban area 55,784), with metal,
engineering and goods vehicle industries. Other towns include
Ambérieu-en-Bugey (12,235) an important rail junction;
Bellegarde-sur-Valserine (11,968) – metallurgy, printing and
clothing; Oyonnax (30,471) – plastics and optical industries.
The nuclear industry is well established and includes the
European Centre CERN at Ferney-Voltaire on the Swiss border,
and a power station at Bugey. Smaller towns have a range of
light industry.

The *Département* is largely agricultural, with pigs, poultry
and cattle being the main sources of activity, with some market
gardening.

Voting patterns show a consistent support for the Centre
Right. In the 1981 and 1988 ÉLECTIONS PRÉSIDENTIELLES, there
were small majorities for Valéry GISCARD D'ESTAING and Jacques
CHIRAC respectively, and the 1992 ÉLECTIONS CANTONALES
confirmed the control of the UNION POUR LA DÉMOCRATIE
FRANÇAISE over the CONSEIL GÉNÉRAL.

Code départemental: 01

AIRBUS-INDUSTRIE
The French and German dominated European consortium
which produces the Airbus. The main French partner is
AÉROSPATIALE.

AIR FRANCE
The largely state-owned international airline, run on
commercial lines. It also owns a number of subsidiary companies,
connected with air travel. Air France serves Europe, America,
Asia and most of Africa, with its greatest traffic in Europe
and to North America. Its fleet is mainly American in origin,
but also includes Airbus, and CONCORDE. From the 1960s it
operated a number of French-built Caravelles.

AIR INTER

The internal airline owned principally by other state-controlled transport interests. It operates jointly with AIR FRANCE and the UNION DES TRANSPORTS AÉRIENS on certain routes, and in competition with private, regional carriers. The fleet is largely composed of Airbus.

AIR LIQUIDE

The largest European company involved in the production and distribution of industrial gases, and also the fifth largest French concern in the chemicals industry.

AISNE

A DÉPARTEMENT in the PICARDIE region, named after the tributary of the Oise which passes through it. The 1990 population was 537,222. The CHEF-LIEU is Laon (urban area 27,431) and other AGGLOMÉRATIONS are Château-Thierry (22,696); Chauny (20,078); Hirson (12,205); St-Quentin (71,887); Soissons (47,305); Tergnier (25,506). The principal employment of the *Département* is in metallurgy and mechanical engineering, while the agricultural bias is towards cereals. The Aisne holds the record for the highest production of sugar beet in France. Unemployment has been relatively high as the traditional industries decline.

The voting patterns show support for the Left, and from 1980–1983 Saint-Quentin had a communist majority in the town council. François MITTERRAND had comfortable majorities here in the 1981 and 1988 ÉLECTIONS PRÉSIDENTIELLES, although the small majority of the Centre Right on the CONSEIL GÉNÉRAL was confirmed in the 1992 ÉLECTIONS CANTONALES.

Code départemental: 02.

AIX-MARSEILLE

There are three universities divided between the two cities of Aix-en-Provence and Marseille. *Aix-Marseille I* (or the *Université de Provence*) has campuses in both cities and provides courses in history, arts and humanities (Aix) and mathematics and science (Marseille) for 22,000 students. *Aix-Marseille II* is based in Marseille and its 19,000 students read economics, pharmacy, medicine, dentistry and social sciences. *Aix-Marseille III*, in Aix, concentrates on law, economics, politics and management, and has 19,000 students.

ALAT See: *AVIATION LÉGÈRE DE L'ARMÉE DE TERRE*

ALBIN MICHEL
A Paris-based publishing house.

ALCOOL
There is a serious problem of alcoholism in France, and government-sponsored measures are being undertaken to reduce it. It is estimated that there are 4.5 million French adults with alcohol dependency, and an increase in alcohol consumption among young people is a disturbing trend.

Licensing laws restrict the sale of alcohol in cafés to minors. Children below 14 may not buy alcohol, nor may unaccompanied children below 16. Spirits may not be sold to under 18s. It is illegal to sell alcohol in sports grounds, swimming pools and other premises where young people gather for leisure activities. Neither is it legal for alcohol to be promoted in advertising or publicity which is aimed at minors.

Transporting alcohol is subject to tax, known as the CONGÉ. Containers of alcohol which do not carry the special *capsule congé* must have tax invoices relating to them raised before they are transported.

In order to exert greater control over the production of alcohol, the traditional hereditary right to distil alcohol, privately held by BOUILLEURS DE CRU, has been abolished. Stills are destroyed by the DOUANES on the death of the licensed owner, or of the surviving spouse.

Alcohol-related disease is quoted as the third most frequent cause of death in France, with particularly high rates in the NORD-PAS-DE-CALAIS, BRETAGNE, and HAUTE-NORMANDIE regions. The incidence of alcoholism is lower in the traditional wine-producing areas of the south. The lowest rate is recorded in CORSE. The proportion of deaths caused by alcohol and cirrhosis of the liver rose in the 1960s, but has declined steadily since

1975. The average annual consumption for each French adult was 32 litres in 1989, a considerable fall from 55 litres in 1979. See also: ALCOOL AU VOLANT

ALCOOL AU VOLANT
It is calculated that in France more than 4,000 road deaths annually are directly related to alcohol consumption. Forty per cent of drivers found responsible for causing death are over the legal limit of alcohol in the blood. There are currently more stringent measures in force in order to reduce this figure.

Since 1983, it has been a criminal offence to drive with more than 80 mg of alcohol in 1 ml of blood, or 40 mg in 1 ml of exhaled breath. Exceeding this limit can lead to a prison sentence of at least one month, up to one year, and/or fines of at least 8,000 francs, as well as temporary or permanent disqualification from driving. If the offence is combined with causing a death or injury, there is automatic disqualification.

There are now further measures in place to restrict the advertising of ordinary quality wines, and to discourage the consumption of alcohol when working or travelling. See also: ALCOOTEST

ALCOOTEST
The alcohol test can be administered by police on drivers at random checks and always in the case of a suspected offence or accident. Either a breath or blood sample is taken. See also: ALCOOL AU VOLANT

ALGÉRIE
An independent republic in North Africa which was part of the French empire, having been colonised steadily from the early nineteenth century. A particularly valuable commodity to France were the oil reserves in the Sahara. Constitutionally, from 1947 until independence in 1962, Algérie was part of France, and contained DÉPARTEMENTS. However, only citizens of French nationality (approximately 10 per cent of the whole) had full political rights. The Muslim African majority were effectively second-class citizens.

A growing nationalist disaffection with the French presence

manifested itself in an increasingly violent struggle for independence, harshly repressed. The period 1954–1962 was marked by a war between French military forces and the *Armée de libération nationale*. The severity of the war (over 180,000 combatants killed, as well as about 35,000 civilians), was a major factor in the downfall of the QUATRIÈME RÉPUBLIQUE. Despite considerable difficulties, including a military officers' revolt in the capital, Alger, and a sustained campaign by right-wing terrorists, the ORGANISATION DE L'ARMÉE SECRÈTE, DE GAULLE received broad support for ending the war by granting independence. This was followed by a mass emigration of Europeans from the country to France, and especially to the south of France. The French army finally left in 1964.

Since 1962, France has maintained generally close if uneasy relations with Algérie. Algerians make up the largest national group of immigrants in France, and tend to suffer most from any racist backlash at times of economic downturn or rise in unemployment. See also: AIDE AU RETOUR; HARKIS; IMMIGRATION; PIED-NOIR

ALLIANCE FRANÇAISE

A private organisation which aims to spread the influence of French culture and language internationally. Its principal activity is by means of language and civilisation courses. It is strongest in South America, in terms of numbers attending courses.

ALLIER

A DÉPARTEMENT in the AUVERGNE region with a population in 1990 of 357,710, named after the tributary of the Loire which runs through it. The population shows a fall of about 30,000 since the mid 1960s. The CHEF-LIEU is Moulins (AGGLOMÉRATION 41,715), an historic town with a wide range of metal and engineering industries, electronics, footwear, musical instruments, animal foodstuffs and security equipment. The other large urban areas are at Montluçon (63,018) – steel, chemicals, tyres, engineering, electronics, clothing and furniture; and VICHY (61,566), a spa town with confectionery, beauty products and food-processing industries, leather goods, plastics, clothing and furniture. The COMMUNE of Saint-Yorre is one of the richest in France, earning five centimes from every bottle of its mineral water.

Rearing sheep and beef and dairy cattle is the principal agricultural activity, and there is some cereal production.

In both the 1981 and 1988 ÉLECTIONS PRÉSIDENTIELLES, François MITTERRAND received a majority of the votes from the Allier, and the DÉPUTÉS elected in 1988 are Socialists or Communists. The SÉNATEURS are from the Centre, and in the 1992 ÉLECTIONS CANTONALES, the Centre Right reaffirmed its control over the CONSEIL GÉNÉRAL.

Code départemental: 03

ALLOCATION
An allowance payable from SÉCURITÉ SOCIALE or other public funds, if certain conditions are met. The allocations listed below cover most cases, although there are some exceptions in detail.

ALLOCATION ASSISTANTE MATERNELLE
Payable by TRIMESTRE at a fixed rate to help pay for a registered child-minder's fees, for a child of three years or younger. The claimant must be a contributor to the appropriate SÉCURITÉ SOCIALE scheme.

ALLOCATION AUX ADULTES HANDICAPÉS
Payable monthly to French nationals and permanent residents from EC member-states, or refugees. Those eligible must be between the ages of 20 and 60, unable to find employment because of at least 80 per cent incapacity and on a low income. It also gives free sickness insurance through the SÉCURITÉ SOCIALE. Entitlement is reviewed every 10 years by the COTOREP, and the allowance is paid by the CAISSE D'ALLOCATIONS FAMILIALES.

ALLOCATION AUX MÈRES DE FAMILLE
Payable monthly to women whose husbands have been SÉCURITÉ SOCIALE contributors, aged 65 or over, who do not receive any other pension, and who have raised at least five children over a period of nine years before the children's sixteenth birthdays.

ALLOCATION AUX VIEUX TRAVAILLEURS SALARIÉS (AVTS)

The standard State old-age pension. Payable to those of 65 years of age and above who have worked and paid contributions to the SÉCURITÉ SOCIALE for at least 25 years, and whose income is not greater than a basic minimum, reviewed annually.

ALLOCATION COMPENSATRICE DE HANDICAP

Payable to a disabled person who is at least 16 years old, of at least 80 per cent incapacity, and who either needs the services of a permanent carer or extra help to carry out employment. The amount depends on circumstances and is paid monthly. The COTOREP administers the fund. Carers benefit from free old-age insurance through the SÉCURITÉ SOCIALE. This allowance can be received in addition to the ALLOCATION AUX ADULTES HANDICAPÉS.

ALLOCATION DE BASE (AB)

The basic unemployment benefit payable in case of involuntary redundancy. The payment is of a proportion of the average wage or salary received in the last year of employment, up to a certain maximum which is lower than the SMIC. The absolute maximum period of benefit is three years nine months, but the proportion of the basic sum paid reduces over this period. Claimants up to the age of 57 have to register their willingness to seek other work. The ASSEDIC administers the *Allocation de base*. See also: ALLOCATION DE FIN DE DROITS

ALLOCATION DE CHÔMAGE See: *ALLOCATION DE BASE*

ALLOCATION D'ÉDUCATION SPÉCIALE

If a disabled child (below 20 years old) needs special education, and fees are paid by the parents or guardians, an allowance is payable.

ALLOCATION DE FIN DE DROITS (AFD)

Payable to the long-term unemployed who no longer qualify for the ALLOCATION DE BASE. The normal maximum entitlement is for two years and three months, depending on age and length of employment. Higher payments are possible for older claimants and for those aged above 57, the payment continues until retirement age. See also: ALLOCATION DE SOLIDARITÉ

ALLOCATION DE GARDE D'ENFANT À DOMICILE
Available to all households where both parents work, and where a nanny is employed at home to care for at least one child aged three years or under. The payment, paid by TRIMESTRE by the CAISSE D'ALLOCATIONS FAMILIALES, covers the cost of the nanny's salary up to a certain maximum. Payments for child-care not covered by this allowance can qualify for tax relief against the IMPÔT SUR LE REVENU. The allowance is halved if combined with the ALLOCATION PARENTALE D'ÉDUCATION.

ALLOCATION DE PARENT ISOLÉ
For a single pregnant woman, or single mother with limited means, this allowance is payable for one year after separation from her partner if she is caring for a child of three years or younger. It is paid monthly by the CAISSE D'ALLOCATIONS FAMILIALES, and gives her the right to free medical care.

ALLOCATION DE SOLIDARITÉ
Payable to the long-term unemployed whose entitlement to the ALLOCATION DE FIN DE DROITS has finished, provided they have worked for at least five years in the 10 years preceding their redundancy, have actively looked for work since, and have no other substantial resources. The ASSEDIC administers the fund, and reviews payments every six months.

ALLOCATION DE SOUTIEN FAMILIAL
Payable to a single parent (until remarried or living with another partner) for the same time as the ALLOCATION FAMILIALE, if the absent partner does not contribute a PENSION ALIMENTAIRE. The CAISSE D'ALLOCATIONS FAMILIALES, which pays the allowance, attempts to recover the payment from the absent partner. The allowance is also paid to a surviving parent or guardian in the event of the death of one or both parents.

ALLOCATION D'INSERTION
Payable to certain groups seeking work, not otherwise entitled

to unemployment benefits, e.g. young people aged below 25, single women, released prisoners, victims of industrial accident or work-related illness, refugees and stateless persons, expatriate workers. Entitlement is for a maximum of 12 months.

ALLOCATION FAMILIALE
Payable to any resident, regardless of nationality, who has at least two children living with him or her, including students, carers or apprentices up to age 20. The allowance is graduated according to the age of the children. The CAISSE D'ALLOCATIONS FAMILIALES or the CAISSE DE MUTUALITÉ SOCIALE AGRICOLE administers the fund.

ALLOCATION LOGEMENT
The CAISSE D'ALLOCATIONS FAMILIALES or the CAISSE DE MUTUALITÉ SOCIALE AGRICOLE administers an additional housing allowance for those who are entitled to a range of other allowances, or to young married couples, young workers, or those with disabled dependants, etc. There are certain conditions regarding the accommodation to be met before an allowance to help payment of rent or mortgage is paid, and the sum payable also depends on a means test. See also AIDE PERSONNALISÉE AU LOGEMENT which replaces this allowance from 1992.

ALLOCATION MILITAIRE
This provides financial compensation to the dependants of a conscript absent on SERVICE MILITAIRE. It is payable by the municipality.

ALLOCATION PARENTALE D'ÉDUCATION
A parent who stops work to care for a new-born or newly-adopted child, and who already looks after two children, is entitled to this allowance until the child is three years old. Returning to work part-time for up to 12 months during this period still entitles the claimant to half-rate benefit. It is only payable to those who have worked for at least two years in the preceding 10, and cannot be claimed in addition to certain other allowances. It can be paid at half-rate in addition to the ALLOCATION DE GARDE D'ENFANT À DOMICILE.

ALLOCATION POUR JEUNE ENFANT
This is payable to a pregnant woman from the fourth month of
pregnancy for nine months without means test, and from then
on until the child's third birthday to a parent with limited means.
The woman must undergo medical examination during
pregnancy and fulfil certain conditions of post-natal care. In the
case of multiple birth, the sum payable is increased until the
children's first birthday.

ALLOCATION RENTRÉE SCOLAIRE
Parents whose children are of compulsory school age (6–16)
can obtain an annual grant, payable in September, from the
CAISSE D'ALLOCATIONS FAMILIALES, provided that they have also
qualified for help in bringing up their children.

ALLOCATION SPÉCIALE VIEILLESSE
Payable to those of 65 years or older who have no other pension
or allowance, and are of limited means. The local municipality
organises payment.

ALOUETTE
A seven-seat helicopter produced by AÉROSPATIALE. Over 3,000
have been built since its introduction in 1959, including those
for military use.

ALPES-DE-HAUTE-PROVENCE
A DÉPARTEMENT in the PROVENCE-ALPES-CÔTE-D'AZUR region,
known until 1970 as Basses-Alpes. The 1990 population was
130,883 and the largest town is Manosque (19,107 inhabitants).
Digne is the CHEF-LIEU (population 16,087). Sparsely populated,
(17 people to one square kilometre) the *Département* is largely
agricultural in its economy, with a specialism in aromatic plants
for the perfume industry. There exist enormous undergound oil
deposits, and the area produces substantial amounts of hydro-
electric power. There is a varied range of tourist attractions,
and water sports and skiing are catered for.

   The people of the *Département* have consistently voted for
the Socialists in recent years, with François MITTERRAND
receiving 53.53 per cent of votes in the 1981 ÉLECTION
PRÉSIDENTIELLE and 53.08 per cent in 1988. The CONSEIL

GÉNÉRAL is, however, finely balanced between the Centre Right and the Left, and in the 1992 ÉLECTIONS CANTONALES Jean-Louis BIANCO, the *Ministre des affaires sociales et de l'intégration*, narrowly lost his seat at Forcalquier.

Code départemental: 04

ALPES-MARITIMES

A fast-growing DÉPARTEMENT in the PROVENCE-ALPES-CÔTE-D'AZUR region with a 1990 population of 971,763, well over double the 1946 figure. The CHEF-LIEU and largest town is Nice (AGGLOMÉRATION 475,459). The Grasse-Cannes-Antibes conurbation has 335,647 inhabitants, and 66,251 live at Menton-Monaco. Other towns outside these areas are Carros (10,747); Vence (18,779).

The *Département* is marked by a large number of well-to-do residents, a lucrative tourist industry, mixed modern industry including a major investment in high-technology at SOPHIA-ANTIPOLIS, right-wing politics, a high crime rate and a fifth of the population over 65 years old.

The votes for Valéry GISCARD D'ESTAING and Jacques CHIRAC in 1981 and 1988 ÉLECTIONS PRÉSIDENTIELLES were 54.37 per cent and 59.02 per cent respectively, and this right-wing strength was further shown in the 1992 ÉLECTIONS CANTONALES, when the only successful FRONT NATIONAL candidate in that election achieved 50.67 per cent in a Nice ward.

Code départemental: 06

ALPHAPAGE

The radiopaging service operated by FRANCE TÉLÉCOM.

ALSACE

The smallest administrative RÉGION in France, on the German/Swiss border, comprising the DÉPARTEMENTS of BAS-RHIN and HAUT-RHIN. Historically Alsace has been closely linked with LORRAINE. Alsace and Lorraine have in modern times been territories of dispute between France and Germany, and after periods of war have been absorbed by the triumphant country.

A distinct regionalism is evident in contemporary Alsace. This is made clearer by a pride in the ALSACIEN dialect, a development of a regional cultural identity, and perhaps a feeling of long-term security encouraged by the Franco-German treaty of 1963.

Alsace does preserve certain local legal and administrative differences from the rest of France. These apply to the laws of property, succession, hunting, commerce and regulations concerning the legal profession, voluntary organisations and social security. A religious concordat exists which gives the churches more privileges and permits the state to pay the salaries of clergy, and railway trains run on the right instead of on the left!

The regional capital is Strasbourg. The region is highly industrialised, with its main industries being mechanical engineering, automobiles, textiles, clothing and steel. There is a substantial production of potassium. Agricultural and food products are cereals, milk, tobacco, wine, as well as 50 per cent of French beer production.

About 30,000 inhabitants cross the German or Swiss frontiers daily to work, particularly in Karlsruhe and Bâle. Politically Alsace has tended to vote for the Right, but in the 1992 ÉLECTIONS RÉGIONALES the VERTS made progress at the expense of the Centre Right.

ALSACE, L'
The daily newspaper published in Mulhouse (BAS-RHIN) with a circulation of about 125,000.

ALSACIEN
A Germanic dialect, spoken in Alsace by 75 per cent of adults, but less frequently by younger people in everyday affairs.

ALSTHOM
A large heavy engineering firm, whose range of products include the TGV railway trains and ocean-going ships.

ALTERNANCE
The CINQUIÈME RÉPUBLIQUE, established by DE GAULLE, had its first test of handing over power peacefully to an opposition group in 1981, when François MITTERRAND won the presidential election. *Alternance* conveys this idea of the smooth handing

over of power from one group to another, as also seen in the
COHABITATION period of 1986–1988. It is also used as a term to
indicate change of mode, such as a balance between practical
experience and classroom work in training schemes.

ALTHUSSER, LOUIS (1918–1990)
A Marxist philosopher who was influential in the development
of structuralism. Althusser was a teacher at the ÉCOLE NORMALE
SUPÉRIEURE.

AMÉNAGEMENT DU TERRITOIRE
In 1981 a ministry to oversee the five-year plans and the
programme of decentralisation was created. It had been realised
that the dominance of the centralised state organisation needed
reform, and a more dynamic way of achieving growth was to
focus on regional and local initiative.

The principal state organ for encouraging decentralisation is
the already existing DATAR. Each RÉGION also has a regional
plan, and a structure of administration which promotes regional
initiatives. See also: FONDS NATIONAL D'AMÉNAGEMENT FONCIER
ET D'URBANISME; PRIME DE DÉVELOPPEMENT RÉGIONAL; SOCIÉTÉ DE
DÉVELOPPEMENT RÉGIONAL

AMENDE FORFAITAIRE
A fine payable if a minor motoring offence has been committed,
without the case coming to court. The fixed penalty can be paid
immediately to the police officer or traffic warden in cash or by
cheque, or within 30 days of the offence by purchasing a TIMBRE-
AMENDE. Except in the case of parking offences, immediate
payment can mean a reduced fine. One has the right of appeal
within the 30-day period.

If there is no appeal, non-payment within 30 days means an
automatic increase in the fine (*amende forfaitaire majorée*),
and the TRÉSOR PUBLIC takes steps to obtain payment. A further
10 day period is available for appeal.

If as a result of an appeal, the case comes before a JUGE, and
the defendant is found guilty, the fine can be further increased
or alternatively reduced below the *amende forfaitaire majorée*.
Again there are 30 days for payment or appeal. In the case of

the latter, the defendant will be called to appear in court.

A more serious offence (e.g. driving without insurance, with excess alcohol, without a driving licence, or where the statutory fine is above 3,000 francs) provides no facility for the above procedure, and the *amende forfaitaire* is not available. See also: ORDONNANCE PÉNALE

AMNISTIE

Since 1965, after each presidential election, the government has presented a bill to the ASSEMBLÉE NATIONALE which becomes an amnesty law, in which certain categories of offenders have their penalties reviewed. These may range from minor motoring offences, where procedures for fines are suspended, to more serious crimes when there may be release from prison or a reduction in the sentence. Equally, certain categories of offences are, by custom, not subject to the amnesty, e.g. terrorist violence, drug-trafficking, fraud, driving under the influence of alcohol. The details of each amnesty depend on the content of the bill, and no two amnesty laws have been the same.

There are occasional amnesties which do not relate directly to the presidential election.

AMNISTIE FISCALE

A device used occasionally by the tax authorities to encourage those who have evaded payment of tax or who have contravened exchange controls to regularise their situation without penalty.

AMOCO CADIZ

In 1978, an oil spillage from this tanker caused massive environmental damage and pollution on the north coast of FINISTÈRE. Thirty thousand birds died and marine life was seriously affected. The final costs of the clean-up operation and losses were estimated to be in the region of 12 billion francs, and measures to recover this from the owners, Standard Oil, and to complete the rehabilitation carried on for at least 10 years.

AMPHITHÉÂTRE

The traditional lecture-theatre of a university, and sometimes used as a nickname (*'les amphis'*) for places of higher education. The *amphithéâtre* at the SORBONNE featured as a centre for student revolt in 1968.

ANAH See: *AGENCE NATIONALE POUR L'AMÉLIORATION DE L'HABITAT*

ANCIENS COMBATTANTS ET VICTIMES DE GUERRE, SECRÉTARIAT D'ÉTAT
The welfare of former service personnel has traditionally featured as a major responsibility within government. Former combatants are entitled to a number of concessions, privileges and allowances, and this department exists to represent their interests as well as those of their families.

ANDORRE
A feudal territory in the Pyrenees (population approximately 45,000), of which the PRÉSIDENT DE LA RÉPUBLIQUE is a co-prince, as is the Bishop of Urgel, Spain. The co-princes are represented by two *Viguiers*, one French, one Spanish, who delegate their legislative powers to two permanent officials. The French official is the PRÉFET of the PYRENÉES-ORIENTALES. A local representative body is the *Conseil général des vallées*. Each year, the President receives the *questia*, a tribute payment of 960 francs, 12 cheeses, 12 capons, 12 partridges and six hams.

ANGERS
The university of Angers has 13,000 students in faculties of arts, economics, humanities, law, medicine, pharmacy and sciences.

ANGOULÊME
This town in the CHARENTE had the unenviable distinction in 1991 of being the first to achieve virtual municipal bankruptcy. A five-year programme of severe measures was adopted to overcome a deficit equal to 27,000 francs per inhabitant.

Angoulême is the site of the annual *Salon international de la* BANDE DESSINÉE, and there is a museum of *bandes dessinées* here.

ANNECY, FESTIVAL D'
An annual festival of cartoon films at Annecy has become a major event in the French cinema calendar.

ANNÉE SCOLAIRE
The school year extends from early September to late June/early July. Wednesday afternoon is free, and a number of schools teach on Saturday mornings. Some schools are now experimenting with a four-day week.

In addition to *jours de* FÊTE LÉGALE, normal breaks are in early November to mark *la* TOUSSAINT (one week), around Christmas and New Year (two weeks), mid-February (two weeks) and early April (two weeks).

The influence of school holiday dates on France is enormous. Dates are fixed nationally, but the ACADÉMIES are arranged in three zones, if only to allow some degree of relief on the transport network, as for many French families the start and end of school holidays are seen as prompts for departure and return. Increasingly the February break is seen as an opportunity for a family skiing holiday.

ANNUAIRE ÉLECTRONIQUE
The national telephone directory is available to all French telephone subscribers on the TÉLÉTEL system, free of charge. This dispenses with the need to produce and distribute so many printed telephone books, and permits the information to be continually updated. To find a number, the user enters the details of the enquiry via a MINITEL terminal and the response is displayed on a screen. Heavy use of the system does incur a charge.

ANOUILH, JEAN (1910–1987)
A dramatist, born in Bordeaux, whose prolific work was both popular and internationally respected. His works include *Le Bal des voleurs* (1938), *Antigone* (1944) and *Becket* (1959).

ANPE See: *AGENCE NATIONALE POUR L'EMPLOI*

ANQUETIL, JACQUES (1934–1987)
A prominent cyclist during the 1950s and 1960s, who won the TOUR DE FRANCE on five occasions, the *Grand Prix des nations* nine times, as well as numerous other events.

ANTENNE 2 See: *FRANCE 2*

ANTILLES

The term generally used to denote the French territories in the Caribbean, GUADELOUPE and MARTINIQUE.

ANTILLES-GUYANE

The university and ACADÉMIE for the ANTILLES and GUYANE, based in Pointe-à-Pitre, in Guadeloupe. The university provides courses in arts, sciences, law, social sciences and medicine, and has 6,500 students.

ANTIOPE

An acronym for *Acquisition numérique et télévisualisation d'images organisées en pages d'écriture*. The service provides Teletext information throughout France.

AOC See: *APPELLATION D'ORIGINE CONTRÔLÉE*

AOÛT, LE 15

The date of the Feast of the Assumption, and a national holiday in France. It is frequently used as the halfway point for August holiday bookings and, particularly if near a weekend, causes heavy traffic congestion on holiday routes.

APATRIDES

France maintains a welcoming tradition towards people who have been made stateless by unsympathetic governments or force of circumstance. See also: OFFICE FRANÇAIS DE PROTECTION DES RÉFUGIÉS ET APATRIDES

À PERCEVOIR (PCV)

The reversed charges service of FRANCE TÉLÉCOM, which is now only possible for international calls.

APL See: *AIDE PERSONNALISÉE AU LOGEMENT*

APPELLATION D'ORIGINE CONTRÔLÉE (AOC)

The quality control system operated by the *Institut national des appellations d'origine des vins et eaux-de-vie*, and supported by legislation. There are severe restrictions on proportions of alcohol, production levels and the soil, in order to retain the AOC label on the very highest quality wines. Only certain wine-producing areas qualify to produce AOC wines, which will identify the exact vineyard of origin.

APPRENTISSAGE
A structured system of apprenticeships to trades exists in France. The normal age of apprentices is between 16 and 20, although some can start at 15, and a minimum 360 hour course at a CENTRE DE FORMATION D'APPRENTIS has to be included. An apprenticeship can last from between one and three years, and a form of contract issued by the CENTRE D'INFORMATION ET D'ORIENTATION has to be signed. An apprentice is entitled to receive a proportion of the SMIC, rising to 60 per cent in the final year. The principal training courses available are in engineering, retail and distributive trades, baking and patisserie, and the caring professions. See also: TAXE D'APPRENTISSAGE

AQUITAINE
The administrative RÉGION in South-West France, incorporating the DÉPARTEMENTS of DORDOGNE, GIRONDE, LANDES, LOT-ET-GARONNE and PYRÉNÉES-ATLANTIQUES. Its historical significance was as a duchy, which in medieval times was the subject of disputes between England and France. The former territories of the present Aquitaine were Agenais, Béarn, the *Pays basque* and Périgord.

The regional capital is Bordeaux, and the overall population is about 2,750,000. About two-thirds of these live in towns and cities. There has been considerable immigration from Mediterranean countries, notably from Portugal, Spain, Morocco and Algeria.

The region produces substantial quantities of oil and natural gas, and supplies 11 per cent of France's requirements of electricity, gas and water. It also has a strong shipbuilding industry, as well as aerospace and armaments production. See also: PAYS BASQUE

ARAGON, LOUIS (1897–1982)
A writer of novels, poetry and history, who was involved in the artistic movements of surrealism and dadaism in the early years of this century. He became a prominent member of the PARTI

COMMUNISTE FRANÇAIS and is renowned as a great poet of the RÉSISTANCE.

ARC See: *ASSOCIATION POUR LA RECHERCHE CONTRE LE CANCER*

ARCHE DE LA DÉFENSE
A construction erected for the BICENTENAIRE *de la Révolution française* as part of the new complex of *La* DÉFENSE in the western suburbs of Paris. See also: GRAND PROJET

ARCHIVES NATIONALES
The collection is a part of the operation of the MINISTÈRE DE LA CULTURE ET DE LA COMMUNICATION. The service was created in 1789, and its latest re-organisation, allowing a degree of decentralisation, was in 1983. The oldest documents are held in Paris (dating back to the fifth century) in the *Hôtel Soubise* and the *Hôtel de Rohan*, while the contemporary archive material is found at Fontainebleau and its overseas archives in Aix-en-Provence. A collection of material related to the world of work is to be placed at Roubaix, and the central microfilm collection is at Espeyran, in the GARD.

Most documents are available for public access after 30 years, with restrictions on some material for reasons of privacy or State security, to a period of between 60 and 150 years.

ARDÈCHE
A DÉPARTEMENT in the RHÔNE-ALPES region, named after a tributary of the Rhône, with a population of 277,579 in 1990. The CHEF-LIEU is Privas (AGGLOMÉRATION 14,473), with textile and confectionery industries. Other urban areas are Annonay (25,123) – textiles, leather, coaches and paper production; Aubenas (24,052) – textiles, engineering and pharmaceuticals; Guilhérand (10,492); Tournon (11,861) – electrical engineering, footwear, textiles, sports and camping equipment, and caravans. There is a nuclear power station at Cruas, and a number of cement works in the valley areas.

The Ardèche is essentially a rural *département*, with agricultural activity in fruit (especially peaches) and wine production and is a popular centre of tourism, with attractions including the river gorges, water-courses and caves.

A marginal majority for François MITTERRAND in the 1981 ÉLECTION PRÉSIDENTIELLE was slightly increased in 1988, but the control of the Centre Right in the CONSEIL GÉNÉRAL was reaffirmed in the 1992 ÉLECTIONS CANTONALES.

Code départemental: 07

ARDENNES

A DÉPARTEMENT in the CHAMPAGNE-ARDENNE region, dominated by the Ardennes plateau, with a population of 296,333 in 1990. There has been a steady population fall since the 1960s. Its CHEF-LIEU and largest conurbation is Charleville-Mézières (often thought by French people to be in Belgium!; 67,213 inhabitants), with iron and steel, food-processing and clothing industries. Other urban areas are Givet (10,017) – adhesives and synthetic fibres; Rethel (10,462) – paper and board, food-processing, engineering and clothing; Sedan (28,992) – textiles, metals and ironworks. Smaller towns have a range of industries, including kitchen equipment, sanitary ware and an underground power station at Revin. At Chooz, there is a joint Franco-Belgian nuclear power station, with another under construction.

The *Département* was important in the early history of French industry, and the basis of its industrial wealth has changed since the comfortable days of iron and steel manufacture. The population has declined, as fewer job opportunities become available, and the *Département* faces the challenge of an ageing, less-qualified population. Support from the European Community has been forthcoming in attempts to reinvigorate the economy. The *Vallée de la Meuse* is a designated industrial renovation area.

This area has been a traditional source of support for the Left in politics, with majorities for François MITTERRAND being strong in both the 1981 and 1988 ÉLECTIONS PRÉSIDENTIELLES. However, the Centre Right has gained control over the CONSEIL GÉNÉRAL, and the 1992 ÉLECTIONS CANTONALES were disastrous for the PARTI SOCIALISTE.

Code départemental: 08

ARGUS, L'

A weekly motoring magazine, specialising in used car prices, with a circulation of 20,000, and with specialist editions for other interests.

ARIANE

The European space programme uses the Ariane rocket to launch satellites from Kourou (GUYANE). A series of Ariane models has been developed by the Arianespace private company, based at Evry (ESSONNE).

ARIÈGE

A DÉPARTEMENT in the MIDI-PYRÉNÉES region, named after the tributary of the Garonne, which flows through it. The population was 136,483 in 1990 and the CHEF-LIEU is Foix, (AGGLOMÉRATION 10,620). The larger urban area of Pamiers (17,060) is an industrial centre, producing special steel. Apart from small pockets of industrial activity, the main picture is one of an agricultural area with a substantial population decline (155,000 in the 1930s), which is depending increasingly on tourism for economic strength. The European Community's regional funds are supporting the textile industry.

Politically, Ariège leans strongly to the Left, and in the ÉLECTIONS PRÉSIDENTIELLES of 1981 and 1988 gave François MITTERRAND among his biggest majorities, and maintains this strength on the CONSEIL GÉNÉRAL where 19 of the 22 seats are held by the PARTI SOCIALISTE.

Code départemental: 09

ARME BLINDÉE ET CAVALERIE

The section of the French army which specialises in tank and mechanised warfare. It includes three kinds of regiments: *cavalerie légère blindée*, with light armoured equipment; tank regiments, concentrated on tanks and support vehicles; and *régiments mécanisés*, which have a combination of such equipment.

ARMÉE DE L'AIR

The general term used to encompass all French military air services, comprising seven high commands: strategic, air defence, tactical, transport, communications, engineering and training, and four aerial regions (Aix-en-Provence, Bordeaux, Metz and Villacoublay).

ARMÉE DE TERRE
The general term used to denote all French ground forces, except the GENDARMERIE NATIONALE, divided into three *corps d'armée*, and other elements such as a rapid action force, the *Division alpine*, and a parachute division. As well as in France, French troops are deployed in the DOM and TOM, in Africa, as part of the UN force in Lebanon, in Berlin and as part of a joint French-German brigade, established in 1988. Within France, the *Armée de terre* is organised in military regions.

ARON, RAYMOND (1905–1983)
A philosopher and columnist in *Le* FIGARO, who had a large popular following, and whose lectures at the COLLÈGE DE FRANCE were guaranteed to attract large audiences. Aron is considered difficult to classify, being a thinker of neither traditional Left nor Right. He wrote about democracy and against totalitarianism.

ARP, HANS (1887–1966)
An artist and sculptor, co-founder of the dada movement, whose work shows a development from the surrealists towards the abstract.

ARRÊTÉ D'INSALUBRITÉ
An order made by the PRÉFET which declares that a property is of sub-standard quality, thus proving entitlement of the occupying owner to an improvement grant (PRIME À L'AMÉLIORATION DE L'HABITAT) and for additional subsidies towards upgrading parts of the building which might otherwise cause health risks. The subsidy is repayable if the owner sells the property within 15 years.

ARRÊTÉ MINISTÉRIEL
These are official decisions made at ministerial level which have the force of law. They are published in the JOURNAL OFFICIEL, and include detailed instructions to FONCTIONNAIRES about how the decisions are to be carried out.

ARRÊTÉ MUNICIPAL
An official decision made by the MAIRE which has the force of a local regulation. The most obvious example would be that of local traffic regulations.

ARRÊTÉ PRÉFECTORAL
An official decision taken by the PRÉFET, who can call upon the police to ensure that it is carried out within the DÉPARTEMENT. For example, a regulation about sales of alcohol on local premises would be made in an *arrêté préfectoral*.

ARRÊTÉ RECTORAL
An official decision taken by the RECTEUR in an ACADÉMIE affecting educational institutions in the area. The document is addressed to the appropriate personnel in the service who are to carry it out.

ARRONDISSEMENT
In Paris, Lyon and Marseille, an *arrondissement* is a sub-division of the city, and has its own MAIRE and CONSEIL D'ARRONDISSEMENT. In this sense, an *arrondissement* has the legal status of a CANTON.

Outside these cities, the *arrondissement* is a sub-division of the DÉPARTEMENT, and the government official who supervises its affairs is the SOUS-PRÉFET. The number of *arrondissements* in a *département* is generally two or three, but there are as many as six, seven or nine in the most highly populated areas. MOSELLE has nine *arrondissements*. There are presently 325 *arrondissements* proper in France, and each of these is composed of a number of COMMUNES. These range from the enormous 397 in the Arras *arrondissement* down to seven in Argenteuil. The *arrondissements* (in this sense) of Paris, Metz and Strasbourg comprise only one *commune* each.

ARTE
A Franco-German cultural television channel, created by agreement between François MITTERRAND and German Chancellor Helmut Kohl, which began transmitting in 1992 on the frequency previously occupied by *la* CINQ.

ARTHUR MARTIN
An electrical goods manufacturer, part of the Electrolux group,

which specialises in items such as cookers, refrigerators, freezers and washing machines for the domestic buyer.

ARTICLE 16

The constitution of the CINQUIÈME RÉPUBLIQUE is set out in articles. *Article 16* gives the PRÉSIDENT DE LA RÉPUBLIQUE the right to assume special powers in exceptional circumstances.

This refers to occasions when the institutions of the republic, the nation's independence, territory or international obligations are placed in immediate danger, and the normal constitutional bodies are unable to act. In such circumstances, the *Président de la République*, after due consultation with the PREMIER MINISTRE, the presidents of the ASSEMBLÉE NATIONALE, the SÉNAT and the CONSEIL CONSTITUTIONNEL, announces his assumption of powers to the nation.

The only time the *Article* has been used to date was in 1961, during the crisis in ALGÉRIE.

ARTILLERIE

The principal artillery units in the ARMÉE DE TERRE are the *Régiments d'artillerie* and *d'artillerie de montagne*, the *Artillerie parachutiste, Régiments Roland* and *Hawk*.

ARTISANAT

A substantial number of French people work in skilled craft trades. The principal organisation which represents their interests is the *Union professionnelle artisanale*, which has about 250,000 members.

ARTS DÉCO

The popular term for the ÉCOLE NATIONALE SUPÉRIEURE DES ARTS DÉCORATIFS.

ARTS ET MÉTIERS

This is the general title for a series of CONCOURS, success at which leads to entry to an ÉCOLE NATIONALE SUPÉRIEURE D'ARTS ET MÉTIERS, providing advanced courses in design engineering of various kinds.

ASCENSION, FÊTE DE L'

A public holiday which, as it falls on a Thursday, usually in

May, provides a good excuse to '*faire le pont*' and make a long weekend's break for many French people.

ASSEDIC See: *ASSOCIATION POUR L'EMPLOI DANS L'INDUSTRIE ET LE COMMERCE*

ASSEMBLÉE NATIONALE
The lower house of the French parliament, also known as the *Chambre des députés*, consisting of 577 DÉPUTÉS (555 from France and 22 from DOM and TOM), meeting in the PALAIS BOURBON in Paris.

The members (minimum age 23) are elected by universal suffrage for a period of five years. The method of electing members is by SCRUTIN MAJORITAIRE, with two rounds of voting if a single candidate does not receive more than 50 per cent of the votes cast on the first round. However, in 1986 members were elected by proportional representation, with *députés* representing a DÉPARTEMENT. (See: SCRUTIN DE LISTE)

The *Assemblée* can be dissolved by the PRÉSIDENT DE LA RÉPUBLIQUE in certain circumstances, but on no more than one occasion in any 12-month period.

The chamber is semi-circular in shape, and members sit to the left or right of the centre in proportion with their political affiliation.

The *Président de l'Assemblée* is elected by its members for the duration of the parliament.

The *Assemblée* can pass laws, vote on the Budget, question ministers, who cannot be *députés*, and pass a motion of censure on the government (which automatically entails the fall of the government). See also: PROJET DE LOI; PROPOSITION DE LOI

ASSIGNATION
A writ used in a civil case, delivered by a HUISSIER.

ASSISTANCE PUBLIQUE
A public hospital service, tracing its history back to the earliest charitable *Hôtel-Dieu* in Paris in the seventh century. It serves mainly the Paris area and ÎLE-DE-FRANCE region.

ASSOCIATION
An organisation of at least two people with common declared

aims. An *association* takes on official status when it formally registers its existence with the local PRÉFECTURE or SOUS-PRÉFECTURE under the law established in 1901. If an *association* is recognised to be of UTILITÉ PUBLIQUE, there are financial advantages but specific supervisory conditions.

ASSOCIATION DES DONNEURS DE VOIX
A charitable foundation, recognised as being of UTILITÉ PUBLIQUE, which produces, and distributes through a free lending service, audio-cassettes of books to blind people.

ASSOCIATION DES UNIVERSITÉS PARTIELLEMENT OU ENTIÈREMENT DE LANGUE FRANÇAISE (AUPELF)
A grouping of 188 institutions and networks in 31 countries, with connections with 400 French Studies departments in non-French-speaking universities. The headquarters are at the *Université de Montréal*, Québec.

ASSOCIATION POUR LA RECHERCHE SUR LE CANCER (ARC)
As its name suggests, this charity works to find cures for cancer. It has three million members.

ASSOCIATION POUR L'EMPLOI DANS L'INDUSTRIE ET LE COMMERCE (ASSEDIC)
These associations, established from 1958 onwards, are the means of providing insurance schemes against unemployment. The CNPF and local union organisations oversee the 48 ASSEDIC in France, and five in the DOM. All employers, except the State, local government and similar bodies, are required to pay contributions of 4.43 per cent of the payroll, while employees pay 2.47 per cent of their wage or salary.

   See also: ALLOCATION DE BASE; ALLOCATION DE FIN DE DROITS; ALLOCATION DE SOLIDARITÉ

ASSOCIATION VALENTIN-HAÜY (AVH)
A charitable organisation which works for the needs of the blind, in particular in maintaining a free lending library of Braille books and musical scores, and spoken books on cassette. There are also periodicals published in Braille, and social and sporting activities

are organised. The association also runs a training centre and a holiday home for the blind and their families.

ASSOMPTION, FÊTE DE L' See: *AOÛT, LE 15*

ASSURANCE AUTO OBLIGATOIRE
This is the minimum car insurance and covers a driver's liability for passengers and third-party risks, but not the driver in person, the car owner, or passengers who are being transported in unsafe circumstances (e.g. in excess of the seats available), or paying passengers. A currently valid insurance certificate has to be displayed in the front windscreen. Contravention of this leads to an AMENDE FORFAITAIRE.

The insurance can be purchased on the open market, and premium rates depend on the firm's tariff, influenced by age of driver, place of residence, etc. The premiums are usually subject to no-claims discounts or claims penalties when renewals are due. Many employees buy their insurance from MUTUELLES PROFESSIONNELLES. See also: BONUS-MALUS

ASSURANCE DE RESPONSABILITÉ CIVILE
This is public liability insurance, compulsory for motorcyclists, who are not covered by ASSURANCE AUTO OBLIGATOIRE. The insurance indemnifies the policy-holder against a wide range of third-party claims for damages, according to the terms of the policy. There are various forms available. Policies covering a whole family are usually provided as part of home insurance packages.

ASSURANCE INVALIDITÉ
If one has been a contributor to the *Régime général* of the SÉCURITÉ SOCIALE for at least 12 months, one is entitled to a PENSION INVALIDITÉ if it is impossible to work because of accident or infirmity.

ASSURANCE MALADIE
Within certain conditions, contributors to the *Régime général* of the SÉCURITÉ SOCIALE are entitled to sickness benefit when unable to work because of poor health, and to reimbursement of a proportion of medical costs. The ASSURÉ SOCIAL pays 5.9

per cent of earnings to cover joint sickness and maternity contributions, the employer 12.6 per cent.

ASSURANCE MATERNITÉ
Provided that at least 10 months' contributions have been made to the *Régime général* of the SÉCURITÉ SOCIALE, and within certain conditions, a woman is entitled to maternity benefit. The ASSURÉ SOCIAL (of either sex) pays 5.9 per cent of earnings to cover joint sickness and maternity contributions, the employer 12.6 per cent.
See also: ALLOCATION POUR JEUNE ENFANT; CONGÉ MATERNITÉ

ASSURANCE PERSONNELLE
It is possible to pay additional contributions to the SÉCURITÉ SOCIALE in order to obtain sickness and maternity benefits, even if otherwise one would not normally qualify by right. This applies to foreign students resident in France who are not contributors to the *Sécurité sociale*, for example.

ASSURANCE RETRAITE
The insurance scheme for old-age pensions is part of the SÉCURITÉ SOCIALE. Some professions have *Régimes spéciaux* which have particular benefits, but all employees can be covered in the *Régime général*. The ASSURÉ SOCIAL pays 7.6 per cent of earnings to cover old-age pension contributions, the employer 8.2 per cent. The employee pays an additional 0.1 per cent to cover early retirement benefits. See also: ALLOCATION AUX VIEUX TRAVAILLEURS SALARIÉS; PENSION DE RETRAITE

ASSURANCES GÉNÉRALES DE FRANCE (AGF)
One of three large, nationalised insurance companies, which operate on a competitive commercial basis and have no privileges in the market.

ASSURANCE VEUVAGE
Depending on the contributions made to the SÉCURITÉ SOCIALE by a deceased partner, a widow or widower can claim benefit, if under the age of 55 years, residing alone in France, and having raised at least one child, and subject to a means test. The benefit is payable for a maximum of three years or, for those aged 50 and above, to the age of 55.

ASSURANCE VIEILLESSE See: *ASSURANCE RETRAITE*

ASSURANCE VOLONTAIRE
In order to obtain old-age pensions and infirmity benefits, it is possible to make additional contributions, if one otherwise would not qualify for the SÉCURITÉ SOCIALE schemes.

ASSURÉ SOCIAL
A contributing member of the SÉCURITÉ SOCIALE, i.e. 100 per cent of the working population, or a person who has made full contributions in the past.

ASTÉRIX
The fictional, cartoon character of a Gaul whose adventures, supported by his faithful village companions, always seem to bring him into conflict with the occupying Romans, invented by GOSCINNY and UDERZO in 1959. After appearing in PILOTE that year, the stories were published separately in large format comic books and their commercial success did much to establish BANDES DESSINÉES as a major force in French book production. Print runs of the latest Astérix books were in millions. The global sales figure is about 200 million to date. The books have been translated into 40 languages.
    An Astérix theme park opened in Plailly (OISE), in 1989.

ATTESTATION D'ASSURANCE
The personal certificate of insurance which, in the case of motor insurance, has to be shown to a police officer if required. Non-presentation of the certificate incurs an automatic AMENDE FORFAITAIRE.

ATTESTATION D'UNION LIBRE
This is a document drawn up by a couple living together which declares that they should be considered as husband and wife.
See also: CERTIFICAT DE CONCUBINAGE

AUBE
A DÉPARTEMENT in the CHAMPAGNE-ARDENNE region, named after the tributary of the Seine which flows through it. The population in 1990 was 289,145. The CHEF-LIEU is Troyes (urban area 122,725) – hosiery, engineering, tyres, electrical and hardware

industries. The other large town is Romilly-sur-Seine (17,789), which has mechanical engineering and railway works. The traditional textile industry in these centres is suffering a decline.

The Aube contributes substantially to cereal production in France, and the food industry is prominent in the *Département*. There is a nuclear power station at Nogent-sur-Seine.

Politically, Aube demonstrates no particular persuasion. In the 1981 ÉLECTIONS PRÉSIDENTIELLES François MITTERRAND gained a tiny majority, raising it slightly in 1988. The Centre Right controls the CONSEIL GÉNÉRAL.

Code départemental: 10

AUBERGE DE JEUNESSE

There are more than 200 youth hostels in France, run by the FUAJ (*Fédération unie des auberges de jeunesse*), which is affiliated to the International Youth Hostel Federation, and more than 150 run by the LFAJ (*Ligue française pour les auberges de jeunesse*).

AUBUSSON

A town in the CREUSE, famous from the sixteenth century for its tapestry. Its period of highest renown was in the eighteenth century when it produced work for the royal household, but it maintains its production. See also: LURÇAT, JEAN

AUCHAN

A chain of hypermarkets founded in 1961, with branches in the USA and Spain as well as its principal base in France. It ranks fourth in the league table of trading space among French hypermarkets. Its largest outlet, at VÉLIZY 2, has 16,000 square metres of trading space.

AUDE

A DÉPARTEMENT on the Mediterranean coast, in the region of LANGUEDOC-ROUSSILLON. The 1990 population was 298,712. The population had been falling since the 1930s and has now begun to climb again, largely as a result of young couples moving to the area.

The CHEF-LIEU is the historic city of Carcassonne (population 43,470) with rubber, chemicals, food-processing industries and a major wine and produce market. The other larger urban areas are Castelnaudary (10,970) with tile-works and brickworks, and an agricultural co-operative; and Narbonne (45,849), a market centre, especially for wines, and with chemical, railway maintenance, agricultural machinery, fertilisers, packaging, uranium treatment, distilling and honey industries.

The principal element of the economy is the food industry, with Aude being the second *département* in France for wine production. There is a growing dependence on tourism.

In elections, Aude follows the traditional pattern of the region in voting for the Left, although some seats were lost to the Centre Right in the 1992 ÉLECTIONS CANTONALES. The FRONT NATIONAL made a strong enough showing in the ÉLECTIONS RÉGIONALES to gain a seat on the CONSEIL RÉGIONAL in 1992.

Code départemental: 11

AUPELF See: *ASSOCIATION DES UNIVERSITÉS PARTIELLEMENT OU ENTIÈREMENT DE LANGUE FRANÇAISE*

AURIOL, VINCENT (1884–1966)
The first PRÉSIDENT DE LA RÉPUBLIQUE of the QUATRIÈME RÉPUBLIQUE, elected on a first ballot by the two houses of parliament in 1947 to serve until 1954. He was a socialist, and a follower of Léon Blum, who headed the first socialist government in France in 1936, in which he was *Ministre des finances*. He joined DE GAULLE in London in 1943, but in protest at the Gaullist régime in 1960, ceased to play a part in active politics.

AURORE, L'
A daily Paris newspaper of the Centre Right, owned by the HERSANT group and, because of falling circulation, since 1985 incorporated into *Le* FIGARO.

AUROUX, LOI
Named after the *Ministre du travail* of the time, Jean Auroux, this act, passed in 1982, increases workers' rights in the firms where they are employed, particularly in relation to better protection for union representatives, observation of health and

safety regulations, and a requirement on medium and large firms to negotiate annually on pay and conditions.

AUTEUIL
A fashionable quarter in the west of Paris, internationally known for the racecourse. See also: NEUILLY-AUTEUIL-PASSY; PARC DES PRINCES

AUTO-ÉCOLE
In order to obtain the PERMIS DE CONDUIRE, a learner driver has to undertake an initial training course of theory and practice in an approved driving school. The second stage of the process does not have to be in a driving school. See also: CONDUITE ACCOMPAGNÉE

AUTO-JOURNAL
A popular motoring magazine (circulation about 275,000) appearing twice a month, with road trials of new models, comparative surveys, etc.

AUTORISATION DE SORTIE DU TERRITOIRE
A minor wishing to leave the country without a parent and not possessing a personal passport must carry a certificate provided by the MAIRIE, which gives the parent's or guardian's permission for him or her to cross the frontier.

AUTORITÉ PARENTALE
Parents have a joint responsibility for their children, and authority over them. Equal responsibility was recognised in a 1970 law, and joint responsibility in 1987.

If the couple are divorced, the parent who has custody normally has responsibility and authority, but the JUGE DES TUTELLES can make other arrangements.

The *Juge des enfants* can call for an investigation if the health, safety or morals of a child are at risk, or if he or she is not being adequately educated. In certain cases, parental rights can be removed temporarily or permanently.

In matters concerning outside bodies, one parent's authority is normally sufficient, and this can be either. In practice, sometimes the father's signature is required, but a mother has the right to object to this, and can insist that her authority is accepted.

Parents are not normally entitled to interfere with their children's relationships with their grandparents.

AUTOROUTES

The system of existing and planned motorways in France covers about 8,000 kilometres, all denoted by the prefix *A*. A number of the roads have names, chosen by means of competitions in 1973.

The means of repaying the public loans raised for the construction and maintenance of motorways is largely by tolls charged according to vehicle type and distance, payable to construction and operating companies who have a concession to collect tolls for 35 years after the road's opening. Most of the network was built and is now operated by SOCIÉTÉS D'ÉCONOMIE MIXTE, and there is one private company, COFIROUTE. Three previous private firms were bought by the SEM. The daily number of vehicles using a motorway section necessary to repay its construction costs and loan repayments is approximately 20,000.

AUVERGNE

A RÉGION of central southern France, comprising the DÉPARTEMENTS of ALLIER, CANTAL, HAUTE-LOIRE and PUY-DE-DÔME. Historically there are three distinct areas included in the present regional territory; as well as Auvergne, there are also Bourbonnais and Velay.

The 1990 population was 1.32 million, a slight drop from 1982. Strongly agricultural in character, the region produces substantial quantities of beef, cereals and dairy products. The regional capital is Clermont-Ferrand, the headquarters of the MICHELIN concern. A number of towns depend largely on the CURE THERMALE trade, and tourism is increasingly important.

Auvergne is low in comparison with other regions of France in its contribution to the Gross National Product, and is now benefitting from additional support from European Community funding, as well as projects aimed at renewing the rural infrastructure.

The Centre Right maintains an absolute majority of seats in

the CONSEIL RÉGIONAL after the 1992 ÉLECTIONS RÉGIONALES,
with Valéry GISCARD D'ESTAING as its Président.

AUXILIA
An association, recognised as of UTILITÉ PUBLIQUE, which works
towards rehabilitating physically handicapped people and prison
inmates through correspondence courses.

AUXILIAIRES DES AVEUGLES
An association, recognised as of UTILITÉ PUBLIQUE, which
provides support to blind people and the visually handicapped
in a number of different ways.

AVEYRON
A DÉPARTEMENT in the MIDI-PYRÉNÉES region, named after the
tributary of the Tarn which runs through it. The Aveyron had
a population of 270,054 in 1990 which shows a massive fall from
the figure of 416,000 a century earlier, in 1886. Its CHEF-LIEU
is Rodez (urban area 39,011) and the other major urban areas
are Decazeville (19,170); Millau (21,788); and Villefranche-de-
Rouergue (12,959). The area is principally rural, with pockets
of industry at Rodez (car components), Decazeville (opencast
coal mining, chemicals) and Millau (gloves, printing). One well-
known product is Roquefort cheese.

Tourism, based on the natural scenic beauty and historic
villages and religious buildings, is important.

The overall political colour of Aveyron is finely balanced
between Left and Right. GISCARD D'ESTAING's marginal majority
in the 1981 ÉLECTION PRÉSIDENTIELLE was overturned by
MITTERRAND in 1988, but the Centre Right have a massive
majority on the CONSEIL GÉNÉRAL.

Code départemental: 12

AVH See: *ASSOCIATION VALENTIN-HAÜY*

AVIATION LÉGÈRE DE L'ARMÉE DE TERRE (ALAT)
Based at Villacoublay (YVELINES), this service provides
helicopters and liaison and reconnaissance aircraft for the army.

AVIGNON ET DES PAYS DE VAUCLUSE, UNIVERSITÉ DE
The university at Avignon provides courses in arts, humanities,

and sciences for 4,000 students. See also: FESTIVAL D'AVIGNON

AVOCAT

A lawyer who practises by preparing cases and defending the accused in court. Only an *avocat* has the right to practise in a TRIBUNAL DE GRANDE INSTANCE, where his or her services are compulsory. The *avocat* has to hold a MAÎTRISE in law, and to have followed successfully a course of professional training. He or she may work in a group practice or individually. *Avocats* are members of a BARREAU who elect a BÂTONNIER as their president. There are 180 *barreaux* in France.

AVOCAT GÉNÉRAL

In a COUR D'ASSISES, the state case is fought by a PROCUREUR-GÉNÉRAL assisted by an *avocat général*.

AVOIR FISCAL

A tax credit amounting to half the value of an investor's annual dividend payments, which can be used to offset the tax payable. If the amount of tax due is less than the credit, a refund is arranged.

AVORIAZ

An Alpine village in HAUTE-SAVOIE near the Italian border which is well known for its *Festival du film fantastique*.

AVOUÉ

A State-appointed lawyer who works solely in the 35 COURS D'APPEL. Before 1972, an *avoué* was also entitled to practise in the TRIBUNAL DE GRANDE INSTANCE.

AVTS See: *ALLOCATION AUX VIEUX TRAVAILLEURS SALARIÉS*

AXE ROUGE

A designated arterial route in Paris, in which there are specific restrictions on parking, so that traffic may flow uninterrupted.

AZNAVOUR, CHARLES (1924–)

An internationally known singer, songwriter and actor of Armenian origin who has become famous through his adoption and development of the French *chansonnier* style into cabaret.

BAC + 3 (etc)

The advertised entry qualification for starting a course or career with this abbreviation means that the candidate must be the holder of a BACCALAURÉAT and to have completed successfully three years of appropriate study after becoming a BACHELIER.

BACCALAURÉAT

The certificate awarded at the end of seven years of secondary education if the student's performance in the final examinations is successful. The courses leading to the *Bac* are arranged in *filières*, and provide various packages of specialisations and continued general courses. Thus all students retain contact with a broad range of subjects beyond the compulsory years of attendance. In recent years the most prestigious option has been the *Bac C*, which is the maths/science specialism. Formerly, the *Bac A* (philosophy) held sway. The other broad series are *B* (economics), *D* (maths/natural sciences), *E* (maths/engineering), *F* (technology), *G* (commerce) and *H* (information technology).

Series F, G and H are classed as *Baccalauréat technologique*, formerly known as *Baccalauréat de technicien*. There is also a wide range of specialist vocational qualifications under the broad title of *Baccalauréat professionnel*.

There is great public interest in the results of the *Bac* each year. The best answers to the philosophy and literature questions are eagerly read in the press, and the detailed results of each LYCÉE in the country are the subject of annual consumer guides for parents.

The pass rate in 1988 was 36 per cent of the whole age-group. In 1991, of those who sat the examinations, 74.7 per cent passed. The declared intention is to achieve attainment at *Bac* level by

80 per cent of the population by the year 2000. In addition to this goal, which has major implications for the education service, the *Baccalauréat* is undergoing a reform in the early 1990s with the intention of reducing the number of possible options from the present 45. See also: CONCOURS GÉNÉRAL

BACHELIER
A holder of a BACCALAURÉAT, the *bachelier* has in theory the right to enrol for higher education courses at a university, without submitting to a selection process. However, the courses chosen must relate to the *Bac* option followed. For some courses in popular universities, there is a limit on places, and not all applicants are able to register.

In order to apply for entrance to the highly sought specialised courses at a GRANDE ÉCOLE, or an ÉCOLE NATIONALE SUPÉRIEURE, further CLASSES PRÉPARATOIRES have to be attended in order to qualify for the CONCOURS.

BADINTER, ROBERT (1928–   )
The GARDE DES SCEAUX from 1981–1986, and later *Président du* CONSEIL CONSTITUTIONNEL. In 1985, the *Loi Badinter* was introduced, giving protection to pedestrians, cyclists and car passengers, who can claim compensation for injuries caused by car drivers, without proving fault.

BAIL
The lease under which a tenant has occupation of a property. A *bail* is normally of three years duration, and this is automatically renewed unless the owner gives notice within the final six months. An owner who needs possession of the property for family reasons can lease it for shorter periods, although the minmum is for one year. See also: LOI MÉHAIGNERIE

BAILLE
The popular name for the ÉCOLE NAVALE at Brest.

BALLADUR, ÉDOUARD (1929–   )
Former *Secrétaire général de l'*ELYSÉE to Georges POMPIDOU, Balladur returned to the world of business before becoming *Ministre de l'économie, finances et privatisation* in the CHIRAC government from 1986–1988.

BANDE DESSINÉE (BD)
The strip cartoon has an enormous following in France.
Stimulated by the success of magazines such as PILOTE and HARA-
KIRI in the 1960s, various artists were able to become household
names, hardback books of cartoon stories became best-sellers,
and the secondhand market is strong. There is an annual
international show at ANGOULÊME, and a convention in Paris.

BANLIEUE
The outer suburbs of a city, beyond the *faubourgs* which are
usually of ancient origin. The *banlieue* is a product of
expansion in the last century and this one. It is sometimes used
as a term to suggest unplanned sprawl and a cultural wasteland.

BANQUE DE FRANCE
Founded in 1800 as the central bank, the *Banque de France* was
nationalised in 1945. It is the government's banker, intervenes
in the international exchange market to protect the franc, and
monitors the performance of other banks. The head of the bank
has the title of *Gouverneur*.

It is the sole issuer of money in France. Its paper factory is
at Vic-le-Comte, and its printing works at Chamallières, both in
PUY-DE-DÔME.

BANQUE NATIONALE DE PARIS (BNP)
The second largest clearing bank in France, the *Banque
nationale de Paris* was nationalised in 1945, and partly
privatised in 1987.

BANQUE PARIBAS
This bank, nationalised in 1982, was partially privatised again
five years later. Its name is derived from its full designation,
Banque de Paris et des Pays-Bas.

BARCLAY
A recording company, founded by Eddie Barclay, whose label
promoted many French popular musicians in the 1950s and later.
Since 1988, Barclay has been part of the German-Dutch
Polygram group of companies.

BARRAULT, JEAN-LOUIS (1910–   )
A theatre director of almost legendary status. After acting as a

member of the COMÉDIE-FRANÇAISE, Barrault founded a theatre
company with his wife, Madeleine Renaud, and then became
director of the THÉÂTRE NATIONAL DE L'ODÉON (1958–1968),
where he was instrumental in establishing the reputations of
Claudel, BECKETT and IONESCO. His company, founded in 1946,
plays in the *Théâtre Renaud-Barrault* in Paris, opened in
1981.

BARREAU
A local legal association to which each practising AVOCAT
belongs. There are 180 of them in France.

BARRE, RAYMOND (1924–   )
After a career in politics and teaching economics at University
of PARIS I, Barre became PREMIER MINISTRE in 1976 and
remained in post until 1981. For two years he was also *Ministre
des finances*. He was a candidate in the ÉLECTIONS
PRÉSIDENTIELLES in 1988 and obtained 16.54 per cent of the vote
in the first round. He has been DÉPUTÉ for the RHÔNE since 1978.

His period of office was marked by austerity measures in an
attempt to control the economy.

BARTHES, ROLAND (1915–1980)
An essayist and critic who was prominent in the emergence of
semiology as applied to literature.

BARZACH, MICHÈLE (1943–   )
One of the most prominent women on the Right of French
politics, Michèle Barzach was MINISTRE DÉLÉGUÉE *à la santé et à
la famille* from 1986–1988. In 1989, she became a member of
the European Parliament, but resigned from the RASSEMBLEMENT
POUR LA RÉPUBLIQUE in 1991 with Michel NOIR.

BASQUE
The Basque language does not have official status in France,
but may be studied in schools within the ACADÉMIES of Aix and
Bordeaux. Just under 2,000 pupils learn it in school, and there
are about 40,000 Basque speakers in France.

The *Pays basque français* has no constitutional recognition.
It is administratively part of PYRÉNÉES-ATLANTIQUES. The

nationalist political parties receive a small but growing proportion of the votes, when they present common lists.

BAS-RHIN

A DÉPARTEMENT of the ALSACE region, with a 1990 population of 953,053. Its CHEF-LIEU is Strasbourg (urban area 388,483), which has developed into a major European centre, being the seat of the European Parliament, the Council of Europe and the European Court of Human Rights. Strasbourg has industrial activity in brewing, tobacco, confectionery, furniture, engineering and toy-making. In addition, it is an important inland port, and is the port with the highest level of exports from France. Other urban areas are Bischwiller (13,899) – textiles, engineering and clothing; Haguenau (33,724) – mechanical and electrical engineering, paper-making; la Broque (11,858); Molsheim (10,101); Niederbronn-les-Bains (12,841) – heating and railway equipment; Obernai (10,666); Saverne (14,969) – engineering and clockmaking; and Sélestat (15,538) – metallurgy, textiles, brushes and leather goods. There are petrol refineries at Reichstett.

The *Département* is France's largest producer of hops and cabbages (especially used in sauerkraut). It also produces sugar-beet, asparagus, tobacco, fruit and vegetables, has a substantial forestry activity, and attracts tourists to the *Parc régional des Vosges du Nord*, as well as to Strasbourg and the fortified Haut-Kœnigsbourg.

The Bas-Rhin has consistently supported the Right in local and national elections, although the majority for Jacques CHIRAC in the 1988 ÉLECTION PRÉSIDENTIELLE was very small.

Code départemental: 67

BASSE-NORMANDIE

The administrative RÉGION comprising the DÉPARTEMENTS of CALVADOS, MANCHE, and ORNE. The population in 1990 was 1.39 million. Caen is the regional capital.

The region is nationally third most important in dairy products and beef cattle, and agriculture still employs a larger than average proportion of the population. The proximity of Paris helps the eastern part of the region, while Cherbourg and the Cotentin peninsular are less strong. Tourism is becoming more important to the local economy, and there are schemes to revitalise the maritime industries.

The Right Wing strengthened their control of the CONSEIL RÉGIONAL in the 1992 ÉLECTIONS RÉGIONALES.

BASSES-ALPES See: *ALPES-DE-HAUTE-PROVENCE*

BASSES-PYRÉNÉES See: *PYRÉNÉES-ATLANTIQUES*

BASTILLE, OPÉRA DE LA See: *OPÉRA DE LA BASTILLE*

BÂTONNIER
An AVOCAT who is elected for two years by the members of the local BARREAU to act as its president, and who represents it at the national conference of *bâtonniers*.

BAYARD-PRESSE
A publisher of newspapers and magazines with a strong Catholic influence. Among its publications are *La* CROIX, NOTRE TEMPS and a series of magazines for young people such as *Astrapi*, *Pomme d'api*, *Phosphore*, and *Okapi*. *Bayard* also publishes books, and has other related interests.

BAZAR DE L'HÔTEL DE VILLE (BHV)
A group of department stores, which has expanded since 1975 from its traditional base in Paris into a chain of DIY stores throughout France.

BAZIN, ANDRÉ (1918–1958)
A film critic whose work in CAHIERS DU CINÉMA in the 1950s inspired many directors, especially François TRUFFAUT.

BAZIN, HERVÉ (1911–   )
A prolific and popular novelist whose works have usually entered the lists of best sellers. His first novel, *Vipère au poing*, is recognised as a modern classic.

BCBG See: *BON CHIC, BON GENRE*

BD See: *BANDE DESSINÉE*

BÉART, GUY (1930–   )
A popular singer in the tradition of the French *chanson*, who

is by training an engineer, a former student of the ÉCOLE
NATIONALE DES PONTS ET CHAUSSÉES. His daughter is the actress,
Émmanuelle Béart.

BEAUBOURG
A quarter of Paris now famous for the *Centre Beaubourg*, the
home of the *Centre national d'art et de culture Georges
Pompidou*, fully opened in 1977. A strikingly designed building,
this is the most popular tourist attraction in France, according
to entrance statistics. It contains a public reference library of
books and other media, the *Musée national d'art moderne*, a
Centre de création industrielle, and IRCAM, directed by Pierre
BOULEZ.

BEAUVOIR, SIMONE DE (1908–1986)
The writer who is world renowned for *Le Deuxième Sexe*, which
appeared in 1949. Her writing encompassed existentialist
works such as *Les Mandarins*, a novel, and she worked closely
with her partner Jean-Paul SARTRE in political and
philosophical activities. From 1974, she was president of the
Ligue du droit des femmes.

BEAUX-ARTS See: *ACADÉMIE DES BEAUX-ARTS; ÉCOLE NATIONALE SUPÉRIEURE DES BEAUX-ARTS*

BÉBÊTE-SHOW
A satirical television show featuring life-size puppets of
politicians and other prominent personalities.

BÉCAUD, GILBERT (1927–   )
A popular singer, who has an international following.

BECKETT, SAMUEL (1906–1989)
The Irish-French dramatist and novelist, whose startling works,
such as *En attendant Godot*, created a sensation when they were
first performed in the 1950s. From 1937 Beckett lived in France,
writing in English and French. He won the Nobel prize for
Literature in 1969.

BÉDÉPHILE
A fan of BANDES DESSINÉES.

BÉGHIN-SAY
One of the largest French industrial concerns, *Béghin-Say*
specialises in sugar products.

BEINEIX, JEAN-JACQUES (1946–   )
A film director who has achieved success with *Diva* and *37.2 le
matin*.

BÉJART, MAURICE (1927–   )
A dancer and choreographer of international fame. He
collaborated with Pierre Schaeffer in creating *Orphée*, an
opéra concret with electronic music in 1953. He has his own
ballet company.

BELC See: *BUREAU POUR L'ENSEIGNEMENT DE LA
LANGUE ET DE LA CIVILISATION*

BELFORT See: *TERRITOIRE DE BELFORT*

BELLON, YANNICK (1924–   )
A woman film director who became well known in the 1970s
with films such as *La Femme de Jean* and *L'Amour violé*.

BELMONDO, JEAN-PAUL (1933–   )
One of the most successful and prolific French film actors, often
taking the role of a genial tough guy. The son of the sculptor,
Paul Belmondo.

BELLECOUR, PLACE
One of the shorthand terms for Lyon, referring to the enormous
open space laid out in the middle of the city in 1714, rebuilt by
Napoléon.

BEP See: *BREVET D'ÉTUDES PROFESSIONNELLES*

BEPA See: *BREVET D'ÉTUDES PROFESSIONNELLES
AGRICOLES*

BEPC See: *BREVET D'ÉTUDES DU PREMIER CYCLE*

BERCY
A south-eastern quarter of Paris, Bercy is the site of the PALAIS
OMNISPORTS and the *Ministère de l'*ÉCONOMIE, FINANCES ET

BUDGET. The TRÈS GRANDE BIBLIOTHÈQUE is being constructed there.

BÉRÉGOVOY, PIERRE (1925–1993)
A former railway employee who entered socialist politics, and rose to become *Secrétaire général de l'*ÉLYSÉE in François MITTERRAND's first government. He was *Ministre des affaires sociales et de la solidarité nationale* from 1982 to 1984, and later *Ministre des finances et du budget*. In 1991 he took on the additional responsibility for the economy in Édith CRESSON's government, and replaced her as PREMIER MINISTRE in April 1992.

BERGERON, ANDRÉ (1922–)
The *Secrétaire général* of the CGT-FO group of unions from 1963–1989. His earlier career was in the printing industry and then as leader of *Force ouvrière* in the book trade.

BERNARD, CLAUDE (UNIVERSITÉ)
The *Université Claude-Bernard* is the official name of *Lyon I*, which specialises in medical, natural and physical sciences, as befits the nineteenth century medical researcher after whom it is named. There are also courses in physical education. There are 22,000 students.

BESANÇON, UNIVERSITÉ DE See: *FRANCHE-COMTÉ, UNIVERSITÉ DE LA*

BESSON, LUC (1959–)
A film director who has achieved international renown for *Subway*.

BETTENCOURT, LILIANE (1924–)
Reportedly the richest person in France, Liliane Bettencourt is the majority shareholder of the cosmetics giant *L'Oréal*. She is married to André Bettencourt, who held ministerial posts in DE GAULLE's governments.

BEURS
This is the generic term given to the children of Arab immigrants born in France, and forming a large second generation community in French cities. Their parents came

from different countries in the MAGHREB. See also: DÉSIR, HARLEM

BHV See: *BAZAR DE L'HÔTEL DE VILLE*

BIANCO, JEAN-LOUIS (1943–   )
A socialist politician who was *Secrétaire général* at the *Palais de l'*ÉLYSÉE from 1982–1991, when he entered Édith CRESSON's government as *Ministre des affaires sociales et de l'intégration*, and was given the portfolio of *Équipement, transports et logement* by Pierre BÉRÉGOVOY in 1992. See also: ALPES-DE-HAUTE-PROVENCE

BIBLIOBUS
A mobile lending library, serving villages and rural areas. There are about 350 of these throughout the country, each serviced from the BIBLIOTHÈQUE CENTRALE DE PRÊT in the DÉPARTEMENT.

BIBLIOTHÈQUE CENTRALE DE PRÊT
Nearly every DÉPARTEMENT has a central lending library which, since 1986, has been under the control of the CONSEIL GÉNÉRAL. This serves collections held in village MAIRIE, or a local school, and the mobile BIBLIOBUS, as well as the BIBLIOTHÈQUE MUNICIPALE of the towns, and those run by voluntary organisations.

BIBLIOTHÈQUE DE FRANCE See: *TRÈS GRANDE BIBLIOTHÈQUE*

BIBLIOTHÈQUE MUNICIPALE
In about 1,300 towns in France a locally-established public library exists. These are now run in collaboration with the services offered by the BIBLIOTHÈQUE CENTRALE DE PRÊT of the DÉPARTEMENT.

BIBLIOTHÈQUE NATIONALE (BN)
The national library, based in Paris, with a history dating back to Charles V in 1386. It became a nationalised concern in 1789, and is now under the supervision of the *Ministère de la* CULTURE. It maintains the DÉPÔT LÉGAL system of copyright deposit, and in addition to book material, has collections of manuscripts, coins, medals, and rare documents of national importance.

As an indication of the size of the stock, there are 13 million items in the printed book collection, 500,000 periodical titles, 650,000 maps, 15 million prints and photographs. In the music branch, combining the collections of the CONSERVATOIRE NATIONAL SUPÉRIEUR DE MUSIQUE and the OPÉRA DE PARIS, there are two million documents. The sound library contains one million items.

Two departments, at Sablé (SARTHE) and Provins (SEINE-ET-MARNE), are engaged on preservation work and duplication of items threatened with decay. The audio-visual media catalogue is available to the public through TÉLÉTEL. See also: TRÈS GRANDE BIBLIOTHÈQUE

BIBLIOTHÈQUE PUBLIQUE D'INFORMATION (BPI)
This is the reference library situated in the *Centre* BEAUBOURG, maintained under the auspices of the *Ministère de la* CULTURE. It receives 14,000 users per day, and has books, periodicals, films, videodiscs, maps, a language laboratory, projection room, records and computer terminals for public use.

BICENTENAIRE
The celebrations designed to commemorate the French Revolution. Paris in particular was the scene of spectacular events in July 1989, but each event of the revolutionary period is covered by the longer term of the *Bicentenaire*.

BICH, BARON MARCEL (1914–   )
A successful entrepreneur and businessman who established and owns most of *Bic-France*, the producer of the inexpensive ball-point pens. The word 'bic' has come to mean any ball-point pen.

BICHAT See: *ENTRETIENS DE BICHAT*

BIDONVILLE
During the late 1950s and early 1960s there were a number of shantytowns on the outskirts of some French cities, deriving their name from oil barrels or *bidons*, which formed the basis of some of the dwellings. These largely housed immigrant families.

BIGE See: *BILLET INTERNATIONAL POUR LES JEUNES*

BILLET DE TRÉSORERIE
A fixed term investment bond of five million francs in a publicly-quoted company, which can be traded in the market.

BILLET INTERNATIONAL POUR LES JEUNES (BIGE)
A train ticket available to those under 26 years old, giving reduced price travel in France and most western European countries.

BIZUTAGE
The initiation ceremonies traditionally imposed on students as they enter a GRANDE ÉCOLE, which have been adopted by students in universities.

BLANCHE PORTE, LA
A mail order firm, selling to households through catalogues from its headquarters in Tourcoing (NORD).

BLESSURE PAR IMPRUDENCE
If one is found guilty of causing injury to another person and thus incapacitating him or her from work for at least three months, there is a possible penalty of imprisonment from 15 days up to a maximum of 12 months.

BNP See: *BANQUE NATIONALE DE PARIS*

BOIS DE BOULOGNE
The parkland area on the western fringe of the city of Paris, owned by the city since 1852. In addition to the wooded areas and open spaces, it contains sports facilities, including the LONGCHAMP racecourse, the Racing-Club premises, the ROLAND-GARROS stadium and the Bagatelle gardens. As well as its stylish reputation, it is also known as the haunt of prostitutes, especially transvestites.

BOISSERIE, LA
The family home of DE GAULLE, situated in Colombey-les-Deux-Églises (HAUTES-MARNE).

BOISSET, YVES (1939–)
A film maker who became known for featuring the Algerian war in his *R.A.S.* (1973).

BON CHIC BON GENRE (BCBG)
The phrase used to denote the life-styles of those who maintain
their upper bourgeois superiority through their tastes and behaviour, rather than by their income. The French equivalent of
the British Sloane Ranger or the American preppy. They know
CQEI (*ce qui est important*) without having a style CQFD (*ce qu'il
fallait démontrer*). See also: COLLIER DE PERLES CARRÉ HERMÈS

BON D'ÉPARGNE
A fixed-term savings certificate, usually for five years, with a
minimum investment of 1,000 francs, available in different
schemes from post offices and banks. Most can be redeemed
after three months. The interest rate is variable.

BON MARCHÉ
A Paris department store, founded by Aristide Boucicaut in the
mid-nineteenth century. It was the first open-access store in
France in which customers could touch goods, which were
clearly priced with tickets, and could return unsatisfactory
purchases for refund or exchange.

BON DU TRÉSOR
A government savings certificate, valid for five years,
redeemable after three months, at a variable interest rate. The
minimum investment is 1,000 francs. For those with high taxable
income, the interest can be taxed at a more favourable rate
through PRÉLÈVEMENT LIBÉRATOIRE.

BONNET PHRYGIEN
One of the symbols adopted by the early revolutionaries, it is
used as the symbolic headwear of MARIANNE.

BONUS-MALUS
The system of discounts and penalties relating to motor
insurance premiums, according to the claims record of the
customer. The normal rate is 5 per cent discount for each year's
accident-free driving, and 25 per cent penalty for each accident.
There are various exceptions.

BORDAS
A Paris-based publisher principally of guides, encyclopaedias
and schoolbooks. Part of the GROUPE DE LA CITÉ since 1988.

BORDEAUX, UNIVERSITÉS DE

The three universities are *Bordeaux I*, with 23,000 students in faculties of law, economics, science, management and planning; *Bordeaux II* with 13,000 in faculties of medicine, pharmacy, social sciences, humanities, languages, computing and physical education; and *Bordeaux III* (officially known as the *Université Michel-de-Montaigne*) with 15,000 students of arts, languages, philosophy, history, geography, communications, environment and geology. *Bordeaux I* and *Bordeaux III* are sited at Talence (GIRONDE).

BORNAGE

The agreed boundary between two properties. This can be established with the help of a GÉOMÈTRE-EXPERT. In the case of dispute, the TRIBUNAL DE GRANDE INSTANCE is competent to resolve it.

BOTTIN

A directory of businesses and private individuals, primarily for the Paris region. It is published by Didot-Bottin.

BOTTIN MONDAIN

The annual directory of the French élite, comprising about 44,000 entries, usually those whose parents were in previous editions. It is published by Didot-Bottin.

BOUCHARDEAU, HUGUETTE (1935–   )

A candidate for the PARTI SOCIALISTE UNIFIÉ in the ÉLECTION PRÉSIDENTIELLE of 1981, achieving the lowest poll in the first round, of 1.1 per cent. She was *Ministre de l'environnement* from 1984–1988.

BOUCHES-DU-RHÔNE

A DÉPARTEMENT in the PROVENCE-ALPES-CÔTE-D'AZUR region, including the Rhône delta from which it derives its name. The 1990 population of 1.76 million makes it the second most highly-populated département in provincial France. Its CHEF-LIEU is Marseille (AGGLOMÉRATION 1.1 million), and other large urban areas are Aix-en-Provence (130,647); Arles (52,126), the most extensive COMMUNE in France; Berre-l'Étang (12,672); Carry-le-Rouet (10,765); Châteauneuf-lès-Martigues (10,911); Château-Renard (11,790); Fos-sur-Mer (11,605); Istres (35,163); la Ciotat (30,620); Martigues (72,375); Miramas (26,998); Saint-Martin-de-Crau (11,040); Salon-de-Provence (41,395); Tarascon (10,826); and Trets (10,375).

The *Département* is highly industrialised, particularly in chemicals, metals, ship repairs and related activities, but its main employment strength is in the service sector. Marseille is the principal French port on the Mediterranean, and has an important international airport. An industrial complex at Fos-sur-mer was established in the 1960s around the gas and oil terminals.

It is also France's first rank producer of rice, vegetables grown under glass and olive oil, and makes a substantial contribution to the country's production of salad vegetables, fruit and wine.

Politically, the Bouches-du-Rhône has traditionally leant towards the Left. Its parliamentary representatives are largely socialist or communist. In recent years, the FRONT NATIONAL has gained ground, especially in Marseille, profiting from friction between native Marseillais and immigrants, of whom there are many from Algérie and Tunisie. There was only a small majority for François MITTERRAND in the 1988 ÉLECTION PRÉSIDENTIELLE. The *Front national* lost ground to the profit of the larger parties in the 1992 ÉLECTIONS CANTONALES in which the PARTI SOCIALISTE consolidated its control of the CONSEIL GÉNÉRAL.

Code départemental: 13

BOUDIN
The regimental march of the LÉGION ÉTRANGÈRE.

BOUILLEUR DE CRU
These are distillers who produce liqueurs and spirits from wines, ciders and other fruit-based alcoholic drinks. Traditionally, private individuals owning fruit trees or vines have had the right to distil 10 litres per annum for their own use, but not for resale, but the hereditary nature of this right was abolished in 1960. Thus, when the holder of the privilege dies, or his or her surviving spouse, the right is lost.

BOULE DE FORT
A variety of the game of *boules*, or PÉTANQUE, also known as
JEU PROVENÇAL, played mainly in the west of France, in which
the playing area is longer than normal.

BOULE LYONNAISE
A variety of the game of *boules*, also known as *sport-boules*, in
which the playing area is smaller than in PÉTANQUE and the
boules larger. The player rolls the *boules* along the ground. The
game is mainly played in the southern part of the country.

BOULE PARISIENNE
A variety of the game of *boules*, or PÉTANQUE, also known as
JEU PROVENÇAL, in which the playing area is in the shape of a
bowl, leading the *boules* towards the jack.

BOULEVARDS, GRANDS
The series of boulevards on the right bank, forming part of the
inner ring of Paris, stretching from the *Place de la Madeleine*
to the *Place de la Bastille*, laid out progessively in the eighteenth
and nineteenth centuries along the former city fortifications.
Those at the western end of the arc are the commercial centre
of the city, and are characterised by department stores,
fashionable cafés, cinemas and restaurants.

BOULEZ, PIERRE (1925–)
A composer and conductor of international stature. His
compositions have included *Le Marteau sans maître*, using the
12-tone scale, and he has directed the *Institut de recherches et
de coordination acoustique* (IRCAM) at BEAUBOURG,
investigating new forms of musical sound.

BOULIN, ROBERT (1920–1979)
A lawyer who became a Gaullist politician, filling a number of
government posts in the 1960s and 1970s, including *Ministre du
travail* from 1978. A press campaign in 1979 alluded to his role
in a property deal, and he died in suspicious circumstances.

BOURGET, LE
A town in the BANLIEUE of Paris, in the DÉPARTEMENT of SEINE-
SAINT-DENIS, famous for its airport, which has largely been

replaced by ROISSY. Le Bourget is now an airport for private
and executive planes. It is the site of the *Musée de l'air*, and of
the Paris Air Show.

BOURGOGNE
The RÉGION, largely based on the former Duchy of Burgundy,
comprising the DÉPARTEMENTS of CÔTE-D'OR, NIÈVRE, SAÔNE-ET-
LOIRE and YONNE. The regional capital is Dijon, and the overall
population is 1.6 million.

Its industrial strength is in rubber and plastics, coal,
metallurgy and electronics, while it is an important provider of
beef (Charolais), dairy products, wine and cereals.

Support from the European Community has helped economic
change in the Morvan area.

Good motorway and rail connections have brought the region
nearer to Paris, and a good number of RÉSIDENCES SECONDAIRES
are to be found here.

The Centre Right controls the CONSEIL RÉGIONAL, but in the
1992 ÉLECTIONS RÉGIONALES the FRONT NATIONAL gained 10 per
cent of the available seats.

BOURSE
One of seven stock exchanges in France, properly called
Bourses de valeurs, the operation of which was reformed in
1988.

Four organisations exercise control over the *Bourses*. AGENTS
DE CHANGE are members of different *Sociétés de Bourse*, which
have the monopoly of dealing. The regulation of these
companies and rules of trading are set by a *Conseil des Bourses
des valeurs*, which guarantees the interests of their clients. The
executive arm of the council is the *Société des Bourses
françaises* which is a limited company. An independent body
which oversees the operation and can intervene is the
Commission des opérations de Bourse.

On the Paris market, most operations are computerised, and
trading hours are normally 10.00 to 17.00. Shares are traded in
the official market (largest firms), and a second market
(medium-sized firms), whereas smaller enterprises' shares

enter the *hors-côte* market (unquoted). See also MARCHÉ RM;
CAC 40; MATIF; MONEP

BOURSE DE LA VOCATION SCIENTIFIQUE ET TECHNIQUE DES FEMMES

This a special four-year study grant of 10,000 francs per year
offered to 50 female students in the CLASSE DE PREMIÈRE, who
are studying one of the Series F options for the BACCALAURÉAT
and who have the intention to become engineers. It is awarded
on application to the *Délégation régionale des droits de la
femme*, as a result of a CONCOURS.

BOURSE D'ENSEIGNEMENT SECONDAIRE

This study grant is awarded, subject to means test, to parents
of students in secondary education (or from age 16 to the students
themselves with parental permission). About 23 per cent of
secondary students receive a grant.

BOURSE D'ENSEIGNEMENT SUPÉRIEUR

A BACHELIER can receive a study grant to enable study at a State
funded institution of higher education, dependent on certain
conditions, including a means test on the parents of the
applicant, not having broken his or her period of study by more
than three years, unless prevented by SERVICE NATIONAL or giving
birth, usually being younger than 26 years old on first application,
and not repeating any years of study supported by the grant. A
new application has to be made for each year of study. The award
of a study grant gives exemption from university fees.

BOURSE D'ÉTUDES

In addition to the three grants detailed above, there is a range
of more specialised grants available for students, including grants
for study towards further degrees and research, travel, studies
abroad and for students otherwise unsupported by a *bourse*
who find themselves in financial difficulties. See also: CENTRE
RÉGIONAL DES ŒUVRES UNIVERSITAIRES ET SCOLAIRES

BOUSSOIS SOUCHON NEUVECEL (BSN)

The largest French food industrial group, with interests in a
wide range of sectors.

BOUYGUES
The largest construction group in the world, the biggest shareholder of which is CRÉDIT LYONNAIS. The Bouygues family still have nearly 8 per cent of the shares. The group also has major interests in the mass media, with a large investment in TF1, for example.

BOXE FRANÇAISE
riety of boxing, also known as *savate*, in which the feet as well as fists may be used. There has been a revival of interest since the 1960s, and in 1976 a ruling *Fédération française de boxe française-savate et disciplines assimilées* took control of the sport.

BPI See: *BIBLIOTHÈQUE PUBLIQUE D'INFORMATION*

BRASSENS, GEORGES (1921–1981)
A poet and singer who achieved an international following. Brassens took a sideways look at society, and did not hesitate to shock mildly in his writing. He retained a strong sense of his Languedoc heritage and the poetic tradition.

BRASSERIE
As well as its meaning of a brewery, this term is also used to denote a simple restaurant where unpretentious meals are served.

BRAUDEL, FERNAND (1902–1985)
An economist and historian, who was an influential member of the '*nouvelle histoire*' group. One of his best-known works, *L'Identité de la France*, was published posthumously.

BRAY-DUNES
The beach of Bray-Dunes, near Dunkerque (NORD), is taken as the most northerly point of France.

BRÉGANÇON
The fort at Brégançon (VAR) is one of the official presidential properties and is used as a holiday residence.

BREL, JACQUES (1929–1978)
Belgian by birth, Brel was an actor and director, but primarily

a singer and composer who achieved international recognition for his powerful and ultimately pessimistic songs.

BRESSON, ROBERT (1907–   )

A film director whose work displays an austere style, often heightened by his use of less experienced actors; for example, *Journal d'un curé de campagne*, based on the novel by Georges Bernanos.

BRETAGNE

A RÉGION comprising the DÉPARTEMENTS of CÔTES-D'ARMOR, FINISTÈRE, ILLE-ET-VILAINE and MORBIHAN. Its population is 2.79 million and it has twice the national proportion of workers in agriculture. The regional capital is Rennes.

Inhabitants in three of its *départements* have among the lowest life expectancy in France, Morbihan being particularly unattractive in this respect (67.3 years for men, 77.4 years for women).

The region provides half the seafish caught by the French fishing industry. A fifth of its population depend directly or indirectly on the maritime economy, which also includes major naval and shipbuilding establishments at Brest and elsewhere.

There are highly developed links with Britain, especially in exports of vegetables, and a long-standing tourist industry. It is the area of the most intense breeding of pigs in France, and also important in cattle and poultry. The effects of European Community quotas have been particularly severely felt in this region.

Rural depopulation has continued to lead to an urbanisation of the population. Industry and commerce are characterised by the dominance of small and medium-sized enterprises.

There are a number of organisations which campaign for either a greater amount of autonomy for the region (e.g. the *Comité d'étude et de liaison des intérêts bretons*, CELIB) or for independence from France (e.g. *Union démocratique bretonne*, UDB). The FLB (*Front de libération de la Bretagne*) is a proscribed organisation, but terrorist acts still occur, usually directed at government buildings.

In the 1992 ÉLECTIONS RÉGIONALES, the Centre Right UNION

POUR LA FRANCE lost its absolute majority, as seats were gained by the FRONT NATIONAL, GÉNÉRATION ÉCOLOGIE and the VERTS on the CONSEIL RÉGIONAL. See also: BRETON

BRETAGNE OCCIDENTALE, UNIVERSITÉ DE
The official name for the university at Brest, with 15,000 students following courses in medicine, sciences, social science, law, economics and oceanography.

BRETÉCHER, CLAIRE (1943–   )
A cartoonist whose weekly strips in *Le* NOUVEL OBSERVATEUR and other work confirm her standing as a symbol of left-wing feminism.

BRETON
The old Celtic language of BRETAGNE, closely connected with Irish, Cornish and Welsh. Its influence can be seen in the place names of the region, but the number of speakers has been steadily declining. In 1982, it was estimated that there were about 700,000 speakers, with about 2,000 homes in which it was the language of communication. These are located principally in the areas of Pont-l'Abbé (FINISTÈRE) and Saint-Brieuc (CÔTES-D'ARMOR).

Since 1951, learning Breton in a secondary school has been possible. In 1986–87, 3,756 pupils were doing so, 83.5 per cent of whom were in private schools. The ACADÉMIES in which this is possible, at least in principle, are those of Nantes, Paris, Rennes and Versailles.

BRETON, ANDRÉ (1896–1966)
The chief of the surrealist movement whose own output was in poetry. His influence was strong over younger writers who continued to create work in more recent years.

BREVET DES COLLÈGES
The general certificate of studies, instituted in 1985, certifying attainment across a broad range of subjects for those ending the PREMIER CYCLE at the COLLÈGE, usually aged 15. The pass rate, based on continuous assessment in all subjects and an examination in French, mathematics and integrated history-

geography, is about 66 per cent of those who enter. It is not necessary to pass in order to transfer to a LYCÉE, but is required as a basic entry qualification for some careers.

BREVET D'ÉTUDES PROFESSIONNELLES (BEP)

A certificate, in the fields of industrial, economic, commercial, administrative or social studies, which is the culmination of a two-year practically-based course in a LYCÉE *d'enseignement professionnel*, normally awarded on the basis of continuous assessment and an examination and possibly some modular credits, at the age of 17. Because of the use of common tests it is possible in some circumstances to sit for the less demanding CERTIFICAT D'APTITUDE PROFESSIONNELLE at the same time, and to be awarded both certificates. The best students can transfer to a CLASSE DE PREMIÈRE in a *Lycée d'enseignement technologique* for a course leading to a BACCALAURÉAT *technologique* or to a BREVET DE TECHNICIEN. There are 85 specialities in the range of BEP available, although by no means is there an equal recruitment for them all. A holder of a BEP can be regarded as an *Ouvrier qualifié*.

BREVET D'ÉTUDES PROFESSIONNELLES AGRICOLES (BEPA)

The minimum certification for employment as a qualified agricultural employee, taken after two years study at a LYCÉE *d'enseignement professionnel agricole* (LEPA) at the age of 17. There are 15 options within the programme. Sixty per cent of candidates are taught at private establishments.

BREVET D'ÉTUDES DU PREMIER CYCLE (BEPC)

This was the general certificate of studies taken at the end of the CLASSE DE TROISIÈME, now replaced by the BREVET DES COLLÈGES.

BREVET DE TECHNICIEN (BT)

A certificate of specialised education obtained after three years of study (one in the CLASSE DE SECONDE *option technologie industrielle*, and two on the BT course) in a special section of a LYCÉE, leading possibly to study for BREVET DE TECHNICIEN SUPÉRIEUR. The field of study, chosen from 67 possibilities, is restricted, and the selection for entry to courses is rigorous. One out of six students drops out during the first year, and one out of the remaining five in the second year.

BREVET DE TECHNICIEN AGRICOLE (BTA)
The equivalent of a BREVET DE TECHNICIEN for agricultural trades, organised in a modular structure. Assessment is 50 per cent by coursework, 50 per cent by examination.

BREVET DE TECHNICIEN SUPÉRIEUR (BTS)
A higher education vocational diploma awarded after two years post-BACCALAURÉAT study, in specific professional fields. There are 71 specialities from which to choose. Study is normally located in a special section of a LYCÉE *d'enseignement professionnel* or *technologique*.

BREVET D'INVENTION
A patent protecting the inventor against unpermitted production of the invention, issued in most cases by the *Institut national de la propriété industrielle*, valid for up to 20 years.

BREVET PROFESSIONNEL See: *TECHNICIEN*

BRUÈRES-ALLICHAMPS
This village in the CHER is one of four locations claiming to be the geographical centre of France. See also: CHAZEMAIS; SAINT-AMAND-MONTROND; VESDUN

BSN See: *BOUSSOIS-SOUCHON-NEUVECEL*

BT See: *BREVET DE TECHNICIEN*

BTA See: *BREVET DE TECHNICIEN AGRICOLE*

BTS See: *BREVET DE TECHNICIEN SUPÉRIEUR*

BUDGET
The government has to publish an annual budget statement which permits the ADMINISTRATION to spend allocated sums, and to gather resources to pay for this. In February, the *Directeur du budget* prepares projection papers for the *Ministre des finances*, from which a plan of action emerges. Consultation

with other ministers takes place, so that in April or May, the
PREMIER MINISTRE makes final decisions about the global sums.
Fine details are worked on until presentation to the ASSEMBLÉE
NATIONALE of the LOI DES FINANCES on the first Tuesday of
October. The bill passes through both houses by the early part
of December. If disagreements between the *Assemblée* and the
SÉNAT cannot be resolved within 70 days, the government can
enact the budget by ORDONNANCE.

BUFFET, BERNARD (1928–   )
A painter and engraver known for his work in depicting human
'*misérabilisme*', either in black and white or colour.

BULL
The state-owned computer and electronics firm. Although
available for privatisation under CHIRAC's programme in 1986, it
remained in state control, and in the early 1990s began to suffer
serious financial problems.

BULLDOZER See: *CHIRAC, JACQUES*

BUREAU D'AIDE SOCIALE See: *AIDE SOCIALE*

BUREAU DE VÉRIFICATION DE LA PUBLICITÉ (BVP)
An association of advertisers and related bodies which
encourages self-discipline among its members in the claims they
make, and acts as a pressure group about legislation affecting
advertising.

BUREAU DE VOTE
A polling station for official elections, in which voters are
provided with a number of ballot papers, from which they
choose their preference, and in a secret booth, insert the chosen
paper into an envelope. The envelope is of a different colour
from that used in the previous election. The envelope is placed
in the ballot box or *urne*, which since 1991 has had to be
transparent.

Some polling stations, in COMMUNES having more than
3,500 inhabitants, are provided with voting machines. Difficulties
with experimental use in the 1970s meant that in the 1988

ÉLECTION PRÉSIDENTIELLE, they were used only in Ajaccio (CORSE).

BUREAU POUR L'ENSEIGNEMENT DE LA LANGUE ET DE LA CIVILISATION (BELC)

A government office, dependent on the *Ministère de l'*ÉDUCATION NATIONALE which, as its name suggests, supports the teaching of French language and culture by the promotion of effective methods and materials.

BUROSSE

An oilfield about 30 kilometres from Pau (PYRÉNÉES-ATLANTIQUES), which could furnish one million tons of fuel per year, i.e. 1 per cent of annual French consumption.

BUT

A chain of furniture retailers, with over 200 outlets, mainly in out-of-town sites.

BUTOR, MICHEL (1926–   )

A critic and novelist, who in his early career, contributed to the '*nouveau roman*' movement, selling almost half a million of his *Prix Renaudot* winner *La Modification*, and who has turned to a more orthodox style in recent years.

BVP See: *BUREAU DE VÉRIFICATION PUBLICITÉ*

CA See: *CONDUITE ACCOMPAGNÉE*

CABINET
The private office of a minister or PRÉSIDENT DE LA RÉPUBLIQUE, combining administrative duties with political advice. A senior position in a cabinet has often led to higher office in government. The numbers involved have risen over the years, and the average number of members of a cabinet is now about 13.

CAC 40
A stock-exchange index of the 40 most quoted shares on the Paris BOURSE, updated every 30 seconds throughout trading hours. The organisation which controls the index is the *Compagnie des agents de change*.

CADA See: COMMISSION D'ACCÈS AUX DOCUMENTS ADMINISTRATIFS

CADRES
The general term used for senior management executives, in private and public sectors, and including FONCTIONNAIRES.

CAECL See: *CAISSE D'AIDE À L'ÉQUIPEMENT DES COLLECTIVITÉS LOCALES*

CAEN BASSE-NORMANDIE, UNIVERSITÉ DE
This university has 23,000 students in faculties of law, economics, politics, humanities, pharmacy, medicine, languages, history, earth and environmental sciences, physical and sports education.

CAHIERS DU CINÉMA
A film journal founded in 1951, particularly influential among

young producers and directors, especially those of the '*Nouvelle Vague*'.

CAISSE D'AIDE À L'ÉQUIPEMENT DES COLLECTIVITÉS LOCALES (CAECL)

A state-controlled funding institution which offers loans to local authorities for them to carry out works not funded by their normal income.

CAISSE D'ÉPARGNE ET DE PRÉVOYANCE (CEP)

A group of state-controlled retail savings institutions, marketed under the symbol of a squirrel, with offices throughout France. The market is principally the private individual, and the CEP offers chequebook accounts, as well as LIVRET savings accounts and those directed especially at home loans, and a range of personal loans.

CAISSE D'ALLOCATIONS FAMILIALES

A local office of the SÉCURITÉ SOCIALE organisation, with the role of administering family allowance entitlements.

CAISSE DE MUTUALITÉ SOCIALE AGRICOLE

A local office similar to the CAISSE D'ALLOCATIONS FAMILIALES but for workers in the agricultural workers' scheme within the SÉCURITÉ SOCIALE.

CAISSE DES DÉPOTS ET CONSIGNATIONS

The state-controlled and guaranteed institution for deposits, e.g. for lawyers' clients' funds, public institutions' accounts, and all funds held by the CAISSE D'ÉPARGNE ET DE PRÉVOYANCE, the SÉCURITÉ SOCIALE, etc. It oversees the financing of public projects, such as the building of AUTOROUTES and public housing, and manages the financial operation of SICAV. Various high-profile financial institutions are subject to its overall control (e.g. CRÉDIT AGRICOLE, CRÉDIT FONCIER DE FRANCE).

CAISSE NATIONALE D'ASSURANCE VIEILLESSE

The department of the SÉCURITÉ SOCIALE which manages the operation of the various ALLOCATIONS relating to old age.

CAISSE NATIONALE D'ÉPARGNE

The state-owned retail savings institution which uses post offices and, in rural areas, postal delivery staff, as its point of contact with clients. A full range of savings accounts is available. See also: LIVRET

CAISSE NATIONALE DE PRÉVOYANCE
A state-owned insurance organisation with about 11 per cent of the life insurance market in France.

CAISSE NATIONALE DES MONUMENTS HISTORIQUES ET DES SITES (CNMHS)
This body administers national historic monuments, is responsible for their finances and management, for developing their tourist potential and for publications about the monuments. It is possible to hire certain monuments on a daily basis through the CNMHS.

CALVADOS
A coastal DÉPARTEMENT in the BASSE-NORMANDIE region, named after the 'Salvador' from the Spanish Armada in 1588, shipwrecked off Arromanches.

The population of Calvados was 618,468 in 1990. The CHEF-LIEU is Caen (urban area 188,799) – metallurgy, steelworks, chemicals, engineering, automobiles, electronics and port activities. Other sizeable urban areas are Bayeux (17,223) – banking administration; Dives-sur-Mer (11,179); Lisieux (28,028) – automotive industry, electrical manufacturing and timber; Luc-sur-Mer (11,513); Ouistreham (12,834), a resort and car-ferry port; Trouville-sur-Mer (18,963); and Vire (15,924) – agricultural market, clothing, dairy, automotive and mechanical engineering industries.

Agricultural strengths are dairy products, beef cattle, and pigs, apples and the Calvados brandy; the fishing industry is also quite important.

The tourist industry is very important, with the *Département*'s proximity to Paris having helped its position in the past, and a direct car-ferry route to England being a recent boost. Some of the coastal resorts expand their numbers phenomenally in the summer months, and are largely made up of second homes, and are thus virtually deserted out of season. Others have adapted to cater for a year-round clientele. The racecourse and casino at Deauville are a regular attraction for moneyed visitors.

Politically, Calvados tends to vote for the Right. Michel D'ORNANO has been nationally the most prominent local politician. However in 1988 François MITTERRAND gained 55 per cent of the vote on the second round. After the 1992 ÉLECTIONS CANTONALES, the Centre Right had 38 out of 49 seats on the CONSEIL GÉNÉRAL.

Code départemental: 14

CAMARADES CHRÉTIENS CRITIQUES
This Catholic pressure group, formerly known as *Échanges et dialogue*, is politically aligned to the Left, and criticises the stance of the Church hierarchy.

CAMIF
A mail-order organisation, based on a primary school teachers' association, *Coopérative des adhérents de la mutuelle des instituteurs de France*, hence its acronym. Its catalogue is published twice a year.

CANAL DU MIDI
Also known as *Canal des Deux-Mers*, this links the Garonne estuary to the Mediterranean, and a continuing programme of work is underway to make the canal navigable to the largest barges.

CANAL PLUS (or CANAL +)
The fourth televison channel available in France, started in 1984. It is run on a paying subscriber basis, although some programmes, supported by advertising, are available without charge. The company, owned mainly by other large firms, has the operating concesssion until 1996. In its charter, it is required only to respect the law, good morals, a balance of opinion and objectivity, and to give a right of reply.

Its programming is dominated by feature films, accessible to subscribers through a decoder.

CANAL RHIN-SAÔNE
A project to link these two rivers, to enable large barges to

travel between Rotterdam and Fos-sur-Mer (BOUCHES-DU-RHÔNE), has met with problems because of the enormous cost involved.

CANARD ENCHAÎNÉ, LE
A satirical weekly paper selling about 500,000, although it fluctuates wildly depending on political events. It jealously guards its independence, accepts no advertising and is vigorous in serious political investigative journalism, unveiling political scandals predominantly affecting the Right.

CANEBIÈRE, LA
A well-known avenue in Marseille, and often used as a nickname for the city.

CANNES
An international film festival is held in this Mediterranean coast town in the VAR each May, the most coveted award being the *Palme d'or*. See also: MIDEM

CANTAL
A mainly rural DÉPARTEMENT in the AUVERGNE region, named after its highest point, *Le Plomb du Cantal*, with a 1990 population of 158,723. This figure is still declining from a peak of 262,000 in the last century. The CHEF-LIEU is Aurillac (urban area 36,069), a market centre with some light industry including umbrella making and food-processing, and there are no other large towns.

Cantal is an important cheese producer, but farming has to be heavily subsidised. It makes a substantial contribution to the hydro-electric power supply of France. It has one of the lowest crime rates. Tourism is becoming a proportionately more important source of wealth. For instance, the cathedral city of Saint-Flour and Eiffel's *Viaduc de Garabit* are major attractions. Cantal has extinct volcanoes and thermal baths of repute.

In politics, Cantal firmly supports the Centre Right, with Valéry GISCARD D'ESTAING and Jacques CHIRAC obtaining comfortable majorities in the 1981 and 1988 ÉLECTIONS PRÉSIDENTIELLES respectively. The UNION POUR LA FRANCE has 21

of the 27 seats on the CONSEIL GÉNÉRAL after the 1992 ÉLECTIONS
CANTONALES.
  Code départemental: 15

CANTON
Basically the constituency area of a member of the CONSEIL
GÉNÉRAL. On average there are 10 COMMUNES in each *canton*,
and about 10 *cantons* in an ARRONDISSEMENT, but extremes of
population density provide numerous special cases. In large
cities, for instance, the *commune* can be divided into a number
of *cantons*, which is the reverse of the norm. The population
of a *canton* can range from 14 to 231,000 (the average is
14,000)!
  Usually there is an office of the GENDARMERIE NATIONALE in
each *canton*. See also: ÉLECTION CANTONALE

CAP See: *CERTIFICAT D'APTITUDE
PROFESSIONNELLE*

CAPCET See: *CERTIFICAT D'APTITUDE AU
PROFESSORAT DES COLLÈGES D'ENSEIGNEMENT
TECHNIQUE*

CAPE See: *CERTIFICAT D'APTITUDE AU
PROFESSORAT D'ÉCOLE*

CAPEGC See: *CERTIFICAT D'APTITUDE AU
PROFESSORAT D'ENSEIGNEMENT GÉNÉRAL DE
COLLÈGE*

CAPES See: *CERTIFICAT D'APTITUDE AU
PROFESSORAT DE L'ENSEIGNEMENT DU SECOND
DEGRÉ*

CAPET See: *CERTIFICAT D'APTITUDE AU
PROFESSORAT DE L'ENSEIGNEMENT TECHNIQUE*

CAPITAL-DÉCÈS
A grant payable to the immediate dependants of a deceased
working contributor to the SÉCURITÉ SOCIALE, or in certain
circumstances to the dependants of an unemployed person.

The amount payable is the equivalent of three months' earnings up to a certain maximum.

CAPITOLE
The nickname for Toulouse, named after the *Place du Capitole*, centre of the medieval and Renaissance city and site of the present HÔTEL DE VILLE.

CAPLP 2 See: *CERTIFICAT D'APTITUDE AU PROFESSORAT DE L'ENSEIGNEMENT TECHNIQUE DU DEUXIÈME GRADE*

CARDIN, PIERRE (1922–   )
The internationally renowned fashion designer, whose business is one of the select group of MAISONS 'COUTURE-CRÉATION'. Since opening his firm in 1947, Cardin has been credited with revolutionising male fashion, and taking the first fashion parade to China and the former USSR. See also: ESPACE PIERRE CARDIN

CARPENTRAS
A town in the VAUCLUSE, with a population of 24,212, which achieved an unenviable renown in 1990 because of an attack by vandals on a Jewish cemetery, giving rise to a wide debate about the level of endemic anti-semitism in France.

CARREFOUR
A hypermarket group, founded in 1959, and now in third position in trading terms in France. It expanded considerably in 1991 by buying the EUROMARCHÉ chain. It also owns hypermarkets in other countries, principally in Spain and Brazil. It owns the largest hypermarket in France, at Portet-sur-Garonne (HAUTE-GARONNE) in the southern Toulouse suburbs, a building with a 24,639m^2 sales floor, and holds the distinction of having opened the first in France, at Sainte-Geneviève-des-Bois (ESSONNE) in the south Paris BANLIEUE in 1963 (4,420m). Carrefour's other interests include *Bricorama* DIY stores, *Eris* restaurants, *Ed* discount stores and part-ownership of BUT electrical and *Castorama* DIY chains.

CARRÉ JEUNE
A concessionary rail card available to those aged 12–25, valid

for one year and allowing four single journeys anywhere on the SNCF network except in the BANLIEUE of Paris, for half price in the PÉRIODE BLEUE and with a 20 per cent reduction in the PÉRIODE BLANCHE.

CARTE AMÉTHYSTE
A card issued to old people resident in the ÎLE-DE-FRANCE, except Paris, giving them 50 per cent reductions (in some cases free travel) on the MÉTRO, buses and suburban trains, and free entrance to leisure facilities in Paris. See also: CARTE RUBIS

CARTE BLEUE
A credit card issued by French banks, participating in the international Visa network. There are about 11 million cardholders in France.

CARTE COUPLE
A concessionary travel card giving a reduction of 50 per cent to the second person in a couple (of any nationality, married or with a CERTIFICAT DE CONCUBINAGE) on all SNCF rail journeys in the PÉRIODE BLEUE.

CARTE DE CIRCULATION DES NON-VOYANTS
A concessionary travel card valid on the Paris suburban transport system. It gives a blind French person, resident for at least three months in the area, half-price travel in second class, and a free place to one accompanying person.

CARTE DE COMBATTANTS
A card issued to ANCIENS COMBATTANTS who served in time of war and fulfil certain conditions (e.g. length of service in a combat unit, having been taken prisoner, or being injured). The card entitles the holder to favourable conditions for early retirement, holidays, reserved occupations, special consideration for loans, etc.

CARTE DE FAMILLE NOMBREUSE
This is one of a number of strategies which have encouraged large families in order to raise the population figures. The card, issued on payment of a fee, is a concession for reduced fares on all SNCF rail services and with special advantages in

the Paris suburban system. It is valid for three or six years. The concession applies to nationals of any European Community member-state. Families with three children below the age of 18, and parents who have had five children (even if no longer living with them), receive reductions from 30 to 75 per cent depending on size of family.

CARTE D'ÉLECTEUR
The voter's card is sent to each elector by the MAIRIE. It is not required to be shown in order to vote, but acts as proof of entitlement to vote if it is presented.

CARTE DE RÉSIDENT
A certificate issued by the *Ministère de l'intérieur*, usually through the police, which gives entitlement to a ten year stay in France and the right to work during that time. It is first issued at the end of the validity of a CARTE DE SÉJOUR on presentation of evidence of means of support and stability, and is automatically rescinded if the holder leaves France for more than three years. Upon renewal, it is re-issued on a permanent basis.

A *Carte de résident* is also issued on a permanent basis to the spouse of a French person, and to immediate dependants (within certain limits), to foreign nationals who are former members of the French forces, stateless persons and certain other categories.

CARTE DE SÉJOUR
Also called a *Carte de séjour temporaire*. A renewable certificate issued by the *Ministère de l'intérieur*, usually through the police, for a period of one year, giving entitlement to stay in France for the purposes of study, work or prolonged visit, and also to those who do not qualify for a CARTE DE RÉSIDENT. Normally, a person intending to work must provide a letter from the employer confirming an offer of employment. Students may seek work during their stay in France to study.

CARTE D'INVALIDITÉ
The *Carte d'invalidité civile* gives concessions to those, regardless of nationality, who have an 80 per cent disability,

including reduced fares on SNCF trains in the PÉRIODE BLEUE for an accompanying person, and free transport of a wheelchair on train and AIR INTER. For those who cannot easily stand, there are extended benefits, such as free VIGNETTE, reserved seats in public transport and exemption from the TAXE D'HABITATION. It is issued by the BUREAU D'AIDE SOCIALE, but can take up to one year to be issued after an application.

The *Carte d'invalidité militaire* applies to the war-wounded with at least 25 per cent disability, and gives concessionary travel on SNCF and RER trains and, depending on severity of handicap, on air travel within France, to and from the DOM and most of Francophone Africa, reduced telephone rentals and some relief on call rates, as well as free entry into national museums. Certain holders of the *Carte d'invalidité militaire* who live in the Paris region are given priority on the RATP transport system. See also: CARTE 'STATION DEBOUT PÉNIBLE'

CARTE ÉMERAUDE
The city of Paris issues this card to old or disabled people who have lived there for at least three years, and whose income is limited. It gives them free travel on the Paris public transport system, free telephone installation, certain help towards home improvements, and free entry to leisure facilities owned by the city, with half-price entry to national monuments.

CARTE GRISE
The registration document for a motor vehicle, issued by the DÉPARTEMENT, which receives the fees payable as part of its local income. The PRÉFECTURE (in Paris, the PRÉFECTURE DE POLICE) is the office which deals with the administration. Changes in ownership have to be notified within two weeks, and incur payment of another fee, halved if the vehicle is more than ten years old. If it is more than five years old, a CONTRÔLE TECHNIQUE has to be satisfactorily passed. An alteration involving a change in *département* means the vehicle has to be re-registered. This also applies to a change of address of the owner which is notifiable within one month, but does not incur a fee.

The *Carte grise* has to be carried by the driver and produced at once if demanded by a police officer. Failure to do so is a

CONTRAVENTION leading to imposition of an AMENDE FORFAITAIRE.

CARTE JEUNE SNCF

All young people between the age of 12 and 26 can obtain this concessionary summer rail travel card on payment of a fee. It allows half-price travel in the PÉRIODE BLEUE from June to September on the SNCF system, except in the Paris BANLIEUE, and on the Dieppe-Newhaven ferry, and in CORSE, free couchette accommodation on night journeys, and two nights' free accommodation in a *Point accueil Jeune*.

CARTE JEUNES

This card is available on payment of a fee to anyone younger than 26 years old, valid from 12 months from September, and entitles the holder to thousands of concessions in eight European countries, including reduced fares on public transport, discounts on restaurant and fast-food meals, insurance, driving lessons, leisure facilities, a free medical service and free legal aid. It is widely available through CAISSES D'ÉPARGNE, post offices, youth hostels and MAIRIES, and many other outlets.

CARTE KIWI

This is a concessionary rail travel card available to children younger than 16 years old, encouraging travel by family groups. A group of four adults travelling with a card holder travels at half-fare on SNCF trains and in Germany (if the tickets are bought in France) in the PÉRIODE BLEUE and PERIODE BLANCHE. The child is guaranteed a seat or free couchette, a free drink, free transport for a pet, and further coupons with incentives to make additional journeys. The accompanying adults receive money-off coupons to encourage them to use other SNCF services.

CARTE NATIONALE DE PRIORITÉ

This card is available without charge to pregnant women, parents of young children, and those who have three children below the age of 16, provided they live with the children, and holders of the MÉDAILLE DE LA FAMILLE FRANÇAISE. According to the circumstances, it is valid for a period of up to three years, and proves entitlement to priority on public transport, in queues in offices and at counters of the ADMINISTRATION.

CARTE NATIONALE D'IDENTITÉ

This card is available for payment of a TIMBRE FISCAL to any person of French nationality, and is issued through a MAIRIE or a COMMISSARIAT DE POLICE. A minor can be issued with a *Carte nationale d'identité*, if the written permission of one parent is given. It is valid for 10 years, and is a convenient way of providing proof of identity in dealings with, for example, public offices and financial institutions, and is occasionally required when writing cheques. It can be used in place of a passport for travel to many countries.

CARTE ORANGE

A travel card available to anyone, which can be bought on a weekly, monthly or annual basis. It gives unlimited travel within the Paris area on bus, MÉTRO and RER trains, depending on the zones in which it is valid. An employer must refund half the cost of the card to employees who live in most of the Paris AGGLOMÉRATION, if the place of residence and the place of work are within the area served by the card.

CARTE PARIS-FAMILLE

A family with three children resident in Paris for a minimum period of three years, and whose income is such that they pay a modest level of IMPÔT, may obtain this card which entitles them to an annual subsidy of 2,000 francs (1990 figure) to help pay for transport, child-minding etc., free entry to Paris leisure facilities, six days' priority per TRIMESTRE in a school canteen or city child-minding service, an ALLOCATION LOGEMENT to help the cost of housing, a rent subsidy or subsidy towards the repayment of a PRÊT POUR L'ACCESSION À LA PROPRIÉTÉ (PAP) up to 10,000 francs monthly (1990 figure), and a reduced electricity bill.

CARTE PARIS-SANTÉ

The city of Paris instituted this facility in addition to the SÉCURITÉ SOCIALE arrangements in 1989. It provides those who are not otherwise covered by the *Sécurité sociale* (e.g. the long-term unemployed) with the basic health-care benefits of the system.

CARTE PASTEL
This is a telephone credit card, issued by FRANCE TÉLÉCOM, allowing calls to be made from a public telephone and charged to a subscriber's account.

CARTE PATHÉ CINÉMA
A 'smart' card which can be used to pre-book seats in a *Pathé* cinema at a preferential rate.

CARTE POSTÉPARGNE
The card is available to anyone of 16 years of age and older, who holds a COMPTE D'ÉPARGNE in the post office, and allows withdrawals in pre-arranged post offices without formality, telegraphic withdrawals from any post office, and acts as a withdrawal card in cash machines.

CARTE RAIL EUROP
This gives entitlement to reduced rate travel by train in a number of European countries, either to a family travelling together (*Carte Rail Europ F*) or to individuals who hold a CARTE VERMEIL (*Carte Rail Europ S*).

CARTE RUBIS
The equivalent of the CARTE AMÉTHYSTE, but relating to travel on buses within the Paris region.

CARTE 'STATION DEBOUT PÉNIBLE'
This card is available to a disabled person who does not qualify for a CARTE D'INVALIDITÉ, if standing is problematic. It is issued through the BUREAU D'AIDE SOCIALE, and gives entitlement to a seat in public transport.

CARTE UGC PRIVILÈGE
A discount card giving various benefits in UGC cinemas, including preferential rates of admission.

CARTE VERMEIL
Any person above 60 years of age is able to obtain this annual concessionary rail card, available on payment of a fee, which

gives a 50 per cent reduction on SNCF tickets for travel in the PÉRIODE BLEUE as well as discounts on SNCF bus services and tours. See also: CARTE RAIL EUROP

CARTIER-BRESSON, HENRI (1908–)
The internationally recognised photographic artist.

CASIER DES CONTRAVENTIONS D'ALCOOLISME
The record of all offences against the laws relating to alcohol consumption and sale are kept at Nantes with the CASIER JUDICIAIRE, and are disclosed only to the legal authorities. See also: ALCOOL

CASIER DES CONTRAVENTIONS DE CIRCULATION
The record of driving offences is held at Nantes with the CASIER JUDICIAIRE, until they are 'spent', usually at least two years after the offence. The details can be disclosed to other courts, as well as to the PRÉFET and the driver's lawyer, if there is a possibility of suspension of a driving licence. A driver is not entitled to request a copy of the record.

CASIER JUDICIAIRE
The central record of convictions and legal judgements, now held on computer in Nantes. It is possible to request a copy of the record held against one's own name, and an approach must be made to the PROCUREUR DE LA RÉPUBLIQUE in order to correct a false record. The record can also be supplied to courts who need to know the record of individuals involved in current cases, and certain details disclosed in confidence to public bodies (e.g. before an appointment to a public post, award of honours). The TRIBUNAL POUR ENFANTS and TRIBUNAL CORRECTIONNEL are able in certain circumstances to ignore the previous record of a minor or young person. See also: CASIER DES CONTRAVENTIONS D'ALCOOLISME; CASIER DES CONTRAVENTIONS DE CIRCULATION

CASINO
One of the largest retail groups in France, with a range of premises from small corner shops to hypermarkets, including the MAMMOUTH chain. Its origins are in a small grocery shop

inside the Casino at Saint-Étienne in 1860. The descendants of the founder still own 30 per cent of the shares. As well as food stores, it now has interests in cafeterias, DIY, food processing factories and a chain of cash and carry stores in USA. Its largest store is a *Géant-Casino* in Marseille (13,875 m²).

CASINO DE PARIS
A Paris theatre on the site of a well-known music hall, the venue for concerts of pop music and light entertainment.

CASINOS
There are nearly 150 gambling casinos in France, overseen by the *Commission supérieure des jeux*, which can close them in the case of irregularity. Minors are excluded and it is possible for an inveterate gambler to ask for a five-year ban on his or her entry, in order to try to break the habit. (About 2,500 people are voluntarily excluded.)

CATALAN
The language spoken by about 25 per cent of Spain's population and by some inhabitants of the Perpignan area (PYRÉNÉES-ORIENTALES) may be studied in schools in the ACADÉMIE of Montpellier. In 1986–1987, 2,576 pupils were following Catalan courses, the vast majority in the public sector.

CATENA
A grouping of hardware businesses throughout France allowing bulk buying through 11 wholesalers by 850 retail enterprises.

CAYATTE, ANDRÉ (1909–1989)
A popular film director who made about 20 feature films, including *Nous sommes tous des assassins* (1952) and *L'Amour en question* (1978).

CB See: *CARTE BLEUE*

CCA See: *COMMISSION DES CLAUSES ABUSIVES*

CCF See: *CRÉDIT COMMERCIAL DE FRANCE*

CCI See: *CHAMBRE DE COMMERCE ET DE L'INDUSTRIE*

CCP See: *COMPTE-CHÈQUES POSTAL*

CD See: *CHEMIN DÉPARTEMENTAL*

CDC See: *CAISSE DES DÉPÔTS ET CONSIGNATIONS*

CDI See: *CENTRE DE DOCUMENTATION ET D'INFORMATION*

CDN See: *CENTRE DRAMATIQUE NATIONAL*

CDS See: *CENTRE DES DÉMOCRATES SOCIAUX*

CDUC See: *COMMISSION DÉPARTEMENTALE D'URBANISME COMMERCIAL*

CE See: *CYCLE ÉLÉMENTAIRE*

CEA See: *COMMISSARIAT À L'ÉNERGIE ATOMIQUE; COMPTE D'ÉPARGNE EN ACTIONS*

CECSMO See: *CERTIFICAT D'ÉTUDES CLINIQUES SPÉCIALES MENTION ODONTOLOGIE*

CEDEX See: *COURRIER D'ENTREPRISE À DISTRIBUTION EXCEPTIONNELLE*

CEG See: *COLLÈGE D'ENSEIGNEMENT GÉNÉRAL*

CEINTURE DE SÉCURITÉ
Wearing seat belts in the front seats of cars registered since 1970, as well as rear seats of those registered since 1978, is a legal requirement, and failure to wear one incurs an AMENDE FORFAITAIRE.

CEINTURE ROUGE
The 'red belt' of Communist dominated COMMUNES in the inner BANLIEUE of Paris, in some state of disrepair following the decline of the PARTI COMMUNISTE FRANÇAIS and the rise of the FRONT NATIONAL.

CENSURE
The *Ministère de la culture* is responsible for decisions on categorizing films for public performance. The decisions are taken by a *Commission de contrôle* representing the cinema

industry, the ministry and the medical and teaching professions. The categories are: unrestricted, restricted to those of 13 years old and above, restricted to adults, and not permitted. There is also an X classification denoting a film with extremely violent scenes. Pornographic films can only be shown in specially licensed premises, and the films and box-office takings on them and on X films are subject to a penal rate of tax.

CENTRE
The administrative RÉGION comprising the DÉPARTEMENTS of CHER, EURE-ET-LOIR, INDRE, INDRE-ET-LOIRE, LOIR-ET-CHER, and LOIRET. It has a population of 2.37 million, and the regional capital is Orléans.

It is the largest cereal-producing region in the European Community. In the 1960s and early 1970s, dynamic development affected the region, especially in giving Orléans the role of regional centre, as a result of the early regionalisation policies, although there is less overtly regional identity than in some more natural geographical groupings. Most industrial concerns are medium and small-sized, and there is no heavy industry. The Centre is important as the site of a number of nuclear power stations. Considerable controversy surrounds the future of the Sologne wetland area, with environmentalists and developers in opposing camps.

The tourist industry, based on the appeal of the Loire Valley and its Renaissance châteaux, is very important. Connections with Paris are easy, with a TGV line open since 1990, and the AUTOROUTE dating from 1968 onwards.

In the 1992 ÉLECTIONS RÉGIONALES, the FRONT NATIONAL and the VERTS made gains, holding the balance of power between the Centre Right and the Left on the new CONSEIL RÉGIONAL.

CENTRE AÉRÉ
A publicly-funded centre where children from the age of three are looked after during the daytime while their parents are at work.

CENTRE COMMERCIAL
A shopping centre, usually on an out-of-town site, where

hypermarkets and large chain discount stores are laid out with free parking facilities.

CENTRE D'ACTION CULTURELLE
These are special centres, of which there are about 30 in total, financed partly by the State and partly by a local authority, which provide facilities for performance, exhibitions, etc., in places where there are few other suitable locations.

CENTRE DE DOCUMENTATION ET D'INFORMATION (CDI)
A resource and information centre located within a school or college, supervised by a *documentaliste* and available to students for personal research or study. The CDI is provided with a full range of library facilities with information technology and access to official literature.

CENTRE DE FORMATION D'APPRENTIS (CFA)
Apprentices between the ages of 16–20 must undertake at least 360 hours of study in a CFA, which provides courses at the level of CLASSE DE TROISIÈME. See also: APPRENTISSAGE; TAXE D'APPRENTISSAGE

CENTRE DE LOISIRS SANS HÉBERGEMENT (CLSH)
A similar venture to the CENTRE AÉRÉ.

CENTRE DE RECHERCHE ET D'ÉTUDE POUR LA DIFFUSION DU FRANÇAIS (CRÉDIF)
A private organisation which has been influential in developing French language teaching methods and courses for foreign learners.

CENTRE DES DÉMOCRATES SOCIAUX (CDS)
A political party of the Centre, founded in 1976. Its immediate predecessors were the *Centre démocrate* (of which the most prominent figure was Jean LECANUET) and the *Centre démocratie et progrès* (leaders Jacques Duhamel and Joseph FONTANET). It works as part of the grouping known as the UNION POUR LA DÉMOCRATIE FRANÇAISE. Its present leader is Pierre MÉHAIGNERIE, and there are about 50,000 paid-up members.

CENTRE D'ÉTUDES, DE RECHERCHE ET D'ÉDUCATION SOCIALISTES (CERES)

A left-wing grouping within the PARTI SOCIALISTE which was a power-base for Jean-Pierre CHEVÈNEMENT, its *Secrétaire général* from 1965 to 1971. Its stance brought it into conflict with the MITTERRAND government, despite Chevènement's membership of both. See also: SOCIALISME ET RÉPUBLIQUE

CENTRE D'INFORMATION ET DE DOCUMENTATION JEUNESSE (CIDJ)

A Paris advice and information centre for young people, run by the *Ministère de la jeunesse et des sports*. It deals with enquiries about education, leisure, travel, careers, training, etc.

CENTRE D'INFORMATION CIVIQUE (CIC)

A Paris information centre which provides information on all matters concerning elections.

CENTRE D'INFORMATION ET D'ORIENTATION (CIO)

There are 585 of these centres throughout France, providing information and advice about educational provision, training and careers. As well as the fully-equipped centres, the CIO provides a support service of advisers, based in schools. The documentation available through the service is provided by ONISEP.

CENTRE D'OPÉRATIONS DES FORCES AÉRIENNES STRATÉGIQUES (COFAS)

The underground command centre of the airborne nuclear forces based at Taverny (VAL-D'OISE).

CENTRE DRAMATIQUE NATIONAL (CDN)

A private, permanent theatre company which has a long-term contract with the State can call itself a *Centre dramatique national*. There were 22 in 1987, distributed throughout France.

CENTRE DRAMATIQUE NATIONAL POUR L'ENFANCE ET LA JEUNESSE

A similar venture to a CENTRE DRAMATIQUE NATIONAL but clearly with a specific target audience. In 1989, these existed at Caen, Lille, Lyon, St-Denis and Sartrouville.

CENTRE HOSPITALIER SPÉCIALISÉ EN PSYCHIATRIE (CHS)

One of about 100 state psychiatric hospitals, which provide the bulk of in-patient psychiatric places.

CENTRE HOSPITALIER UNIVERSITAIRE (CHU)

A teaching hospital attached to the medical faculty of a university.

CENTRE INTERNATIONAL DES ÉTUDIANTS ET STAGIAIRES (CIES)

A voluntary body dependent on various ministries, which provides lodging, social and counselling services to foreign students in France and Francophone Africa, and organises training facilities and international meetings within the COOPÉRATION programmes.

CENTRE INTERNATIONAL D'ÉTUDES PÉDAGOGIQUES (CIEP)

A publicly-funded body which promotes international studies, as well as research into teaching methods and means of developing innovatory approaches.

CENTRE MÉDICAL DE LONG SÉJOUR (CMLS)

A state-funded long-stay hospital.

CENTRE NATIONAL DE DOCUMENTATION PÉDAGOGIQUE (CNDP)

The publications office of the *Ministère de l'*ÉDUCATION NATIONALE for materials directly concerning the teaching profession. Its headquarters are in Paris but it also supplies every CENTRE RÉGIONAL DE DOCUMENTATION PÉDAGOGIQUE, CENTRE DÉPARTEMENTAL DE DOCUMENTATION PÉDAGOGIQUE, and even three *Centres locaux de documentation pédagogique*. There is a mail order service.

CENTRE NATIONAL D'ENSEIGNEMENT À DISTANCE (CNED)

Dependent on the *Ministère de l'*ÉDUCATION NATIONALE, this

organisation provides a range of correspondence courses, supported by audio-visual media and TÉLÉTEL, for all levels, from primary education to specialist training for entry to certain careers in the ADMINISTRATION. There are seven centres, each with its own specialisms: Grenoble, Lille, Lyon, Rennes, Rouen, Toulouse, Vanves, with a sub-branch at Poitiers. There are about 260,000 students.

CENTRE NATIONAL DE LA CINÉMATOGRAPHIE (CNC)

The organisation dependent on the *Ministère de la* CULTURE which has the responsibility for providing state support for the cinema and television industry.

Its income is based on a tax on cinema box-office receipts, on part of the television REDEVANCE and 4 per cent of television programme companies' income, as well as direct government funding.

Its support takes the form of subsidies to organisations promoting French cinema, funds for further investment to the makers of fictional and animated films for television, subsidies for new programme makers, etc.

CENTRE NATIONAL DE LA RECHERCHE SCIENTIFIQUE (CNRS)

A financially autonomous body set up in 1939 in order to carry out research in its own laboratories, or in association with universities and other research organisations. The CNRS employs 17,000 research staff and 8,500 technicians and administrators.

CENTRE NATIONAL DES INDÉPENDANTS ET PAYSANS (CNIP)

A Right of Centre political grouping founded in 1949 by René COTY and Roger Duchet. At the time of the birth of the CINQUIÈME RÉPUBLIQUE in 1958, it was the second largest party in the ASSEMBLÉE NATIONALE and the SÉNAT. Its power declined in the 1960s with the growth of the RÉPUBLICAINS INDÉPENDANTS, but it participated in the Raymond BARRE governments in the late 1970s. It presently has only 20 representatives in parliament, but there is a substantial CNIP presence in municipal and CONSEIL GÉNÉRAL composition.

CENTRE NATIONAL DES INDUSTRIES ET DES TECHNIQUES (CNIT)
An enormous exhibition centre at *La* DÉFENSE, built in the 1950s on a triangular plan, designed by Bernard ZEHRFUSS.

CENTRE NATIONAL DES JEUNES AGRICULTEURS (CNJA)
A union organisation taking the form of a pressure group within the FNSEA, reflecting the views of farmers and agricultural workers below the age of 35. It has 80,000 members, and has been influential in forming policy of the parent organisation.

CENTRE NATIONAL D'ÉTUDES SPATIALES (CNES)
A participating institution in the European space programmes, this is the state-funded space research institution. It has three space centres: at Toulouse, Évry (ESSONNE), and the launch station at Kourou (GUYANE). See also: ARIANE

CENTRE OPÉRATIONNEL DE LA DÉFENSE AÉRIENNE (CODA)
A national command network of 'early warning' defences which acts as France's detection system for incoming missiles. It transmits information to COFAS.

CENTRE RÉGIONAL DES ŒUVRES UNIVERSITAIRES ET SCOLAIRES (CROUS)
Each university has a CROUS attached to it. The organisation deals with all matters of student welfare, and its affairs are run by committees which reflect the various student bodies for whose members it works.

CEP See: *CAISSE D'ÉPARGNE ET DE PRÉVOYANCE; CERTIFICAT D'ÉTUDES PRIMAIRES; CERTIFICAT D'ÉTUDES PROFESSIONNELLES*

CÉRÉMONIAL DU SOUVENIR
The national remembrance events focus on the tomb of the unknown soldier, a victim of World War I, whose remains lie under the *Arc de Triomphe* in Paris, and are constantly guarded by a special military detachment. Each evening the permanent flame is ceremonially relit by ANCIENS COMBATTANTS, and the

Last Post sounded. On 11 November each year, there is a public holiday to commemorate the 1918 Armistice, and there are national and local ceremonies to mark the occasion, involving members of the government, local elected representatives, uniformed services and *Anciens Combattants*.

CERES See: *CENTRE D'ÉTUDES, DE RECHERCHE ET D'ÉDUCATION SOCIALISTES*

CÉRÈS
The Greek goddess of agriculture has frequently been used as a symbolic representation of France, emphasising the enormous agricultural wealth of the country.

CERGY-PONTOISE
A VILLE NOUVELLE in the VAL-D'OISE, with 139,121 inhabitants in 1990, near to the older towns of Cergy and Pontoise. It was developed as part of the regional plan to disperse the growing population of the ÎLE-DE-FRANCE region in an organised infrastructure. There is the relatively small *Université de Cergy-Pontoise* (within the ACADÉMIE of Versailles) with 2,000 registered students following courses in arts, applied languages, law, economics and sciences.

CERTIFICAT D'APTITUDE AU PROFESSORAT D'ÉCOLE
The qualification necessary to become a PROFESSEUR DES ÉCOLES obtained after training in an INSTITUT UNIVERSITAIRE DE FORMATION DES MAÎTRES.

CERTIFICAT D'APTITUDE AU PROFESSORAT D'ENSEIGNEMENT GÉNÉRAL DE COLLÈGE (CAPEGC)
A teaching certificate introduced in 1982 entitling teachers to work in a COLLÈGE. Candidates must have completed four years of professional training, and either had to hold the DEUG in one of the two subjects entered for in the CAPEGC, or to have had three years' teaching experience as a qualified INSTITUTEUR. The normal maximum age limit was 30. The course included subject studies and pedagogical training, and required the holder to teach for 10 years in a state institution. No teachers were recruited for the CAPEGC after 1986. The holder is a *Professeur d'enseignement général de collège*.

CERTIFICAT D'APTITUDE AU PROFESSORAT DE L'ENSEIGNEMENT DU SECOND DEGRÉ (CAPES)

This is the normal teaching certificate for qualifying as a PROFESSEUR in a secondary school, applicable to all levels from 1986. The training course takes two years, and entry to the course is for holders of a LICENCE D'ENSEIGNEMENT, and for those who hold an equivalent diploma and who have five years' teaching experience. The course is based in an INSTITUT UNIVERSITAIRE POUR LA FORMATION DES MAÎTRES. The examination is by CONCOURS, and the pass rate ranges from approximately 50 to 100 per cent, depending on the subject specialism. The holder of a CAPES, called a *Professeur certifié*, teaches for 18 hours per week (20 hours in the case of art or music teachers), and agrees to teach in a state institution for 10 years.

CERTIFICAT D'APTITUDE AU PROFESSORAT DE L'ENSEIGNEMENT TECHNIQUE (CAPET)

This is the equivalent to the CAPES for teachers of technical subjects.

CERTIFICAT D'APTITUDE AU PROFESSORAT DE LYCÉE PROFESSIONNEL (CAPLP)

The teaching qualification entitling teachers to work in a LYCÉE *d'enseignement professionnel*. There were two grades of CONCOURS, but only the more advanced (CAPLP 2) is now available, and requires candidates to have a LICENCE or five years' teaching experience and a DUT, or five years' professional experience as a CADRE.

CERTIFICAT D'APTITUDE AU PROFESSORAT DES COLLÈGES D'ENSEIGNEMENT TECHNIQUE (CAPCET)

A teaching certificate formerly available by CONCOURS entitling the holder to teach practical subjects in a LYCÉE *d'enseignement professionnel*.

CERTIFICAT D'APTITUDE AU PROFESSORAT TECHNIQUE (CAPT)

A teaching certificate formerly available by CONCOURS entitling the holder to teach technical subjects in a LYCÉE *d'enseignement professionnel*.

CERTIFICAT D'APTITUDE PROFESSIONNELLE (CAP)

A professional qualification achieved normally after three years of study in a LYCÉE *d'enseignement professionnel*. There are more than 300 possible CAP syllabuses, each directly related to vocational requirements.

CERTIFICAT DE CONCUBINAGE

A document which can be provided by the MAIRIE, which certifies that the unmarried couple mentioned are living together as man and wife. There is no legal obligation on a *Mairie* to supply the certificate. It is accepted as sufficient evidence to obtain a CARTE COUPLE, and certain other minor benefits. See also: ATTESTATION D'UNION LIBRE

CERTIFICAT DE SYNTHÈSE CLINIQUE ET THÉRAPEUTIQUE (CSCT)

A medical qualification taken in the later stages of training before students select their specialisms or general practice.

CERTIFICAT D'ÉTUDES CLINIQUES SPÉCIALES MENTION ODONTOLOGIE (CECSMO)

An advanced certificate in dentistry, taken by dentists after qualification and further study.

CERTIFICAT D'ÉTUDES PRIMAIRES (CEP)

A major achievement of the *Troisième République*, the former certificate awarded after the years of compulsory schooling, before the expansion of secondary education to all. It is still available to adults who are working towards elementary qualifications.

CERTIFICAT D'ÉTUDES PROFESSIONNELLES (CEP)

A basic educational qualification awarded after one year of study at some LYCÉES *d'enseignement professionnel*, and leading to unskilled employment.

CERTIFICAT D'INVESTISSEMENT (CI)

A share of a company which does not confer voting rights on the owner. A CI will trade at about a third or half below the price of a full share.

CERTIFICAT D'URBANISME
A planning document available to the owner or tenant of a property on request from the MAIRIE which gives information about mains services, etc., and states the possible developments that are permitted for a specific property.

CES See: *COLLÈGE D'ENSEIGNEMENT SECONDAIRE*

CÉSAR
The French 'Oscars', awarded each February since 1976 to cinema personnel, by their peers in the *Académie des arts*, and named after the sculptor who designed the statuettes. There are 19 categories of award.

CETELEM
A charge card company which runs the *Carte Aurore*.

CFA See: *CENTRE DE FORMATION D'APPRENTIS; COMMUNAUTÉ FINANCIÈRE AFRICAINE; COMMUNAUTÉ FRANÇAISE D'AFRIQUE*

CFDT See: *CONFÉDÉRATION FRANÇAISE DÉMOCRATIQUE DU TRAVAIL*

CFE-CGC See: *CONFÉDÉRATION FRANÇAISE DE L'ENCADREMENT DE LA CONFÉDÉRATION DES CADRES*

CFP See: *COMMUNAUTÉ FRANÇAISE DU PACIFIQUE; TOTAL – COMPAGNIE FRANÇAISE DES PÉTROLES*

CFTC See: *CONFÉDÉRATION FRANÇAISE DES TRAVAILLEURS CHRÉTIENS*

CGC See: *CONFÉDÉRATION GÉNÉRALE DES CADRES*

CGE See: *COMPAGNIE GÉNÉRALE D'ÉLECTRICITÉ; GÉNÉRALE DES EAUX*

CGPME See: *CONFÉDÉRATION GÉNÉRALE DES PETITES ET MOYENNES ENTREPRISES*

CGT See: *CONFÉDÉRATION GENÉRALE DU TRAVAIL*

CHABAN-DELMAS, JACQUES (1915–   )

A distinguished politician, MAIRE of Bordeaux since 1947, who served as PREMIER MINISTRE under DE GAULLE from 1969 and under Georges POMPIDOU to 1972 and held a number of other ministerial posts in the QUATRIÈME RÉPUBLIQUE. He was one of the earliest politicians to rally to De Gaulle during the Second World War. From 1958, Chaban-Delmas was *Président* of the ASSEMBLÉE NATIONALE until his prime ministerial appointment, and again for the periods 1978–1981 and 1986–1988. He was unsuccessful against Valéry GISCARD D'ESTAING in the presidential elections of 1974. As well as his political career, he has maintained a glittering record of sporting achievements, having been an international rugby player and later in life taking a leading role in veteran tennis championships.

CHABROL, CLAUDE (1930–   )

A film director whose speciality has been in creating a sense of suspense and menace, and in focusing on portraits of provincial life. Among his best-known of more than 30 films are *Le Boucher* (1969), *Le Beau Serge* (1958) and *L'Inspecteur Lavardin* (1986).

CHAILLOT

The *Théâtre national de Chaillot* is a major Paris playhouse, since 1968 supported by public funds as the home of the THÉÂTRE NATIONAL POPULAIRE. Since reconstruction in 1975, the building has two theatres, the larger one doubling as a concert hall.

CHAMBERY, UNIVERSITÉ DE See: *SAVOIE, UNIVERSITÉ DE*

CHAMBRE CIVILE See: *TRIBUNAL DE GRANDE INSTANCE*

CHAMBRE CORRECTIONNELLE See: *TRIBUNAL DE GRANDE INSTANCE*

CHAMBRE D'AGRICULTURE DÉPARTEMENTALE

Each DÉPARTEMENT has a representative body elected by local farmers and agricultural organisations to give advice to local planners, and to maintain certain local rulings. They are financially dependent on the government and on a levy upon landowners.

CHAMBRE DE COMMERCE ET DE L'INDUSTRIE (CCI)

There are a number of different levels of *Chambre de commerce et de l'industrie*, covering the whole of France. They are public bodies, funded partly by the TAXE PROFESSIONNELLE, but mostly by the government, and represent the interests of the business community in dealings with the ADMINISTRATION. In addition, they manage ports, airports, bus stations, warehouses, exhibition centres and educational establishments, particularly those with a management training role, such as business schools.

CHAMBRE DES DÉPUTÉS

The former term for the lower house of parliament, since 1946 known as ASSEMBLÉE NATIONALE.

CHAMBRE DES MÉTIERS

There are a number of *Chambres des métiers*, representing the interests of various craft industries, mainly on the basis of one per DÉPARTEMENT.

CHAMBRE DES MISES EN ACCUSATION

The formal stage in a legal case to be brought before a COUR D'ASSISES after the JUGE D'INSTRUCTION has completed investigations, and has named a person as INCULPÉ. The *Chambre des mises en accusation* examines the evidence to ascertain whether there is a case to answer. It can dismiss the case, or confirm the findings of the *Juge d'instruction*, whereupon the *inculpé* becomes an *accusé*, and the case is referred to the *Cour d'assises*. It is also a means whereby an *inculpé* can appeal against the *Juge d'instruction's* decision. See also: PRÉVENU

CHAMPAGNE-ARDENNE

The administrative RÉGION comprising the DÉPARTEMENTS of ARDENNES, AUBE, HAUTE-MARNE and MARNE, with a population in 1990 of 1.34 million. The regional capital is Châlons-sur-Marne. Agriculturally the region is important for crops, cereals and beet accounting for over 80 per cent of its agricultural revenue.

The Champagne wine trade, based in Reims and Epernay, is highly controlled by a small number of large firms, dominated by the Moët group. Production has quadrupled over 25 years, reaching 232 million bottles in 1990.

Other industries are less dominant and, where they were large, tend to be in decline, whereas tourism has become important over the years.

Champagne-Ardenne has been relatively prosperous, with an above-average level of income per household, but there has recently been a slight decline in the working population.

The Centre Right consolidated its control of the CONSEIL RÉGIONAL in the 1992 ÉLECTIONS RÉGIONALES, but the FRONT NATIONAL and VERTS also made gains, largely at the expense of the PARTI SOCIALISTE.

CHAMPION
A national chain of grocery supermarkets and hypermarkets, part of the PROMODÈS group of companies.

CHAMPIONNAT DE FRANCE DE FOOTBALL
Established in 1894, and now comprising a competition between the 20 clubs of the first division, the championship is based on points, and the winning club plays in the European Cup Winners' Cup, with second and third playing in the UEFA Cup. The clubs in nineteenth and twentieth place are relegated to the second division.

CHAMPS-ÉLYSÉES
The fashionable world-famous shopping and commercial avenue in Paris, on the site of part of the royal hunting forest.

CHAMPS-SUR-MARNE
The *Château de Champs-sur-Marne* (SEINE-ET-MARNE) is government property, reserved for the use of the PREMIER MINISTRE. In fact, it is normally used as a government guest house for distinguished foreign visitors.

CHAR, RENÉ (1907–1988)
A famous RÉSISTANCE poet who broke away from the surrealist

group and became more lyrical and humanist, his style
remaining rather elliptical.

CHARBONNAGES DE FRANCE
The central co-ordinating body which oversees the operation
of the three nationalised coal-producing firms, which are
regionally grouped. The coal industry is in decline, and is
heavily subsidised by government funds. A restructuring plan
was put into operation in 1984, with the aim of closing
uneconomic mines, reducing manpower and turning the
industry into profit. The only surviving production is from opencast mining. Subsidiary businesses to exploit sales and by-
products are also controlled by *Charbonnages de France*.

CHARENTE
A DÉPARTEMENT in the POITOU-CHARENTES region, named after
the river which flows through it, with a 1990 population of
342,268. The CHEF-LIEU is ANGOULÊME (urban area 101,107). The
other centre of population is COGNAC (27,474).

Charente is largely agricultural, with its main activities being
dairy and beef production, wheat, maize and sunflower growing
and the production of wine and brandy. The towns have mixed
light industry, and the smaller ones retain their craft-based
traditions, and tourism is increasingly important. There are
well-known festivals of folk music at Confolens, of detective films
at Cognac, and cartoons and jazz at Angoulême, a former
centre of paper-making.

Politically, Charente generally supports the Left. Since the
financial troubles at Angoulême, however, the Right is in the
ascendancy, and this was confirmed by the ÉLECTIONS
CANTONALES and RÉGIONALES of 1992.

Code départemental: 16

CHARENTE-MARITIME
A coastal DÉPARTEMENT in the POITOU-CHARENTES region,
including a number of inshore islands, named after the river
which flows into the Atlantic at la Rochelle, its CHEF-LIEU. The
Département's population in 1990 was 527,124. The la
Rochelle AGGLOMÉRATION is home to 100,264, and it is a busy

commercial and fishing port with historical connections to France's imperial expansion. There are a number of engineering firms with plants here (including ALSTHOM, PEUGEOT), and the town is an important tourist centre. Other urban areas are Rochefort (35,047), a port and garrison town, with boatbuilding, wood veneer and aeronautic industries; Royan (29,194), a seaside resort; and Saintes (27,003) – telecommunications equipment, agricultural co-operative.

Agricultural activity is dominated by crops such as sunflowers, vines, cereals, and dairy products. Charente-Maritime produces 60 per cent of French oysters. There has been considerable development of the islands and their connections with the mainland in recent years, including a bridge to the *Île de Ré*, opened in 1988.

In politics, the *Département* has leant toward the Left but is represented in the ASSEMBLÉE NATIONALE by parties of both Left and Right, and the ÉLECTIONS CANTONALES of 1992 confirmed the control of the Centre Right over the CONSEIL GÉNÉRAL.

Code départemental: 17

CHARGE SOCIALE

The general term for deductions from salary and wages payments made by employers to cover compulsory contributions to SÉCURITÉ SOCIALE, ASSURANCE CHÔMAGE, etc. The term also includes employers' contributions.

CHARLIE-HEBDO

A weekly cartoon magazine for adults, founded in 1970. A monthly version started in 1982, and has a circulation of over 50,000. The magazine does not accept advertising, and has been influential in setting trends, sometimes taking the risk of offending the public.

CHASSE, LA

Hunting has a wide and increasing following in France. About 10,000 hunt with horses and hounds and there are at least one million French hunt followers. 1.8 million go shooting (18 per cent of whom are farmers), and this number has declined slightly since the introduction of a proficiency test in order to obtain a licence. All forms of hunting are controlled by law, and certain species are totally protected by legislation, and the numbers of others which may be hunted are limited.

The owner of a property has the right to hunt on it, and can give permission to anyone else. Hunting without such permission is illegal.

The hunting season for each DÉPARTEMENT is fixed by the PRÉFET. There are particular exceptions to the law in ALSACE. See also: PERMIS DE CHASSE

CHÂTELET
Named after a fortress previously situated in central Paris, this is now best known as an enormous MÉTRO station, linked to Châtelet-les-Halles. It is the largest underground railway station in the world, and the busiest in terms of annual passenger movements on the Paris network (33 million), at the intersection of six lines.

CHAZEMAIS
If one includes CORSE in one's calculations, this village in the ALLIER claims to be the centre of France. See also: BRUÈRES-ALLICHAMPS; SAINT-AMAND-MONTROND; VESDUN

CHEF DE L'ÉTAT See: *PRÉSIDENT DE LA RÉPUBLIQUE*

CHEFS-D'ŒUVRE EN PÉRIL
An annual award jointly funded by the *Ministère de la* CULTURE and other donors in order to support the work of conservation of ancient monuments, usually awarded to a private individual.

CHEF-LIEU
The principal town of either an ARRONDISSEMENT or a DÉPARTEMENT. The CHEF-LIEU of an *arrondissement* is the seat of a SOUS-PRÉFET. It thus has the alternative title of SOUS-PRÉFECTURE.

The *chef-lieu* of the *département* is the seat of the PRÉFET, and thus is sometimes called the PRÉFECTURE, as is also the building where he or she works.

CHEMIN COMMUNAL
An unclassified road, maintained by the COMMUNE.

CHEMIN DÉPARTEMENTAL See: *ROUTE DÉPARTEMENTALE*

CHÈQUE BARRÉ
A crossed cheque can normally only be paid into a postal cheque account. These cheques are issued free of charge by banks.

CHÈQUE CERTIFIÉ
A cheque which, at the request of the customer, is certified by the bank and is thereby guaranteed for a week.

CHÈQUE NON-BARRÉ
A normal cheque, issued by a bank, against a tax of five francs per cheque, and valid for a year. Banks have to supply the ADMINISTRATION with the names of all account holders to whom such cheques are issued.

CHÈQUE POSTAL See: *COMPTE-CHÈQUES POSTAL*

CHÈQUE-RESTAURANT
A personalised voucher giving entitlement to a meal on a working day at a restaurant which is a member of the scheme, up to the limit of the voucher, issued by employers if there is no canteen at the work-place. The employee can contribute 50 per cent of the value of the voucher in addition. In theory, only one voucher is accepted per meal.

CHÈQUE SANS PROVISION
It is illegal to issue cheques which cannot be paid because the account is not adequately funded. A first offender will be denied the right to issue cheques for 30 days if the amount overdrawn is refunded to the bank. Further contraventions of the rule mean a one-year ban on issuing cheques on any account held. A bank will, however, always honour a cheque below 100 francs if presented within one month, and will then take steps to recover the money paid from the customer.

Recipients of such cheques can report the offence to a HUISSIER, who automatically institutes proceedings if the matter is not resolved within 20 days. The case is then referred to the TRIBUNAL DE GRANDE INSTANCE.

If the bank has erroneously alleged that the account is

inadequately funded, it can be liable for a fine from 2,000 to 60,000 francs.

CHÈQUE-VACANCES

A voucher redeemable through holiday firms, issued by an employer as a result of an employee's savings and the employer's contribution. The group of employees to whom these are issued pay below a restricted ceiling of income tax. The cheques are issued in units of 10, 50 and 100 francs, and are reimbursed to holiday firms by the CAISSE DES DÉPOTS.

CHER

A DÉPARTEMENT in the CENTRE region, named after the tributary of the Loire which runs through it, with a 1990 population of 321,548. The CHEF-LIEU is Bourges, which is also the centre of the largest urban area (92,719) with employment in iron foundries, mechanical and aeronautic engineering, rubber, munitions and printing industries. Other centres of population are SAINT-AMAND-MONTROND (13,961) – metallurgy, hosiery, jewellery, packaging, printing, leather, food-processing and ceramics; and Vierzon (35,049) – metals, clothing, porcelain, chemicals, pottery, and textiles.

The *Département* is primarily agricultural, and cereals, maize, tobacco and wine are important. It is the largest producer of oil-producing crops, especially sunflowers, rape and mustard, as well as lentils and goat's milk.

There is a large cement plant at Beffes, and the Cher has the distinction of producing a third of French porcelain, largely at Mehun-sur-Yèvre and Vierzon. Other industry is mixed, ranging from traditional craft activities to radio-telescopes (at Nançay).

Tourism is increasingly important, and the *Département* has a rich resource of Renaissance châteaux.

Cher generally votes Left of Centre, but in recent years, Centre Right candidates have taken control of the CONSEIL GÉNÉRAL.

Code départemental: 18

CHÉREAU, PATRICE (1944–   )

A theatre, opera and film director who achieved early

prominence with his direction of Wagner's Ring Cycle in conjunction with BOULEZ at Bayreuth. He has worked with Roger PLANCHON at the THÉÂTRE NATIONAL POPULAIRE at Villeurbanne (RHÔNE), and became resident director at the *Théâtre des amandiers* in Nanterre (HAUTS-DE-SEINE).

CHEVAUX (CV)

The fiscal measure which reflects the size and power of a vehicle's engine, and thus places it on a scale of varying tax rates. The normal range is between 2CV, a small engined, lightly-powered car, and 22CV, a large powerful sports car. See also: VIGNETTE

CHEVÈNEMENT, JEAN-PIERRE (1939–)

A socialist politician, DÉPUTÉ for the TERRITOIRE DE BELFORT from 1973, who was *Secrétaire général* of the think-tank and pressure group, CERES, from 1965–1971. He uses this group as his personal power-base within the PARTI SOCIALISTE. After a number of junior ministerial posts, he became *Ministre de l'*ÉDUCATION NATIONALE in 1984–1986, and *Ministre de la* DÉFENSE NATIONALE from 1988 resigning over the Gulf War in 1991. He has written a number of books about modern socialism.

CHEYSSON, CLAUDE (1920–)

An ÉNARQUE who rose through the ADMINISTRATION into politics, having been a chief adviser of Pierre MENDÈS-FRANCE when the latter was PRÉSIDENT DU CONSEIL from 1954–1955. After a period as an Ambassador, he went into private industry and then became a European Commissioner, and in 1981, he became Minister for Foreign Affairs in MITTERRAND'S first government (a post then called *Ministre des relations extérieures*), until 1984.

CHIRAC, JACQUES (1932–)

A politician of the Right who became a DÉPUTÉ for the CORRÈZE in 1967, in the same year entering the government as employment minister. He rapidly climbed through the ranks of the Gaullist party, and after periods in various senior ministries, became PREMIER MINISTRE in 1974 during the presidency of Valéry GISCARD D'ESTAING, resigning in 1976. He headed the

Gaullist *Union des démocrates pour la République* from 1974, and founded its replacement party, the RASSEMBLEMENT POUR LA RÉPUBLIQUE in 1976. In 1977, he became the first elected MAIRE DE PARIS since 1871. He was unsuccessful in the ÉLECTIONS PRÉSIDENTIELLES of 1981 amd 1988, achieving 46 per cent of the vote in the second round in 1988, but served a second term as *Premier Ministre* from 1986 to 1988. Chirac's nickname of '*Le Bulldozer*' is a recognition of his dynamic style.

CHÔMAGE
The overall rate of unemployment at the end of 1990 was 9 per cent, with 2.5 million unemployed. The DÉPARTEMENTS with rates higher than 12 per cent were all coastal: BOUCHES-DU-RHÔNE, CHARENTE-MARITIME, GARD, HÉRAULT, NORD, PAS-DE-CALAIS, PYRÉNÉES-ORIENTALES and VAR. Those with less than 6 per cent unemployed were AIN, AVEYRON, BAS-RHIN, ESSONNE, HAUTE-SAVOIE, HAUT-RHIN, JURA, LOZÈRE, MAYENNE, and YVELINES. See also: ALLOCATION DE BASE; SÉCURITÉ SOCIALE

CHRONOPOST
An express document and parcel service guaranteeing delivery within 24 hours to any address in France. The service is run by a subsidiary of the PTT, the *Société française de messagerie internationale*, in which TRANSPORT AÉRIEN TRANSRÉGIONAL has a 34 per cent holding.

CHS See: *CENTRE HOSPITALIER SPÉCIALISÉ EN PSYCHIATRIE*

CHSCT See: *COMITÉ D'HYGIÈNE, DE SÉCURITÉ ET DES CONDITIONS DE TRAVAIL*

CHU See: *CENTRE HOSPITALIER UNIVERSITAIRE*

CIC See: *CENTRE D'INFORMATION CIVIQUE; CRÉDIT INDUSTRIEL ET COMMERCIAL*

CIDEX See: *COURRIER INDIVIDUEL À DISTRIBUTION EXCEPTIONNELLE*

CIDJ See: *CENTRE D'INFORMATION ET DE DOCUMENTATION JEUNESSE*

CIEP See: *CENTRE INTERNATIONAL D'ÉTUDES PÉDAGOGIQUES*

CIES See: *CENTRE INTERNATIONAL DES ÉTUDIANTS ET STAGIAIRES*

CINÉ-CLUB
There are more than 11,000 *ciné-clubs* in France, with over 1 million members. A club is permitted to show films two years after their public exhibition, or after they have been shown on television.

CINÉMATHÈQUE FRANÇAISE
The national film library with a museum and two film theatres. The archive is kept at Bois-d'Arcy (YVELINES) as part of the *Service des archives du film*, which also collects all film material received by the BIBLIOTHÈQUE NATIONALE as part of the DÉPÔT LÉGAL. The *Cinémathèque* library has a collection of printed and photograph material, equipment, posters, sets and costumes. Its film programme is shown at the *Palais de* CHAILLOT and *Centre* BEAUBOURG, as well as at festivals and events throughout France and abroad.

CINQ, LA
The privately-owned fifth television channel, from 1987 controlled by the HERSANT and Berlusconi groups, each of which held 25 per cent of the shares. In 1990, control passed to the HACHETTE group. It was required to include in its output 40 per cent of French-made programmes, and 60 per cent from within the European Community. *La Cinq* went bankrupt and ceased operation in 1992.

CINQUANTE MILLIONS DE CONSOMMATEURS
The monthly publication of the publicly-funded INSTITUT NATIONAL DE LA CONSOMMATION, which has a circulation of 250,000. The magazine gives comparative reviews of products and consumer advice. See also: QUE CHOISIR?

CINQUIÈME RÉPUBLIQUE
The *régime* established in 1958 by the adoption of the present CONSTITUTION, based largely on the principles of Charles DE

GAULLE in order to provide a strong executive, as a reaction to the weak governmental position experienced under the QUATRIÈME RÉPUBLIQUE. See also: ARTICLE 16; ASSEMBLÉE NATIONALE; PREMIER MINISTRE; PRÉSIDENT DE LA RÉPUBLIQUE; SÉNAT; SEPTENNAT

CIO See: *CENTRE D'INFORMATION ET D'ORIENTATION*

CIRCONSCRIPTION
The term usually means an electoral constituency in any election for public office. It is also used in the title *Circonscription d'action régionale* to denote the area in which a PRÉFET DE RÉGION has authority over all civil matters in time of war, and which has the same borders as a DIVISION MILITAIRE.

CITÉ DES SCIENCES ET DE L'INDUSTRIE
This centre with a permanent exhibition and display areas for temporary exhibitions, at la Villette in the suburbs of Paris, receives over four million visitors annually. Its main attractions include the GÉODE. The project was originally conceived in 1977 as a replacement for the market which by tradition provided Paris with its main meat supply, and the *Cité* was opened to the public in 1985.

CITROËN
The motor vehicle manufacturer, founded by André Citroën in 1919, which pioneered all-steel bodies, front-wheel drive, and a range of individualistic designs which typified French car production in the immediate post-war period. The longest-running model, the 2CV, was first produced in 1939, at the very moment war was declared. Citroën's main factory was at Levallois, in the Paris suburbs, but this closed in 1988. It has other plants at Caen, Metz and Rennes.

In 1976, Citroën was taken over by PEUGEOT, but still retains its identity within the group. Its models in more recent years have shown less individuality and have achieved higher sales.

CLASSE DE CINQUIÈME See: *CYCLE D'OBSERVATION*

CLASSE DE DÉTERMINATION See: *CLASSE DE SECONDE*

CLASSE DE NEIGE
Schools have the opportunity to take whole classes to the
mountain areas in the skiing season, to combine ski tuition
and normal school work in state-provided establishments.

CLASSE DE PREMIÈRE
The LYCÉE class for pupils aged 16–17, and thus the second year
of the BACCALAURÉAT course. The curriculum is more specialised
than that followed in the CLASSE DE SECONDE, for it is on entry
to the *Première* that the final choice of *filière* is made. An
examination in French as part of the *Bac* is compulsory at the
end of the *Première* year.

CLASSE DE QUATRIÈME See: *CYCLE D'ORIENTATION*

CLASSE DE SECONDE
Also called the *Classe de détermination*, the class in the LYCÉE
for pupils aged 15–16. It is the entry class to BACCALAURÉAT
courses, and the curriculum takes the form of a common core
with options.

The core consists of French (between four and five hours
weekly, according to options chosen), mathematics (two hours
30 minutes to four hours), history/geography/civics (three to
four hours), a first foreign language (two hours 30 minutes
to three hours), physics and chemistry (two to three hours),
biology and geology (30 minutes to two hours), physical
education and sport (two hours), and often a second foreign
language.

The range of options available in any *lycée* depends on its
special character, and the *Baccalauréat* courses it offers. Certain
options are obligatory for entry into particular courses.

CLASSE DE SIXIÈME See: *CYCLE D'OBSERVATION*

CLASSE DE TROISIÈME See: *CYCLE D'ORIENTATION*

CLASSE PRÉPARATOIRE
This is an intensive two-year post-BACCALAURÉAT course,
usually provided in a LYCÉE, in preparation for the entry
CONCOURS for a GRANDE ÉCOLE. The course is specific to the
concours, and certain prestigious *lycées* largely base their

reputation on their success rate in such courses. 287 lycées, including 63 private establishments, provide such courses. An elaborate *argot* has arisen around the *Classes préparatoires*, which are a major step in the process of upper middle-class success and security. Thus *Bizuths* (first year students), *Khâgne*, HYPOKHÂGNE (literary), and *Taupins* (maths/physics) indicate various stages of study in the different '*classes prépas*'. The HEC *classes préparatoires* are aimed at entry into any business school.

CLASSE PRÉPARATOIRE À L'APPRENTISSAGE (CPA)
This is a very different kind of course from those in the CLASSE PRÉPARATOIRE, despite its similar name. These courses are provided for pupils of 14–15 years of age who have only reached the standard of general education normally expected of 13 year olds, at the end of the *Classe de cinquième*. This situation is usually as a result of REDOUBLEMENT. They lead towards apprenticeships and are provided in a COLLÈGE, a LYCÉE *d'enseignement professionnel* or a CENTRE DE FORMATION D'APPRENTIS. The course structure alternates between 30 hours in class, and 30 hours at a work placement. See also: ALTERNANCE; APPRENTISSAGE; CLASSE PRÉ-PROFESSIONNELLE DE NIVEAU

CLASSE PRÉ-PROFESSIONNELLE DE NIVEAU (CPPN)
This is a similar to the CLASSE PRÉPARATOIRE À L'APPRENTISSAGE, but is based full-time in a COLLÈGE or a LYCÉE *d'enseignement professionnel*. After one year, a pupil can enter a CAP course, or transfer to the CPA. After two years, it is possible to take up an apprenticeship. See also: APPRENTISSAGE

CLASSE TERMINALE See: *TERMINALE, CLASSE*

CLE See: *COMPAGNIE LYONNAISE DES EAUX*

CLERC, JULIEN (1947–   )
The professional name of a popular singer who has found a new career as a film actor, notably in *Van Gogh*, the 1991 feature film made by Maurice PIALAT.

CLERMONT-FERRAND, UNIVERSITÉS DE
There are two universities, *Clermont-Ferrand I* (or the

Université d'Auvergne) with 10,000 students specialising in law, economics, medicine, pharmacy and dentistry, and *Clermont-Ferrand II* (*Université Blaise Pascal*), which has 14,000 students in faculties of arts, humanities, science and physical education.

CLÔTURE
Every property owner has the right to enclose his or her property, but cannot deny right of way to a neighbour who is thus prevented from having access to his or her own premises. In built-up residential areas, one can be required by a neighbour to contribute to the cost of erecting and maintaining separating walls or fences. This obligation only applies if the demand is made before the construction is started. See also: BORNAGE

CLSH See: *CENTRE DE LOISIRS SANS HÉBERGEMENT*

CLUB MED
A highly successful holiday organisation which began as an association in 1950, setting up holiday villages. One of its co-founders was Gilbert TRIGANO. The business now has about 250 sites including 140 villages in 35 countries, and has expanded into cruises and hotels. The *Club Med* became a limited company in 1957.

CM See: *COURS MOYEN*

CMLS See: *CENTRE MÉDICAL DE LONG SÉJOUR*

CNAL See: *COMITÉ NATIONAL D'ACTION LAÏQUE*

CNC See: *CENTRE NATIONAL DE LA CINÉMATOGRAPHIE*

CNCL See: *COMMISSION NATIONALE DE LA COMMUNICATION ET DES LIBERTÉS*

CNDP See: *CENTRE NATIONAL DE DOCUMENTATION PÉDAGOGIQUE*

CNEC See: *COMITÉ NATIONAL DE L'ENSEIGNEMENT CATHOLIQUE*

CNED See: *CENTRE NATIONAL D'ENSEIGNEMENT À DISTANCE*

CNES See: *CENTRE NATIONAL D'ÉTUDES SPATIALES*

CNIL See: *COMMISSION NATIONALE DE L'INFORMATIQUE ET DES LIBERTÉS*

CNIP See: *CENTRE NATIONAL DES INDÉPENDANTS ET PAYSANS*

CNIT See: *CENTRE NATIONAL DES INDUSTRIES ET DES TECHNIQUES*

CNJA See: *CENTRE NATIONAL DES JEUNES AGRICULTEURS*

CNMHS See: *CAISSE NATIONALE DES MONUMENTS HISTORIQUES ET DES SITES*

CNP See: *CAISSE NATIONALE DE PRÉVOYANCE; COMMISSION NATIONALE DE PLANIFICATION*

CNPF See: *CONFÉDÉRATION NATIONALE DU PATRONAT FRANÇAIS*

CNRS See: *CENTRE NATIONAL DE LA RECHERCHE SCIENTIFIQUE*

COB See: *COMMISSION DES OPÉRATIONS BE BOURSE*

CODA See: *CENTRE OPÉRATIONNEL DE LA DÉFENSE NATIONALE*

CODE
A collection of statutes, laws and all legally binding documents relating to a particular branch of the law or human activity. Among the most frequently referred to are the following:

The oldest is the *Code civil*, originally adopted in 1804, and since amended as necessary, which is the collection of laws and statutes relating to civil law. It is sometimes also called the *Code Napoléon*, after its originator.

The *Code de la nationalité* has often been amended to reflect government measures concerning IMMIGRATION.

The *Code de la route* enshrines all law concerning road users, and familiarity with it is necessary to obtain a PERMIS DE CONDUIRE.

The *Code du travail* includes all current employment legislation, the *Code électoral* lays down procedures and laws in all public election matters, and the *Code pénal* incorporates all statutes regarding the criminal law.

CODEC
A major co-operative group of food retailers, with over 850 hypermarkets, supermarkets and smaller shops, sometimes using the alternative identity of *Lion*. It found itself in serious difficulties in 1990. See also: SYSTÈME U

CODE NATIONAL D'ALERTE
This is a siren code signifying a warning of enemy action or other emergency affecting the safety of the population. Sirens are tested on the first Wednesday of the month (every two months in Paris and near suburbs) at midday.

CODE POSTAL
A five-figure numerical code which identifies the town or village of the local postal sorting office, preceding the town name in an address. The first two digits show the DÉPARTEMENT's code. The sorting office code is shown in the last three digits, and the larger the office, the more likely it is to end in 00 or 0. A code ending in 000 is the CHEF-LIEU of a *département*. Private addresses in Paris, Lyon and Marseille have their ARRONDISSEMENT number as the last two figures of the code. Large business users have individual codes. See also: CEDEX; CIDEX

CODER See: *COMMISSION DE DÉVELOPPEMENT ÉCONOMIQUE RÉGIONAL*

CODEVI
A tax-free fixed-rate investment account, created in 1983, open only to tax-paying private investors and their partners, and for the purpose of supporting industrial development. The acronym CODEVI is short for *Compte pour le développement industriel*. The account, up to a maximum investment of 15,000

francs, can be obtained through a bank, a CAISSE D'ÉPARGNE or a post office.

COEFFICIENT D'OCCUPATION DU SOL (COS)
This is a planning measurement which determines the legal size limit of a building in relation to the land area of the property.
See also: PLAN D'OCCUPATION DES SOLS

COFAS See: CENTRE D'OPÉRATIONS DES FORCES AÉRIENNES STRATÉGIQUES

COFIROUTE
The only remaining private company operating a motorway concession. It operates nearly 700 kilometres of toll motorway.
See also: AUTOROUTE

COGEMA See: COMPAGNIE GÉNÉRALE DES MATIÈRES NUCLÉAIRES

COGNAC
This town in the CHARENTE, as well as being synonymous with the local brandy, is the setting for an annual detective film festival.

COHABITATION
The term used for the period from 1986 to 1988, when the right-wing parties had a majority in the ASSEMBLÉE NATIONALE, although the president was Socialist. *Cohabitation* describes the working relationship between Jacques CHIRAC and François MITTERRAND.

COHN-BENDIT, DANIEL (1945–   )
A German citizen, now a Frankfurt city councillor, who rose to prominence in 1968 as one of the leaders of the student movement which provoked the May events. He was expelled from France and refused entry for 10 years.

COLBERT, COMITÉ
Named after the seventeenth century financier, the *Comité Colbert* is an ASSOCIATION of 70 firms producing luxury goods including high fashion, perfume and porcelain or providing services such as luxury hotels, opera houses and quality wines.

COLISSIMO

A special parcel rate operated by the PTT guaranteeing delivery the next day if within the same DÉPARTEMENT, and within 48 hours anywhere else in France. Credit is given to the user if these targets are not achieved.

COLLECTIVITÉ LOCALE/TERRITORIALE

The generic term for any local public authority, whether COMMUNE, MUNICIPALITÉ, DÉPARTEMENT or RÉGION. See also: COMMUNAUTÉ URBAINE

COLLÈGE

The state school for pupils aged 11–15. The *collège* is the standard route for pupils of this age group, and its curriculum and organisation are national.

There is basically a common core curriculum (TRONC COMMUN) with certain optional additions at various stages. Hours and programmes of study are laid down nationally, but the *collège* arranges its own timetable and organisation of methods of teaching.

Homework of between one to two hours daily will be set. Marks for all results are recorded on a standard scale out of 20, an average mark of below 10 being considered that of a child in difficulty. The aim will be to maintain an average performance of between 10 and 13.

At the end of their time in the *collège*, pupils are assessed for the award of the BREVET DES COLLÈGES.

The teaching staff is composed of those who fall into the following categories: PROFESSEUR CERTIFIÉ or PROFESSEUR D'ENSEIGNEMENT GÉNÉRAL DES COLLÈGES. Sixty per cent are women. The head is a PRINCIPAL who is a former teacher, but who is a full-time administrator. See also: CLASSE DE TROISIÈME; COLLÈGE D'ENSEIGNEMENT GÉNÉRAL; COLLÈGE D'ENSEIGNEMENT SECONDAIRE; CONSEIL DE CLASSE; CONSEIL DES PROFESSEURS; CYCLE D'OBSERVATION; CYCLE D'ORIENTATION; LYCÉE; REDOUBLEMENT

COLLÈGE DE FRANCE

Created in 1530 by François 1er and now the responsibility of the *Ministère de l'*ÉDUCATION NATIONALE, the *Collège de France* is a self-governing body of eminent specialists in sciences, arts, philosophy, humanities and law, who give free classes to the general public in Paris.

COLLÈGE D'ENSEIGNEMENT GÉNÉRAL (CEG)
Now replaced by the COLLÈGE, the CEG was a secondary school for those pupils aged 11–15 who had not been admitted to a selective LYCÉE. It was itself a replacement for the elementary school catering for the older pupil, and was being progressively replaced by the COLLÈGE D'ENSEIGNEMENT SECONDAIRE.

COLLÈGE D'ENSEIGNEMENT SECONDAIRE (CES)
The immediate precursor of the COLLÈGE, the CES was a lower comprehensive secondary school for pupils of 11–15, and provided education during these years for most French children. In some areas, the LYCÉE would provide for this age group, and thus the CES did not apply to the whole of the population.

COLLIER DE PERLES CARRÉ HERMÈS
A reference to the classic fashion adopted by the young upper bourgeois set classified by BON CHIC BON GENRE.

COLOMBEY-LES-DEUX-ÉGLISES See: *LA BOISSERIE*

COLONEL-FABIEN, PLACE DU
The address of the PARTI COMMUNISTE FRANÇAIS headquarters in Paris. *Fabien* was the code name for the first Communist saboteur against the German occupation in Paris.

COLONIE DE VACANCES
A holiday village or summer camp for children, usually subsidised by state funds, and staffed as a rule by students who act as *moniteurs* and *animateurs*. The *Colonie de vacances* has been the inspiration for many songs and films, having entered modern French folklore.

COLUCHE (1944–1986)
The stage name of Michel Colucchi, a popular comedian, famous for lampooning public figures and taking the part of the downtrodden Parisian working man. Coluche founded the

Restaurants du cœur which provide meals for the very poor.
He was killed in a motorcycle accident.

COMÉDIE FRANÇAISE
A national theatre company, founded in 1680 by Louis XIV's
action of merging two existing companies. Since 1799, the
Comédie Française has performed in the *Salle Richelieu* in Paris,
as well as on tour, and its activities centre on plays of the
established tradition, mainly French, but including some in
translation.

Its present constitution gives the company members
(approximately 30) the status of *sociétaire* for a term of between
10 and 30 years, the most senior being the *doyen*. The *sociétaires*
take a share of the profits, with the newest member being given
the largest individual share. There are also *pensionnaires* on
short-term contracts and honorary members.

COMITÉ DE LA RÉGLEMENTATION BANCAIRE
The body which oversees the operation of the banking industry,
and rules over matters of credit and banking liquidity. It is
composed of the *Ministre de l'*ÉCONOMIE, the governor of the
BANQUE DE FRANCE and four other members.

COMITÉ D'ENTREPRISE
Since 1945, any business with more than 50 employees has had
to have a *comité d'entreprise*, which includes the head of the
enterprise or his or her representative, and a number of
employees' representatives, fixed according to a sliding scale. All
employees of 16 years of age and above, who have been on the
payroll for at least three months, are eligible to vote for
candidates, who must be at least 18, and employed there for 12
months.

If there are more than 25 CADRES, they have their own
representatives on the *comité*. Union organisations present
lists of candidates, and the first round of voting is only final if
more than 50 per cent of those entitled to vote do so. If a second
round is held, the lists can be presented by other groups.

The *comité d'entreprise*'s major function is to represent the
interests of the workforce and to participate in the discussion of

plans for the business, in which case it must be consulted. It must receive a report from the employer once a year. It also has the responsibility of organising social and cultural facilities. In larger enterprises, the *comité* can call for reports to be commissioned, and sub-committees to work on economic matters. It has 0.2 per cent of the wages bill as its budget.

Abuse of a *comité d'entreprise* can lead to a fine and/or imprisonment. See also: COMITÉ D'HYGIÈNE, DE SÉCURITÉ ET DES CONDITIONS DE TRAVAIL

COMITÉ DES PARENTS
A representative body of parents of children at each ÉCOLE PRIMAIRE. Membership is dominated by national groupings of parents, especially the FCPE (FÉDÉRATION DES CONSEILS DE PARENTS D'ÉLÈVES DES ÉCOLES PUBLIQUES).

COMITÉ D'HYGIÈNE, DE SÉCURITÉ ET DES CONDITIONS DE TRAVAIL (CHSCT)
Since 1982, each enterprise with over 50 employees must have a CHSCT, which is responsible for consulting with the employer about measures to protect employees from health and safety risks at work. See also: COMITÉ D'ENTREPRISE

COMITÉ INTERMINISTÉRIEL
An ad-hoc grouping of ministers and SECRÉTAIRES D'ÉTAT, chaired by the PREMIER MINISTRE, convened in order to discuss particular matters of common interest.

COMITÉ NATIONAL D'ACTION LAÏQUE (CNAL)
A powerful pressure group, supported by left-wing parties, which resists moves to support private schools, and particularly those of religious foundations. It was influential in mobilising opinion against aspects of the *Plan* SAVARY in 1984.

COMITÉ NATIONAL DE L'ENSEIGNEMENT CATHOLIQUE (CNEC)
A Catholic pressure group formed to further the interests of the private education sector, prominent in its ability to mobilise opinion against aspects of the *Plan* SAVARY in 1984. See also: UNION NATIONALE DES ASSOCIATIONS DE PARENTS D'ÉLÈVES DE L'ENSEIGNEMENT LIBRE

COMMISSAIRE DE LA RÉPUBLIQUE
From 1982 to 1988, the post of PRÉFET was renamed
Commissaire de la République, as a reminder of the period of
the *Libération* of 1944. The PRÉFET DE RÉGION held the title
Commissaire de la République de région.

COMMISSAIRE DE POLICE
A senior non-uniformed police officer in the POLICE NATIONALE.
The *Commissaire* rank is sub-divided into three grades, in
descending order of seniority: *Commissaire divisionnaire* (385 in
1988); *Commissaire principal* (770); and *Commissaire de police*
(893, including 118 women), out of a total non-uniformed force
of 110,732. 30 per cent of posts of this rank are reserved for
women, as from 1986. Recruitment to a post of *Commissaire* is
by CONCOURS, open to holders of a LICENCE. In preparation for
the *concours*, candidates attend the *École supérieure de police*
at Saint-Cyr-au-Mont-d'Or (RHÔNE). A *Commissaire* performs
the functions of OFFICIER DE POLICE JUDICIAIRE.

COMMISSAIRE-PRISEUR
A qualified auctioneer, who must have a legal qualification and
have followed a three-year training course before passing a
professional examination. The auctioneer is independent and
has to follow a legally fixed rate of commission. The numbers
of posts are controlled by law. There are 330 *études*, including
64 in Paris, employing a total of 420 *commissaires-priseurs*,
including 50 women, who were first admitted in 1975. See also:
DROUOT

COMMISSARIAT À L'ÉNERGIE ATOMIQUE (CEA)
Created in 1945, this is the government agency which oversees
all development of atomic energy. Its industrial wing is
dominated by its subsidiary COGEMA. It also has responsibility
for research, safety and nuclear waste. See also: ÉLECTRICITÉ DE
FRANCE

COMMISSARIAT DE POLICE
A police station under the supervision of a COMMISSAIRE DE
POLICE.

COMMISSARIAT GÉNÉRAL AU PLAN

The administrative organisation responsible for drawing up and executing the five-year economic and development PLAN, headed by a *Commissaire au Plan*, responsible to the PREMIER MINISTRE. See also: COMMISSION NATIONALE DE PLANIFICATION

COMMISSION BANCAIRE

A committee composed of the governor of the BANQUE DE FRANCE, the director of the TRÉSOR, and four other members, with the responsibility of monitoring the financial situation of banking establishments, and of ordering investigations into credit institutions. It can take disciplinary measures, and in serious cases can withdraw the approved status of a banking firm.

COMMISSION D'ACCÈS AUX DOCUMENTS ADMINISTRATIFS (CADA)

This body is able to investigate refusals of the ADMINISTRATION to supply copies of documents, except those in a personal file. If there is a further refusal to comply with the findings of CADA, it is possible to take legal action, either through a TRIBUNAL ADMINISTRATIF, or through the MÉDIATEUR. See also: COMMISSION NATIONALE DE L'INFORMATIQUE ET DES LIBERTÉS

COMMISSION DE CONCILIATION

These exist in each DÉPARTEMENT in order to resolve disputes about rental increases at the time of lease renewal. The *Commission de conciliation* proposes a solution, but if this is not acceptable, the case can then go to a TRIBUNAL D'INSTANCE.

COMMISSION DE DÉVELOPPEMENT ÉCONOMIQUE RÉGIONAL (CODER)

A consultative body set up in each RÉGION in 1964 to aid the first PRÉFETS DE RÉGION. It was composed of representatives of CHAMBRES DE COMMERCE ET DE L'INDUSTRIE, CHAMBRES D'AGRICULTURE, professional and union organisations, local authorities and others. From 1973, the CODER was replaced by the EPR (*Établissement public régional*) which had enhanced powers and indicated a move towards more determined DÉCENTRALISATION.

COMMISSION DÉPARTEMENTALE D'URBANISME COMMERCIAL (CDUC)

Set up by the LOI ROYER in 1982, these bodies, composed of nine local councillors, nine representatives of commercial interests and two consumers, make decisions on allowing or refusing the establishment of large retail outlets in the DÉPARTEMENT.

COMMISSION DES CLAUSES ABUSIVES (CCA)

A consumer protection body set up in 1978, and connected with the *Ministère de l'*ÉCONOMIE ET DES FINANCES, which takes action on illegally restrictive clauses in contracts and order forms.

COMMISSION DES OPÉRATIONS DE BOURSE (COB)

The autonomous regulatory body which oversees all stocks and shares markets. See also: BOURSE; MATIF; MONEP; SICAV

COMMISSION MIXTE PARITAIRE

If a parliamentary bill cannot be agreed upon after the necessary two readings in both the ASSEMBLÉE NATIONALE and the SÉNAT, a *Commission mixte paritaire* can be formed by the PREMIER MINISTRE (seven members of each house) to produce a revised text. If each house then approves this text, it becomes law.

COMMISSION NATIONALE DE LA COMMUNICATION ET DES LIBERTÉS (CNCL)

Founded in 1986 to replace the HAUTE AUTORITÉ DE LA COMMUNICATION AUDIO-VISUELLE, it had members nominated by the presidents of the ASSEMBLÉE NATIONALE and of the SÉNAT, by the CONSEIL D'ÉTAT, the COUR DES COMPTES, the ACADÉMIE FRANÇAISE, and by the media. Its role was to ensure free competition and freedom of expression in the media, to guarantee the rights of individuals and to represent French interests in international broadcasting negotiations. It apppointed the heads of the public broadcasting services and ruled on political broadcasts, licensed private radio and television channels and specified operating conditions. In 1989, the CNCL was replaced by the CONSEIL SUPÉRIEUR DE L'AUDIO-VISUEL.

COMMISSION NATIONALE DE L'INFORMATIQUE ET DES LIBERTÉS (CNIL)
A body created in 1978 to ensure that laws relating to information technology are known to users and to individuals whose details are kept in databases. Database holders have to register these with CNIL. Individuals have certain rights of access to their personal files. It is illegal for an individual's religious and political opinions to be recorded in databases, with certain exceptions for the police and defence forces. Alleged breaches of the code are dealt with by a process similar to that used by CADA.

COMMISSION NATIONALE DE PLANIFICATION (CNP)
An advisory committee which is consulted at each stage of the construction of the PLAN. It is dominated by the *Présidents de* RÉGION, representatives of professional and union organisations and public sector directors. See also: COMMISSARIAT GÉNÉRAL AU PLAN

COMMISSION PERMANENTE
A parliamentary committee with a specialist brief which examines the text of proposed laws in detail before they are discussed in the main chamber. A *rapporteur* appointed by the *Commission permanente* presents the findings of the committee to the house. There are six *Commissions permanentes* for each of the two houses of the Parliament. See also: COMMISSION SPÉCIALE

COMMISSION RÉGIONALE DU PATRIMOINE HISTORIQUE, ARCHÉOLOGIQUE ET ETHNOLOGIQUE (COREPHAE) See: *IMMEUBLE CLASSÉ*

COMMISSION ROGATOIRE
A warrant signed by a judge which authorises an officer of the POLICE JUDICIAIRE or magistrate to act on his or her instructions. The *Commission rogatoire* must give precise details of names and actions to be taken. See also: PERQUISITION

COMMISSION SPÉCIALE
A parliamentary committee which is established to consider the

text of proposed laws outside the remit of the COMMISSIONS PERMANENTES.

COMMISSION TECHNIQUE D'ORIENTATION ET DE RECLASSEMENT PROFESSIONNEL (COTOREP)

A national agency, with local offices, which rules on levels of disability. There are currently three categories of disabled workers recognised by COTOREP: A – temporarily disabled, B – moderately disabled, C – seriously disabled. The category influences the level of entitlement in terms of support for retraining and re-employment.

COMMUNAUTÉ FINANCIÈRE AFRICAINE (CFA)

The group of African countries which use a currency based on the CFA franc, established in 1945 in the French colonies. This comprises the states of Bénin, Burkina Faso, Cameroun, Centrafrique, Congo, Côte-d'Ivoire, Gabon, Guinée équatoriale, Mali, Niger, Sénégal, Tchad and Togo. See also: ZONE FRANC

COMMUNAUTÉ FRANÇAISE

The *Communauté* was established by *Article 12* of the Constitution of the CINQUIÈME RÉPUBLIQUE in 1958, replacing the *Union française*. It was an association of France, its Algerian and Sahara territories and the DOM and TOM and remaining colonial territories, by then internally autonomous. Progressively, from 1960, all territories except the DOM and TOM became fully independent.

COMMUNAUTÉ FRANÇAISE DU PACIFIQUE (CFP)

The group of French territories which have more autonomy than the TOM, and which use the CFP franc. These comprise NOUVELLE CALÉDONIE and POLYNÉSIE FRANÇAISE.

COMMUNAUTÉ LÉGALE

The legal status of a married couple who did not sign a marriage contract. A clear distinction is made between items owned by each partner and those owned jointly.

COMMUNAUTÉ UNIVERSELLE

The contract of marriage signed in order to obtain this legal status renders all the possessions of both parties into common ownership.

COMMUNAUTÉ URBAINE
A group of COMMUNES, usually in an AGGLOMÉRATION, linked together from 1966 in order to provide more coherent local planning. They are in the areas of Bordeaux, Brest, Cherbourg, le Creusot-Montceau-les-Mines, Dunkerque, Lille-Roubaix-Tourcoing, Lyon, Le Mans, Orléans and Strasbourg. The prominent exception is Marseille. See also: SYNDICAT DE COMMUNES

COMMUNE
The basic administrative unit of France for local government purposes. Each *commune* has a MAIRE and a CONSEIL MUNICIPAL, and is grouped with others into a CANTON. There are over 36,000 *communes* in France, ranging from 25 with fewer than 10 inhabitants (seven actually uninhabited), to 37 with over 100,000, including Paris, which is a *commune* in its own right. See also: AGGLOMÉRATION; ARRONDISSEMENT; SYNDICAT DE COMMUNES

COMPAGNIE FRANÇAISE DES PÉTROLES (CFP) See: *TOTAL*

COMPAGNIE GÉNÉRALE See: *COMPAGNIE GÉNÉRALE MARITIME ET FINANCIÈRE*

COMPAGNIE GÉNÉRALE D'ÉLECTRICITÉ (CGE)
A nationalised firm which dominates the French electrical equipment industry, and ranks third in the world in that sector.

COMPAGNIE GÉNÉRALE DES EAUX (CGE) See: *GÉNÉRALE DES EAUX*

COMPAGNIE GÉNÉRALE DES MATIÈRES NUCLÉAIRES (COGEMA)
The industrial wing of the COMMISSARIAT À L'ÉNERGIE ATOMIQUE. It has powers of supervision over the entire industrial nuclear cycle, including the treatment of nuclear waste.

COMPAGNIE GÉNÉRALE MARITIME ET FINANCIÈRE (GMF)

Usually referred to as the *Compagnie générale*, this is a major maritime operator, formed in 1977 from the merger of the *Compagnie des messageries maritimes* and the *Compagnie générale transatlantique*, the two principal French shipping lines.

COMPAGNIE LYONNAISE DES EAUX See: *LYONNAISE DES EAUX*

COMPAGNIES RÉPUBLICAINES DE SÉCURITÉ (CRS)

A sector of the POLICE NATIONALE, trained specifically in measures to restore public order in the case of riots and disturbances, but also with responsibilities for policing the AUTOROUTES, mountain safety and coastal lifeguard duties. One company, based at Vélizy, (YVELINES) is on ceremonial duties providing escorts for official processions and the national police band.

COMPAGNON DE LA LIBÉRATION

A member of the ORDRE DE LA LIBÉRATION, the exclusive group who were deemed to have demonstrated an exceptional contribution to the Liberation of 1944. Apart from an award to Churchill in 1958, and a posthumous award to King George VI in 1960, no new members joined the *Ordre* after 1946. Of the original 1,059 *Compagnons de la Libération*, about 300 remain alive.

COMPLÉMENT FAMILIAL

A supplementary monthly payment to low-earning taxpayers for the support of families with at least three children over the age of three years. See also: ALLOCATION POUR JEUNE ENFANT

COMPROMIS DE VENTE See: *PROMESSE DE VENTE SYNALLAGMATIQUE*

COMPTE BANCAIRE

Personal bank accounts in France can be grouped into two major categories. A *compte de dépôts* permits the issue of cheques, payable immediately, if a *compte de chèques à vue* is held, whereas if the account is a *compte à terme* interest is earned, but repayment is subject to a fixed term notice. The second category, a *compte sur livret* is a savings account, but without cheque facilities. Some banks provide special accounts for young people, but without cheque facilities.

COMPTE D'ÉPARGNE EN ACTIONS (CEA)
A facility available to investors from 1983 to 1988, whereby a tax reduction was allowed on the purchase of shares in French companies.

COMPTE-CHÈQUES POSTAL (CCP)
A popular form of personal current account banking in France, operated by the PTT. Cheques are issued free of charge, statements are provided on a daily basis or less frequently, day to day operations are conducted through post offices organised by regional centres. A full range of automated and additional services is provided. See also: VIDÉOPOSTE

COMPTE ÉPARGNE-LOGEMENT
A regular tax-free savings account with a bank, CAISSE D'ÉPARGNE or other finance house. After a minimum period of 18 months, depending on the interest earned, and subject to safeguards relating to ability to repay, the saver is entitled to a low-interest loan repayable over a period of up to 15 years towards the purchase or improvement of a dwelling. The *Compte épargne-logement* has a limit on deposits of 100,000 francs, and on loans of 300,000 francs. See also: PLAN ÉPARGNE LOGEMENT

COMPTE ODYSÉE
A form of the COMPTE-CHÈQUES POSTAL, adapted for young people aged 13–18.

COMPTE POUR LE DÉVELOPPEMENT INDUSTRIEL See: *CODEVI*

COMPTOIRS MODERNES
A major retailing group with its strength in the northern half of France, comprising neighbourhood shops under the *Comod* name, and STOC supermarkets.

COMTE DE PARIS
The Orléanist claimant to the throne of France, the most direct descendant of Louis-Philippe 1er holds the title, *Comte de Paris*. The present claimant, Henri d'Orléans, born in 1908, stated his claim in 1941 in Morocco, during his exile from 1926 to 1950, when the law banning residence in France of heads of its former ruling houses and eldest sons was repealed. It is still legally possible to expel them if they incite disorder. His direct heirs are his son, Henri, Comte de Clermont (1933–   ), and grandson Jean, Duc de Vendôme (1965–   ). See also: DUC D'ANJOU

CONCERTS LAMOUREUX
A musical ASSOCIATION founded in 1881 by Charles Lamoureux in order to manage a symphony orchestra now named *Orchestre des concerts Lamoureux*, resident at the *Salle* PLEYEL.

CONCERTS PASDELOUP
A musical ASSOCIATION founded in 1861 by Jules-Étienne Pasdeloup which manages symphony concerts from October to March at the *Salle* PLEYEL and the *Salle* GAVEAU.

CONCESSIONS DE PARIS
The collective term given to the commercial operations licensed by the city authorities in Paris. Among the best known are the TOUR EIFFEL, racecourses at AUTEUIL, LONGCHAMP and VINCENNES, and the *Palais des sports*, but they also include catering concessions in public areas, and newspaper kiosks. The *Concessions de Paris* also include arrangements for the use of the pavements by cafés and other traders.

CONCIERGE
The traditional role of the *concierge*, who acts as permanent guard on the entrance ways to apartment and office blocks, is tending to be replaced by non-resident caretakers. The word *concierge* is increasingly replaced by the term '*gardien d'immeuble*'.

CONCILIATEUR
A voluntary official in each CANTON who is recruited from the ranks of retired professionals whose duties are to facilitate the

informal resolution of disputes, so that they do not result in court cases.

CONCORDE
The supersonic aeroplane built by the Anglo-French consortium in the 1960s and 1970s, and bought only by AIR FRANCE and British Airways. The French partner in the consortium is AÉROSPATIALE. The four Air France aircraft in regular service operate between Paris and New York.

CONCOURS
A competitive examination (including scrutiny of qualifications) used by the ADMINISTRATION to recruit staff. It is particularly bound up with the academic system, which is used as a recruitment route for posts as FONCTIONNAIRES. Usually, a *concours* is open to any number of candidates who have the relevant pre-qualifications, but a fixed number of posts will be available. Because of this, sometimes the success rate is very low. Those who do not have posts within the service sit the *Concours externe*, and special conditions apply to serving *fonctionnaires* seeking promotion who take the *Concours interne*.

CONCOURS EXTERNE See: *CONCOURS*

CONCOURS GÉNÉRAL
This CONCOURS is open to the best pupils in the CLASSE DE PREMIÈRE and the CLASSE TERMINALE in state LYCÉES, nominated by their teachers, and leads to the award of prizes in each qualifying subject. About 2 per cent of those entered receive prizes.

CONCOURS INTERNE See: *CONCOURS*

CONCOURS 'LE PRIX DU MAIRE'
A competition, sponsored by TOTAL oil, open to rural COMMUNES who have enhanced the environment by the elimination or improvement of a building offensive to the eye.

CONDUITE ACCOMPAGNÉE (CA)
A learner driver over the age of 16, having passed the theoretical stage of the driving course in an approved driving

school, may practise on any road, except an AUTOROUTE, if accompanied by a qualified driver aged 28 or more with at least three years' driving experience and with no major endorsements. The driving test itself cannot be taken until the candidate is 18. There are valuable insurance premium discounts for those who learn to drive in this way.

CONFÉDÉRATION DES SYNDICATS LIBRES (CSL)
A union with about 250,000 members, formed in 1977, with the principal aim of co-management and worker participation in the running of enterprises.

CONFÉDÉRATION FRANÇAISE DE L'ENCADREMENT DE LA CONFÉDÉRATION DES CADRES (CFE-CGC)
A white-collar union, recruiting members from the CADRES, founded in 1944, and under its present title since 1981. It has almost half a million members.

CONFÉDÉRATION FRANÇAISE DÉMOCRATIQUE DU TRAVAIL (CFDT)
With almost a million paid-up members, this is one of the larger French unions, consulted by government bodies in economic planning, etc. It has existed under its present title since 1964, having broken away from the CFTC. Its main support lies in areas which have traditional Catholic ties, but its ideology is determinedly allied to the PARTI SOCIALISTE, with which it has, however, no constitutional link.

CONFÉDÉRATION FRANÇAISE DES TRAVAILLEURS CHRÉTIENS (CFTC)
Founded in 1919, this was a major but moderate union, which lost the bulk of its members in 1964 with the formation of the CFDT. Now it maintains a moderate stance and refuses political links with any party grouping. It has about 250,000 members.

CONFÉDÉRATION GÉNÉRALE DES CADRES (CGC)
This was a prominent, non-militant white-collar union which was the largest representation of managers' interests until its merger in 1979 into the CONFÉDÉRATION FRANÇAISE DE L'ENCADREMENT DE LA CONFÉDÉRATION DES CADRES.

CONFÉDÉRATION GÉNÉRALE DES PETITES ET MOYENNES ENTREPRISES (CGPME)

A representative organisation for small employers, which forms part of the larger CNPF. It speaks for about 1,500,000 small businesses, and its character and direction were closely defined by its founder Léon Gingembre from its formation in 1944.

CONFÉDÉRATION GÉNÉRALE DU TRAVAIL (CGT)

In some ways the most prominent of French unions. It was founded in 1895, and thus was the first national grouping of workers' interests of significance. It has a history of highly politicised activity, ranging from its early identification with revolutionary socialism to its present stance of sympathy with more moderate socialist politics. One of its main principles is independence from political parties, but many of its organisers are also well-known within the PARTI COMMUNISTE FRANÇAIS. The CGT has a falling membership, estimated in 1989 at about 700,000, most of whom are not Communists. See also: FORCE OUVRIÈRE

CONFÉDÉRATION NATIONALE DU PATRONAT FRANÇAIS (CNPF)

An umbrella organisation which groups geographical and specialist sectors to represent employers' interests, with a claim to be able to speak for over a million enterprises. The CONFÉDÉRATION GÉNÉRALE DES PETITES ET MOYENNES ENTREPRISES (CGPME) is an example of a more specialist component part. It operates as a pressure group in influencing legislation and public opinion. Apart from regular meetings of its standing committees and executive, it organises *assises nationales* at least once every three years.

CONFÉDÉRATION PAYSANNE

Formed in 1987 by a merger of national and local unions, as a single representative organisation for peasant farmers. Its members obtained a fifth of the seats on CHAMBRES D'AGRICULTURE DÉPARTEMENTALES in 1989.

CONFÉRENCE ADMINISTRATIVE RÉGIONALE

A statutory committee of PRÉFETS in a RÉGION chaired by the

PRÉFET DE RÉGION with the task of co-ordinating their activities.

CONFORAMA
A discount furnishing retailer, with large premises usually in suburbs or green-field sites.

CONGÉ
The term used for time off from usual working practice, and more especially for holiday entitlement. See also: ALCOOL

CONGÉ D'ADOPTION
When a child is adopted, one adoptive parent (usually the mother) is entitled to 10 weeks' unpaid leave from work, and to the same level of support as for a CONGÉ DE MATERNITÉ.

CONGÉ DE FORMATION
After six months' service for an employer, a worker with two years' experience in his/her field of work is entitled to leave of absence for further training. The employee continues to be paid a proportion of normal earnings, financed through a levy on all firms with more than 10 employees.

CONGÉ DE MATERNITÉ
Statutory maternity benefit in France is of 16 weeks duration (six weeks pre-natal, 10 weeks post-natal), and this is extended to 26 weeks (eight weeks pre-natal, 18 weeks post-natal) if the birth is of the third child or later. Extensions are automatic in the case of multiple births, and possible if there are complications or for other medical reasons. See also: ASSURANCE MATERNITÉ.

CONGÉ D'ENSEIGNEMENT ET DE RECHERCHE
After two years' service for an employer, a worker is entitled to up to 12 months' unpaid leave of absence for the purpose of professional study or research. The employer is entitled to defer an application if too many are made at one period.

CONGÉ D'EXAMEN
If entitled to CONGÉ DE FORMATION, an employee can also take 24 hours' paid leave in a year to sit an examination for the training received.

CONGÉ INDIVIDUEL DE FORMATION See: *CONGÉ DE FORMATION*

CONGÉ JEUNES TRAVAILLEURS
Unqualified employees below the age of 25, with three months' service, may have 200 hours' paid leave of absence a year, in order to obtain training. Upon completion of the course, the employee is then immediately entitled to CONGÉ DE FORMATION.

CONGÉ PARENTAL D'ÉDUCATION
A parent is entitled to up to two years' unpaid leave of absence in order to care for a child below the age of three. This period begins at the expiry of CONGÉ DE MATERNITÉ or CONGÉ D'ADOPTION. See also: ALLOCATION PARENTALE D'ÉDUCATION

CONGÉS PAYÉS
Since 1982, each employee has been entitled to annual paid leave of 30 days, calculated on the basis of two and a half days' holiday per month worked. This restriction does not apply to those under 22, who have full holiday entitlement. At least 12 days must be taken betwen May and October, including an unbroken period of at least two weeks, and a maximum of four weeks. In addition, women below the age of 21 have an additional entitlement of two days per dependant child. Many schemes provide more than these minimum statutory entitlements.

The effect is to close many businesses for a full month in the summer, holiday periods often beginning, July 1, 15, or August 1, 15. Accordingly, around these dates there is frequently enormous traffic congestion on holiday routes.

CONGÉ SABBATIQUE
Employees with three years' service and six years' experience are able to claim unpaid sabbatical leave for 6–11 months, no more frequently than once every six years. Small enterprises may object to such arrangements, in which case, the dispute is resolved by the CONSEIL DE PRUD'HOMMES.

CONJOINT
One's married or unmarried partner (feminine: *conjointe*). See

also: ATTESTATION D'UNION LIBRE; CERTIFICAT DE CONCUBINAGE

CONSEIL CONSTITUTIONNEL
A major organ of State with the role of safeguarding the constitution, especially in regulating the elections of the PRÉSIDENT DE LA RÉPUBLIQUE and of referenda, in ruling on disputes about elections to the ASSEMBLÉE NATIONALE, and in verifying that the constitution is not contravened by legislative measures. It must be consulted if the *Président de la République* wishes to invoke ARTICLE 16, and is the body which impeaches the *Président* if that is necessary. Its discussions are secret, and only its findings are made public. The *Conseil constitutionnel* sits in the PALAIS-ROYAL.

It consists of nine members, each in office for nine years (three each appointed by the *Président de la République*, the *Président de l'Assemblée nationale*, and the *Président du* SÉNAT), and former *Présidents de la République*, although neither DE GAULLE nor GISCARD D'ESTAING attended. No serving member of the government, of the *Assemblée nationale* or *Sénat*, or of the CONSEIL ÉCONOMIQUE ET SOCIAL may be a member.

CONSEIL D'ADMINISTRATION
The board of directors or management of an enterprise or voluntary body. In a COLLÈGE or LYCÉE, its composition is determined by law: the head of the establishment, seven teachers, five administrators, three parents, 5–7 pupils and five representatives of the local community. It is required to agree a budget, to make regulations for the internal organisation, and to advise on educational matters. It has disciplinary powers.

CONSEIL D'ARRONDISSEMENT
Since 1982, in Paris, Lyon and Marseille, each ARRONDISSEMENT has a council, elected at the same time as the CONSEIL MUNICIPAL. The *Conseil d'arrondissement* has limited powers over housing and local amenities.

CONSEIL DE CABINET
A meeting of ministers and SECRÉTAIRES D'ÉTAT, chaired by the

PREMIER MINISTRE, called only in exceptional circumstances. See also: CONSEIL DES MINISTRES

CONSEIL DE CLASSE
In a COLLÈGE or LYCÉE, each class has a committee which is chaired by the head teacher or his or her representative. The *Conseil de classe* includes the teachers of the class, two parent members, two pupils (*délégues de classe*) and can be attended by the school support staff (e.g. the CONSEILLER D'ÉDUCATION). Its role is to discuss the general progress of the class, and matters arising from the CONSEIL DES PROFESSEURS.

CONSEIL D'ÉCOLE
In an ÉCOLE PRIMAIRE, this committee is composed of the CONSEIL DES MAÎTRES, the parents' committee, the school psychologist, school doctor and social worker, and is responsible for the internal organisation of the school, and for determining learning support programmes.

CONSEIL DE L'ORDRE
A committee of the Order of the LÉGION D'HONNEUR, which assists the *Grand Chancelier* in maintaining his role of the central administration. All grades of the *Ordre* are represented on the *Conseil*.

CONSEIL DE PARIS
Because Paris is both a COMMUNE and a DÉPARTEMENT, its elected *Conseil de Paris* has two functions. In its role as CONSEIL MUNICIPAL, it elects the MAIRE DE PARIS, and has overall control over finance (including setting the IMPÔT LOCAL), transport and planning. It has the normal powers of a CONSEIL GÉNÉRAL, and the *Maire de Paris* is the chief executive of the *Département*. See also: CONSEIL D'ARRONDISSEMENT; CUMUL DES MANDATS

CONSEIL DE PRUD'HOMMES
A local industrial tribunal with the role of ruling in certain cases of dispute over contracts of employment. Equal numbers of employers' and employees' representatives are elected to office for five years. A *Conseil de prud'hommes* sits in specialised sections.

CONSEIL DES BOURSES DE VALEURS See: *BOURSE*

CONSEIL DES MAÎTRES
The statutory committee of teachers in an ÉCOLE PRIMAIRE.

CONSEIL DES MINISTRES
The cabinet meeting of all ministers and the PREMIER MINISTRE, chaired by the PRÉSIDENT DE LA RÉPUBLIQUE, normally held at the PALAIS DE L'ÉLYSÉE on Wednesdays, and followed by a public statement. SECRÉTAIRES D'ÉTAT only attend on specific invitation. See also: CONSEIL DE CABINET

CONSEIL DES PROFESSEURS
Each term in a COLLÈGE or LYCÉE, the teaching staff meet to discuss the progress of each pupil, and to propose measures which are then considered by the CONSEIL DE CLASSE.

CONSEIL D'ÉTAT
A major organ of State, which dates back to the *Constitution de l'an VIII* (1799). It has a dual function, firstly to advise the government, in effect the PREMIER MINISTRE, on each PROJET DE LOI and ORDONNANCE which it intends to introduce, and secondly, to act as an final appeal court in administrative cases. It has a watching brief over the actions of the ADMINISTRATION.

  Because of the detailed nature of much of its work, it is staffed by specialists in different fields. It recruits its *auditeurs* only from the ÉCOLE NATIONALE D'ADMINISTRATION, and the higher ranks of *Maîtres des requêtes* and *Conseillers* are dominated by promotion from *auditeur*. It is independent of government, but the *Premier Ministre* or the GARDE DES SCEAUX can chair its general meetings. The *Conseil d'État* is based in the PALAIS-ROYAL.

CONSEIL ÉCONOMIQUE ET SOCIAL
A consultative body, protected by the Constitution, composed of 230 members representing the major industrial, business and social groups. The members are provided by trade unions, employers' groups, nationalised industries, farmers' organisations, co-operatives, the MUTUALITÉ movement, voluntary bodies, DOM and TOM. There are also individuals

personally nominated because of their expertise, as well as government representatives. A person cannot also be a member of the CONSEIL CONSTITUTIONNEL.

The role of the *Conseil économique et social* is to discuss economic and social issues, to react to government PROJETS DE LOI, and to encourage understanding between government and interested sectors. It has no competence in budgetary matters. Its decisions are published in the JOURNAL OFFICIEL.

CONSEIL GÉNÉRAL
The body of elected representatives for the DÉPARTEMENT. Each *Conseiller général* is elected for six years. Half the *Conseil général* is elected on a three-year cycle.

A *Président du Conseil général* is elected by its members, and is the chief executive of the *Département*. The *Conseil* also elects a *Bureau* of between four and 10 *Vice-Présidents*. Meetings are held at least once a TRIMESTRE, normally in public, at the HÔTEL DU DÉPARTEMENT. If for any reason, the *Conseil général* cannot function, the government can dissolve it, and allows its *Président* executive powers with the consent of the PRÉFET until a new *Conseil* is elected within two months. Under the CINQUIÈME RÉPUBLIQUE, this has happened only in the case of the BOUCHES-DU-RHÔNE, in 1974.

The principal roles of the *Conseil général* (enlarged since the DÉCENTRALISATION programme of 1982), are to deal with all business affecting its département, including the management of staff and property, the road network, housing, school grants, economic development, strategic planning, and maintaining the infrastructure within the PLAN. It is not entitled to make political resolutions. See also: CUMUL DES MANDATS; ÉLECTIONS CANTONALES

CONSEIL JURIDIQUE ET FISCAL
Legal and tax advisers are subject to regulations set up in 1971 and monitored by the PROCUREUR DE LA RÉPUBLIQUE.

CONSEIL MUNICIPAL
Elected for six years by the inhabitants of a COMMUNE, the *Conseil municipal* in turn elects the MAIRE. The method of the

Conseil's election depends on the size of the *commune*. Up to 30 per cent of the members can become *Adjoints* to the *Maire*.

It meets at least four times a year at the MAIRIE. Its role is to agree a budget for the *commune*, and manage the organisation of local services, such as streets, nursery and primary schools, leisure facilities, refuse collection. The level of administration available and extent of functions varies considerably depending on the size of the *commune*. See also: ÉLECTIONS MUNICIPALES; SYNDICAT INTERCOMMUNAL; COMMUNAUTÉ URBAINE

CONSEIL NATIONAL DES PROGRAMMES
A body within the *Ministère de l'*ÉDUCATION NATIONALE, set up in 1989 to make recommendations about the school curriculum to the minister. The establishment of this body removed much of the influence of the INSPECTEURS GÉNÉRAUX DE L'ÉDUCATION NATIONALE over the control of the curriculum.

CONSEIL NATIONAL DU CRÉDIT
The consultative body chaired by the *Ministre de l'*ÉCONOMIE ET DES FINANCES, with the governor of the BANQUE DE FRANCE as vice-chairman. It includes 51 members representing all economic sectors, and is concerned with overall monetary and credit policy.

CONSEIL RÉGIONAL
These were established in 1985. Members are elected directly for six years, with a DÉPARTEMENT being the constituency. Almost every *département* has twice as many *Conseillers généraux* as it does DÉPUTÉS. The size ranges from the 197 members for ÎLE-DE-FRANCE to the 31 for GUYANE.

The *Conseil régional* meets at least once per TRIMESTRE, and is able to delegate some of its powers to its elected executive team, which is supposed to reflect the political balance of the overall *Conseil*, as well as a geographical balance.

The *Président* has executive powers, and is responsible for the management of the region's resources, liaising with the PRÉFET DE RÉGION where necessary.

The *Conseil régional* is able to initiate development plans and co-ordinate the work of lower COLLECTIVITÉS LOCALES, and can engage in collaborative ventures with other regions. See also: CUMUL DES MANDATS; ÉLECTIONS RÉGIONALES

CONSEIL SUPÉRIEUR DE LA MAGISTRATURE
An advisory body directly responsible to the PRÉSIDENT DE LA RÉPUBLIQUE for nominating candidates for appointments as senior law officers, and for advice on the nominations of the GARDE DES SCEAUX for less senior posts. It is also the law officers' disciplinary body.

CONSEIL SUPÉRIEUR DE L'AUDIOVISUEL (CSA)
Established in 1989, as a replacement for the COMMISSION NATIONALE DE LA COMMUNICATION ET DES LIBERTÉS, this body's membership is appointed in equal numbers by the PRÉSIDENT DE LA RÉPUBLIQUE, the *Président* of the SÉNAT, and the *Président* of the ASSEMBLÉE NATIONALE. There are nine members in all, none of whom can hold elected office or any other employment.

The CSA exists in order to guarantee impartiality and freedom of speech on radio and television, to stimulate competition and high quality of programmes, and to ensure the promotion of French language and culture in the broadcast media. It has a monitoring role over broadcast advertising, and is consulted when international broadcasting agreements are negotiated.

It appoints senior personnel to the public sector companies, and draws up the rules for party political broadcasts. It oversees the licensing of private broadcasting companies and their wavelength allocations.

CONSEIL SUPÉRIEUR DE L'ÉDUCATION NATIONALE
A national consultative body with a history dating back to 1808. It advises the *Ministre de l'*ÉDUCATION NATIONALE on all matters concerning the service, and acts as an appeal tribunal of last resort for administrative or disciplinary disputes affecting the personnel or students.

CONSEILLER D'ÉDUCATION
A member of staff in a COLLÈGE or a LYCÉE who does no teaching, but is responsible for the general discipline of the

pupils, and for recording and investigating non-attendance, etc.

CONSEILLER D'ORIENTATION
A member of staff in a COLLÈGE or a LYCÉE who is responsible for giving careers and course advice to pupils. The *conseiller d'orientation* also takes part in meetings which recommend class groupings.

CONSERVATOIRE DU LITTORAL ET DES RIVAGES LACUSTRES
Set up in 1975 to safeguard the environment of the coastline and shores of larger lakes, it has powers of acquisition of threatened areas, and owns about 50,000 hectares over 500 kilometres of coastline. It is partly funded by ÉLECTRICITÉ DE FRANCE.

CONSERVATOIRE NATIONAL DES ARTS ET MÉTIERS
A network of 55 institutes serving 64,000 adults who follow further professional courses. See also: FORMATION CONTINUE

CONSERVATOIRE NATIONAL SUPÉRIEUR DE MUSIQUE
Two colleges are entitled to use this prestigious title: one in Paris, founded in 1795, the other in Lyon dating from 1979. Both train musicians and dancers for professional life, and recruit through CONCOURS. About 10 per cent of candidates are admitted to the Paris *Conservatoire*.

CONSERVATOIRE NATIONAL DE RÉGION
There are 31 music colleges providing advanced courses, administered through the *Ministère de la* CULTURE.

CONSIGNE
The arrangement whereby one deposits an article in a specially designed area. For example, this can be for left-luggage at a station or airport, or for the return of recyclable bottles or liquid gas containers at a supermarket.

CONSOMMATEURS
Since the late 1960s, the consumer movement has been growing in influence in France. There are numerous monitoring groups checking prices, competition, standards, etc., national

organisations with group and individual membership, and the government's own INSTITUT NATIONAL DE LA CONSOMMATION. See also: FÉDÉRATION NATIONALE DES COOPÉRATIVES DE CONSOMMATEURS; UNION FÉDÉRALE DES CONSOMMATEURS; NORMES FRANÇAISES

CONSTAT
A factual report certified by a HUISSIER, which can be used as evidence in legal proceedings. In the case of a car accident where injury occurs, the police draw up the *constat*.

CONSTAT AMIABLE
A report jointly agreed by the parties concerned which can be used to resolve motor insurance claims if there is injury.

CONSTITUTION
The present constitution of France is that of the CINQUIÈME RÉPUBLIQUE, which dates from 1958, with certain minor amendments. See also: ARTICLE 16; ASSEMBLÉE NATIONALE; CONSEIL CONSTITUTIONNEL; PREMIER MINISTRE; PRÉSIDENT DE LA RÉPUBLIQUE; SÉNAT

CONTINENT
A medium-sized chain of hypermarkets in the PROMODÈS group of companies.

CONTRAT DE TRAVAIL
There is no legal obligation to have a written contract of employment except if it is for a fixed-term job, an apprenticeship or for temporary work. However, many CONVENTIONS COLLECTIVES exist which require a contract of employment. There is usually a probationary period agreed when a contract is drawn up, and the normal period is for one month (three months for CADRES).

A fixed-term contract, or *contrat de travail à durée limitée*, can be agreed for a maximum period of two years, and can be renewed twice. If it is not renewed, the employee can claim a redundancy payment of 5 per cent of normal gross earnings.

CONTRAVENTION
An offence, often punishable by fixed penalty. It can range

from hunting offences to breaking traffic regulations, in which case a PROCÈS-VERBAL is drawn up. See also: AMENDE FORFAITAIRE.

CONTRÔLE D'IDENTITÉ

The police are permitted to check the identity of anyone who is suspected of a breach of the law, considered able to help in enquiries, or wanted by the police. There is also a more extensive right to check anyone in order to prevent a breach of public order. It is this provision which allows random identity checks. Presentation of a CARTE NATIONALE D'IDENTITÉ is sufficient, or of any document bearing the person's photograph.

A person unable to prove his/her identity can be detained by the police for four hours while further checks are made by an officer of the POLICE JUDICIAIRE, and possibly fingerprints and photographs taken. Anyone detained has the right to contact the PROCUREUR DE LA RÉPUBLIQUE (this is compulsory if a minor is detained), or one's family or another person. Minors must be accompanied by a parent, and in all cases a PROCÈS-VERBAL must be made out. All papers relating to the check must be destroyed within six months, if no further proceedings are taken.

CONTRÔLE JUDICIAIRE

An alternative to imprisonment, whereby a convicted person has to report regularly to the authorities, and is temporarily deprived of certain freedoms, for example by surrendering his or her passport, or driving licence, by restricting travel to certain areas or by denying contact with certain individuals. Imprisonment is used if the conditions of the *Contrôle judiciaire* are breached.

CONTRÔLE TECHNIQUE

A test of a vehicle's condition, when it is five years old, valid for three years. Until 1990, this test was only required when the vehicle was sold.

CONVENTION COLLECTIVE

A written agreement made by unions and employers' organisations about working conditions in a particular industry, with advantages to employees which go beyond the national legal entitlements. The scope of the *Convention collective* may be national or restricted to a certain RÉGION or DÉPARTEMENT. A particular enterprise may adopt an existing *Convention collective*.

CONVOCATION AU COMMISSARIAT

One can be required to attend a police station only if the police are investigating a FLAGRANT DÉLIT or if a COMMISSION ROGATOIRE is enacted.

CONVOI EXCEPTIONNEL

A wide or long load being taken by road transport.

COOPÉRATION ET DU DÉVELOPPEMENT, MINISTÈRE DE LA

This ministry oversees the official co-operation programmes, particularly in relation to Francophone countries in Africa, to counteract the dwindling French influence of the early 1970s. The Ministry funds posts in teaching, administration, health services, agricultural technology, energy, telecommunications, as well as in military and security fields. There are also programmes controlled by the *Ministère des* AFFAIRES ÉTRANGÈRES, but in a wider range of countries. It is possible to fulfil one's SERVICE NATIONAL as part of a *Coopération* programme, if equipped with the appropriate skills.

COOPÉRATIVE AGRICOLE

Many small farmers are members of *Coopératives agricoles*, which exist in order to preserve the independence of members at the same time as benefitting from the advantages of larger units. There are, for instance, over 4,000 cooperatives which deal with the business aspects of farming. More than two million farmers are members of these organisations. One of the largest, the *Union laitière normande* accounts for 10 per cent of milk production in France. Another, SODIMA, runs the international *Yoplait* and *Candia* dairy produce brands. Well over half the production of milk, butter, cereals, cattle and pigs is handled by *Coopératives agricoles*.

COOPÉRATIVE DE CONSOMMATEURS See: *CODEC; ROND-POINT; SYSTÈME U*

COPROPRIÉTÉ

The form of contract necessarily entered into by an owner of a flat. The *Règlement de copropriété* sets out the agreement about common and private areas of the building, the conditions of ownership, the arrangements about service charges and administration of the common areas. There must be an annual meeting of co-owners and the details of voting arrangements among them are laid down in a law passed in 1965, amended in 1985.

COQ FRANÇAIS

A symbol of France, deriving, it is thought, from a Latin pun (galus = Gallic; gallus = cockerel) which has become more popular in the last two centuries. Since 1848, it features on the seal of the *République*, and has appeared on postage stamps and coins. It is perhaps best known as the symbol chosen for sports teams, especially rugby, in international matches.

CORA

A medium-sized chain of hypermarkets.

CORAIL

Air-conditioned railway carriages, gradually introduced on conventional main-line services in France from 1975.

COREPHAE See: *IMMEUBLE CLASSÉ*

CORRÈZE

A rural DÉPARTEMENT of the LIMOUSIN region with a 1990 population of 237,859, named after the tributary of the Vézère river which runs the whole of its course here. The Corrèze has suffered from depopulation although the trend downwards was temporarily arrested in the early 1980s. The three urban areas of any size are Tulle, the CHEF-LIEU (17,164) – animal foodstuffs, arms, engineering and accordeon making; Brive-la-Gaillarde (63,760) – metallurgy, electronics, furniture and food-processing; and Ussel (11,448) – aluminium smelting, hosiery and timber industries.

The principal agricultural activities are in sheep, cattle and pig rearing, and there are crops of tobacco, fruit and vegetables.

Tourists are attracted by a number of ancient villages and the lakes created by hydro-electric schemes. A considerable proportion of the Corrèze is woodland. The state-owned stud founded by Colbert is found at Pompadour.

The *Département* has a strongly Centre Right CONSEIL GÉNÉRAL, but it gave a large majority to François MITTERRAND in the 1981 ÉLECTION PRÉSIDENTIELLE, much reduced in 1988. One of its DÉPUTÉS is Jacques CHIRAC.

Code départemental: 19

CORSE

The island of Corsica, part of France since 1768, which is now an administrative RÉGION, including the two DÉPARTEMENTS of CORSE-DU-SUD and HAUTE-CORSE. It has a population of 249,596, more than half of whom live in the urban areas surrounding the regional capital, Ajaccio, and the other city, Bastia. More than 10 per cent of the population are in immigrant communities, coming particularly from Morocco and Italy.

The principal economic activity is in the service sectors, with a large proportion of the region's income based on tourism. Agricultural production is of citrus fruits, peaches, potatoes, kiwi fruits, chestnuts, olives and wine. A major programme of state-supported agricultural development has been in place since the 1950s. According to the 1982 census, fewer than 52 per cent of principal residences in the region met full standards of modern amenities. This compared with 66 per cent for France as a whole.

The region has traditionally provided substantial numbers of FONCTIONNAIRES who find posts on the mainland. Large numbers of Corsicans are to be found in the Paris police force, for example.

Because of the special cultural identity of Corsica, and in recognition of the sometimes violent expression of the desire for autonomy, the region was given in 1982 greater powers than others. The CONSEIL RÉGIONAL therefore has direct lines of contact with the PREMIER MINISTRE, and additional powers in agricultural and transport planning and over educational matters. The Corsican language may be studied in the island's schools, and courses are followed by about 3,000 pupils.

CORSE-DU-SUD

A DÉPARTEMENT in the CORSE region which, as its name indicates, covers the southern half of the island. Its population in 1990 was 118,174 and the CHEF-LIEU is Ajaccio, the only large town (58,315).

The principal single source of employment is tourism, but there are small fishing and cork industries, and significant agricultural production of fruit, vegetables and flowers.

The mainstream political support is for the Right, but the various Corsican nationalist organisations also command a level of support. Local elections are more intensely contested than those of national level, in which a greater deal of opportunism seems to determine voting patterns.

Code départemental: 20A

CORSE PASCAL PAOLI, UNIVERSITÉ DE

The smallest university in France is sited in Corte (HAUTE-CORSE), and has faculties of human and natural sciences and law. It has 2,300 students.

COS See: *COEFFICIENT D'OCCUPATION DU SOL*

COSTA-GAVRAS (1933–   )

A Greek-born film director whose main work has been in the French cinema. His best-known films have been political thrillers, such as *Z* and *État de siège*.

CÔTE D'AZUR

A term coined in 1888 to denote the Mediterranean coastline between Bec de l'Aigle to the Italian frontier, territorially part of the DÉPARTEMENTS of ALPES-MARITIMES and VAR.

CÔTE D'OR

A DÉPARTEMENT in the BOURGOGNE region (population 493,867), of which the CHEF-LIEU is Dijon (AGGLOMÉRATION 226,025) – pharmaceuticals, mustard, tobacco, plastics, rubber, engineering, electronics, household appliances, precision instruments and automotive industries. The only other urban area of any size is Beaune (21,289), a centre of the wine-trade, and printing, board, electronics, plastics and jewellery industries.

There is relatively little industrial activity, most of the
employment being accounted for in agriculture and service
sectors. Cereal and wine production dominate the economic
activity, and there is a major element of tourism. Because of
good communications with Paris, there is some daily commuting
to the capital.

Politically, the Côte-d'Or elects a balance of DÉPUTÉS from
both Right and Left. In both 1981 and 1988 ÉLECTIONS
PRÉSIDENTIELLES, it voted for François MITTERRAND with virtually
the same proportion of votes (52.53 per cent and 52.59 per cent).
The Centre Right's control of the CONSEIL GÉNÉRAL was however
confirmed in the 1992 ÉLECTIONS CANTONALES.

Code départemental: 21

CÔTES-D'ARMOR

A DÉPARTEMENT, as befits its former name, *Côtes-du-Nord*, on
the north coast of the BRETAGNE region (population 538,423),
with its CHEF-LIEU at Saint-Brieuc (AGGLOMÉRATION 83,871), a
port with a metallurgy industry, 50 per cent of the production
of water-heaters in France, and an international repute for its
household and paint brush production. Other large urban areas
are Dinan (24,416); Guingamp (22,416); and Lannion (16,958).

The maritime economy dominates the coastal area, the sea
being a rich source of shellfish, especially oysters and mussels.
Saint-Brieuc lands 10,000 tons of fish a year, and its hinterland
catches 30 per cent of the national consumption of *coquilles
Saint-Jacques*. The tourist industry has also developed leisure
activities and marinas connected with the sea.

As in other Breton *départements*, agriculture is important to
Côtes-d'Armor, and cattle, pigs, poultry and market gardening
are the dominant factors. The *Département* is in first place for
egg production. Saint-Paulin is a local cheese, and Plancoët a
source of mineral water.

The *Centre national d'études de télécommunications* and its
planetarium are situated at Pleumeur-Bodou, and there are
developing electronic industries in some of the towns.

Male inhabitants of the *Côtes-d'Armor* have one of the lowest
life expectancies in France: 68.4 years. The electors voted for

Socialist politicians in the 1980s, with 59.36 per cent of the vote going to François MITTERRAND in the 1988 ÉLECTIONS PRÉSIDENTIELLES. It was the only *département* in north west France to retain Socialist control of its CONSEIL GÉNÉRAL after the 1992 ÉLECTIONS CANTONALES.

Code départemental: 22

CÔTES-DU-NORD See: *CÔTES-D'ARMOR*

COTISATION DE CHARGES SOCIALES
Both employer and employee pay contributions for the SÉCURITÉ SOCIALE schemes. The proportions of gross salary paid are as follows (the first column shows the percentage paid by the employer, the second by the employee):

Sickness and maternity	12.6	5.9
Additional retirement benefits	2.88	1.92
Unemployment	4.43	2.47
Retirement pension	8.2	7.6

There are additional contributions charged to employers for other benefits, and the proportions are different for those not in full-time employment. See also: COTISATION SOCIALE GÉNÉRALISÉE

COTISATION SOCIALE GÉNÉRALISÉE (CSG)
A reform introduced by the ROCARD government in the 1991 budget, with the aim of taking contributions to SÉCURITÉ SOCIALE funds from investment income as well as from wages and salaries. The additional funds in the CSG are devoted to the ALLOCATION FAMILIALE.

COTOREP See: *COMMISSION TECHNIQUE D'ORIENTATION ET DE RECLASSEMENT PROFESSIONNEL*

COTY, RENÉ (1882–1962)
The last PRÉSIDENT DE LA RÉPUBLIQUE of the QUATRIÈME RÉPUBLIQUE, who in 1958 called DE GAULLE to take the role of PRÉSIDENT DU CONSEIL in order to solve the crisis provoked by the situation in ALGÉRIE. Coty was a lawyer from Le Havre, who entered local and then national politics, became minister for reconstruction in 1947, and was elected as *Président de la*

République as a compromise candidate after 13 ballots in 1953. When the CONSTITUTION of the CINQUIÈME RÉPUBLIQUE took effect in 1958, he thus became the first *Président de la République* but resigned a few months later.

COUPOLE
The nickname for the ACADÉMIE FRANÇAISE. '*Sous la Coupole*' refers to its meetings under the dome of its building.

COUR D'APPEL
There are 35 *Cours d'appel* in France and the DOM and TOM, one in each legal region. The court is competent to hear appeals from lower courts in civil, criminal and industrial cases. A civil case can go to appeal where the damages awarded are more than 13,000 francs, and a criminal case if the sentence is more than five days' imprisonment or a fine of 160 francs. An appeal can be sought by either side in the original case. After a *Cour d'appel* has pronounced its decision, the only further appeal possible is to the COUR DE CASSATION.

COUR D'ASSISES
The criminal court, one in each DÉPARTEMENT, which tries cases referred to it by the JUGE D'INSTRUCTION and a CHAMBRE DES MISES EN ACCUSATION. There are three judges (one *président*, and two *assesseurs*) and nine citizens who are JURÉS. An AVOCAT GÉNÉRAL conducts the case against the *accusé*. The jury and judges deliberate together after the evidence has been heard, and the verdict is based on a two-thirds majority of the 12, the sentence, if applicable, on a simple majority, and damages to the innocent victim by the judges alone. The staff of the court includes a HUISSIER and a GREFFIER. The only appeal possible against the verdict of a *Cour d'assises* is to the COUR DE CASSATION.

Crimes against the State security, and crimes of terrorism are tried in a *Cour d'assises*, but without a jury. In such cases, the *président* sits with six *assesseurs*, all of whom are professional judges.

Minors aged 16 and 17 are brought before a *Cour d'assises pour mineurs* which has no jurors. The *président* and *assesseurs* are all specialists in cases affecting children.

COUR DE CASSATION
This higher court of appeal, which meets in civil, criminal, commercial and social sections, does not decide on the facts of cases, but on the legality of decisions made by lower courts in cases which are referred to it. The *Cour de cassation* can reject an appeal, overturn the decision of the lower court, or require a retrial. If after a retrial, the case returns to the *Cour* for appeal, the full *Cour de cassation* meets (25 members) to pronounce a verdict, or to send for further retrial in which case the lower court has to comply with the legal interpretation of the *Cour de cassation*.

COUR DES COMPTES
The public body which audits national public expenditure. COLLECTIVITÉS LOCALES are audited by regional bodies, the *Chambres régionales des comptes*, but in case of appeal, the *Cour des comptes* is the body of ultimate responsibility.

The *Cour des comptes* reports when it is not satisfied that public money and resources have been properly used or accounted for in the ADMINISTRATION, SÉCURITÉ SOCIALE, ENTREPRISES PUBLIQUES, etc., and produces an annual report for the PRÉSIDENT DE LA RÉPUBLIQUE and PARLEMENT. The press coverage given to such reports is usually enough to prompt reforms in procedures.

COURRIER DE L'OUEST, LE
A daily newspaper, published in Angers (MAINE-ET-LOIRE), with a daily circulation of 107,000.

COURRIER D'ENTREPRISE À DISTRIBUTION EXCEPTIONNELLE (CEDEX)
The system of special postal codes for enterprises which receive over 600 items of mail a day, which entitles them to special delivery procedures.

COURRIER INDIVIDUEL À DISTRIBUTION EXCEPTIONNELLE (CIDEX)
In rural areas, post delivery boxes are grouped together on road sides, allowing a more frequent mail delivery than to individual addresses.

COURRIER POSTE RESTANTE
A highly developed service is provided, used particularly heavily in holiday periods, whereby mail sent to a local post office is held for up to a fortnight until collected by the addressee.

COURS DE PROMOTION SOCIALE
An adult class designed either to enable a person to work for qualifications missed while at school, or for mature entry to universities and higher education institutions. See also: CONGÉ DE FORMATION; FORMATION CONTINUE

COURS ÉLÉMENTAIRE See: *CYCLE ÉLÉMENTAIRE*

COURS LÉGAL
The coins and banknotes which are of legal tender. These are banknotes issued by the BANQUE DE FRANCE, and bearing the currently valid designs, and the coins circulated by the *Administration des monnaies et médailles*. See also: POUVOIR LIBÉRATOIRE DES PIÈCES

COURS MOYEN See: *CYCLE MOYEN*

COURS PRÉPARATOIRE See: *CYCLE PRÉPARATOIRE*

COURSE CAMARGUAISE
This is the form of bullfighting popular in the GARD, HÉRAULT and BOUCHES-DU-RHÔNE, in which the *razeteur* has to grasp a ribbon from a bull's forehead. A number of trophies are available for best *razeteurs*; the *trophée taurin*, sponsored by the MIDI LIBRE, is awarded to the best bull at the end of the season.

COURSE LANDAISE
A form of bullfighting practised in South West France. Since the beginning of this century, cows have been used. Points are awarded for the bullfighter's skill in avoiding the charging animal.

COUVE DE MURVILLE, MAURICE (1907–)
A Gaullist politician who was the last PREMIER MINISTRE under DE GAULLE's presidency from 1968 to 1969. He had previously

served as *Ministre des* AFFAIRES ÉTRANGÈRES for ten years from 1958, and for a few weeks as *Ministre des* FINANCES.

CP See: *CYCLE PRÉPARATOIRE*

CPA See: *CLASSES PRÉPARATOIRES À L'APPRENTISSAGE*

CPCH See: *COLLIER DE PERLES, CARRÉ HERMÈS*

CPPN See: *CLASSES PRÉ-PROFESSIONNELLES DE NIVEAU*

CRAZY HORSE
An internationally known night club in Paris created in 1951, with spectacular floor shows.

CRÈCHE COLLECTIVE
Staffed by qualified personnel, a *crèche collective* takes children aged from two months to three years for daytime care, from as early as 6.30 a.m. to 7.00 p.m. on weekdays, with rates dependent on the income of the parents.

CRÈCHE PARENTALE
A crèche organised by a group of parents, but subject to regulations and monitoring by the DDASS.

CRÉDIF See: *CENTRE DE RECHERCHE ET D'ÉTUDE POUR LA DIFFUSION DU FRANÇAIS*

CRÉDIT AGRICOLE
A retail banking organisation, traditionally strong in rural areas, based on mutual principles through a federation of regional banks, all using the title *Crédit agricole*. There are 87 regional offices with about 3,000 branches. In terms of assets, it is the largest French and European bank, and holds about 16 per cent of the country's reserves on deposit. As a public sector bank, it is ultimately subject to the controls of the CAISSE DES DÉPÔTS ET CONSIGNATIONS.

CRÉDIT COMMERCIAL DE FRANCE (CCF)
A medium-sized bank, in public ownership from 1982 but privatised in 1987.

CRÉDIT D'ÉQUIPEMENT DES PETITES ET MOYENNES ENTREPRISES
A state-owned financing organisation, subject to the controls of the CAISSE DES DÉPÔTS ET CONSIGNATIONS, which lends funds for the development of small and medium-sized businesses and service sector industries.

CRÉDIT DU NORD
A retail bank, more than 50 per cent owned by the State since 1982.

CRÉDIT FONCIER DE FRANCE (CFF)
A state-owned financing organisation, subject to the controls of the CAISSE DES DÉPÔTS ET CONSIGNATIONS, which lends funds to private developers to fund public projects.

CRÉDIT GRATUIT
Interest-free credit is subject to certain regulations: it cannot be advertised except at the point of sale, and the price must be held for at least one month before the credit is available. There must be a reduction possible for full payment in cash. A fortnight's delay is prescribed before the credit agreement is signed, with further delays for reconsideration before it is binding.

CRÉDIT IMMOBILIER See: *PRÊT POUR L'ACCESSION À LA PROPRIÉTÉ; PRÊT D'ÉPARGNE-LOGEMENT; PRÊT CONVENTIONNÉ*

CRÉDIT INDUSTRIEL ET COMMERCIAL (CIC)
A banking group, nationalised in 1982, now under the control of the State-owned insurance group, GAN.

CRÉDIT LOCAL DE FRANCE (CLF)
A bank controlled by the CAISSE DES DÉPÔTS ET CONSIGNATIONS which finances COLLECTIVITÉS LOCALES for approved projects. It was partly privatised in 1991.

CRÉDIT LYONNAIS
The third largest banking organisation in France, nationalised in 1945. It has the second largest international network of branches of any bank in the world.

CRÉDIT MUNICIPAL
The official name for the network of regulated pawnbrokers, also known as *monts-de-piété*, since the first one was established in Avignon in 1577, which will lend on a short-term basis on the security of deposited goods.

The services offered are wider than those of a pawnbroker, however, extending into banking accounts, savings bonds and CODEVI, etc.

CRÉDIT MUTUEL
A national savings organisation run on mutual lines with local banks, grouped into 20 regional federations. There are about four million members, and the funds account for about 4 per cent of the country's reserves.

CRÉDIT NATIONAL
A State-owned financing organisation, subject to the controls of the CAISSE DES DÉPÔTS ET CONSIGNATIONS, which lends funds to industrial borrowers.

CRÉPEAU, MICHEL (1930–   )
A politician active in the MOUVEMENT DES RADICAUX DE GAUCHE, who was a candidate in the 1981 ÉLECTION PRÉSIDENTIELLE, but was eliminated after the first round with 1.76 per cent of the votes. He was a member of the MAUROY and FABIUS governments from 1981–1986, and was successively in charge of *Environnement*, *commerce*, *l'*ARTISANAT, and *justice*. His local base is La Rochelle (CHARENTE-MARITIME), where he has been MAIRE since 1971.

CRESSON, ÉDITH (1934–   )
The first woman to hold the office of PREMIER MINISTRE, to which she was appointed in 1991. She joined the PARTI SOCIALISTE in 1975 and became a member of the European Parliament in 1979. In the MAUROY and FABIUS governments 1981–1986, she was *Ministre de l'*AGRICULTURE then *du redéploiement et du commerce extérieur*, and in ROCARD's cabinet, *Ministre des affaires européennes* from 1988 to 1990. Her move to MATIGNON was widely interpreted as a move by François MITTERRAND to improve the Socialists' chances in the 1993 ÉLECTIONS LÉGISLATIVES, but

she was highly unpopular and resigned after the ÉLECTIONS CANTONALES and RÉGIONALES in 1992.

CREUSE

A DÉPARTEMENT in the LIMOUSIN region, named after the tributary of the Vienne that flows through it. The population in 1990 was 131,346, less than half its peak in 1891 of almost 285,000. The demographic pattern shows a considerably older population than for the country as a whole, emphasised by the immigration of retired people from elsewhere. The CHEF-LIEU is Guéret (population 14,706) and the second largest town is AUBUSSON, famous for its tapestries (the *École nationale de la tapisserie* is situated here) with 5,097 inhabitants.

The economic activity is dominated by agriculture, especially in cattle and sheep rearing. There is no large industrial concern, but many small, traditional industries.

The Creuse is subject to a number of initiatives to revive it, but there are compensations for its relative backwardness for its residents – it has among the lowest crime and divorce rates in France.

Politically, Creuse voted for François MITTERRAND decisively in 1981 and 1988, and traditionally votes for the Left. Against the national trend in the 1992 ÉLECTIONS CANTONALES, the PARTI SOCIALISTE increased its majority on the CONSEIL GÉNÉRAL.

Code départemental: 23

CRIME See: *DÉLIT*

CROISADE DES AVEUGLES

An ASSOCIATION D'UTILITÉ PUBLIQUE with 12,000 members, providing Braille and cassette magazines for the blind, and supportive and social activities.

CROIX, LA

Published by BAYARD-PRESSE, *La Croix* is a daily Roman Catholic newspaper, founded in 1880, with a circulation of about 105,000. About 90 per cent of its sales are to subscribers, three-quarters of whom live outside the Paris region. It claims a readership of 300,000, with 84 per cent coming from managerial and professional classes.

CROIX D'ANJOU See: *CROIX DE LORRAINE*

CROIX DE GUERRE
A military decoration, awarded only in the two World Wars, and for action in military operations during 1918–1921. As well as individuals, certain COMMUNES were awarded the *Croix de guerre* in the same periods. The town which received the greatest number of decorations was VERDUN.

CROIX DE LA LIBÉRATION
The insignia worn by a COMPAGNON DE LA LIBÉRATION. Five towns were also awarded the decoration: Grenoble, Île de Sein, Nantes, Paris and Vassieux-en-Vercors.

CROIX DE LORRAINE
Also known as the *Croix d'Anjou*, this symbol, with the double horizontal crosspieces originating from the *Ducs d'Anjou et Lorraine* in the fifteenth century, was adopted in 1940 by the Free French forces who followed DE GAULLE. It was subsequently used by De Gaulle as a personal emblem, and a very large one was erected at COLOMBEY-LES-DEUX-ÉGLISES by public subscription after his death.

CROIX DU COMBATTANT VOLONTAIRE
Volunteers who served in the World Wars or Resistance or in the colonial campaigns of the 1950s are entitled to wear this medal.

CROUS See: *CENTRE RÉGIONAL DES ŒUVRES UNIVERSITAIRES ET SOCIALES*

CROZIER, MICHEL
A sociologist who came to prominence with the publication of *La Société bloquée* in the 1960s, reflecting on the need to reform what he saw as an archaically centralised stratification of French society.

CRS See: *COMPAGNIES RÉPUBLICAINES DE SÉCURITÉ*

CSA See: *CONSEIL SUPÉRIEUR DE L'AUDIOVISUEL*

CSCT See: *CERTIFICAT DE SYNTHÈSE CLINIQUE ET THÉRAPEUTIQUE*

CSG See: *COTISATION SOCIALE GÉNÉRALISÉE*

CSL See: *CONFÉDÉRATION DES SYNDICATS LIBRES*

CULTURE ET COMMUNICATION, DES GRANDS TRAVAUX ET DU BICENTENAIRE, MINISTÈRE DE LA

A somewhat inelegant name for a ministry which has considerable prestige and importance. It has a major influence over the funding of the arts. Under François MITTERRAND it co-ordinates the often presidentially inspired schemes for major developments, and has been responsible for all the public events to commemorate the French Revolution. In 1991, Édith CRESSON made the minister, Jack LANG, who had been in post from 1981 to 1986 and again from 1988, government spokesman as well.

Other ministers have included André MALRAUX, its first incumbent from 1959, Maurice DRUON and François LÉOTARD.

CUMUL DES MANDATS

There is a restriction on the combination of elected posts a person can hold at any one time. Thus, a DÉPUTÉ cannot be a SÉNATEUR, and neither can hold more than one of the following positions at the same time as the parliamentary seat: Member of the European Parliament, CONSEIL RÉGIONAL, CONSEIL GÉNÉRAL, CONSEIL DE PARIS, *Assemblée territoriale*, MAIRE of a COMMUNE with more than 20,000 inhabitants or MAIRE-ADJOINT of a city with more than 100,000.

CURE THERMALE

Treatment in a spa which can be partially or wholly funded by the SÉCURITÉ SOCIALE, depending on the nature of the complaint and the contributions paid.

CURIE, PIERRE ET MARIE (UNIVERSITÉ)

The official name of the *Université Paris VI*, which specialises in natural sciences and medecine, having the largest Paris medical faculty. There are 36,000 students.

CURSUS
The overall course package taken in order to qualify for a degree.

CV See: *CHEVAUX*

CYCLE D'OBSERVATION
The first two years spent in a COLLÈGE, in the *Classe de sixième* and *Classe de cinquième*, when all pupils receive a common curriculum. The weekly timetable takes up four and a half days, and consists of 24–27 hours of lessons, (which last 55 minutes), including four and a half hours of French, three hours of mathematics, two and a half hours of history/geography, three three hours of a foreign language, chosen by the parents (84 per cent choose English).

Certain subjects are taught in mixed ability classes, others are subject to a test to organise the teaching groups. A child may have to repeat the *Classe de sixième* before entry to the second year of collège. Only about half the population enter the *Classe de cinquième* at the age of 12.

During the *Classe de cinquième*, pupils' progress is closely monitored so that a firm recommendation can be made for the appropriate route to be followed in the CYCLE D'ORIENTATION. There is a set procedure which gives parents certain rights of choice. See also: REDOUBLEMENT

CYCLE D'ORIENTATION
The last stage of the COLLÈGE, in the *Classe de quatrième* and the *Classe de troisième*. During this period all pupils follow 24½ hours each week of the TRONC COMMUN of subjects, with additional options depending on the *orientation* of the course. The *Tronc commun* includes four and a half hours of French, four hours of mathematics, three hours of history/geography, three hours each of two foreign languages. In addition, each pupil can expect two hours homework daily. Most of the *Classe de quatrième* pass into the *Classe de troisième*, during which the ORIENTATION SCOLAIRE process is fairly intense, as pupils, parents and staff consult and decide about possible routes to follow after the *collège*. See also: CLASSE DE SECONDE; CYCLE D'OBSERVATION; LYCÉE; REDOUBLEMENT

CYCLE ÉLÉMENTAIRE (CE)

Also called *Cours élémentaire*, this can be further divided into CE1 and CE2, showing the two years of a child's life between the ages of 7 and 9 spent in an ÉCOLE PRIMAIRE. The weekly timetable includes eight hours of French, six hours of mathematics, three hours of science and technology, two hours of history and geography, one hour each of civics, music and plastic arts, and five hours of physical education and sport. See also: CYCLE MOYEN; CYCLE PRÉPARATOIRE

CYCLE MOYEN (CM)

Also called *Cours moyen*, and like the CYCLE ÉLÉMENTAIRE can be further divided into CM1 and CM2, corresponding to the two years between the ages of 9 and 11 spent in the ÉCOLE PRIMAIRE. The curriculum is similar to that in the *Cycle elémentaire*. The teacher decides if the child should transfer at the end to the COLLÈGE and the CYCLE D'OBSERVATION. A child will do this in any case no later than age 12. Sixty per cent enter the *collège* without repeating a year. See also: REDOUBLEMENT

CYCLE PRÉPARATOIRE (CP)

Also known as the *Cours préparatoire*, this is the infants year in an ÉCOLE PRIMAIRE, and takes children at the minimum statutory age of six years. Most children have already attended an ÉCOLE MATERNELLE. There is a maximum of 25 children in a CP class, where they spend their time mastering basic skills. The 27 hour week is spent in French (10 hours), mathematics (six hours), science and technology (two), physical education and sport (five) and one hour each for history/geography, civics, music and plastic arts.

CYCLOMOTEUR

A motorised cycle with an engine capacity of 49 cc or less. The rider does not need a PERMIS DE CONDUIRE, and may ride one from the age of 14, but access to an AUTOROUTE is not permitted. Insurance is compulsory, a helmet must be worn, and speed is limited to 45 kph, using cycle lanes where provided. See also: SOLEX

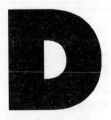

DA See: *DIVISION AÉROMOBILE; DIVISION ALPINE*

DAB See: *DISTRIBUTEUR AUTOMATIQUE DE BILLETS*

DARTY
A family-controlled chain of household electrical goods stores, which has made the Darty family one of the richest in France.

DASSAULT-BRÉGUET
A major participant in the French aerospace industry, formerly owned by its founder, the vigorous Marcel Dassault (1892–1986). Since the 1982 nationalisation programme, however, the majority of shares have been in public control. Dassault-Bréguet employs 60,000, mainly in manufacturing military aeroplanes and equipment, including the MIRAGE series.

DATAR See: *DÉLÉGATION À L'AMÉNAGEMENT DU TERRITOIRE ET À L'ACTION RÉGIONALE*

DATE DE PÉREMPTION
The 'use by' date on perishable goods.

DAUPHINÉ LIBÉRÉ, LE
A daily newspaper published in Grenoble (ISÈRE), with a circulation of about 360,000 throughout the RHÔNE-ALPES region except for the Lyon area. Its publisher, the *Groupe du Progrès-Dauphiné*, is part of the larger HERSANT empire. There is a Sunday edition with a circulation of 428,000.

DB See: *DIVISION BLINDÉE*

DCEM See: *DEUXIÈME CYCLE D'ÉTUDES MÉDICALES*

DCPJ See: *DIRECTION CENTRALE DE LA POLICE JUDICIAIRE*

DDASS See: *DIRECTION DÉPARTEMENTALE DE L'ACTION SANITAIRE ET SOCIALE*

DEA See: *DIPLÔME D'ÉTUDES APPROFONDIES*

DÉBIT DE TABAC

A specially licensed vendor of tobacco and cigarettes, often combined with a newsagents or café business, and designated by the red cigar sign outside. A *débit de tabac* also sells postage stamps, TIMBRES-AMENDES and TIMBRES FISCAUX. See also: SOCIÉTÉ NATIONALE DE L'EXPLOITATION INDUSTRIELLE DES TABACS ET ALLUMETTES

DEBRAY, RÉGIS (1941–)

A left-wing journalist and novelist, who was imprisoned in Bolivia from 1967 to 1970 for activities associated with Che Guevara, having been saved from the death sentence through the personal intervention of DE GAULLE. His more recent influence was as an adviser to François MITTERRAND about Third World affairs, but since leaving that post he has devoted most of his time to writing.

DEBRÉ, LOI

A law passed in 1959 which permits state subsidies to be paid to private schools. It caused the resignation of the *Ministre de l'*ÉDUCATION NATIONALE, and was supported personally by the PREMIER MINISTRE, Michel DEBRÉ.

DEBRÉ, MICHEL (1912–)

The principal architect of the CONSTITUTION and a former PREMIER MINISTRE under DE GAULLE from 1959 to 1962, and holder of major ministerial posts from 1966 to 1973. A right-wing independent candidate in the ÉLECTIONS PRÉSIDENTIELLES of 1981, he was eliminated in the first round with 1.32 per cent of the vote. A prolific writer on political affairs, he is regarded as an authoritative figure in interpreting the Gaullist view. His political power-base was in the INDRE-ET-LOIRE for which he was a SÉNATEUR from 1948 to 1958, and MAIRE of Amboise from 1966 to 1989. He was also DÉPUTÉ for RÉUNION from 1963 to 1988.

DÉCENTRALISATION
The move away from the overdominant influence of Paris in the ADMINISTRATION, much discussed in the 1970s, but only taking effect in the 1980s, especially after the laws of 1982 and 1983 setting up strong regional bodies. See also: CODER; RÉGION

DÉCÈS
In the case of a family bereavement, an employee has the legal right of one or two days' paid leave, and this is often increased in the terms of a CONVENTION COLLECTIVE.

The COMMUNE must permit its residents to be buried in the municipal cemetery without charge. See also: DÉCLARATION DE DÉCÈS; DROITS DE SUCCESSION

DÉCLARATION DE DÉCÈS
Once a death occurs, a doctor must sign a *Certificat de décès*. For death by natural cause, this is signed by any doctor if in a rural area, but in towns of any size, the *médecin d'*ÉTAT CIVIL must do this. The MAIRIE must be informed, in person, of the need for this to be done. If the death is by any other cause only a police doctor can sign.

The death is then registered by a *Déclaration de décès* at the *Mairie*, within one working day. The LIVRET DE FAMILLE has to be produced, or suitable proof of identity of the dead person, together with the *Certificat de décès*. The person registering the death has to return to the *Mairie* to sign the *Acte de décès*, and if necessary to collect copies of it.

DÉCLARATION DE NAISSANCE
The father, doctor, midwife or anyone attending the birth must register a birth within three working days, either at the MAIRIE or at the hospital if such facilities are possible. The LIVRET DE FAMILLE and the medical certificate have to be produced.

DÉCLARATION DE PERTE
A formality to be completed at a PRÉFECTURE, COMMISSARIAT DE POLICE or MAIRIE, which declares the loss of a possession. If identity papers have been lost, usually two adult witnesses are required to confirm the person's identity.

DÉCLARATION DE RECONNAISSANCE D'ENFANT NATUREL

This formality ensures that the parents of an illegitimate child can, if they wish, be duly recognised in the appropriate records. The child is able to claim SÉCURITÉ SOCIALE benefits from his or her parents' contributions, and also has DROITS DE SUCCESSION. The formality of making such a declaration which is made at a MAIRIE or before a NOTAIRE, does not give rights of AUTORITÉ PARENTALE.

DÉCLARATION DE SUCCESSION

Except in the case of a surviving spouse or child, or where the inheritance is valued at less than 10,000 francs, it is necessary to complete a *Déclaration de succession* for tax purposes which identifies all the beneficiaries of a will. This has to be done within six months of the death, and requires the completion of a tax form, usually part of the NOTAIRE's work in executing the will.

DÉCLARATION D'UTILITÉ PUBLIQUE See: *UTILITÉ PUBLIQUE*

DÉCLARATION PRÉALABLE DE CONSTRUCTION

A simplified procedure for obtaining planning permission to build in certain circumstances. To qualify, the work must be restoration, or a small outbuilding, or an open swimming pool, glasshouse, repairs to a listed building, or a small extension. A form is completed and returned to the MAIRIE, and within one month, a reply will be given either allowing the construction, rejecting it, or setting conditions.

DÉCOLONISATION

The process undergone in the 1940s and 1950s when France withdrew its colonial administration from its former colonies, with varying degrees of enthusiasm. After the Brazzaville conference of 1944, there was greater representation of local populations, and in 1946 the Empire became the *Union française*. There was growing pressure for independence in the African colonies, and also in Indo-China, where war had broken out in 1946, resulting eventually in humiliation for France at Dien-Bien-Phu in 1954, and total independence for Cambodia,

Laos and Vietnam. By 1960 all the African colonies had become independent, and in 1958 the Union was itself supplanted by the COMMUNAUTÉ FRANÇAISE. Territories which later became independent were *Afars et Issas* and the Comoro Islands and there have been active political movements in NOUVELLE-CALÉDONIE. See also: ALGÉRIE; FRANCOPHONIE

DÉCRET MINISTÉRIEL
A decision taken by the PREMIER MINISTRE in order to execute the legislation agreed by the parliament. It is relayed to the various *Ministres* who are responsible for carrying it out in their own areas of responsibility.

DÉCRET PRÉSIDENTIEL
A decision taken personally by the PRÉSIDENT DE LA RÉPUBLIQUE, and not subject to parliamentary approval. For example, the appointment of the PREMIER MINISTRE is by *Décret présidentiel*. The decisions taken in the CONSEIL DES MINISTRES are also *décrets*, signed by the *Président de la République* and counter-signed by the *Premier Ministre*.

DE DIETRICH
A large mechanical engineering enterprise, still controlled by its original family owners.

DÉFENSE, LA
A predominantly business quarter of the north western Paris BANLIEUE, built around the monument commemorating the defence of Paris in 1870–1871, into which vast investment was poured between the 1960s and 1980s. Concentration of multi-national groups into the 40 skyscraper development managed to preserve the traditional skyline of central Paris at the same time as promoting the image of Paris as an ultramodern city for offices. See also: ARCHE DE LA DÉFENSE

DÉFENSE NATIONALE, MINISTÈRE DE LA
A major department of State, accounting for about 15 per cent of government expenditure. The ministers in recent times have not always had the smoothest of careers, Charles HERNU having resigned in 1985 over the RAINBOW WARRIOR affair, and Jean-

Pierre CHEVÈNEMENT in 1991 about differences over the Gulf War.

DEFFERRE, GASTON (1910–1986)

A Socialist politician, MAIRE of Marseille, where he owned two newspapers of opposing political views, from 1953 to 1986. He was a minister in the QUATRIÈME RÉPUBLIQUE, as well as in the MITTERRAND governments, in which he served as *Ministre d'État de l'*INTÉRIEUR *et de la* DÉCENTRALISATION from 1981 to 1984, and the *Ministre du* PLAN *et de l'*AMÉNAGEMENT DU TERRITOIRE from 1984 to 1986. He was the PARTI SOCIALISTE candidate in the 1969 ÉLECTION PRÉSIDENTIELLE.

DE GAULLE, CHARLES (1890–1970)

The founder and first PRÉSIDENT DE LA RÉPUBLIQUE of the CINQUIÈME RÉPUBLIQUE. After a military career, he established the FRANCE LIBRE movement by making a radio appeal to the French people from London on 18 June 1940. He was supported by Winston Churchill against American hostility in his assertion of speaking on behalf of France during the war. In 1944, De Gaulle was able to establish his control over the French ADMINISTRATION of liberated France, and was accepted as the new leader by various factions in the RÉSISTANCE, and recognised de facto by the Allies as leader of the provisional government. He resigned office in 1946, but maintained a solitary self-imposed exile awaiting the call back to power.

This occurred in 1958, when the crisis in ALGÉRIE seemed insoluble. He was appointed PRÉSIDENT DU CONSEIL, demanded and was given exceptional powers, introduced the CONSTITUTION of the *Cinquième République*, becoming *Président de la République* in 1959, re-elected by universal suffrage in 1965. He survived at least five attempts on his life, and resigned in 1969 when he lost the RÉFÉRENDUM on regionalisation, taking no further part in active political life.

DE GAULLE, CHARLES (UNIVERSITÉ)

The title of the *Université de Lille III* at VILLENEUVE-D'ASCQ (NORD), which specialises in human sciences, arts and literature. It has nearly 5,000 students.

DÉGRADATION CIVIQUE
The withdrawal of certain citizens' rights from an individual, such as the right to vote, which can be imposed as part of court sentence.

DÉLAI DE RÉFLEXION
The period of at least three days which must follow the signing of a credit agreement, so that the purchaser has the opportunity to change his/her mind.

DÉLÉGATION À L'AMÉNAGEMENT DU TERRITOIRE ET À L'ACTION RÉGIONALE (DATAR)
The State agency with a mission to invigorate regional economies, founded in 1963. Without a strong overall regional policy, its first 10 years concentrated on investing in grand industrial schemes outside the Paris region, e.g. Fos-sur-Mer (BOUCHES-DU-RHÔNE) to replace disappearing agricultural jobs.

Its role in the 1970s and 1980s followed the pattern of developing regional policy. See also: DÉCENTRALISATION; OREAM; TECHNOPOLES

DÉLÉGATION AUX RISQUES MAJEURS
A state agency under the tutelage of the *Ministre de l'environnement*, with the role of identifying areas of major disaster risk and taking steps to prevent these occurring. These include industrial risks such as in southern Toulouse, the chemicals complex south of Lyon, and the area of Lillebonne (SEINE-MARITIME), and natural disaster risks of climate, and mountain, forest or river areas.

DÉLÉGATION GÉNÉRALE POUR L'ARMEMENT (DGA)
The section of the armed forces which tests, builds and researches armaments for all branches of the military, and investigates export possibilities for armaments.

DÉLÉGUÉ DE SITE
An elected representative of employees in a small enterprise (fewer than 11 employees) working in conjunction with other businesses on site where there are 50 employees or more (e.g. building site, market), who negotiates with the management on their behalf. See also: DÉLÉGUÉ DU PERSONNEL

DÉLÉGUÉ DU PERSONNEL
When an enterprise employs more than 11 employees, the law provides for a pro-rata scale of workers' elected representatives to negotiate on their behalf, with 15 hours per month paid for by the employer for this activity.

They must meet the management at least once a month, and are entitled to call in union officials to advise them. See also: DÉLÉGUÉ DE SITE

DÉLIT
A criminal offence against the person, property or common good, such as fraud, manslaughter, indecency, burglary, etc., but not as serious as a crime, which entails the use of arms, grievous injury, or incitement to riot, treason, etc. The punishments that a court can impose on those found guilty are prescribed within a minimum and maximum for each kind of offence. See also: CONTRAVENTION; FLAGRANT DÉLIT

DÉLIT DE FUITE
The offence of not stopping after causing a road accident. The minimum sentence is two months in prison and/or an AMENDE of 2,000 francs.

DÉLIT DE PRESSE
A published provocation to commit an offence is punishable by a law passed in 1981. It is under this heading that publicly insulting the Head of State is classed as a criminal offence.

DELLUC, LOUIS (PRIX)
A film prize, awarded to a new French film each year, in memory of Louis Delluc (1890–1924), an early film director, regarded as the first specialist cinema journalist.

DELORS, JACQUES (1925–   )
An economist who entered politics in 1969 as an adviser to Jacques CHABAN-DELMAS, the then PREMIER MINISTRE. He joined the PARTI SOCIALISTE, and became *Ministre de l'*ÉCONOMIE ET DES FINANCES in the MAUROY government from 1981 to 1984, also taking the post of MAIRE of Clichy (HAUTS-DE-SEINE) in 1983. In 1985, he became President of the European Commission.

DÉMARCHAGE À DOMICILE
There are restrictions on the kind of door-to-door business that is permitted. As a safeguard for the consumer, any contract signed at home is subject to a week's delay in which the client can change his/her mind. Certain kinds of business are forbidden.

DÉMEMBREMENT DE LA PROPRIÉTÉ
A legal arrangement by which temporary occupants of a property retain rights of use and residence until their death, but cannot pass them on to anyone else. It is often used in blocks of flats for retired people.

DEMY, JACQUES (1931–1990)
A film director, best known for films deriving from the musical comedy tradition, such as *Les Parapluies de Cherbourg* (1964) and *Les Demoiselles de Rochefort* (1967).

DENEUVE, CATHERINE (1943–   )
A popular film actress who has had a large number of leading roles since the 1960s, having played in more than 40 features.

DÉPARDIEU, GÉRARD (1948–   )
A film actor who, after a life of petty crime, took acting classes, and since his début in the early 1970s has become one of the most famous and prolific film stars, with renowned performances in *Danton*, *Jean de Florette*, *Manon des sources* and *Cyrano de Bergerac*, entering the international arena with *Green Card* in 1990.

DÉPARTEMENT
The unit of local government based largely on the division of France in the Revolution, when 83 *départements* were established, formed broadly on natural and historical divisions, reflected in their names usually of rivers or mountains. There are now 96 *départements* in metropolitan France, as well as the DOM. In 1964, the two *départements* of the greater Paris area were reorganised into seven, there were some boundary changes in the RHÔNE-ALPES region in 1967, and CORSE was divided into two *départements* in 1975. The most populated is

NORD (2.53 million) and the least populated is LOZÈRE (72,814).

Each *département* has a CHEF-LIEU, also called the PRÉFECTURE, where the government representative, the PRÉFET is the ultimate figure of local authority for all aspects of the ADMINISTRATION. The *Préfet's* role has changed and become more consultative with the DÉCENTRALISATION policies, and there is now greater responsibility given to the local representatives. See also: ARRONDISSEMENT; CANTON; COMMUNE; CONSEIL GÉNÉRAL; RÉGION

DÉPARTEMENT D'OUTRE-MER (DOM)
Since 1946, GUADELOUPE, GUYANE, MARTINIQUE and RÉUNION have been overseas DÉPARTEMENTS, and SAINT-PIERRE-ET-MIQUELON was a DOM until 1985, when it became a COLLECTIVITÉ TERRITORIALE. ALGÉRIE was divided into three DOM until its independence in 1962.

In general, a DOM can be regarded in the same way as a *département*, and since 1982, each has also been a RÉGION in its own right.

DÉPARTEMENTS ET TERRITOIRES D'OUTRE-MER, MINISTÈRE DES
A ministry which looks after the interests of overseas possessions in Paris, with the smallest ministerial budget.

DÉPÊCHE DU MIDI, LA
A daily newspaper published in Toulouse, with a circulation of almost 250,000, having a dominant sales position in the MIDI-PYRÉNÉES region.

DÉPÔT DE GARANTIE
The sum deposited by a tenant, equivalent to two months' rent, returnable at the end of tenancy if no further sums are owing, and no damage has been incurred.

DÉPÔT DU TEXTE
When legislation is proposed, the first stage is to place the text of the PROJET DE LOI or a PROPOSITION DE LOI in the office of the ASSEMBLÉE NATIONALE and the SÉNAT.

DÉPÔT LÉGAL
All publications available for public purchase or distribution,

in printed, pictorial, photographic, audio or visual form, except for purely administrative or advertising purposes, are subject to the *Dépôt légal*. Copies of the items have to be delivered to the BIBLIOTHÈQUE NATIONALE, and in modern publications, the date of this is given in printed copies.

DÉPUTÉ
Under the CINQUIÈME RÉPUBLIQUE, there are 577 members of the ASSEMBLÉE NATIONALE (555 for metropolitan France, 22 for the DOM), elected for five years. Each *député* must be at least 23 years of age, and cannot hold a government post at the same time. A *député* who dies, or who is appointed to the government is replaced by a SUPPLÉANT, elected at the same time as the *député*. Certain senior members of the ADMINISTRATION and State enterprises are ineligible to be *députés*. See also:
CIRCONSCRIPTION; CUMUL DES MANDATS; ÉLECTIONS LÉGISLATIVES; SCRUTIN

DERNIÈRES NOUVELLES D'ALSACE, LES
A daily newspaper, published in Strasbourg, with a circulation of 222,000.

DES See: *DIPLÔME D'ÉTUDES SPÉCIALISÉES*

DESCARTES, RENÉ (UNIVERSITÉ)
The official title of the *Université Paris V*, which has more than 3,500 students, specialising in biomedical science, psychology, law, technology, physical education and social sciences.

DÉSIR, HARLEM (1959–   )
The leader of the pressure group SOS-Racisme, and a prominent campaigner against racist attitudes.

DESS See: *DIPLÔME D'ÉTUDES SUPÉRIEURES SPÉCIALISÉES*

DEST See: *DIPLÔME D'ÉTUDES SUPÉRIEURES TECHNIQUES*

D'ESTAING, VALÉRY GISCARD See: *GISCARD D'ESTAING, VALÉRY*

DÉTENTION PROVISOIRE
In cases where a suspect held is accused of serious offences, it is possible for the suspect to be detained for up to four months, with the period being renewed if necessary. During the detention, the detainee has greater privileges than a convicted prisoner, but can be denied visits and mail by a JUGE D'INSTRUCTION. If after detention the person is found not guilty, compensation can be claimed. See also: GARDE À VUE

DETTE DE L'ÉTAT
The sum of all the deficits in the BUDGET, and, because of a special Franco-Swiss convention of 1969, including the external debt owed to Switzerland.

DEUG See: *DIPLÔME D'ÉTUDES UNIVERSITAIRES GÉNÉRALES*

DEUST See: *DIPLÔME D'ÉTUDES UNIVERSITAIRES DE SCIENCES ET TECHNIQUES*

DEUXIÈME CYCLE D'ÉTUDES MÉDICALES (DCEM)
A four-year stage in a university medical course, including clinical work in hospitals, for the later stages of which the student is paid. See also: CENTRE HOSPITALIER UNIVERSITAIRE; DIPLÔME D'ÉTUDES SUPÉRIEURES; PREMIER CYCLE D'ÉTUDES MÉDICALES

DEUX-ROUES
Any two-wheeled vehicle using the public roads, motorised or not. Pedal cycles and CYCLOMOTEURS must carry an identity plate with the name and address of the owner.

DEUX-SÈVRES
A DÉPARTEMENT in the POITOU-CHARENTES region, with a population in 1990 of 346,280, named after the two rivers which pass through it. The CHEF-LIEU is Niort (urban area 61,131), a centre for the insurance industry, and other towns are Bressuire (17,827), with its economy dominated by the meat industry; Parthenay (17,214), a market centre; and Thouars (15,921), producing agricultural machinery. All these centres also have small-scale light industry, and there are chemical and cement works in other centres. There is a broadly based

agricultural economy, and a growing tourist sector. There is no single large employer in the *Département*.

Deux-Sèvres has the distinction of offering its male inhabitants the longest life expectancy in the whole of France: 73.2 years, almost two years above the average. Economically, it is the least advanced *Département* in the region.

Politically, the voters of Deux-Sèvres changed allegiance between 1981 and 1988, as they moved away from the Right. In 1981, GISCARD D'ESTAING drew 52.4 per cent of their vote, whereas in 1988, MITTERRAND gained 53.66 per cent. Their parliamentary representatives are split between Right and Left, and in the 1992 ÉLECTIONS CANTONALES the Centre Right retained its local control.

Code départemental: 79

DGA See: *DÉLÉGATION GÉNÉRALE POUR L'ARMEMENT*

DGCCRF See: *DIRECTION GÉNÉRALE DE LA CONCURRENCE, DE LA CONSOMMATION ET DE LA RÉPRESSION DES FRAUDES*

DGSE See: *DIRECTION GÉNÉRALE DE LA SÉCURITÉ EXTÉRIEURE*

DI See: *DIVISION D'INFANTERIE*

DIJON, UNIVERSITÉ DE
The *Université de Bourgogne* has 22,000 students and faculties in law, politics, economics, sciences, human sciences, medicine, pharmacy, arts, languages and physical education.

DIMA See: *DIVISION D'INFANTERIE DE MARINE*

DIPLÔME D'ÉTAT DE DOCTEUR EN MÉDÉCINE
Awarded after the three *Cycles d'études médicales*, taking at least eight years post-BAC, and the qualification to practise as a medical practitioner. See also: DEUXIÈME CYCLE D'ÉTUDES MÉDICALES

DIPLÔME D'ÉTAT DE DOCTEUR EN PHARMACIE
The qualification to practise as a pharmacist, awarded after six years post-BAC study.

DIPLÔME D'ÉTUDES APPROFONDIES (DEA)

Awarded after a year's post-MAÎTRISE study. Such studies are partly more specialist, partly a training for research, thus leading on to study for a DOCTORAT. See also: DIPLÔME D'ÉTUDES SUPÉRIEURES SPÉCIALISÉES

DIPLÔME D'ÉTUDES ÉCONOMIQUES GÉNÉRALES

A post-BAC qualification in economics, replaced in 1973 by the DEUG.

DIPLÔME D'ÉTUDES JURIDIQUES GÉNÉRALES

A post-BAC qualification in law, replaced in 1973 by the DEUG.

DIPLÔME D'ÉTUDES SPÉCIALISÉES (DES)

Awarded after the third *Cycle d'études médicales* for those training to become specialists, the specialists' course lasting four or five years beyond the six years already covered in the two previous stages. The DES is necessary to practise as a medical specialist.

DIPLÔME D'ÉTUDES SUPÉRIEURES SPÉCIALISÉES (DESS)

As the DIPLÔME D'ÉTUDES APPROFONDIES, awarded after one or two years of post-MAÎTRISE study, but with a greater vocational bias, and with less expectation of the student's move into research for a doctorate.

DIPLÔME D'ÉTUDES UNIVERSITAIRES DE SCIENCES ET TECHNIQUES (DEUST)

Awarded after two years post-BAC university study, introduced in 1984. There is a vast range of courses and specialisms provided, but in each case, the course package is self-contained, and can lead to entry into professional life or a move on to a course for a LICENCE. See also: DIPLÔME D'ÉTUDES UNIVERSITAIRES GÉNÉRALES; DIPLÔME UNIVERSITAIRE DE TECHNOLOGIE

DIPLÔME D'ÉTUDES UNIVERSITAIRES GÉNÉRALES (DEUG)

A similar two-year post-BAC university qualification to the DEUST, except that it is offered in all non-scientific subject areas. The DEUG replaced a number of other qualifications in 1973, and a more flexible course pattern was introduced in 1984. There are compulsory and optional courses as part of the offer, and the principal subject area chosen by the student is mentioned on the certificate. The DEUG can lead to further study for a LICENCE or MAÎTRISE, other qualifications, or to entry into professional life.

DIPLÔME UNIVERSITAIRE DE TECHNOLOGIE (DUT)
Awarded after two years' post-BAC study at an INSTITUT UNIVERSITAIRE DE TECHNOLOGIE, less specialised than BREVET DE TECHNICIEN SUPÉRIEUR, but more vocationally based than a DEUST. The course includes a placement on work experience in the subject area chosen. There are about 40 options from which to choose, not all offered in every IUT.

DIPLÔME UNIVERSITAIRE D'ÉTUDES LITTÉRAIRES (DUEL)
A qualification awarded after two years' university study towards an arts LICENCE, replaced by the DEUG in 1973.

DIPLÔME UNIVERSITAIRE D'ÉTUDES SCIENTIFIQUES (DUES)
A qualification awarded after two years' university study towards a science LICENCE, replaced by the DEUG in 1973, and later by the DEUST in 1984.

DIRECTEUR DE CABINET See: *CABINET*

DIRECTION CENTRALE
The headquarters establishment of any branch of the ADMINISTRATION.

DIRECTION CENTRALE DE LA POLICE JUDICIAIRE (DCPJ)
The national headquarters of the serious crimes division of the POLICE NATIONALE.

DIRECTION DE LA SURVEILLANCE DU TERRITOIRE (DST)
An anti-espionnage intelligence agency, part of the POLICE NATIONALE, which keeps watch over foreign diplomats and their

staff. See also: DIRECTION GÉNÉRALE DE LA SÉCURITÉ EXTÉRIEURE; RENSEIGNEMENTS GÉNÉRAUX; SERVICE DE DOCUMENTATION EXTÉRIEURE ET DE CONTRE-ESPIONNAGE

DIRECTION DÉPARTEMENTALE DE LA CONCURRENCE, DE LA CONSOMMATION ET DE LA RÉPRESSION DES FRAUDES (DDCCRF)

Each DÉPARTEMENT has a local office of this government agency. See also: DGCCRF

DIRECTION DÉPARTEMENTALE DE L'ACTION SANITAIRE ET SOCIALE (DDASS)

The office which distributes AIDE SOCIALE where necessary, and which should become redundant eventually as the SÉCURITÉ SOCIALE gradually covers the entire population.

DIRECTION GÉNÉRALE DE LA CONCURRENCE, DE LA CONSOMMATION ET DE LA REPRESSION DES FRAUDES (DGCCRF)

The State agency under the tutelage of the *Ministère de l'*ÉCONOMIE ET DES FINANCES set up with local offices in each DÉPARTEMENT to protect consumers and to implement and monitor consumer legislation, and to provide support for consumers' groups.

DIRECTION GÉNÉRALE DE LA SÉCURITÉ EXTÉRIEURE (DGSE)

The military intelligence service, under the control of the *Ministère de la* DÉFENSE NATIONALE. It was connected with the RAINBOW WARRIOR affair. See also: DIRECTION DE LA SURVEILLANCE DU TERRITOIRE; RENSEIGNEMENTS GÉNÉRAUX; SERVICE DE DOCUMENTATION EXTÉRIEURE ET DE CONTRE-ESPIONNAGE

DISQUE AUTOMOBILE

In town centres where free parking facilities exist, a time disc is used in a controlled ZONE BLEUE, on which the driver shows the time of arrival. If the vehicle is not removed after the permitted period, the driver can be fined. The disc is now being replaced by a time stamped ticket issued at a machine called a *horodateur*.

DISSOLUTION DE L'ASSEMBLÉE NATIONALE

The ASSEMBLÉE NATIONALE can be dissolved by the PRÉSIDENT DE LA RÉPUBLIQUE, after consulting with the PREMIER MINISTRE and the *Présidents* of the two chambers. This was most recently done in 1981 and in 1988, both occasions when François MITTERRAND was elected as *Président de la République*. New ÉLECTIONS LÉGISLATIVES have to be held.

DISTRIBUTEUR AUTOMATIQUE DE BILLETS (DAB)

Many banks now have automatic cash machines available outside bank opening hours. See also: GUICHET AUTOMATIQUE DE BANQUE

DISTRICT

A group of COMMUNES which pool their housing and fire-fighting services, and take over any services previously organised by a SYNDICAT DE COMMUNES in that area. There were 168 *districts* in 1989. See also: AGGLOMÉRATION; COMMUNAUTÉ URBAINE

DIVISION AÉROMOBILE (DA)

The 6,000 personnel of the 4ème *Division aéromobile* based at Nancy (MEURTHE-ET-MOSELLE) with a specialism in helicopters, are part of the army's FORCE D'ACTION RAPIDE.

DIVISION ALPINE

The 27ème *Division alpine*, based at Grenoble (ISÈRE), is part of the army's FORCE D'ACTION RAPIDE and has 9,000 men specially trained for difficult terrain.

DIVISION BLINDÉE (DB)

Each armoured division in the French army, composed of 10,000 men, is trained for conventional, nuclear and chemical warfare.

DIVISION D'INFANTERIE (DI)

Each infantry division is composed of 7,500 men.

DIVISION D'INFANTERIE DE MARINE (DIMA)

The 9ème *Division d'infanterie de marine* is part of the army's FORCE D'ACTION RAPIDE, and is based at Saint-Malo (ILLE-ET-

VILAINE). It has 8,000 men, specially trained for rapid transporting to action.

DIVISION LÉGÈRE BLINDÉE (DLB)

The 7,500 men of the 6ème *Division légère blindée*, part of the army's FORCE D'ACTION RAPIDE, are based at Nîmes (GARD).

DIVISION PARACHUTISTE (DP)

Based at Toulouse (HAUTE-GARONNE), the 11ème *Division parachutiste* has 13,000 soldiers.

DIVORCE

The divorce laws were liberalised in 1975. There are now three forms of divorce: by mutual consent after a minimum period of six months' marriage, by the demand of one partner after six years' separation, or because of faults committed by one partner (adultery, unreasonable behaviour, violence, etc.).

The case is heard by a JUGE DES AFFAIRES MATRIMONIALES in a TRIBUNAL DE GRANDE INSTANCE. See also: GARDE DE L'ENFANT; PENSION ALIMENTAIRE; PENSION DE RÉVERSION; SÉPARATION DE CORPS

DJA See: *DOTATION AUX JEUNES AGRICULTEURS*

DJIBOUTI

A city and territory in the Horn of Africa, acquired by France in 1862, and known from 1892 to 1967 as *Côte française des Somalis*. It took the statute of a TOM in 1946. After a referendum in 1967, greater autonomy was granted and the name of *Territoire français des Afars et des Issas* was adopted. Inter-tribal and anti-French disturbances marked the 1970s. In 1977 Djibouti became independent, and in 1981 became a one-party State. The population is about half a million, of which the Issas form 47 per cent and the Afars 37 per cent.

France maintains a military base, takes well over half the exports, and is the source of almost a third of imported goods.

DLB See: *DIVISION LÉGÈRE BLINDÉE*

DOCKS DE FRANCE

A national chain of general stores, supermarkets and cafeterias, with a number of different names used in various regions and for certain activities. Overall, the group commands fifth place in annual turnover in the retail sector.

DOCTORAT

An advanced academic qualification, obtainable through a number of routes. A *doctorat* can be obtained by those who have followed the medical, pharmacy or dentistry courses beyond DIPLÔME D'ÉTAT level, and by those who have completed a MAÎTRISE followed by a DIPLÔME D'ÉTUDES APPROFONDIES or a DIPLÔME D'ÉTUDES SUPÉRIEURES SPÉCIALISÉES. Holders of a MAGISTÈRE or a *Diplôme d'ingénieur* can move directly into studies for a *doctorat*.

DOILLON, JACQUES (1944–)

A film director of the new generation, known for his intimist work such as *Un Sac de billes* (1975).

DOISNEAU, ROBERT (1912–)

A photographer whose evocative views of romantic couples in Paris have established a popular reputation, but who is also known for his scenes of working-class Paris and his industrial photography for RENAULT.

DOM See: *DÉPARTEMENT D'OUTRE-MER*

DOMAINE DE L'ÉTAT

The overall collection of state-owned property, including lands and buildings, and including also the property held temporarily when a person dies intestate.

DOMAINE PUBLIC

Property held in public ownership, and which normally cannot be sold, because of its particular nature or use. The property is usually available for public use, e.g. coastline, waterways, roadways, airports and schools, etc.

DOMICILE

The declared place of residence of an individual, over which the person has rights of protected privacy. These rights include an absolute right of privacy between the hours of 21.00 and

06.00 and all day on a *jour de* FÊTE LÉGALE, except for police access in a case of FLAGRANT DÉLIT, or under a JUGE's warrant, or a HUISSIER acting under court instructions. A change in *domicile* has to be notified so that all personal documents and records can be amended.

DONATION-PARTAGE
An irrevocable settlement in which one declares the division of wealth between one's children in the event of death. It has to be drawn up by a NOTAIRE, and gives tax advantages to the beneficiaries. If the *Donation-partage* includes a personally owned business, the beneficiaries can include others, either within or outside the family.

DORDOGNE
A DÉPARTEMENT in the AQUITAINE region, with a population of 386,354, named after the tributary of the Vézère. The CHEF-LIEU is Périgueux (urban area 59,842), an industrial centre, and other towns are Bergerac (31,794), a centre for the food and tobacco industry; Sarlat (9,909), a market and light industrial centre; and Terrasson-la-Villedieu (10,628) – rubber, plastics, paper goods and food-processing.

The Dordogne's main economic activity is in tourism, specialist food industries and in footwear. It is the largest producer of strawberries in France, the second in walnuts, tobacco and footwear production, and is known for its truffles, *foie gras* and wines. It is more densely provided with châteaux than any other *département*, and has renowned natural features such as the caves of Lascaux and the sites of Cro-Magnon. Its tourist industry is distinctive for the many GÎTES RURAUX.

In both the 1981 and 1988 ÉLECTIONS PRÉSIDENTIELLES, the Dordogne voted decisively for François MITTERRAND, but in 1992 the CONSEIL GÉNÉRAL fell to the control of the Centre Right for the first time this century.

Code départemental: 24

D'ORMESSON, COMTE JEAN LEFÈVRE (1925–) See: *ORMESSON, COMTE JEAN D'*

D'ORNANO, COMTE MICHEL (1924–1991)
A politician of the RÉPUBLICAINS INDÉPENDANTS, MAIRE of

Deauville (CALVADOS) 1962–1977, a post which his widow Anne now holds, DÉPUTÉ for Calvados from 1968, and holder of various ministerial posts in GISCARD D'ESTAING'S government 1974–1981. He was a candidate for the position of MAIRE DE PARIS in 1976.

DOSSIER MÉDICAL
The medical file of a patient is kept by the hospital which gives treatment, and since 1975 the patient has the right to see it by making a request to a medical practitioner.

DOTATION AUX JEUNES AGRICULTEURS (DJA)
In order to encourage the establishment of young people in farming, grants are available to farmers younger than 35 (and slightly older in certain cases) who satisfy certain conditions of minimum training (from 1992, this must be at least at the level of BREVET DE TECHNICIEN AGRICOLE), and who commit themselves to at least one year's farming, and at least 10 years' management if not directly farming personally. There are certain tax reductions available to holders of a DJA, which in 1990 was at least 52,000 francs, and can be as much as 162,000 francs.

DOUANES
The Customs administration, responsible for monitoring imports at the frontiers, and throughout the country for ensuring that appropriate duties are paid. They have the right of entry to any premises with a court order to search for goods fraudulently obtained. See also: DOMICILE

DOUBS
A DÉPARTEMENT in the FRANCHE-COMTÉ region, on the border with Switzerland, named after its main river, a tributary of the Saône. The population is 484,770, and the CHEF-LIEU is Besançon (AGGLOMÉRATION, 122,623), a centre of micro-engineering and clockmaking. Other urban areas are the Montbéliard conurbation (128,194), which includes the PEUGEOT headquarters at Sochaux, and Pontarlier (19,781).

It is the automobile and light industries which dominate the employment patterns, although the bulk of the area is rural, and includes part of the Jura mountain range. Dairy produce, including Emmenthal and Comté cheeses, is the principal agricultural activity, and there is a considerable tourist industry, especially in the forest and mountain areas, with some winter sports.

Politically, the urban conurbations have tended to be supportive of the Left, and in both ÉLECTIONS PRÉSIDENTIELLES in 1981 and 1988, François MITTERRAND received a majority of votes, but the CONSEIL GÉNÉRAL has a majority of Centre Right members.

Code départemental: 25   See also: SAUGEAIS

DP See: *DIVISION PARACHUTISTE*

DPU See: *DROIT DE PRÉEMPTION URBAINE*

DROIT DE BAIL
A tax of 2.5 per cent of the annual rental of an unfurnished property, if this is more than 2,500 francs, paid by the landlord.

DROIT DE CHASSE
A landowner has certain hunting rights over his or her property, and a tenant farmer has personal rights, which can be restricted by the owner, over the land occupied. Different rules exist in the MOSELLE, BAS-RHIN and HAUT-RHIN, where the COMMUNE has greater powers. The hunter owns the game killed by him or her. See also: CHASSE

DROIT DE GRÈVE
Since the Constitution of the QUATRIÈME RÉPUBLIQUE in 1946, each worker has had the right to strike, and it is illegal for an employer to penalise or dismiss a striker simply for exercising that right. See also: DROIT SYNDICAL

DROIT D'ENREGISTREMENT
A duty payable when certain legal documents are registered with the ADMINISTRATION, usually those needing the services of a NOTAIRE.

DROIT DE PRÉEMPTION URBAINE See: *ZONE D'INTERVENTION FONCIÈRE*

DROIT DE TIMBRE
The purchase of a TIMBRE FISCAL from a DÉBIT DE TABAC is the means by which certain duties or fees can be paid for documents, such as passports.

DROIT-ÉCONOMIE ET SCIENCES SOCIALES, UNIVERSITÉ DE (PARIS) See: *PANTHÉON-ASSAS (UNIVERSITÉ)*

DROIT SYNDICAL
The CONSTITUTION of 1958, confirming that of 1946, guarantees the right of a worker to join a trade union, if he or she so wishes, and to leave it without penalty at any time. An employer is not allowed to discriminate against members of a trade union. If there are more than 50 employees, the law provides that union representatives are entitled to time for union activities within the workplace, the amount depending on the size of the workforce.

DROITS DE SUCCESSION
The taxes payable on a deceased person's estate. Certain parts of the estate are exempt, and certain outstanding debts can be excluded. Beneficiaries of the will then have a right to certain bequests before a maximum is reached beyond which tax is payable. A spouse or a child will have to pay between 5 per cent and 40 per cent, those outside the family up to 60 per cent.

DRÔME
A DÉPARTEMENT in the RHÔNE-ALPES region, with a population in 1990 of 414,072, taking the name of a tributary of the Rhône. The CHEF-LIEU is Valence (urban area 89,485), a centre for precision engineering, electronics, chemicals and textiles. Other towns are Livron-sur-Drôme (12,903); Montélimar (31,260), famous for its nougat; Pierrelatte (11,770), the site of a nuclear power station; and Romans-sur-Isère (49,212), where the economy is dominated by shoes and leather goods, but suffers from foreign competition.

Much of the Drôme is taken up by the *Vercors drômois*, an upland forest area and regional park. Agricultural activity produces wines, lavender, poultry, honey, olives and fruit. The Côtes-du-Rhône and Ermitage wines come from the Drôme.

Tourism is an important contributor to the local economy, focusing on natural features such as gorges, forests and mountain passes, as well as picturesque villages, châteaux and museums. Winter sports facilities are also available.

In the ÉLECTIONS PRÉSIDENTIELLES in 1981 and 1988, the electors of the Drôme supported François MITTERRAND, and all its DÉPUTÉS and SÉNATEURS from 1988 have been Socialist, but the Right gained control of the CONSEIL GÉNÉRAL in 1992.

Code départemental: 26

DROUOT

The generic term for the main auction houses in Paris, based on the original *Salle Drouot* in the rue Drouot. The new salesroom at the same address sees 7,000 visitors per day, and has offshoots in Montmartre (*Drouot nord*) and in the northern suburbs at La-Plaine-Saint-Denis, there is a car market, *Drouot véhicules*. Many stamp dealers have established premises in the rue Drouot and its immediate area.

DRUON, MAURICE (1918–)

A popular novelist who was *Ministre des affaires culturelles* from 1973 to 1974, and for short periods a DÉPUTÉ for Paris and a member of the European Parliament. His novel *Les Grandes familles*, a GONCOURT prize-winner of 1948, has been made into a film, and *Les Rois maudits*, a seven-volume novel, became a successful television series. Since 1985 he has been permanent secretary of the ACADÉMIE FRANÇAISE.

DST See: *DIRECTION DE LA SURVEILLANCE DU TERRITOIRE*

DUBY, GEORGES (1919–)

An historian familiar to television viewers; a specialist in medieval France.

DUC D'ANJOU

The head of the Bourbon family, directly descended from the dynasty of the *Ancien Régime*, through the royal house of

Spain. The present *Duc d'Anjou*, Louis-Alphonse (1974–   ), took the title in 1981 on the death of his father. If he were to become king, he would take the title *Louis XX*. See also: COMTE DE PARIS

DUEL See: *DIPLÔME UNIVERSITAIRE D'ÉTUDES LITTÉRAIRES*

DUES See: *DIPLÔME UNIVERSITAIRE D'ÉTUDES SCIENTIFIQUES*

DURAS, MARGUERITE (1914–   )
Novelist, playwright and screenplay writer, who achieved popularity only in later life with a GONCOURT winner in 1984, *L'Amant*. A modern classic is *Moderato Cantabile* (1958), and she wrote the screenplay for Alain RESNAIS's film *Hiroshima mon amour*.

DURÉE DU TRAVAIL
In 1982, the legal working week became 39 hours, with five weeks' annual paid holiday. This length of the week may not be exceeded by employees under the age of 18, whose working day cannot be longer than eight hours, and who are not permitted to work night shifts. Adults may work up to 10 hours a day, to a maximum of 48 hours in a week. An overnight break must be at least 12 hours in duration.

DUT See: *DIPLÔME UNIVERSITAIRE DE TECHNOLOGIE*

EA See: *ÉCOLE DE L'AIR*

ÉCHOS, LES
A press and media group owned by the Pearson group, publisher of Britain's Financial Times since 1988. Its Paris daily newspaper, *Les Échos*, which specialises in financial and economic news, has a circulation of about 88,000.

ÉCLAIREUSES ET ÉCLAIREURS
Scouting organisations for young people are divided into lay bodies and those connected with religious confessions. The *Éclaireuses et Éclaireurs de France*, with about 35,000 members, is open to all and forbids religious and political connections. The *Fédération des éclaireurs et éclaireurs unionistes de France* (10,000) is a Protestant group, and the Jewish youth movement is the *Éclaireuses et Éclaireurs israélites de France*, with about 5,000 members. See also: GUIDES DE FRANCE; SCOUTS DE FRANCE

ÉCOLE CENTRALE
There are two institutions, the *École centrale Paris* (full title *École centrale des arts et manufactures*, nicknamed '*Piston, centrale*'), actually sited in the suburbs at Châtenay-Malabry (HAUTS-DE-SEINE) Paris, and the *École centrale de Lyon*, at Ecully (RHÔNE), which use the name *École centrale*, both recruiting their students through a post-BAC CONCOURS shared with the *École supérieure d'électricité* (or *Supélec*) at Gif-sur-Yvette (ESSONNE) and the *École supérieure d'optique* (or *Supoptic*) at Orsay in the same DÉPARTEMENT. Both these last institutions are privately-owned. The *concours* used by these GRANDES ÉCOLES is often called the *Concours Supélec*. Only one in five candidates was admitted in 1990.
  They offer advanced courses in engineering, but with an

emphasis on maintaining a high level of general cultural education, with a view to providing an elite force of technocrats in public service and industry.

ÉCOLE DE L'AIR (EA)

The higher education college of the ARMÉE DE L'AIR, situated at Salon-de-Provence (BOUCHES-DU-RHÔNE), and providing a range of long-term training courses for officers and technicians. It is also the base for the flying team, the '*Patrouille de France*'.

ÉCOLE DES BARRES See: *ÉCOLE NATIONALE SUPÉRIEURE AGRONOMIQUE*

ÉCOLE DES HAUTES ÉTUDES COMMERCIALES (HEC)

In 1990, 15 per cent of those who presented themselves for the second time at the CONCOURS HEC were admitted to the *École des hautes études commerciales* at Jouy-en-Josas (YVELINES), a GRANDE ÉCOLE run by the CHAMBRE DE COMMERCE ET DE L'INDUSTRIE de Paris. Only 5 per cent of candidates were admitted at their first attempt. There are about 220 CLASSES PRÉPARATOIRES throughout France for this *concours*.

The same *concours*, but with different coefficients (weightings in papers) is used by the *Écoles supérieures de commerce* (ESC) *de Paris* and *de Lyon*, and the *École supérieure des sciences économiques et commerciales* (ESSEC) at Cergy-Pontoise (VAL-D'OISE), a private institution under the control of the *Chambre de commerce et de l'industrie de Versailles*.

The various ESCAE (*Écoles supérieures de commerce et d'administration des entreprises*) have their own examinations, as do another group of similar establishments under the *Écricome* umbrella.

These are the leading management and business schools in France, and their graduates must do part of their studies abroad, as well as learn two foreign languages to a high level.

ÉCOLE ÉLÉMENTAIRE

The glory of the *Troisième République*, the *École élémentaire* provided free compulsory primary education from 1881, and this was often the vehicle for the establishment of the Republican ethos in COMMUNES throughout France, notably in disputes with

Church authorities and influence. The primary stage is now conducted in an ÉCOLE PRIMAIRE, but some individual establishments still retain the original name.

ÉCOLE EUROPÉENNE DES AFFAIRES (EAP)
Formerly known as the *École des affaires de Paris*, established by the CHAMBRE DE COMMERCE ET DE L'INDUSTRIE *de Paris* in 1974, its courses, to which students are recruited by the CONCOURS for HEC or ESSEC, provide facilities for study in Oxford, Berlin and Madrid as well as in Paris.

ÉCOLE LIBRE
The term used to denote private sector schools, independent of state control in management and regulation. The majority of such schools are run by the ÉGLISE CATHOLIQUE. All qualifications remain under state regulation. See also: LOI DEBRÉ; SAVARY, ALAIN.

ÉCOLE MATERNELLE
The vast majority of French children attend a publicly-funded nursery school before the statutory age of six years. The *École maternelle* is open to children from the age of two years. If there is no separate establishment, there will be nursery classes available in a primary school for those of five years of age.

ÉCOLE MILITAIRE
A number of special academies use the title *École militaire*. Principal among them are the *École spéciale militaire* (ESM), the officer training college of the ARMÉE DE TERRE at Coëtquidan (MORBIHAN), although still often referred to as Saint-Cyr, because of its previous occupation of the royal palace there, the naval *École militaire de la Flotte* (EMF) based at Poulmic (FINISTÈRE) and the *École militaire de l'Air* (EMA) at Salon-en-Provence (BOUCHES-DU-RHÔNE), which form similar functions for those services. There is also the *École militaire interarmes* (EMIA), also at Coëtquidan, which trains reserve officers and non-commissioned officers for full commissions. See also: ÉCOLE NAVALE

ÉCOLE NATIONALE D'ADMINISTRATION (ENA)
A GRANDE ÉCOLE, set up in 1945 to train an elite force of public

administrators. It recruits by CONCOURS from holders of a LICENCE or graduates of another *Grande École* or INSTITUT D'ÉTUDES POLITIQUES, or experienced FONCTIONNAIRES. About one in 10 applicants are accepted, and they then follow a highly structured 29 month course. Its graduates, '*énarques*', are required to work for the State for 10 years, and the choice of career is determined by their placing in the final pass list.

One third of top-ranking *fonctionnaire* posts are now filled by *énarques*. As part of the DÉCENTRALISATION, the ENA is being moved to Strasbourg (BAS-RHIN).

ÉCOLE NATIONALE DE MUSIQUE
There are 82 establishments with the title *École nationale de musique*, funded by the State.

ÉCOLE NATIONALE DES CHARTES (ENC)
Based in Paris, the specialist GRANDE ÉCOLE for training archivists and museum curators, entered by CONCOURS after two years in a CLASSE PRÉPARATOIRE, of which there are only three in the whole of the country. Students who commit themselves to 10 years' service are entitled to draw a salary.

ÉCOLE NATIONALE DES PONTS ET CHAUSSÉES (ENPC)
Commonly called '*Les ponts*', this college trains public civil engineers and information scientists. It was established in Paris in 1747. The CONCOURS, the *Concours Mines-Ponts-Télécom*, is also the means of entry to the *Écoles nationales supérieures des mines* which provide courses for managers and administrators in commerce and industry, and the *Écoles nationales supérieures des télécommunications*.

ÉCOLE NATIONALE D'INGÉNIEURS (ENI)
There are five ENI, at BELFORT, Brest (FINISTÈRE), Metz (MOSELLE), Saint-Étienne (LOIRE) and Tarbes (HAUTES-PYRÉNÉES), recruiting by CONCOURS those who have obtained BAC E or F, and who want training for senior engineering posts.
See also: ÉCOLE NATIONALE SUPÉRIEURE D'INGÉNIEURS

ÉCOLE NATIONALE D'INGÉNIEURS DE TRAVAUX AGRICOLES (ENITA)
Rather similar to the ENI, these five colleges train engineers and

technicians for agricultural (Bordeaux, Clermont-Ferrand and Dijon), horticultural (Angers), and food-processing (Nantes) industries.

ÉCOLE NATIONALE DU CIRQUE
A private establishment in Paris with a programme of study for those aged eight years old and above, leading to a CERTIFICAT D'APTITUDE PROFESSIONNELLE in circus performing arts.

ÉCOLE NATIONALE SUPÉRIEURE AGRONOMIQUE (ENSA)
About a third of the applicants for the CONCOURS '*Agro*' for agricultural and environmental engineers are accepted in the eight ENSA, including the *Institut national agronomique* (INA) in Paris. The *École des Barres*, at Nogent-sur-Vernisson (LOIRET) is the smallest, specialising in forestry and water management courses.

ÉCOLE NATIONALE SUPÉRIEURE D'ARTS ET MÉTIERS (ENSAM)
This has regional centres for its first two years of its three-year courses, the final year being spent in Paris. Entry is by CONCOURS, and students qualify in design engineering.

ÉCOLE NATIONALE SUPÉRIEURE DES ARTS DÉCORATIFS (ENSAD)
Often called *Arts déco*, this Paris fine arts and design school was founded in 1766, and recruits by CONCOURS, taking about one-tenth of applicants for its four-year courses.

ÉCOLE NATIONALE SUPÉRIEURE DES BEAUX-ARTS (ENSBA)
With its origins tracing back to the seventeenth century royal academies of sculpture, painting and architecture, the present *Beaux-Arts* in Paris retains its role as a leading art school for creative artists.

ÉCOLE NATIONALE SUPÉRIEURE D'INGÉNIEURS (ENSI)
The 29 ENSI are grouped geographically and by specialism, and a number are situated on university campuses. After entry

by CONCOURS, students train for three or four years in applied sciences.

ÉCOLE NATIONALE SUPÉRIEURE DES MINES See: *ÉCOLE NATIONALE DES PONTS ET CHAUSSÉES*

ÉCOLE NATIONALE SUPÉRIEURE DES TÉLÉCOMMUNICATIONS See: *ÉCOLE NATIONALE DES PONTS ET CHAUSSÉES*

ÉCOLE NATIONALE VÉTÉRINAIRE (ENV)
About one third of the candidates for the CONCOURS '*Véto*' are admitted to one of the four *Écoles nationales vétérinaires*, at Maisons-Alfort (VAL-DE-MARNE), Marcy-l'Étoile (RHÔNE), Toulouse (HAUTE-GARONNE) or Nantes (LOIRE-ATLANTIQUE), where four-year courses are provided. Seventy per cent of the graduates enter private practice.

ÉCOLE NAVALE (EN)
Part of the complex at Poulmic (FINISTÈRE), the *École navale*, also known as '*La Baille*', trains naval officer cadets, who pass out as *Enseigne de vaisseau de 2ème classe*. See also: ÉCOLE MILITAIRE

ÉCOLE NORMALE
A training college for teachers, often originally single-sex establishments. The *Écoles normales* produced INSTITUTEURS and teachers for lower secondary classes. In 1991, they were absorbed into the INSTITUTS UNIVERSITAIRES DE FORMATION DES MAÎTRES.

ÉCOLE NORMALE SUPÉRIEURE (ENS)
About 3,000 students attend courses at the four ENS. The only one outside the Paris conurbation is the *École normale supérieure scientifique de Lyon*. There are ENS at Cachan (VAL-DE-MARNE) and at the split campus of Fontenay-Saint-Cloud (HAUTS-DE-SEINE), but the most famous is in Paris itself with an additional campus at Montrouge (Hauts-de-Seine). Known as '*Norm sup*' or '*rue d'Ulm*', this has a history dating back to 1794, and is an amalgamation of separate colleges for men and women. It is a prestigious training establishment for teachers

and researchers, recruiting by CONCOURS, with many glittering names among its former students, called '*normaliens*', including POMPIDOU, PEYREFITTE, Bergson and Jaurès.

ÉCOLE POLYTECHNIQUE

The summit of the GRANDES ÉCOLES, under the control of the *Ministère de la défense*, and founded in 1794. The *École polytechnique* carries the nickname '*X*', and is now sited at Palaiseau (ESSONNE). It has perhaps the most rigorous of all CONCOURS for entry to a *Grande École*, and its graduates are more or less guaranteed a place in France's élite of industrialists or administrators. Its particular bias is towards engineering. Its students, who have the rank of reserve military officers, are paid a salary. Tuition fees are demanded from graduates who do not enter State service. Former *polytechniciens* include Valéry GISCARD D'ESTAING.

ÉCOLE PRIMAIRE See: *ÉCOLE ÉLÉMENTAIRE*

ÉCOLE SPÉCIALE MILITAIRE (ESM) See: *ÉCOLE MILITAIRE*

ÉCOLE SUPÉRIEURE DE COMMERCE (ESC) See: *ÉCOLE DES HAUTES ÉTUDES COMMERCIALES*

ÉCOLE SUPÉRIEURE DE COMMERCE ET D'ADMINISTRATION DES ENTREPRISES (ESCAE) See: *ÉCOLE DES HAUTES ÉTUDES COMMERCIALES*

ÉCOLE SUPÉRIEURE D'ÉLECTRICITÉ (ESE) See: *ÉCOLE CENTRALE*

ÉCOLE SUPÉRIEURE DES SCIENCES ÉCONOMIQUES ET COMMERCIALES (ESSEC) See: *ÉCOLE DES HAUTES ÉTUDES COMMERCIALES*

ÉCONOMIE, FINANCES ET BUDGET (MINISTÈRE DE L')

One of the three *Ministères d'État*, signifying its importance. It moved its headquarters in 1989 to new buildings on the banks of the Seine at BERCY in South-East Paris. In 1991 in the cabinet of Édith CRESSON, the ministry became a super-ministry incorporating the former separate *Ministères de l'industrie, du*

commerce extérieur, de la poste et des télécommunications and
du commerce et de l'artisanat under Pierre BÉRÉGOVOY.

ÉCOUTE TÉLÉPHONIQUE
Telephone tapping can legally be authorised by a COMMISSION
ROGATOIRE, but illegal tapping is punishable by a prison sentence
of up to one year, or a fine of up to 60,000 francs.

ÉCUREUIL
The sign of the squirrel is the logo of the CAISSE D'ÉPARGNE ET
DE PRÉVOYANCE, and the term *Écureuil* is sometimes used to
denote the network.

EDF – GDF See: *ÉLECTRICITÉ DE FRANCE; GAZ DE FRANCE*

ÉDUCATION NATIONALE, JEUNESSE ET SPORTS (MINISTÈRE DE L')
One of the three *Ministères d'État*, which indicates the
importance attached to education as part of the essence of the
Republic.

ÉGALITÉ DE SALAIRE
It is illegal for an employer to discriminate between workers on
the ground of sex when fixing rates of pay.

ÉGLISE CATHOLIQUE
The largest Christian church in France, traditionally a Catholic
country, and known in the nineteenth century as the elder
daughter of the Church. Since 1905, the Church has been
entirely separated from the State, which jealously maintains
its secular nature, although there is much less mutual suspicion
than in former times. There are 95 dioceses divided into apostolic
regions, with 18 archdioceses. See also: ÉCOLE LIBRE

ÉGLISE RÉFORMÉE DE FRANCE
The largest Protestant church in France, with about 400,000
practising members, and 460 clergy.

ÉLECTEUR
Every French national aged 18 and above is entitled to cast a
vote in an election, provided that he or she is not a declared

bankrupt, or has not had the *droit de vote* suspended as part of a judicial sentence. The elector's name must appear on the local voters' list, which is updated annually in December. French people living abroad may vote in ÉLECTIONS PRÉSIDENTIELLES and in a RÉFÉRENDUM through embassies and consulates. Women became electors in 1944, and military personnel in 1945. The age of majority was lowered from 21 in 1974. See also: DEGRADATION CIVIQUE; VOTE PAR PROCURATION

ÉLECTION
Elections for public office are always held on a Sunday, usually for 10 hours, with a week's delay between first and second rounds (a fortnight in the case of ÉLECTIONS PRÉSIDENTIELLES). Counting of votes starts immediately after the voting closes. There are strict rules about campaigning, which is in any case forbidden on election day. Opinion poll results cannot be published in the preceding week.

Voters collect individual candidates' voting slips from tables at the polling station, and in secret place the slip of their choice in an envelope which is then placed in a ballot box. If the slip is placed in the envelope in public, the vote is considered to be void.

Voting machines may be used, but they have not been popular, and their use is rare. See also: AFFICHAGE; CARTE D'ÉLECTEUR; SCRUTIN

ÉLECTIONS CANTONALES
The term used for the election of members of the CONSEIL GÉNÉRAL. Held every three years to elect half the *Conseil général*, the elections use the SCRUTIN UNINOMINAL MAJORITAIRE. One member per CANTON is elected.

ÉLECTIONS LÉGISLATIVES
Parliamentary elections for DÉPUTÉS, held every five years, unless the ASSEMBLÉE NATIONALE is dissolved in mid-term. The normal method has been the SCRUTIN UNINOMINAL MAJORITAIRE, but in 1986, as an experiment, the SCRUTIN DE LISTE method was used.

ÉLECTIONS MUNICIPALES

The elections to the CONSEIL MUNICIPAL in each COMMUNE, held every six years. If a *commune* has fewer than 3,500 inhabitants, the SCRUTIN UNINOMINAL MAJORITAIRE is used, but larger *communes* use the SCRUTIN À MODE MIXTE method. If a seat becomes vacant between elections, the candidate in the previous election who has the greatest number of votes, but who was not elected, assumes the vacant seat.

ÉLECTIONS PRÉSIDENTIELLES

Held every seven years. An absolute majority is essential for a candidate to be elected, and this is normally as a result of a second round, when only two candidates are left in the contest. Candidates must be of French nationality, at least 23 years of age, have complied with SERVICE NATIONAL obligations, not have been found guilty of serious offences, be nominated by at least 500 elected holders of public office, and have paid a deposit of 10,000 francs. Each candidate has an equal share of television and radio time in the campaign which lasts a fortnight. The campaign costs are subsidised by the State if the candidate obtains at least 5 per cent of the votes cast. See also: AMNISTIE; PRÉSIDENT DE LA RÉPUBLIQUE

ÉLECTIONS RÉGIONALES

Held every six years, using the SCRUTIN PROPORTIONNEL, in order to elect members of the CONSEIL RÉGIONAL.

ÉLECTIONS SÉNATORIALES

A third of the SÉNAT is elected every three years, using the method of SCRUTIN DE LISTE MAJORITAIRE if the DÉPARTEMENT has fewer than five SÉNATEURS, and the SCRUTIN PROPORTIONNEL in other cases.

ÉLECTRICITÉ DE FRANCE (EDF)

The State-owned utility which is responsible for generating and distributing power supply. It has a monopoly over distribution, and generates 97 per cent of the electricity consumed in France.

ELF AQUITAINE

A State-owned petroleum company, part of the *Entreprise de recherches et d'activités pétrolières* (ERAP) organisation. The largest French oil company, it controls the Elf and Antar brand names, and operates in 32 countries. It is the second largest French industrial concern in terms of turnover.

ELLE
A women's weekly magazine, with a circulation of 360,000, and since 1986 with American, British and Spanish editions.

ÉLUS LOCAUX
Elected members of either the CONSEIL GÉNÉRAL, the CONSEIL MUNICIPAL, or the CONSEIL RÉGIONAL. See also: CUMUL DES MANDATS

ÉLYSÉE, PALAIS DE L'
The official residence and office of the PRÉSIDENT DE LA RÉPUBLIQUE, situated off the *avenue des* CHAMPS-ÉLYSÉES in Paris. The address is 55 rue du Faubourg-Saint-Honoré. It has played a part in the fortunes of royalty and emperors, as well as aristocrats and presidents since the eighteenth century, taking on its current role in 1876.

EMA See: *ÉCOLE MILITAIRE*

ÉMANCIPATION
The status of a person aged 16 or 17, who either because he or she is married, or has parental consent, assumes most of the rights of an adult who has attained majority. The status is granted by a JUGE DES TUTELLES of the TRIBUNAL D'INSTANCE. The person becomes a '*mineur émancipé*', and is no longer subject to AUTORITÉ PARENTALE.

EMF See: *ÉCOLE MILITAIRE*

EMIA See: *ÉCOLE MILITAIRE*

EMMANUEL, PIERRE (1916–1984)
A poet known for his work expressing the conflicts experienced by a committed Christian, e.g, in *Babel* (1952) and *Jacob* (1970).

EMMANUELLI, HENRI (1945–)
A banker and Socialist politician, a DÉPUTÉ for the LANDES, elected *Président* of the ASSEMBLÉE NATIONALE in 1992.

EMMAÜS
A charitable organisation, founded in 1954 by Abbé Pierre, with the objective of supporting underprivileged families and individuals. It has a worldwide mission, with 250 local groups in France, who collect old clothing, paper and furniture for resale.

EN See: *ÉCOLE NAVALE*

ENA See: *ÉCOLE NATIONALE D'ADMINISTRATION*

ÉNARQUE See: *ÉCOLE NATIONALE D'ADMINISTRATION*

ENC See: *ÉCOLE NATIONALE DES CHARTES*

ÉNERGIE ÉOLIENNE
Experimental stations to harness wind for producing energy have been built on the Atlantic and Channel coasts and in the lower Rhône valley. The *Centre national d'essais éoliens* is at Lannion (CÔTES-D'ARMOR).

ÉNERGIE GÉOTHERMIQUE
The overall production of thermally generated power is less than 1 per cent of the national production. There is a considerable concentration of this in the Paris basin.

ÉNERGIE NUCLÉAIRE
France has a highly developed nuclear energy sector. The programme is controlled by the COMMISSARIAT À L'ÉNERGIE ATOMIQUE, and in 1990, there were nearly 60 nuclear power stations, generating well over two-thirds of France's electricity supply. The decision to concentrate on nuclear sources was taken in 1974 as a reaction to the international oil crisis, but there has been considerable opposition to the programme in recent years, and the rate of increase in production has slowed.

ÉNERGIE SOLAIRE
The aim is to provide 5 per cent of France's energy needs from solar sources by the year 2000.

ENI See: *ÉCOLE NATIONALE D'INGÉNIEURS*

ENITA See: *ÉCOLE NATIONALE D'INGÉNIEURS DE TRAVAUX AGRICOLES*

ENS See: *ÉCOLE NORMALE SUPÉRIEURE*

ENSA See: *ÉCOLE NATIONALE SUPÉRIEURE AGRONOMIQUE*

ENSAD See: *ÉCOLE NATIONALE SUPÉRIEURE DES ARTS DÉCORATIFS*

ENSAM See: *ÉCOLE NATIONALE SUPÉRIEURE D'ARTS ET MÉTIERS*

ENSBA See: *ÉCOLE NATIONALE SUPÉRIEURE DES BEAUX-ARTS*

ENSEIGNEMENT
The term used to cover the whole educational system, including schools, colleges and universities. See also: COLLÈGE; ÉCOLE ÉLÉMENTAIRE; ÉDUCATION NATIONALE; LYCÉE; UNIVERSITÉ

ENSI See: *ÉCOLE NATIONALE SUPÉRIEURE D'INGÉNIEURS*

ENTREPRISE PUBLIQUE
Any commercially operated business in public ownership (e.g. SOCIÉTÉ NATIONALE DES CHEMINS DE FER FRANÇAIS). See also: ÉTABLISSEMENT PUBLIC INDUSTRIEL ET COMMERCIAL

ENTRETIENS DE BICHAT
An annual medical conference in Paris, attracting thousands of participants, named after the *Hôpital Bichat* where it started in 1947.

ENV See: *ÉCOLE NATIONALE VÉTÉRINAIRE*

ENVOI CONTRE REMBOURSEMENT
The guaranteed delivery service with a flat-rate refund in case of loss.

ENVOI EN VALEUR DÉCLARÉE (VD)
The registered letter service for valuable items, providing insurance for loss.

EPIC See: *ÉTABLISSEMENT PUBLIC INDUSTRIEL ET COMMERCIAL*

EPR See: *COMMISSION DE DÉVELOPPEMENT ÉCONOMIQUE RÉGIONAL (CODER)*

ÉPURATION
The period of official score-settling that took place mainly in 1945–1946 when those found guilty of collaborating with the occupying forces suffered judicial penalties, ranging from capital punishment to loss of civic rights. About two million were found guilty. The final proceedings of the special *Haute Cour de justice* took place in 1960.

ÉQUIPE, L'
The daily sports newspaper published in Paris by the Amaury group, with a circulation sometimes reaching 250,000.

ERAP See: *ELF AQUITAINE*

ESC See: *ÉCOLE DES HAUTES ÉTUDES COMMERCIALES*

ESCAE See: *ÉCOLE DES HAUTES ÉTUDES COMMERCIALES*

ESM See: *ÉCOLE MILITAIRE*

ESPACE PIERRE-CARDIN
The former *Théâtre des ambassadeurs* in Paris was redesigned in 1970 by CARDIN and took his name.

ESSEC See: *ÉCOLE DES HAUTE ÉTUDES COMMERCIALES*

ESSONNE
A DÉPARTEMENT of the ÎLE-DE-FRANCE region, created in 1964 by the reorganisation of the former Paris region. The Essonne, named after a minor tributary of the Seine, takes in the southern outskirts of greater Paris as well as the rural, largely dormitory area beyond. It has a population of 1.08 million and the most populous COMMUNES are its CHEF-LIEU, Évry, which is a VILLE NOUVELLE, and itself comprises four *communes* (urban area

45,531); Athis-Mons (29,123); Corbeil-Essonnes (40,345);
Draveil (27,867); Étampes (25,981); Grigny (24,920); Les Ulis
(27,164); Massy (38,574); Palaiseau (28,395); Sainte-Geneviève-
des-Bois (31,286); Savigny-sur-Orge (33,295); and Viry-
Châtillon (30,600). The highest density of population is at Juvisy-
sur-Orge, where over 5,500 people live in each square
kilometre.

The Essonne is home to a number of GRANDES ÉCOLES, and
research institutes, laboratories and high-tech industries
predominate. SNECMA has a large plant at Évry. The
Département retains its picturesque character in its rural area,
and Étampes and Montlhéry are tourist centres.

Women living in the Essonne have the third highest life
expectancy in France: 79.9 years (shared with those in the
ALPES-MARITIMES). During 1968–1975, the Essonne experienced
the highest number of immigrants of any *département* – largely
from central Paris, and coinciding with the development of Évry
and expanding communes.

In both 1981 and 1988 ÉLECTIONS PRÉSIDENTIELLES, the Essonne
voted firmly for MITTERRAND, and its parliamentary
representatives are mainly Socialist. The composition of the
CONSEIL GÉNÉRAL, however, shows a large majority for the Right,
dominated by the RASSEMBLEMENT POUR LA RÉPUBLIQUE,
confirmed in the 1992 ÉLECTIONS CANTONALES.

Code départemental: 91

ESTAING, VALÉRY GISCARD D' See: *GISCARD D'ESTAING, VALÉRY*

EST RÉPUBLICAIN, L'

The daily newspaper published in Nancy, with a circulation of
250,000, dominating the market in LORRAINE except for
MOSELLE, and most of the FRANCHE-COMTÉ. The Sunday edition
sells about 325,000.

ÉTABLISSEMENT D'ACTION CULTURELLE

A cultural centre officially recognised by the *Ministère de la*
CULTURE and directly supported by its *Direction du théâtre et
des spectacles*. The centre must make a distinctive contribution

to the national or international achievement in its field in order to qualify for State support, and must be managed by an ASSOCIATION.

ÉTABLISSEMENT PUBLIC INDUSTRIEL ET COMMERCIAL (EPIC)

A publicly-owned body which operates on commercial lines. One is the *Établissement public des voies navigables*, founded in 1991, which oversees the operation of all navigable waterways. See also: ENTREPRISE PUBLIQUE

ÉTABLISSEMENT PUBLIC RÉGIONAL (EPR) See: *COMMISSION DE DÉVELOPPEMENT ÉCONOMIQUE RÉGIONAL (CODER)*

ÉTAIX, PIERRE (1928–)

Circus clown, film actor and director, Étaix is well known for his references to the legendary comic tradition in films such as *Le Soupirant* (1962), *Yoyo* (1964) and *Le Grand Amour* (1970).

ÉTAT CIVIL

A citizen's entitlement to rights as a French national, as certified by documents such as birth and marriage certificates, provided by the MAIRIE. See also: CARTE NATIONALE D'IDENTITÉ; CASIER JUDICIAIRE; LIVRET DE FAMILLE

ÉTAT DE SIÈGE

Article 36 of the CONSTITUTION provides that at a time of grave national danger, the CONSEIL DES MINISTRES is able to declare a state of siege in part or the whole of the country for a period of up to 12 days, after which renewal of the DÉCRET has to be approved by parliament. During this time, the military authorities can be given exceptional police powers. See also: ÉTAT D'URGENCE

ÉTAT D'IVRESSE See: *ALCOOL AU VOLANT*

ÉTAT D'URGENCE

More severe than the ÉTAT DE SIEGE, this is when civil authorities are given special powers. The *État d'urgence* was invoked in

ALGÉRIE in 1960, and in France to deal with the Algerian crisis for 15 months from 1961 to 1962. Extension beyond 12 days entails passing a special law.

ÉTAT-MAJOR
The central command of the armed forces, headed by the *Chef d'État-Major des armées*, who is the military adviser to the government, with representatives of the three services as assistants. The chief of staff is responsible to the PRÉSIDENT DE LA RÉPUBLIQUE and the government for the command of all military forces, subject to special arrangements for the FORCES NUCLÉAIRES.

ÉTIQUETAGE
Laws on labelling consumer goods are subject to European Community directives. The prices of prepacked goods have to be expressed in kilos or litres. Perishable goods must also indicate a *date limite de consommation* (DLC) and tinned food, medicines, etc., must show a *date limite d'utilisation optimale* (DLUO). See also: APPELLATION D'ORIGINE CONTRÔLÉE; NORMES FRANÇAISES

ÉTRANGERS
The term tends to be used to denote any resident or visitor not born of French parents, or who has not taken out French nationality. The issue is closely bound with continuing controversy over IMMIGRATION. Estimates of the number of foreigners in France fluctuate depending on the definition one is using, and are notoriously unreliable because of this.

ÉTUDIANT, L'
A monthly magazine about student life, with a wide range of supplementary publications on careers advice, information for parents, etc.

EURE
A DÉPARTEMENT in the HAUTE-NORMANDIE region, with a 1990 population of 513,818, named after the tributary whose confluence with the Seine is at Pont-de-l'Arche. The CHEF-LIEU is Évreux (urban area 54,654) and other centres of population

are Bernay (11,873); Gisors (10,359); Louviers (20,705); Pont-Audemer (12,913); Vernon (28,416). Despite its relative proximity to Paris, the *Département's* inhabitants live mainly in rural areas, although mixed, light industrial activity outweighs agriculture as a source of employment. Agricultural activity is mainly concerned with wheat, cattle and dairy produce.

The village of Thierville has the distinction of the only French village with no war dead in either the Franco-Prussian War of 1870 or the two World Wars. There are numerous abbeys and châteaux, adding to the tourist attraction of the Eure.

In politics, there is great rivalry with the other, dominant *département* in the region, SEINE-MARITIME. The DÉPUTÉS are split between Right and Left, the SÉNATEURS between Centre and Right. Voting was in favour of MITTERRAND in 1981 and 1988 by a very small margin. Three-quarters of the seats on the CONSEIL GÉNÉRAL are held by the Centre Right.

Code départemental: 27

EURE-ET-LOIR

A DÉPARTEMENT of the CENTRE region, with a population of 396,064 in 1990. Its name is derived from two rivers which pass through it – the Eure flowing into the Seine, and the Loir, a tributary of the Sarthe. The CHEF-LIEU is Chartres (AGGLOMÉRATION 84,627), and other sizeable urban areas are Châteaudun (14,511); Dreux (48,191); and Nogent-le-Rotrou (12,745).

The Eure-et-Loir, one of the driest areas of the country, comes first in the league of wheat producers in France. The towns are centres of light engineering, but retain their historic and, especially Chartres, ecclesiastical heritage.

In the ÉLECTION PRÉSIDENTIELLE of 1981, the voters of Eure-et-Loir gave Valéry GISCARD D'ESTAING a slight majority, but supported MITTERRAND in 1988. The parliamentary representation reflects this balance with no overall dominance of either Right or Left. A Centre Right coalition controls the CONSEIL RÉGIONAL, strengthened by the result of the ÉLECTIONS CANTONALES in 1992.

Code départemental: 28

EUROMARCHÉ
A chain of hypermarkets, formerly owned by the PRINTEMPS group which established them as participants in a central purchasing organisation in 1968, bought in 1991 by CARREFOUR.

EUROPE I
A French language commercial radio station, broadcasting on long wave and FM from Saarland, in Germany, with an estimated audience of 15 million. In 1987, it received 33 per cent of the national advertising on radio. During the 1950s there were disputes about wavelengths, and from 1959 to 1986, the French State had a financial interest through SOFIRAD. Just over half the French listeners who tune into one station only, choose *Europe I*, i.e. almost four million. The successful diet is a mixture of news, varieties, sport and light music.

ÉVÉNEMENT DU JEUDI, L'
A weekly news magazine launched with phenomenal success in 1984, rising within three weeks from a circulation of 25,000 to 160,000, which it maintains.

ÉVIAN, ACCORDS D'
The agreement signed at Évian-les-Bains (HAUTE-SAVOIE) in 1962, ending the Algerian war, and ratified by RÉFÉRENDUM.

ÉVRY-VAL-D'ESSONNE, UNIVERSITÉ DE
A small university establishment with 1,000 students at Évry (ESSONNE) with courses in economics, mathematics, social science and sciences.

EXAMEN MÉDICAL PRÉNUPTIAL
In the two months preceding a planned wedding, each partner must normally obtain medical certificates from a doctor. The examination includes blood tests for blood group compatibility, screening for venereal diseases and tuberculosis. See also: MARIAGE CIVIL

EXODE RURAL
The massive population movement from rural areas to towns and cities which occurred throughout the twentieth century, and which accelerated after 1945, especially among young

families, and with a particular intensity from south-western regions. Some DÉPARTEMENTS have lost half their rural population in a hundred years, even taking into account immigration.

EXPRESS, L'
A weekly news magazine, formerly taking a left-wing stance, founded by Jean-Jacques SERVAN-SCHREIBER in 1953 as an offshoot of *Les* ÉCHOS, and sold in 1977 to James Goldsmith. Its current circulation is 555,000. The publishing firm *Groupe Express* has built up a number of titles, and is part of the *Générale Occidentale* group.

EXTERNE
The term given to a day-pupil at a LYCÉE or COLLÈGE where there are boarding facilities for boarders in an INTERNAT.

A parallel distinction is made in the hospital service between resident and non-resident junior doctors, and in CONCOURS between those for internal and external candidates.

FABIUS, LAURENT (1946–)
A Socialist politician who rose rapidly from being a DÉPUTÉ for the SEINE-MARITIME in 1978 through posts within the PARTI SOCIALISTE, and then in ministerial office to become PREMIER MINISTRE from 1984 to 1986. In 1988, he became the youngest *Président* of the ASSEMBLÉE NATIONALE this century. He commands an influential power-base within the *Parti socialiste*, and became its *premier secrétaire général* in 1992.

FACTURE TÉLÉPHONIQUE
The account for telephone service is payable every two months. A detailed account is available on payment of a special fee, and monthly bills can be provided on request. Bills not settled within three weeks can lead to the service being suspended.

FACULTÉ
The commonly used term for university, although technically, universities are no longer organised in *facultés*. See also: UNITÉ DE FORMATION ET DE RECHERCHE

FAMILLE NOMBREUSE See: *ALLOCATION AUX MÈRES DE FAMILLE; CARTE NATIONALE DE PRIORITÉ; MÉDAILLE DE LA FAMILLE FRANÇAISE*

FAURE, EDGAR (1908–1988)
A lawyer, novelist and economic historian who entered politics before the Second World War, active in the FRANCHE-COMTÉ region, but also holding ministerial posts in the QUATRIÈME RÉPUBLIQUE, including PRÉSIDENT DU CONSEIL on two occasions. In the CINQUIÈME RÉPUBLIQUE, Faure was perhaps best known for his role as *Ministre de l'*ÉDUCATION NATIONALE in framing the 1968 LOI FAURE which reformed the higher education system. He was *Président de l'*ASSEMBLÉE NATIONALE from 1973 to 1978.

FAUSSES FACTURES, AFFAIRES DES See: *URBA,*
AFFAIRE

FAUTEUIL
A numbered seat in the ACADÉMIE FRANÇAISE. When a place is
vacant, the election is to fill the particular seat. *Le 41*ème
fauteuil is an expression denoting all the famous authors who
have not been elected.

FAVART, SALLE
The opera house used by the *Théâtre musical de Paris* at the
Châtelet.

FAYARD
A general publishing house, now part of the HACHETTE group.

FCP See: *FONDS COMMUN DE PLACEMENTS*

FCPE See: *FÉDÉRATION DES CONSEILS DE PARENTS*
D'ÉLÈVES DES ÉCOLES PUBLIQUES

FÉDÉRATION D'ÉCOLES SUPÉRIEURES D'INGÉNIEURS
ET DE CADRES (FESIC)
A co-ordinating body with responsibilities over 19 private
Catholic higher education establishments, and which organises
their common CONCOURS.

FÉDÉRATION DE L'ÉDUCATION NATIONALE (FEN)
The largest single union organisation for teachers in the State
education system, claiming to represent an estimated
membership of 400,000. Individuals join one of the member
unions, not FEN itself. There are various political strands
within its composition, the largest being sympathetic to the
PARTI SOCIALISTE, but without direct ties. The FEN also functions
as a major commercial venture, providing services for its
associations' members.

FÉDÉRATION DES CONSEILS DE PARENTS D'ÉLÈVES
DES ÉCOLES PUBLIQUES (FCPE)
The largest pressure group representing parents of children in
state schools, claiming to speak for 600,000 families. Its local
groups have the majority of parents' seats on CONSEILS D'ÉCOLE.

See also: UNION NATIONALE DES ASSOCIATIONS DE PARENTS D'ÉLÈVES
DE L'ENSEIGNEMENT LIBRE

FÉDÉRATION DES FAMILLES DE FRANCE
A consumer pressure group, founded in 1921, which publishes
the monthly *Familles de France*, with a circulation of 20,000.

FÉDÉRATION FRANÇAISE DE L'AGRICULTURE (FFA)
A farmers' organisation, with 75,000 members, created in 1969
by a right-wing group which split off from the FNSEA.

FÉDÉRATION NATIONALE DES ACHATS (FNAC)
Founded in 1953 by two former militant Trotskyists, FNAC
started as an organisation for selling photographic equipment,
but in the 1970s developed bookshops, record and hi-fi stores
throughout France on a co-operative discount basis. Its Paris
bookshops are enormous, and throughout France it accounts
for 10 per cent of all book sales. In 1985, the control of FNAC
was taken over by a MUTUELLE for FONCTIONNAIRES.

FÉDÉRATION NATIONALE DE SYNDICATS D'EXPLOITANTS AGRICOLES (FNSEA)
The largest farmers' grouping, claiming more than 700,000
member families, who join local associations. FNSEA virtually
functions as the official union of farmers, and is fully consulted
by the ministry, especially when the right-wing parties are in
office. A recent former secretary, François Guillaume, moved
into the government as *Ministre de l'*AGRICULTURE in 1986. See
also: FÉDÉRATION FRANÇAISE DE L'AGRICULTURE

FÉDÉRATION UNIVERSITAIRE ET POLYTECHNIQUE DE LILLE
A private higher education establishment with 13,000 students,
providing courses in arts, economics, humanities, management,
medicine, sciences, technology and theology.

FÉLIX POTIN
A large chain of self-service stores of varying size, part of the
Primistères group.

FÉMINA, PRIX
An annual literary prize, founded in 1904, awarded in

November by a jury of women. The sales of the prizewinner sometimes exceed those of the GONCOURT winner. The *Fémina étranger* has been awarded since 1986 for a novel written by a foreign woman.

FEN See: *FÉDÉRATION DE L'ÉDUCATION NATIONALE*

FERMETURE ANNUELLE
Because of the traditional pattern of month-long summer holidays, many businesses close entirely for a period, usually between 15 July and 15 August, or for the whole of July or August.

FERNANDEZ, DOMINIQUE (1929–)
A novelist whose first prominent work, *Porporino ou les mystères de Naples*, appeared in 1974, and who went on to win the *Prix* GONCOURT in 1982 with *Dans la main de l'Ange*.

FERRAT, JEAN (1930–)
A singer in the *chansonnier* tradition.

FERRÉ, LÉO (1916–)
A well-known singer whose popular mixture of poetry and music developed out of the intellectual milieu of Paris night-clubs in the 1950s.

FESIC See: *FÉDÉRATION D'ÉCOLES SUPÉRIEURES D'INGÉNIEURS ET DE CADRES*

FESTIVAL D'AVIGNON
An annual music and drama festival founded by Jean VILAR in 1947 with the intention of widening the audience for cultural events, and the precursor of the now common international arts festival. The present *Festival d'Avignon* also comprises film, dance, poetry and other performing arts.

FESTIVAL DE BOURGES
An annual event, started in 1976, promoting young talent in French song of all kinds, held in Bourges (CHER). The event takes place in the spring and is often called '*le Printemps de Bourges*'.

FÊTE DE L'HUMANITÉ
An annual social event held by the PARTI COMMUNISTE FRANÇAIS each autumn in La Courneuve (SEINE-SAINT-DENIS) in the northern part of the CEINTURE ROUGE.

FÊTE DU BLEU, BLANC, ROUGE
The FRONT NATIONAL holds its annual social celebration at Le BOURGET a week after the FÊTE DE L'HUMANITÉ.

FÊTE LÉGALE
An official public holiday, currently comprising all Sundays, 1 January, Easter Monday, Ascension Day, Whit Monday, 1 May, 8 May, 14 July, 15 August, 1 November, 11 November and 25 December. Only on 1 May do all workers have the right to demand a holiday with pay, but except in the case of continuous process industries, all workers below the age of 18 must be given time off.

FÊTE NATIONALE
The annual celebrations on 14 July mark the symbolic date of the fall of the Bastille in 1789 and the *Fête de la Fédération* a year later. In Paris it is traditionally marked by a military parade in the CHAMPS-ÉLYSÉES in front of the PRÉSIDENT DE LA RÉPUBLIQUE, and throughout France by civic events, public balls, fireworks displays and fairs.

FEUILLE DE SOINS
A document identifying medical treatment given and to which a patient attaches the *vignettes*, or manufacturer's label, of prescribed medicines obtained, so that a refund may be sought from the SÉCURITÉ SOCIALE.

FFA See: *FÉDÉRATION FRANÇAISE DE L'AGRICULTURE; FORCES FRANÇAISES EN ALLEMAGNE*

FHCP See: *FOULARD HERMÈS, COLLIER DE PERLES*

FICHE D'ACCUEIL
An hotel registration form. It is not legally required to prove

one's identity in order to obtain an hotel room. See also: FICHE
DE POLICE

FICHE DE POLICE
Foreign nationals can be required to complete a police
registration form at an hotel, and will have to prove their identity.
See also: FICHE D'ACCUEIL

FICHIER DES MAL-LOGÉS
The unofficial record of those who are poorly housed or
homeless.

FIGARO, LE
The respected right-wing Paris daily newspaper, which because
it was suspended by the VICHY régime in 1942, was allowed to
retain its pre-war title after 1944. Its origins date back to 1826,
and it has published daily since 1866; it is the oldest Paris daily.
Le Figaro was purchased by Robert HERSANT in 1975. Since
1985, it has incorporated *L'Aurore*, and has a circulation of
433,500. Its announcements of births, marriages and deaths are
the register of Paris social life. Business news is printed on pink
pages called '*Fig-Éco*'. There is also a substantial weekly colour
magazine.

FILIPACCHI
A media group, founded by the journalist and publisher Daniel
Filipacchi, with interests in popular magazines (including
PARIS-MATCH, Penthouse and OK!), RADIO LIBRE and books.

FINANCES, MINISTÈRE DES See: *ÉCONOMIE,
FINANCES ET BUDGET*

FINISTÈRE
The most western DÉPARTEMENT of BRETAGNE, with a 1990
population of 838,662. Unusually, Finistère is not named after
a river but is a modern form of the Latin *Finis terrae*. Pointe
de Corsen, near Brest, is considered the most westerly point
on the French mainland. The CHEF-LIEU is Quimper (59,420), a
major distribution centre, and other large urban areas are the
naval port of Brest (201,480); Concarneau (24,760), a fishing
port; Douarnenez (16,457), a centre of the canning industry;

Landerneau (14,269) – food-processing and paper production; Morlaix (25,810), a port and industrial centre; and Quimperlé (10,748), with food-based industries.

The *Département* also includes a number of inhabited offshore islands. Its tourist appeal is enormous because of its coastline, nature reserves and the *Parc naturel régional d'Armorique*. Much of the tourist trade focuses on campsites and self-catering GÎTES.

It is the major producer of artichokes and cauliflowers, second in production of beans, carrots and pigs, third in cattle and peas, and sixth for eggs. Finistère catches more than half the shellfish in France, and 20 per cent of the national fresh and frozen fish product.

There is rainfall in Finistère on more days than anywhere else in France (201 days). The life expectancy for men is the fourth lowest (68 years), probably more due to excess of alcohol rather than water!

In political terms, Finistère changed allegiance in the ÉLECTIONS PRÉSIDENTIELLES in 1988, supporting MITTERRAND, after giving GISCARD D'ESTAING a slight majority in 1981, whereas its parliamentary representation reflects its more traditional Centre Right allegiance. The CONSEIL RÉGIONAL is dominated by the Right, and is remarkable for having only one woman member.

Code départemental: 29

FIP
A local Paris radio station run by RADIO FRANCE, broadcasting uninterrupted music.

FITERMAN, CHARLES (1933–   )
A Communist politician who rose through the ranks of the PARTI COMMUNISTE FRANÇAIS officials, entered the ASSEMBLÉE NATIONALE in 1978, and became *Ministre des* TRANSPORTS from 1981 to 1984. In 1990 and 1991 he provided a major challenge to Georges MARCHAIS for control of the party.

FLAGRANT DÉLIT
Any crime, DÉLIT or INFRACTION which is in the process of being

committed when the adult offender is apprehended. A *flagrant délit* allows the police powers of search on premises or in a vehicle. The offender is brought before the PROCUREUR DE LA RÉPUBLIQUE who decides whether to involve a JUGE D'INSTRUCTION or to pass the case directly to court. A defendant then has the right of five days' delay to prepare a defence. Any citizen has the right of arrest if the *flagrant délit* is theft, but the arrested person can take action for damages if the arrest is without cause.

FLAMMARION
An independent Paris publishing firm, named after its founding family.

FLAMME See: *CÉRÉMONIAL DU SOUVENIR*

FN See: *FRONT NATIONAL*

FNAC See: *FÉDÉRATION NATIONALE D'ACHATS*

FNE See: *FONDS NATIONAL DE L'EMPLOI*

FNS See: *FONDS NATIONAL DE SOLIDARITÉ; FORCE DE FRAPPE*

FNSEA See: *FÉDÉRATION NATIONALE DES SYNDICATS D'EXPLOITANTS AGRICOLES*

FO See: *FORCE OUVRIÈRE*

FOLIES-BERGÈRES
An enormous theatre in Paris, opened in 1869, and providing spectacular dance shows.

FONCTION PUBLIQUE ET RÉFORMES ADMINISTRATIVES, MINISTÈRE DE LA
The government ministry which is responsible for the efficient running of the ADMINISTRATION and the effective implementation of the regional policy.

FONCTIONNAIRE
A government employee, recruited by CONCOURS, and who having succeeded in that process, is guaranteed generous rights

of tenure. There is a strict hierarchy of salaries, the 'GRILLE', in which differentials correspond to qualifications.

FONDATION CLAUDE-POMPIDOU
A charitable organisation, named after the wife of Georges POMPIDOU, which provides volunteer help in clubs for old people, in families where there are disabled children, and in hospitals.

FONDATION DE FRANCE
A private charitable organisation, of UTILITÉ PUBLIQUE, with a general role of helping those in need, as well as supporting cultural, scientific and environmental schemes, and aiding Third World projects. Donations of up to 5 per cent of taxable income are free of tax. The *Fondation de France* has 500,000 donors and in 1988 distributed 150 million francs in aid.

FONDS COMMUN DE PLACEMENTS (FCP)
A unit trust for investment on the BOURSE. Investments can be made by individuals or companies, and are placed in specialised shares. Sums of between 100 and 10,000 francs can be invested, subject to an initial minimum. See also: SICAV

FONDS DE GARANTIE AUTOMOBILE
An emergency fund, provided partly by motor insurance companies and partly from court fines and sums recovered from offenders, in order to compensate those injured or whose property has been damaged by uninsured or unidentified drivers.

FONDS NATIONAL DE L'EMPLOI (FNE)
Financial support is available from the FNE for a redundant worker to seek work in another part of France (*Aide à la mobilité géographique*), for a worker who chooses half-time work to avoid redundancy (*Allocation spéciale mi-temps*), and for a worker who accepts a lower paid job (*Allocation temporaire dégressive*), if the firm concludes an agreement with the *Fonds national de l'emploi* through a standard CONVENTION.

FONDS NATIONAL DE SOLIDARITÉ
This is an additional source of support within the SÉCURITÉ SOCIALE system which enables old people of severely limited means to have an extra *allocation supplémentaire*, and entitles them to a CARTE ÉMERAUDE, or its equivalent in other cities.

FONTANET, JOSEPH (1921–1980)

A lawyer who entered centrist politics in the QUATRIÈME RÉPUBLIQUE, and who held ministerial posts in the CINQUIÈME RÉPUBLIQUE, notably as *Ministre de l'*ÉDUCATION NATIONALE on two occasions in the 1970s. He left politics for business in 1978, and was assassinated in mysterious circumstances in 1980.

FORCE D'ACTION RAPIDE

The section of the conventional armed forces which groups together the 4ème DIVISION AÉROMOBILE, 6ème DIVISION LÉGÈRE BLINDÉE, 9ème DIVISION D'INFANTERIE DE MARINE, 11ème DIVISION PARACHUTISTE and the 27ème DIVISION ALPINE with the mission to respond immediately to incidents.

FORCE DE FRAPPE

The nuclear strike capability of France, since the time of DE GAULLE, jealously guarded as independent of any alliance. The present official title is *Forces nucléaires stratégiques* (FNS), composed of *Forces aériennes* (FAS), *Forces océaniques* (FOST) and the *Air-sol longue portée* (ASLP). The ground-to-ground mobile ballistic programme was abandoned in 1991.

FORCE OCÉANIQUE STRATÉGIQUE (FOST) See: *FORCE DE FRAPPE*

FORCE OUVRIÈRE (FO)

The official title of this moderate trade union is *CGT-FO Force ouvrière*, but it severed its links with the CONFÉDÉRATION GÉNÉRALE DU TRAVAIL as long ago as 1947. Its local associations and federations group about 400,000 members (although it does not publish figures), largely recruited from the lower ranks of public employees. Its stance is fairly pragmatic, and determinedly anti-Communist.

FORCES NUCLÉAIRES STRATÉGIQUES (FNS) See: *FORCE DE FRAPPE*

FORMATION CONTINUE

Universities and some GRANDES ÉCOLES provide continuing education programmes. See also: FORMATION PROFESSIONNELLE

FORMATION PROFESSIONNELLE
Apart from pre-vocational courses provided in LYCÉES, there
are centres where training for particular occupational activities,
under the control of the *Ministère de l'*ÉDUCATION NATIONALE,
caters for about 400,000 trainees per year, financed jointly by
business and State and local authorities. See also: CONGÉ DE
FORMATION; FORMATION CONTINUE

FORUM DES HALLES
A shopping development, partly underground, on the site of
Les Halles, the former food market serving Paris.

FOST See: *FORCE DE FRAPPE*

FOS-SUR-MER See: *BOUCHES-DU-RHÔNE*

FOUCAULT, MICHEL (1926–1984)
A structuralist philosopher and essayist, prominent for his
opposition to existentialism, and for his 1961 book *Histoire de
la folie à l'âge classique*, who died of AIDS.

FOUGERON, ANDRÉ (1913–   )
A painter, who with others founded the '*Réalisme progressiste*'
movement in 1948.

FOULARD HERMÈS, COLLIER DE PERLES (FHCP)
A social label for the upper bourgeois young women dressing
in conventional style, also variously known as CPCH (*Collier
de perles, Carré Hermès*). See also: BON CHIC BON GENRE

FOULARDS, AFFAIRE DES
In 1989, the secular character of the LYCÉE was tested by a
number of Muslim schoolgirls who insisted on wearing scarves
in school against the instructions of their PROVISEURS.

FOURIER, JOSEPH (UNIVERSITÉ)
The official name of the *Université Grenoble I*, at the campus
of Saint-Martin-d'Hères (ISÈRE), and specialising in sciences,
medicine, pharmacy, and physical education for its 15,000
students. Fourier was a mathematician who in 1812 discovered
that vibration could be represented by a trigonometrical series.

FOURRIÈRE
The police car pound, where vehicles removed from an illegal parking place are kept for reclaim by their owners. An owner can only avoid paying the removal fee if the towing truck has not left the depot, in which case a PROCÈS-VERBAL is issued. Vehicles unclaimed for 45 days can be sold. The proceeds of the sale are paid to the owner after deduction of daily penalties, valuation and sale fees. However, a vehicle with a resale value of less than 3,000 francs is scrapped after only 10 days, at the owner's expense.

FOYER DE JEUNES TRAVAILLEURS
Low-cost hostels for young workers of any nationality, also available to students of limited means between the ages of 16 and 25.

FRANCE 2
A publicly-owned television channel formerly known as *Antenne 2*, based in Paris, once part of the ORTF. It was retained in public hands when other channels (e.g. TF 1) were sold off. It claims to be the leading television channel for quality and audience size.

FRANCE 3 (F3)
The regionally based third television channel, a State-owned company with the requirement to give access to a diverse range of beliefs and thought, to promote regional variety (only four hours a day of national programming permitted) and the restriction that it cannot devote more than one-seventh of its transmission time to films.

FRANCE CULTURE
A 24-hour FM stereo radio service provided by RADIO FRANCE focusing on serious talk programmes.

FRANCE DIMANCHE
A popular Sunday newspaper, published in Paris, with a circulation of about 700,000, which has fallen since a peak of well over a million in 1970. Its character is rather sensationalist,

dwelling on human interest stories, media stars, popular medicine, and claiming to expose scandal and injustice. Its market research has found that 90 per cent of its sales are to women, and estimates its readership at three million.

FRANCE INFO
A 24-hour radio news station run by RADIO FRANCE, set up in 1987, and networked to 80 French towns and cities, reaching 75 per cent of the population, and its audience is growing.

FRANCE INTER
The popular light entertainment radio station of RADIO FRANCE, broadcasting on long wave, medium wave and FM.

FRANCE LIBRE
The name of DE GAULLE's organisation during the Second World War which set itself up in opposition to the VICHY régime and the German occupation.

FRANCE-LOISIRS
A publishing organisation selling books and discs directly to the public, half owned by the German firm, Bertelsmann, and half by PRESSES DE LA CITÉ. Sales are by post through its book clubs and by a network of shops. Editions of previously published works are produced and sold at about 75 per cent of the original prices.

FRANCE MUSIQUE
The 24-hour FM stereo radio station concentrating on classical music and jazz, run by RADIO FRANCE.

FRANCE PLUS
An organisation which promotes the interests of those whose parents were immigrants to France, particularly those from Africa.

FRANCE-RÉGIONS 3 (FR3) See: *FRANCE 3 (F3)*

FRANCE-SOIR
A popular Paris newspaper, published by the HERSANT group. It has a falling circulation of about 350,000, compared with over 1,110,000 in 1960.

FRANCE TELECOM
The State-owned monopoly running all aspects of public
telecommunications services in France, separated from the PTT
which previously controlled it. See also: MINITEL; TÉLÉTEL

FRANCHE-COMTÉ
The administrative RÉGION on the border with Switzerland,with
a population of 1.09 million in 1990. The constituent
DÉPARTEMENTS are DOUBS, JURA, SAÔNE and the TERRITOIRE DE
BELFORT. The regional capital is Besançon.

Although its employment is mainly in industrial activity, in
aspect, the Franche-Comté is predominantly rural, and indeed
42 per cent of its area is forest. Dairy produce is also a vital
part of the regional economy, particularly milk, and cheese. The
income of households in the region is less than 1 per cent below
the average for the whole of France.

The political complexion is fairly evenly balanced between
Left and Right, and Edgar FAURE was a powerful force in the
region. In the 1992 ÉLECTIONS RÉGIONALES, the Left lost seats to
the benefit of the FRONT NATIONAL, GÉNÉRATION ÉCOLOGIE and the
VERTS.

FRANCHE-COMTÉ, UNIVERSITÉ DE
The university at Besançon (DOUBS) with 19,000 students
following courses in arts, economics, law, medicine,
pharmacy, social sciences and science.

FRANC-MAÇONNERIE
There are approximately 80,000 freemasons in France. The
lodges with the greatest number of members are the *Grand
Orient de France* (30,000 members), the *Grande Loge de France*
(18,000) and the *Grande Loge nationale de France*, (14,000). The
Grande Loge féminine de France has 7,120 women members.

There are politicians of both Left and Right who are
freemasons, and many members of the police force, justice
system and insurance firms.

FRANCOPHONIE
The French-speaking world, including parts of Belgium and
Switzerland, Luxembourg and Monaco, as well as Québec, but

principally those countries which have a more or less dependent relationship on France because of imperial history. A MINISTRE DÉLÉGUÉ in the *Ministère des* AFFAIRES ÉTRANGÈRES has special responsibility for *Francophonie*, and leads government efforts in promoting the French language on an international basis. See also: ALLIANCE FRANÇAISE

FRESNES
A COMMUNE in the southern BANLIEUE of Paris, well-known for its prison. It was a German detention camp in the occupation, and the site of some trials and executions of collaborationists during the ÉPURATION.

FROMAGES DE LA RÉPUBLIQUE
The perks of those in high public office or sometimes as part of a contract for a firm working for the State, or having been granted a concession.

FRONTALIER
A person living within 15 kilometres of the frontier who may work in the country across the border. Special formalities regarding SÉCURITÉ SOCIALE and residence arrangements apply in such cases, and there are different dispensations for regular seasonal workers who cross national boundaries. Special customs restrictions apply to those who travel across the frontier for work.

FRONT NATIONAL (FN)
A right-wing political organisation, founded in 1972 by Jean-Marie LE PEN, who still leads the party. Slow to gain power against the established parties, it received support in the 1980s, especially in working-class urban areas, in ÉLECTIONS MUNICIPALES, European elections and in 1986 took 9.65 per cent of the votes in the ÉLECTIONS LÉGISLATIVES, with strong support in the Marseille area. In the 1988 ÉLECTIONS PRÉSIDENTIELLES, Le Pen took 14.38 per cent in the first round.

It made further advances in the ÉLECTIONS RÉGIONALES and ÉLECTIONS CANTONALES IN 1992, polling almost 14 per cent of the vote for regional seats, but in the second round for the *Élections cantonales*, agreements between most of the other parties forced down its proportion of the vote to 6.35 per cent.

On the far Right, the FN has called for repatriation of immigrants, restoration of capital punishment, priority of employment for French people, and a reduction in State powers. Its populist stance has won it over 100,000 members.

FUTUROSCOPE

A futuristic theme park at Jaunay-Clan, near Poitiers (VIENNE), opened in 1987, which receives about 400,000 visitors a year.

GAB See: *GUICHET AUTOMATIQUE DE BANQUE*

GALERIES LAFAYETTE
A chain of department stores, founded in 1899. The Paris
flagship store was built just before the First World War. The two
families holding the majority of the shares also control the
NOUVELLES GALERIES and BAZAR DE L'HÔTEL DE VILLE chains.

GALLIMARD
A general publishing house, founded by Gaston Gallimard
(1881–1975), who had the good fortune of publishing many
of the major names in modern French literature, partly through
the literary journal *La Nouvelle Revue française*.

GAN See: *GROUPE DES ASSOCIATIONS NATIONALES*

GARANTIE CONTRACTUELLE
The guarantee that accompanies many manufactured items,
giving a time limit for claims for malfunction, etc. See also:
GARANTIE LÉGALE; NORMES FRANÇAISES

GARANTIE DÉCENNALE
The 10-year guarantee concerning the construction dating from
the day of purchase of a new house or flat. See also: GARANTIE
DE PARFAIT ACHÈVEMENT

GARANTIE DE PARFAIT ACHEVÈMENT
A guarantee available to buyers of new houses and flats,
available for one year from the date of purchase, by which the
builder will repair free of charge any faults which become
apparent during that period and which were not visible at the
time of purchase, but which are due to the construction of the
property. See also: GARANTIE DÉCENNALE

GARANTIE LÉGALE

Every item bought is guaranteed by law against faults which
make it unfit for its intended use, provided the fault is serious,
impossible to ascertain at the time of purchase, and not resulting
from the purchaser's action. In order to obtain redress from the
seller, the buyer has to prove the existence of the fault, but this
statutory protection has no time limit. See also: GARANTIE
CONTRACTUELLE; NORMES FRANÇAISES

GARAUD, MARIE-FRANÇOISE (1934–   )

A lawyer and politician of the Right, who worked in the CABINET
of Georges POMPIDOU from 1967–1974. A member of the COUR
DES COMPTES in the 1970s and again from 1985, she joined the
RASSEMBLEMENT POUR LA RÉPUBLIQUE on its formation, but left it
to stand in the 1981 ÉLECTIONS PRÉSIDENTIELLES, when she gained
2.58 per cent of the vote in the first round. She heads a political
grouping, the *Institut international de géopolitique*, but was not
elected to a seat in the ASSEMBLÉE NATIONALE in 1986.

GARD

A DÉPARTEMENT of the LANGUEDOC-ROUSSILLON region, named
after the tributary of the Rhône which passes through it. It had
a population of 585,049 in 1990, and its CHEF-LIEU is Nîmes
(urban area 138,527), where the textile industry, including the
original denim, is a traditional strength. Other major towns are
Alès (71,585), a coal mining and industrial centre; Bagnols-sur-
Cèze (17,872); Beaucaire (13,400); and la Grand-Combe
(11,991). There are a number of smaller industrial centres.

Employment is provided by agriculture and industry.
Traditional products such as Roquefort cheese, fruit, silk, wine
and honey combine with a nuclear power station at Bagnols,
the PERRIER water industry at Vergèze and steel and glassworks
at Laudun, for example. There is also a thriving tourist industry,
based on the appeal of the mountainous terrain, the Camargue
and Roman remains such as at Pont-du-Gard and Nîmes.

The Gard was badly hit by unemployment because of the
declining fortunes of the steel industry from the mid-1980s,
and the area received support from the European Community.

The voters strongly supported MITTERRAND in the 1981

Presidential contest, less so in 1988. The Left, however, still control the CONSEIL RÉGIONAL.

Code départemental: 30

GARDE À VUE

The police are able to detain an arrested adult for 24 hours without warrant for questioning. During this time, the detainee is not a prisoner, but neither is he or she free, and may not call on the services of an AVOCAT. However, a medical examination can be demanded by the detainee. A body search is permitted to obtain evidence, but a search of premises requires further authorisation, unless the case is a FLAGRANT DÉLIT. After 24 hours, the detainee must be freed or taken before the PROCUREUR DE LA RÉPUBLIQUE who can order an extension of up to 48 hours.

In the case of suspected drug trafficking, terrorism or offences against the State, this period can be further extended. See also: DÉTENTION PROVISOIRE

GARDE CHAMPÊTRE

A full-time or part-time employee of a small COMMUNE who carries out minor duties of public order, perhaps acting as a messenger of the MAIRE, or in checking the arrangements concerning elections. Traditionally, the *garde champêtre* would beat a drum in the street to announce local news and meetings.

GARDE DES SCEAUX

The title of the *Ministre de la* JUSTICE, dating from the time of the feudal monarchs, when the chancellor of the courts was the guardian of the royal seals.

GARDE RÉPUBLICAINE

Part of the GENDARMERIE NATIONALE, with the special functions of ceremonial duties, security of public buildings, escorts for State and visiting dignitaries, and prestigious occasions. Its numbers include its own band and the choir of the French army.

GARDIEN DE LA PAIX

The lowest grade of police officer in the POLICE MUNICIPALE.

GARDIEN D'IMMEUBLE See: *CONCIERGE*

GARNIER, PALAIS
The main opera house in Paris, home of the OPÉRA DE PARIS, said to be the masterpiece of its designer, Charles Garnier (1825–1899).

GARY, ROMAIN (1914–1980)
A Russian-born Jewish novelist who took French nationality in 1945, was a COMPAGNON DE LA LIBÉRATION having been a pilot in the Free French forces, became the French consul in Los Angeles, won the *Prix* GONCOURT twice (once under the pseudonym Émile Ajar), made films, and took his own life after the suicide of his wife.

GAULLISTE
Either as adjective or noun, attributing an allegiance to the political camp of Charles DE GAULLE, either in his lifetime, or as a member of the one of the political parties and groupings which claim to continue his direction. See also: CHIRAC; CINQUIÈME RÉPUBLIQUE; POMPIDOU; RASSEMBLEMENT POUR LA RÉPUBLIQUE; UNION DES DÉMOCRATES POUR LA RÉPUBLIQUE

GAULOISE
The archetypal French cigarette, taking on this identity in 1910, having been previously known as Hongroise, which has been reformulated over recent years in order to have less tar content. There is a whole range of cigarettes in the Gauloise stable, including *Disque bleu*. See also: GITANE; SEITA

GAULT-MILLAU
An annual hotel and restaurant guide, published since 1972, and edited by two journalists, Henri Gault and Christian Millau, whose verdict is eagerly awaited by gastronomes. See also: MICHELIN

GAUMONT
A film production company founded by Léon Gaumont in 1895.

GAVEAU, SALLE
A concert hall in Paris, seating 1,000, opened in 1907 and renovated in 1983.

GAZ DE FRANCE (GDF)
The State-owned gas exploitation and supply enterprise. It does not manufacture gas, but its role is to ensure a supply and distribution network. As part of its operations, there are subsidiary companies to develop special projects and for investment abroad. Gas is imported from the Norwegian fields in the North Sea, ALGÉRIE, Netherlands, USSR and West African countries.

GDF See: *GAZ DE FRANCE*

GÉANT CASINO See: *CASINO*

GENDARMERIE NATIONALE
A section of the military which has police duties outside the areas covered by POLICE MUNICIPALE. The *Gendarmerie nationale* is organised in brigades, grouped into a company in each ARRONDISSEMENT and a '*groupement*' in each DÉPARTEMENT. There are also specialist units, and the *Gendarmerie mobile*, organised in squadrons. The *Gendarmerie nationale* has its own training establishments at Melun for officers, and at Châtellerault, Maisons-Alfort, Montluçon and Berlin for non-commissioned officers. See also: GARDE RÉPUBLICAINE; POLICE NATIONALE

GÉNÉRALE DES EAUX
A private enterprise utility, based on its core business of providing water supplies. It is the third largest service industry in Europe.

GÉNÉRATION ÉCOLOGIE
A political party founded in 1989 by Brice LALONDE as a breakaway group from the VERTS. It gained 104 seats in the 1992 ÉLECTIONS RÉGIONALES, one fewer than the *Verts*.

GENET, JEAN (1910–1986)
A novelist and dramatist whose work often shocked, as it was based partly on his experience in the criminal underworld, and was blatant in declaring his homosexuality, and often snubbed convention.

GENEVOIX, MAURICE (1890–1980)

A novelist whose writing is often based in the traditional provincial France. His best-known work is Raboliot, winner of the *Prix* GONCOURT in 1925.

GÉODE

A 1,000 square metre, hemispheric cinema screen in the CITÉ DES SCIENCES ET DE L'INDUSTRIE, composed of a steel-tubed framework covered by over 6,000 curved triangles in stainless steel.

GERS

A DÉPARTEMENT of the MIDI-PYRÉNÉES region, named after a minor tributary of the Garonne. It has a declining population (174,566 in 1990) which has fallen steadily since peaking in the mid-nineteenth century at over 300,000. The CHEF-LIEU is Auch (23,136). The next largest town is Condom (7,717). The industrial activity is small-scale, traditional and of local significance only.

Agriculture dominates the employment scene. The principal agricultural commodities are wheat and maize, but there are also wines, *eaux-de-vie*, cattle, pigs and poultry of significant degree. Perhaps because industry is less important, the Gers has not suffered from unemployment as seriously as some other areas.

Traditionally, the *Département* has supported Socialist politics, although in 1986, centrist SÉNATEURS were elected. In both 1981 and 1988 ÉLECTIONS PRÉSIDENTIELLES François MITTERRAND received good majorities here. However, the Left lost control of the CONSEIL GÉNÉRAL in 1992.

Code départemental: 32

GERTRUDE

A traffic management system operating in Paris, primarily with the notion of linking traffic signals so that a steady flow of traffic is produced. The acronym stands for *Gestion électronique de la régulation du trafic routier défiant les embouteillages*. See also: AXE ROUGE

GIBERT

A major Paris academic bookshop with some provincial

branches. The title of the present business, a descendant of the original in 1886, is *Gibert jeune*.

GIC See: *GRAND INVALIDE CIVIL; GROUPEMENT INTERMINISTÉRIEL DE CONTRÔLE*

GIG See: *GRAND INVALIDE DE GUERRE*

GIRARDOT, ANNIE (1931–)
A popular film actress with about 30 films to her credit.

GIRONDE
A DÉPARTEMENT of the AQUITAINE region, dominated by its CHEF-LIEU, Bordeaux, which in its AGGLOMÉRATION accounts for 685,456 of the *Département's* 1.2 million inhabitants. Bordeaux's economy is that of a port, a regional commercial and administrative centre, and a centre of the wine trade with a substantial industrial activity based on aviation, defence, textiles, computers and electrical engineering. Other major urban areas are Arcachon (39,931) – shipbuilding, oysters and seaside resort; and Libourne (26,597), a wine centre.

Almost half of the *Département*, which is in any case the largest in France, is covered in woodland. The name comes from the estuary of the Garonne and Dordogne rivers, now an important site for oil terminals and refineries and a nuclear power station. The Gironde produces the greatest amount of APPELLATION D'ORIGINE CONTRÔLÉE and VDQS wine, and is fourth in national wine production of all grades. Tourism is an important element, especially on the Atlantic coast.

In both the 1981 and 1988 ÉLECTIONS PRÉSIDENTIELLES, François MITTERRAND obtained a firm majority in the Gironde. Most parliamentary representatives are PARTI SOCIALISTE members (with Jacques CHABAN-DELMAS a notable exception), and after the 1992 ÉLECTIONS CANTONALES, the Socialists and Communists had a majority of one seat on the CONSEIL GÉNÉRAL.
Code départemental: 33

GIROUD, FRANÇOISE (1916–)
A Swiss-born former journalist for *l'*EXPRESS, novelist and politician, who held junior governmental posts under GISCARD

D'ESTAING's presidency, and became vice-president of the Centrist party, UNION POUR LA DÉMOCRATIE FRANÇAISE on its inauguration in 1978.

GISCARD D'ESTAING, VALÉRY (1926–   )

A former PRÉSIDENT DE LA RÉPUBLIQUE (1974–1981), whose early career after successfully passing through the ÉCOLE POLYTECHNIQUE and as an ÉNARQUE followed the classic technocrat line. He entered politics in the late 1950s, rising quickly to become *Ministre des* FINANCES from 1962 to 1966, and from 1969 to 1974. He set up the Centre Right *Républicains indépendants* group in 1966, and was the first non-Gaullist *Président* of the CINQUIÈME RÉPUBLIQUE. His generally liberal policies were tarnished by various scandals affecting members of the government towards the end of his SEPTENNAT, and personal allegations regarding the gift of diamonds from the Central African dictator, President Bokassa.

After his defeat in 1981 by a margin of 3.52 per cent, he moved into local politics, and started a remarkable political comeback, becoming a DÉPUTÉ in 1984 for the PUY-DE-DÔME. In 1986 he was elected *Président du* CONSEIL RÉGIONAL for the AUVERGNE, and in 1988 became the president of the UNION POUR LA DÉMOCRATIE FRANÇAISE.

GISCARDIEN

The adjective describing GISCARD D'ESTAING, or as a noun, one of his supporters.

GITANE

A cigarette brand introduced in 1910, more expensive and with stronger tobacco than its main rival, GAULOISE. There are two versions, '*papier blanc*' and '*papier maïs*'. See also: SEITA

GÎTE RURAL

A farmhouse which has been turned into country holiday cottage. A scheme of classification and a booking service is operated by the *Fédération nationale des gîtes de France* through the branches within the *départements*.

GLUCKSMANN, ANDRÉ (1937–   )

A post-Marxist philosopher, one of the '*nouveaux philosophes*', a very influential figure whose 1975 work, *La Cuisinière et le mangeur d'hommes*, was a strong pamphlet against totalitarianism. His *Les Maîtres penseurs* was a best-seller in 1977.

GMF See: *COMPAGNIE GÉNÉRALE MARITIME ET FINANCIÈRE*

GODARD, JEAN-LUC (1930–)
A film director who became a major figure in the 1960s, after his first noted film, *À bout de souffle* (1959). Godard is perhaps the most famous director of the New Wave movement, but he withdrew from film-making between 1967 and 1980.

GONCOURT, PRIX See: *ACADÉMIE GONCOURT*

GOSCINNY, RENÉ (1926–1977)
The co-writer of the ASTÉRIX and *Lucky Luke* cartoon books.

GRÂCE
The PRÉSIDENT DE LA RÉPUBLIQUE has the power to pardon those found guilty by courts. If a judgement is considered too repressive, it can be reduced by this measure. See also: AMNISTIE

GRACQ, JULIEN (1910–)
The pseudonym of a novelist, critic and poet who refused the 1951 *Prix* GONCOURT for *Le Rivage des Syrtes*. His work is characterised by much imagination and is highly influenced by surrealism. He is recognised as a master of style.

GRANDE COURONNE
The outer ring of COMMUNES which form the AGGLOMÉRATION of Greater Paris.

GRANDE ÉCOLE
A higher education establishment which recruits by specialist CONCOURS, with a high reputation for both educational and social prestige. The *Grandes Écoles* are often considered to be the summit of the French educational system. See also: CLASSE PRÉPARATOIRE; ÉCOLE CENTRALE; ÉCOLE DES HAUTES ÉTUDES COMMERCIALES; ÉCOLE NATIONALE D'ADMINISTRATION; ÉCOLE

NATIONALE DES CHARTES; ÉCOLE NORMALE SUPÉRIEURE; ÉCOLE POLYTECHNIQUE

GRANDE VÉNERIE
A local horse-mounted hunt, of which there exist nearly 200 in France, a growing number reflecting the interest in hunting. Fox-hunting is the largest single category of hunting within this classification. See also: CHASSE; PETITE VÉNERIE

GRAND INFIRME CIVIL (GIC) See: *GRAND INVALIDE CIVIL*

GRAND INVALIDE CIVIL (GIC)
Disabled people who have lost the use of one or both legs, as well as the blind or the mentally disabled who need a companion to accompany them can benefit from a GIC sticker, giving the police some discretion in applying parking regulations, and entitling the holders to use specially reserved spaces. The sticker has to be renewed after three years. See also: CARTE D'INVALIDITÉ; CARTE 'STATION DEBOUT PÉNIBLE'

GRAND INVALIDE DE GUERRE (GIG)
A concession similar to that of the GRAND INVALIDE CIVIL is available to those disabled through war injuries, if the certificate of disablement states '*Station debout pénible*'. See also: CARTE D'INVALIDITÉ; CARTE 'STATION DEBOUT PÉNIBLE'

GRAND LIVRE DU MOIS
The second largest book-club in France, jointly owned by a group of publishers, including LAFFONT and ALBIN MICHEL.

GRAND-PALAIS
The exhibition hall near the CHAMPS-ÉLYSÉES in Paris, completed in 1900, for the *Exposition universelle*, now the site of major touring international art exhibitions.

GRAND PRIX DE LA SACEM
SACEM, the SOCIÉTÉ DES AUTEURS, COMPOSITEURS ET ÉDITEURS DE MUSIQUE, awards an annual prize to French artists and firms in areas of its expertise.

GRAND PRIX DE PARIS
A horse race run at LONGCHAMP on the last Sunday in June, with a prize of one million francs.

GRAND PRIX DE ROME
An annual prize for recorded music, awarded by the *Académie de France* in Rome.

GRAND PRIX DU CINÉMA FRANÇAIS LOUIS-LUMIÈRE
Founded in 1934, and annually awarded to the best French film of the year.

GRAND PRIX MUSICAL DE LA VILLE DE PARIS
An annual award of 40,000 francs given by the city to a French composer, or a composer who has worked for the most part in France.

GRAND PROJET
The term used to describe the monumental developments often nurtured by the PRÉSIDENT DE LA RÉPUBLIQUE against considerable public criticism. They have included the ARCHE DE LA DÉFENSE, *Pyramide du* LOUVRE, and the TRÈS GRANDE BIBLIOTHÈQUE.

GRAND-ROBERT
A highly respected six-volume dictionary of the French language. See also: ROBERT, DICTIONNAIRE

GRANDS BOULEVARDS
The earliest Paris avenues which took the name *boulevard*, on the line of the former city defences, and laid out as a place for fashionable promenades and riding between 1660 and 1705 between the current *Place de la Madeleine* and the *Place de la République*. They are now a centre of commercial activity.

GRASSET
A Paris publisher of literature, now part of the HACHETTE group.

GRÉCO, JULIETTE (1927–   )
A Paris night-club and cabaret singer who sang modern poetry, and who personified the sophisticated image of young, cultured France in the 1950s.

GREEN, JULIEN (1900–   )
A novelist, dramatist and essayist, born in France of American parents, who continues to write in old age. His latest books are situated in the Deep South of the USA. He has kept and published a journal since 1928.

GREFFIER
An officer of a court of law who acts as executive in carrying out court decisions, and is responsible for its administration. See also: TRIBUNAL

GRENELLE, CONSTAT DE
An agreement between trade unions and government in 1968 which provided across-the-board rises in wages and salaries, and reduced working hours, thus serving to end the unions' participation in the student and worker disturbances. It was signed at the *Ministère du* TRAVAIL in the *rue de Grenelle* in Paris.

GRÉVIN, MUSÉE
The Paris waxworks museum, founded in 1882 in the *boulevard Montmartre*, one of the GRANDS BOULEVARDS. Arthur Grévin was the artistic director. The business has established a number of smaller waxworks in other locations in France.

GRILLE DE LA FONCTION PUBLIQUE
The salary and conditions scale of the ADMINISTRATION, divided into four categories which depend on the educational qualifications of the FONCTIONNAIRES. There is also another category reflecting posts of special responsibility, the *Catégorie hors-échelle*.

GROUPE AXA
An insurance grouping of MUTUELLES organisations and some private insurers.

GROUPE DE LA CITÉ
A major publishing conglomerate wholly owning LAROUSSE, NATHAN, BORDAS, PRESSES DE LA CITÉ and half of FRANCE LOISIRS.

GROUPE DES ASSOCIATIONS NATIONALES (GAN)
A State-controlled insurance company operating on a

commercial basis. See also: CRÉDIT INDUSTRIEL ET COMMERCIAL (CIC)

GROUPE DES BANQUES POPULAIRES
A private sector clearing bank, the eighth in France in terms of assets.

GROUPEMENT D'ÉTABLISSEMENT POUR LA FORMATION CONTINUE (GRETA)
A local consortium of educational institutions which offers a range of post-experience training courses, part-time preparation for professional and other qualifications, etc., with a special focus on providing for the young unemployed, migrant workers and women seeking a return to employment. There are nearly 400 GRETA.

GROUPEMENT INTERMINISTÉRIEL DE CONTRÔLE (GIC)
A co-ordinating organisation which supervises telephone tapping carried out for the State. See also: ÉCOUTE TÉLÉPHONIQUE

GUADELOUPE
A volcanic island group in the Carribean Windward Islands, occupied by French settlers since 1635, and since 1946 a DÉPARTEMENT D'OUTRE-MER. It also has the status of a RÉGION. The population is 387,000, with a large concentration in the lower age groups. The CHEF-LIEU is Basse-Terre (AGGLOMÉRATION 52,600), whereas the centre of the economic activity is Pointe-à-Pitre (141,300). There are more natives of Guadeloupe residing in metropolitan France than on the islands themselves.

The economy is based on sugar cane, rum, bananas, cement manufacture and tourism, with 65 per cent of the working population employed in service industries. Economic ties with metropolitan France are strong.

Most of the French major political parties have connected groups in Guadeloupe, and there are independence movements. In the 1988 ÉLECTION PRÉSIDENTIELLE, François MITTERRAND obtained a more than comfortable majority of 69.4 per cent of the votes cast. Parties of the Left retained

control of the CONSEIL GÉNÉRAL in 1992, when a member of the
Union pour la libération de la Guadeloupe was also elected.
   Code départemental: 971

GUIBERT, HERVÉ (1955–1991)
A writer and photographer whose novels attracted attention for
their personal content. He wrote two accounts of AIDS from
which he was suffering when he committed suicide.

GUICHARD, BARON OLIVIER (1920–   )
An administrator and politician who headed DE GAULLE'S private
office in the 1950s. He held various ministerial posts in the De
Gaulle, POMPIDOU and GISCARD D'ESTAING governments, notably
at ÉDUCATION NATIONALE in 1972 and as GARDE DES SCEAUX from
1976 to 1977.

GUICHET AUTOMATIQUE DE BANQUE (GAB)
An automatic bank machine, dispensing notes and carrying out
other functions, a development from the DISTRIBUTEUR
AUTOMATIQUE DES BILLETS.

GUIDES DE FRANCE
The Catholic organisation of girl guide organisations, divided
into *Jeannettes* (8–11 year olds), *Guides* (12–14), *Caravelles* (15–
16) and *Jeunes en marche* (17–19). There are 70,000 members.
See also: ÉCLAIREUSES ET ÉCLAIREURS DE FRANCE; SCOUTS DE FRANCE

GUYANE
A territory in South America, first settled by French people in
1637, but having been disputed on a number of occasions since
then. A DÉPARTEMENT D'OUTRE-MER since 1946, and now also
with the status of a RÉGION. The population is 114,678, 65 per
cent of whom live in the CHEF-LIEU, Cayenne. There is a variety
of cultural communities in Guyane, and the bulk of the
inhabitants live on the coastal strip.
   The economy depends on the continued success of the
European ARIANE space programme based at Kourou. With a
small agricultural and forestry base, Guyane is dependent on
imports for even basic foodstuffs.
   In the 1988 ÉLECTIONS PRÉSIDENTIELLES, 60.38 per cent of the

votes cast in the second round went to François MITTERRAND. In local politics, the *Parti socialiste guyanais* has an absolute majority in the CONSEIL GÉNÉRAL.

Code départemental: 973

HABACHE, AFFAIRE

In early 1992, the Arab terrorist leader Georges Habache entered France for urgent medical treatment, with the permission of junior immigration officers, to the great embarrassment of the government.

HABITATION À LOYER MODÉRÉ (HLM)

Public housing available for rent, built and managed by OPAC (*Offices publics d'aménagement et de construction*) or OPHLM (*Offices publics d'HLM*). There are also private concerns carrying out these functions, supported by state loans (*Sociétés anonymes d'HLM*) and co-operative ventures run by *Sociétés coopératives de production d'HLM*. There are over 1,000 different management bodies.

About 13 million people live in HLM, paying no more than 40 per cent of the equivalent free market rent. Tenants may purchase an HLM property, but are not allowed to resell within five years. Tenants of an association have privileged rights of purchase of empty HLM over other potential buyers.

HABY, LOI

René Haby (1919–   ) was *Ministre de l'*ÉDUCATION NATIONALE from 1974 to 1978, and his reform of schools in 1975 is called the *Loi Haby*. Over a number of stages, it extended nursery education to all, instituted the TRONC COMMUN in the ÉCOLE PRIMAIRE and the COLLÈGE, and confirmed the idea of providing extra help to children who found difficulties. It allowed students to choose to drop a subject from their programme in the CLASSE TERMINALE and set up the LYCÉE *d'enseignement professionnel*.

HACA See: *HAUTE AUTORITÉ DE LA COMMUNICATION AUDIOVISUELLE*

HACHETTE
A publishing and media combine, with a strong presence in general literature, educational publishing and children's books, distribution, printing and information technology. Its distribution depot at Maurepas (YVELINES) can hold 50 million items.

HALLYDAY, JOHNNY (1943–   )
A popular singer who adopted the rock and roll style of American and British performers in the late 1950s when le *yé-yé* arrived in France, and has managed to retain his popularity. His private life is of constant interest to readers of the tabloid press.

HALTE-GARDERIE
A day-care facility for children below the age of six years old. See also: CENTRE AÉRÉ; CENTRE DE LOISIRS SANS HÉBERGEMENT

HANIN, ROGER (1925–   )
A PIED-NOIR who is a popular film and television actor, featuring mainly in thriller series.

HARA-KIRI
The first monthly BANDE DESSINÉE for adults, founded in 1960, later banned and replaced by CHARLIE-HEBDO.

HARCÈLEMENT SEXUEL
Up to 36 per cent of French women, according to polls, claim to have suffered sexual harassment at work.

HARKIS
The Algerian soldiers who fought in the French forces at the time of the Algerian war, and who after the independence of ALGÉRIE were offered residence in France.

HATIER
A Paris-based educational publisher.

HAUTE ALSACE, UNIVERSITÉ DE
The official title of the university at Mulhouse (HAUT-RHIN), which specialises in natural, pure and human sciences, as well as arts, and has 5,000 students.

HAUTE ASSEMBLÉE
A commonly used term to refer to the SÉNAT.

HAUTE AUTORITÉ DE LA COMMUNICATION AUDIO-VISUELLE (HACA)
In existence from 1982 to 1986, this body had the role of overseeing the operations of the state-owned broadcasting media, and of licensing the RADIOS LIBRES. It was largely ineffective in its role of arbiter for local radio, and was replaced by the COMMISSION NATIONALE DE LA COMMUNICATION ET DES LIBERTÉS.

HAUTE-BRETAGNE, UNIVERSITÉ DE
The title for Rennes II university, which teaches languages, arts, history, politics, human sciences, education to 15,500 students.

HAUTECOMBE, ABBAYE DE
By a quirk of history, in this twelfth century abbey, occupied by Benedictines since 1922, not all French laws apply. When Nice and Savoie became part of France in 1860, it was agreed that the abbey would remain under religious jurisdiction for ever. It is the place of burial of certain of the Italian royal house, including Umberto II (1904–1983).

HAUTE-CORSE
The DÉPARTEMENT, formed in 1982, which covers the northern half of CORSE. Its population was 131,563 in 1990, a considerable drop from the 1975 figure of 161,208. The CHEF-LIEU is Bastia (AGGLOMÉRATION 45,087) and there is no other large town.
   Code départemental: 20B   See also: CORSE-DU-SUD

HAUTE-GARONNE
A DÉPARTEMENT of the MIDI-PYRÉNÉES region, with a population of 925,958 in 1990. More than half of these (608,427) live in the AGGLOMÉRATION of Toulouse, the CHEF-LIEU, a centre of aeronautics, chemicals, electronics and other light industry, as well as a major educational and tourist centre. Other urban areas are Muret (18,134), whose mixed industry includes the manufacture of hypodermic syringes, and Saint-Gaudens

(13,604). With the territory extending into the Pyrenees to the Spanish border, the bulk of the area is rural and sparsely populated.

Toulouse is the site of the highest temperature ever recorded in France (44° Celsius, August 1923). The Haute-Garonne has the fourth highest life expectancy for men.

Employment is marked by the dominance of service industries. Agricultural products are wheat, maize and cattle, and considerable amounts of wine are produced.

François MITTERRAND maintained his lead of around 60 per cent in the 1981 and 1988 ÉLECTIONS PRÉSIDENTIELLES, and the parliamentary representation is dominated by the Left. The Socialists have an absolute majority on the CONSEIL GÉNÉRAL as well, but lost seats in the 1992 ÉLECTIONS CANTONALES to the Centre Right.

Code départemental: 31

HAUTE-LOIRE

A mainly rural DÉPARTEMENT of the AUVERGNE region, with a population of 206,568 in 1990. It has been steadily falling since a peak in 1886 of over 320,000. The CHEF-LIEU is Le Puy, an important religious centre, with 40,937 inhabitants in the urban area. The second largest town is Brioude, with a population of 7,285.

Industry tends to be traditional in nature – lace, textiles, dyeing, basketry, etc., with light industry and tourism playing a quite important part. Food-processing has developed in recent years. Agriculture is the largest single source of employment, the Haute-Loire producing veal, dairy produce, sheep and some cereals.

In 1981, the Haute-Loire supported GISCARD D'ESTAING in the ÉLECTION PRÉSIDENTIELLE with 56.02 per cent of the vote, and Jacques CHIRAC with 51.24 per cent in 1988. The Centre and Right have similarly gained in parliamentary elections, and the UNION POUR LA DÉMOCRATIE FRANÇAISE outnumbers all other party groups in the CONSEIL GÉNÉRAL.

Code départemental: 43

HAUTE-MARNE

A DÉPARTEMENT of the CHAMPAGNE-ARDENNE region, named after

the Marne river, the source of which is found in the southern part, with a population of 204,255 in 1990. The CHEF-LIEU is Chaumont (AGGLOMÉRATION 27,988), a commercial and light industrial centre, and other urban areas are Langres (10,399) – engineering; and Saint-Dizier, (35,838) – steel-making. Bourbonne-les-Bains receives many spa treatment patients.

The Haute-Marne is predominantly agricultural in aspect, and is quite important for dairy produce. Tourists are attracted by the developing water-sports facilities (including those at the largest of France's lakes, the *Lac du Der-Chantecocq*), its forests, and the DE GAULLE family home of LA BOISSERIE at Colombey-les-Deux Églises.

The second lowest temperature ever recorded in France was −33 degrees Celsius at Langres in 1879.

Politically, Haute-Marne is by tradition more concerned with local issues. In 1988, François MITTERRAND slightly increased his 1981 majority proportion of the poll in the ÉLECTION PRÉSIDENTIELLE, whereas the RASSEMBLEMENT POUR LA RÉPUBLIQUE's control over the CONSEIL GÉNÉRAL was given further strength in the 1992 ÉLECTIONS GÉNÉRALES.

Code départemental: 52

HAUTE-NORMANDIE
The administrative RÉGION incorporating the DÉPARTEMENTS of EURE and SEINE-MARITIME on either side of the Seine river at its lowest point. The population of the region in 1990 was 1.73 million. Rouen is the regional capital. There is a continuing controversy about merging with BASSE-NORMANDIE.

Near to Paris, but also a coastal region, it has influences pulling it in both directions. Its character, too, is split: the traditional Norman countryside supporting agricultural production, and a maritime economy based on fishing and port activity, with the outskirts of the Paris-dominated commuter and residential belt.

Haute-Normandie manages to produce a higher than average proportion of the gross national product per inhabitant, who are accordingly relatively well-off. However, it has suffered considerably from unemployment since the mid-1970s. Political

power in the CONSEIL RÉGIONAL after the 1992 ÉLECTION
RÉGIONALE was finely balanced between Right and Left in a
hung council, and GÉNÉRATION ÉCOLOGIE, VERTS and FRONT
NATIONAL all made significant progress.

HAUTES-ALPES

As may be imagined from its name, a mountainous
DÉPARTEMENT of the PROVENCE-ALPES-CÔTE-D'AZUR region, indeed
the highest in France, with a population in 1990 of 113,272. The
CHEF-LIEU is Gap (33,438), and the other significant urban area
is Europe's highest town at over 1300 metres, Briançon
(15,073).

Agricultural activity concentrates on sheep, cattle, pigs and
fruit production, while there is a substantial timber industry,
as well as hydro-electric power production. Its principal
individual source of income is the Alpine tourist industry, with
particular features of regional nature parks and reserves, as well
as winter sports.

The highest COMMUNE in Europe is Saint-Véran, in the *Parc
régional du Queyras*.

Political representatives in parliament are balanced between
Right and Left. This fine balance is demonstrated by voting for
the PRÉSIDENT DE LA RÉPUBLIQUE. The small majority in the
ÉLECTION PRÉSIDENTIELLE in 1981 gained by François
MITTERRAND was overturned by Jacques CHIRAC in 1988 into a
proportion of 50.32 per cent of the poll, and this swing to the
Right was repeated in the 1992 ÉLECTIONS CANTONALES.

Code départemental: 05

HAUTE-SAÔNE

A DÉPARTEMENT of the FRANCHE-COMTÉ region, with a population
of 229,659 in 1990, named after the Saône river which passes
through the area. The CHEF-LIEU is Vesoul (urban area 26,266),
the location of metal works and PEUGEOT car works, and other
urban areas are Gray (12,017); Lure (11,062); and Luxeuil-les-
Bains (12,850), the latter three being centres for engineering
and metallurgy.

Employment is dominated by the industrial base but, in
addition, agricultural products include milk and cheese, wheat,

barley, oats and maize. Tourist attractions are ancient churches and Le Corbusier's chapel at Ronchamp, folk museums and skiing. A number of religious pilgrimages attract visitors.

The DÉPUTÉS and SÉNATEURS for the Haute-Saône are of the Right Wing, but the majority obtained by François MITTERRAND increased between the ÉLECTIONS PRÉSIDENTIELLES in 1981 and 1988. The Centre Right controls the CONSEIL GÉNÉRAL.

Code départemental: 70

HAUTE-SAVOIE

A DÉPARTEMENT in the RHÔNE-ALPES region, named after the kingdom which was incorporated into France only in 1860, and of which it was part. The Haute-Savoie had a population of 568,256 in 1990, 122,622 of whom inhabited the AGGLOMÉRATION of its CHEF-LIEU, Annecy, known as a tourist centre, but also supporting wide range of small industries. Other urban areas are Annemasse, immediately abutting the Swiss frontier at Geneva (70,989); Bonneville (15,317); Chamonix-Mont-Blanc (11,648); Cluses (34,753); Rumilly (11,379); Sallanches (14,294); and Thonon-les-Bains (55,078, including ÉVIAN). Because of the terrain, there are relatively few villages, but a number of winter-sports resorts have grown up.

Much of the industrial activity is based on precision engineering (clocks, weighing machines, cutlery, etc) and on exploiting the electrical generating resources of the Alps. The spa towns of the shore of *Lac Léman* are important health resorts.

Agricultural activity is not of a significant level, because of the nature of the area.

The Haute-Savoie is solidly centrist and to the Right in politics, in its parliamentary representation, its CONSEIL GÉNÉRAL, and in its majority votes for GISCARD D'ESTAING and Jacques CHIRAC in the 1981 and 1988 ÉLECTIONS PRÉSIDENTIELLES.

Code départemental: 74

HAUTES ÉTUDES COMMERCIALES (HEC) See: *ÉCOLE DES HAUTES ÉTUDES COMMERCIALES*

HAUTES-PYRÉNÉES

A DÉPARTEMENT in the MIDI-PYRÉNÉES region, on the border with
Spain, with a population of 224,754 in 1990. The CHEF-LIEU is
Tarbes (urban area 74,639) – engineering, electronics, and other
centres of population are Bagnères-de-Bigorre (11,805) a spa
town; and Lourdes (16,300), a centre for pilgrimages, having
the third largest number of hotel bedrooms in France. The
basilica is the largest church in the country. The *Département*
has 22 electricity power stations, and there is some aluminium
production at Lanemezan, as well as aerospace at Ossun. The
country's highest television transmitter is at the *Pic du Midi
de Bigorre* (2,865 metres).

Agricultural activity produces maize, poultry, fruit, pigs, wine
and *foie gras*. The *Parc national des Pyrénées* covers a significant
area of the mountains, and winter sports are important.

Two small areas of the Hautes-Pyrénées are entirely
surrounded by the adjacent PYRÉNÉES-ATLANTIQUES.

Politically, the Hautes-Pyrénées consistently supports the
Left, and in the 1981 and 1988 ÉLECTIONS PRÉSIDENTIELLES,
François MITTERRAND obtained comfortable majorities. There
were right-wing gains on the CONSEIL GÉNÉRAL in the ÉLECTIONS
CANTONALES in 1992, but it remains in left-wing control.

Code départemental: 65

HAUTE-VIENNE

A largely rural DÉPARTEMENT in the LIMOUSIN region, named
after the river which rises in the neighbouring CORRÈZE. The
population is 353,586, almost half of whom (170,064) live in the
AGGLOMÉRATION of Limoges, the CHEF-LIEU. It is a city famous
for its porcelain, but there is wide range of other industries
present in the urban area. The only other town with a population
over 10,000 is Saint-Junien (glovemaking, chemicals), where
the number of inhabitants has fallen to 10,604. This population
drift from the country areas is a major problem. Life expectancy
is relatively high, women having the fifth highest expectancy in
France: 79.8 years.

Sheep are the main source of agricultural activity, there being
850,000 animals in the *Département*.

There are uranium mines and processing plants at Bessines-sur-Gartempe and Razès. Oradour-sur-Glane was the scene of a massacre of villagers by SS troops in 1944.

The Haute-Vienne is traditionally a support of the Left (Limoges, sometimes called the Rome of Socialism, participated vigorously in the insurrections of 1848 and the Commune of 1871, and the CONFÉDÉRATION GÉNÉRALE DU TRAVAIL was formed there in 1895). DÉPUTÉS and SÉNATEURS are entirely from the PARTI SOCIALISTE, and in both the 1981 and 1988 ÉLECTIONS PRÉSIDENTIELLES, François MITTERRAND obtained among his highest levels of support. In the 1992 ÉLECTIONS CANTONALES, the *Département* went against the national trend by maintaining its level of support for the Socialists and Communists, the latter using the title ADS, '*Alternative, démocratie, socialisme*'.

Code départemental: 87

HAUT-RHIN

A DÉPARTEMENT in the ALSACE region, on the border marked by the Rhine with Germany and Switzerland, with a population of 671,319 in 1990. The CHEF-LIEU is Colmar, (urban area 83,816). Other urban areas are Guebwiller (26,020); Mulhouse (223,856); Munster (11,123); Saint-Louis, abutting the Swiss city of Basel (19,547); and Thann-Cernay (28,885).

Most of these industrial centres depend on well-established chemicals, textiles, heavy engineering and food processing enterprises. Mulhouse also has a large PEUGEOT car works. A nuclear power station is situated on the Rhine at Fessenheim.

There are also smaller historic villages which have a strong tourist attraction, deriving their prosperity from the substantial wine production. Because of Alsace's important strategic and economic position in international disputes, there are also numerous military memorials which provide their own constant stream of visitors.

Apart from wine production, agricultural activity is practically insignificant.

The Haut-Rhin presents women with one of the lowest life expectancies in France: 77.3 years.

Politically, the area is traditionally a supporter of the Right, its parliamentary representation almost entirely from the RPR or Centre groups. In 1981 it voted for GISCARD D'ESTAING in the ÉLECTION PRÉSIDENTIELLE, but in 1988 just transferred allegiance to François MITTERRAND who obtained 50.15 per cent of the vote.

Code départemental: 68

HAUTS-DE-SEINE

An almost entirely urbanised DÉPARTEMENT of the ÎLE-DE-FRANCE, encompassing the western and north-western PETITE CEINTURE of Paris. It was formed in 1964, and now has a population of 1.39 million. Nanterre, the CHEF-LIEU, well-known for being the site of the Paris-X university, has 84,565 inhabitants. Other large COMMUNES are Antony (57,771); Asnières-sur-Seine (71,850); Bagneux (36,364); Bois-Colombes (24,415); Boulogne-Billancourt (101,743); Châtenay-Malabry (29,197); Châtillon (26,411); Clamart (47,214); Clichy (48,030); Colombes (78,513); Courbevoie (65,389); Fontenay-aux-Roses (22,992); Gennevilliers (44,818); Issy-les-Moulineaux (46,127); La Garenne-Colombes (21,754); Le Plessis-Robinson (21,289); Levallois-Perret (47,548); Malakoff (30,959); Meudon (45,339); Montrouge (38,106); Neuilly-sur-Seine (61,768); Puteaux (42,756); Rueil-Malmaison (66,401); Saint-Cloud (28,597); Sèvres (21,990); Suresnes (35,997); Vanves (25,967); and Villeneuve-la-Garenne (23,824).

The *communes* range from the fashionable middle-class mainly residential domain of Neuilly through commercial and business quarters such as *La* DÉFENSE which straddles the boundary between Courbevoie and Puteaux, to highly industrialised areas such as Gennevilliers with metalworks, automotive engineering, chemicals and electronics plants and an inland port.

The political makeup of the *Département* reflects the same diversity, and DÉPUTÉS and SÉNATEURS are drawn from all ranges of political colour. In the 1981 and 1988 ÉLECTIONS PRÉSIDENTIELLES, the Hauts-de-Seine changed its marginal majority allegiance from GISCARD D'ESTAING (51.18 per cent in 1981) to François MITTERRAND (51.43 per cent in 1988). The RASSEMBLEMENT POUR LA RÉPUBLIQUE has a substantial majority

on the CONSEIL GÉNÉRAL and gained more seats in the 1992
ÉLECTIONS CANTONALES.

Code départemental: 92   See also: PASQUA, CHARLES

HAVAS

A major advertising and travel agency network, based on the
earlier press agency which had been founded in 1835 and
absorbed into AGENCE FRANCE PRESSE in 1944. Havas was
nationalised at the same time but sold off to the private sector
in 1987.

HEC See: *ÉCOLE DES HAUTES ÉTUDES COMMERCIALES*

HÉLIAS, PIERRE-JAKEZ (1914–   )

A university teacher and novelist who has been active in
promoting the BRETON language, and whose most famous work,
Le Cheval d'orgueil (1975), a saga of his Breton ancestors, was
a huge best-seller.

HÉLION, JEAN (1904–1987)

A surrealist painter and sculptor who was a major protagonist
of Pop Art. He escaped from a prison camp in 1942 and lived
in USA until 1947. His *carnets* have been published.

HÉRAULT

An rapidly expanding DÉPARTEMENT of the LANGUEDOC-
ROUSSILLON region, with a population of 794,603 in 1990. The
CHEF-LIEU is Montpellier (urban area 236,788), with engineering,
electronics, textiles and food industries, and the home of the
oldest medical university, dating from 1021. The town holds the
record of having the second highest temperature ever recorded
in France, 42.8 degrees Celsius in 1904. Other urban areas are
Béziers (76,344), a centre for the wine trade; Lattes (10,203);
Lunel (20,705); Mauguio (11,487); and Sète (62,768), a port
and fishing centre, specialising in the wine trade, with chemical,
oil and clothing industries.

The Hérault is the single largest wine-producing area in the
world, and accounts for almost 15 per cent of the French
production. Fruit and vegetables are also important. Tourism

is of growing influence, and there has been a sustained urban development of the coastal resorts such as Agde, La Grande-Motte and Palavas-les-Flots in the last 30 years. Sailing is popular on the CANAL DU MIDI, and there has been a growth in the number of RÉSIDENCES SECONDAIRES, especially owned by Dutch people.

The political complexion of the Hérault traditionally favours the Left. François MITTERRAND received a comfortable majority in the 1981 and 1988 ÉLECTIONS PRÉSIDENTIELLES. The Left held on to its control of the CONSEIL GÉNÉRAL in 1992, against the national trend.

Code départemental: 34

HERNU, CHARLES (1923–1990)
A Socialist politician and former member of the RÉSISTANCE, with a power base as MAIRE of Villeurbanne (RHÔNE), who rose to international prominence as *Ministre de la* DÉFENSE NATIONALE from 1981 until his resignation over the RAINBOW WARRIOR affair in 1985.

HERSANT, ROBERT (1920–   )
A member of the European Parliament and owner of an enormous press and media empire. Hersant controls both national and local newspaper titles, and various subsidiary concerns which were acquired as the group has expanded. Among the best known are *Le* FIGARO, *Le* PROGRÈS, FRANCE-SOIR, and JOURS DE FRANCE. He was also the chairman of *La* CINQ television station. Partly in order to restrict his growing control of so many newspapers, amendments were made to the law in 1984, in what is known as the *Affaire Hersant*.

HEURES CREUSES
Off-peak hours. By choosing the ÉLECTRICITÉ DE FRANCE *Tarif consommation heures creuses*, it is possible to pay a lower rate for energy consumed within an eight-hour off-peak period.

HEURES SUPPLÉMENTAIRES
Employees working more than 39 hours in a week are entitled to overtime rates of 125 per cent for the first eight hours, and 150 per cent for any hours above that. See also: DURÉE DU TRAVAIL

HINAULT, BERNARD (1954–   )

A professional racing cyclist who won many tournaments (including the TOUR DE FRANCE on five occasions) and was the first to win the three major trophies of the *Tour de France*, *Tour of Italy* and *Grand Prix des nations* in one year, 1982. He was not very popular with journalists as he was very outspoken.

HLM See: *HABITATION À LOYER MODÉRÉ*

HÔPITAL PRIVÉ PSYCHIATRIQUE (HPP)

A private sector hospital working within the public service. About a quarter of psychiatric beds available to the public are through this arrangement.

HORS TAXE

Goods or services which are free of duty. This usually refers to international travellers' duty-free concessions, but there are special regulations concerning certain frontier areas. See also: DOUANES; FRONTALIER

HOSSEIN, ROBERT (1927–   )

A theatre director who has become a prominent exponent of '*théâtre de grand spectacle*', showing with great success dramas such as *Notre-Dame de Paris* and *La Liberté ou la mort*.

HÔTEL DE PRÉFECTURE

A simple hotel, usually quite small, classified by local tourist services organised by the DÉPARTEMENT.

HÔTEL DE TOURISME

An hotel which is part of the classification system operated by the *Secrétariat d'état au tourisme*, which is a non-judgemental measure of the facilities available.

HÔTEL DU DÉPARTEMENT

The headquarters of the administrative services in a DÉPARTEMENT, under the control of the *Président* of the CONSEIL GÉNÉRAL.

HÔTEL MATIGNON See: *MATIGNON*

HPP See: *HÔPITAL PRIVÉ PSYCHIATRIQUE*

HUISSIER
A legal officer appointed by the GARDE DES SCEAUX, who has the role of carrying out court decisions, of drawing up a CONSTAT, of executing a SAISIE. Since 1986, the minimum qualification for appointment as *huissier* has been a law LICENCE, followed by specialist training. A *huissier* can also take on extra privileged roles, such as officiating at auctions, becoming an insurance agent, or secretary of a COOPÉRATIVE AGRICOLE.

HUMANITÉ, L'
The daily newspaper of the PARTI COMMUNISTE FRANÇAIS, founded in 1904 by the Socialist leader, Jean Jaurès, and clandestinely published during World War II. Its sales have fallen steadily and its circulation has dropped well below the 1989 figure of 95,000 since the collapse of Communism in the former USSR.
   See also: FÊTE DE L'HUMANITÉ

HUPPERT, ISABELLE (1953–   )
A film star who has acted important parts in a number of films, such as *Rosebud*, *La Dentellière*, *Sac de nœuds*, *Madame Bovary*.

HYMNE NATIONAL
The revolutionary *La Marseillaise* has been the official national anthem since 1879, taking on the character of military march rather than song in 1887. In 1974, GISCARD D'ESTAING decided that on State occasions, the earlier version should be used, but this decision caused great controversy and was reversed in 1981 by the Socialist government.

HYPOKHÂGNE
The slang term for the first year CLASSE PRÉPARATOIRE working towards the CONCOURS for ÉCOLE NORMALE SUPÉRIEURE entry, the second year being known as '*khâgne*'.

HYPOTHÈQUE
A mortgage loan, secured on a property. A NOTAIRE has to countersign the loan documents to give it legal status. Usually, interest only is repaid during the loan period, with the principal repaid as a lump sum at the end.

IBIS
A large hotel chain, incorporating the *Urbis* brand name for city centre hotels. *Ibis/Urbis* is owned by the ACCOR group.

ICI PARIS
A sensational tabloid weekly newspaper with a circulation of 422,000, and claiming a readership of a million and a half. The sales have fallen from about 700,000 in the early 1960s.

IDEN See: *INSPECTEUR DE L'ÉDUCATION NATIONALE*

IDENTITÉ, CARTE D' See: *CARTE NATIONALE D'IDENTITÉ*

IEN See: *INSPECTEUR DE L'ÉDUCATION NATIONALE*

IET See: *INSPECTEUR DE L'ENSEIGNEMENT TECHNIQUE*

IFOP See: *INSTITUT FRANÇAIS D'OPINION PUBLIQUE*

IGEN See: *INSPECTEUR GÉNÉRAL DE L'ÉDUCATION NATIONALE*

IGN See: *INSTITUT GÉOGRAPHIQUE NATIONAL*

ÎLE-DE-FRANCE
The administrative RÉGION based on PARIS, and also incorporating the DÉPARTEMENTS of ESSONNE, HAUTS-DE-SEINE, SEINE-ET-MARNE, SEINE-SAINT-DENIS and YVELINES. Before 1976, this area was officially known as the *Région parisienne*.

Not surprisingly it has the highest density (887 people per square kilometre) and population (10.66 million) of all the regions, and its inhabitants, increasingly referred to as the

'*Franciliens*', are those with the highest per capita income and standard of living. Because of the status of the capital, which clearly affects the character of the region, its PRÉFET DE RÉGION has special powers of co-ordinating public transport systems and economic planning, and is also *Préfet de Paris*.

With 18 per cent of the population, the Île-de-France generates 27 per cent of the gross national product, far outstripping the region in second position, Rhône-Alpes. This imbalance is one of the major reasons underlying the regionalisation policies. Special restrictions are placed on new industrial enterprises being established in the region, except in the VILLES NOUVELLES. The effect of such measures has been to slow the rate of growth of the region, and to divert growth to others.

The CONSEIL RÉGIONAL of the Île-de-France has 209 members, the largest in the country. In the 1992 ÉLECTIONS RÉGIONALES, the Right increased their majority, the PARTI SOCIALISTE lost 27 seats, with a lower percentage of the poll than the FRONT NATIONAL, who are now the second largest party group on the *Conseil*, after the RASSEMBLEMENT POUR LA RÉPUBLIQUE which has 50 seats. The GÉNÉRATION ÉCOLOGIE and VERTS gained 22 and 15 seats respectively.

ÎLE DE LA CONFÉRENCE
An island in the Bidassoa estuary on the frontier with Spain at Hendaye (PYRÉNÉES-ATLANTIQUES), formerly considered as the joint property of the royal houses of France and Spain, and now administered by each country for six months in turn. See also: ÎLE DES FAISANS

ÎLE DES FAISANS
This island is near the ÎLE DE LA CONFÉRENCE and is administered under the same arrangements.

ILLE-ET-VILAINE
A DÉPARTEMENT of the BRETAGNE region, named after the two rivers which meet at its CHEF-LIEU, Rennes. The Ille-et-Vilaine has a population of 798,715. Of these, 245,065 live in the Rennes AGGLOMÉRATION, which is a centre for the motor industry

(CITROËN), mechanical engineering, printing and information technology industries. The other main urban areas are Dinard (15,707); Fougères, (25,066); Saint-Malo (48,057); and Vitré (14,486).

The maritime influence of the Channel coast is still important in the local economy (oysters from Cancale, fishing, boatbuilding and naval institutions at Saint-Malo, beach resort at Dinard, etc.), but the inland towns have other industrial bases (e.g. shoes and clothing at Fougères, metallurgy and electronics at Redon). Agricultural activity is dominated by cattle, pigs and poultry breeding and the dairy industry as well as the cultivation of vegetables and cereals.

The Right and Centre are strong in local political allegiances, and so it was remarkable that GISCARD D'ESTAING'S 54.18 per cent share of the vote in the 1981 ÉLECTION PRÉSIDENTIELLE was turned into a 54.21 per cent share for François MITTERRAND in 1988.

Code départemental: 35

ILM See: *IMMEUBLE À LOYER MOYEN*

ÎLOT, L'
A voluntary organisation for the care of freed prisoners and for those who are in need of social support. The organisation runs hostels, overnight shelters and day centres.

IMMATRICULATION, PLAQUE D'
The registration plate which must be carried on a motor vehicle. The final two figures are the code of the DÉPARTEMENT of the residence of the owner, and each vehicle is re-registered at change of ownership, or change of *département* of residence.
See also: CARTE GRISE; VIGNETTE

IMMATRICULATION (SÉCURITÉ SOCIALE)
An employee's SÉCURITÉ SOCIALE record is filed under a registration number coded according to the date and place of birth. Without this number, it is impossible to exercise one's right to benefits. An employer's registration number is also coded according to the size and nature of the enterprise.

IMMEUBLE À LOYER MOYEN (ILM)
A building containing moderate rent accommodation, similar to but more expensive than the more common HABITATION À LOYER MODÉRÉ.

IMMEUBLE CLASSÉ
A protected building by ARRÊTÉ of the *Ministre de la* CULTURE. The first step towards listing a building for protection is to apply to the PRÉFET DE RÉGION who consults with the local *Commission régionale du patrimoine historique, archéologique et ethnologique* or COREPHAE.

IMMIGRATION
There is persistent controversy in France over the issue of ÉTRANGERS. A confused situation relating to perceptions of nationality and race, especially concerning those not of West European origin is prone to exploitation by politicians. All political parties are affected by this, and the frequency with which the issue of so-called *immigrants* (anyone) or *immigrés* (usually non-white) is raised possibly has more to do with the parties' motives than anything else. The concentration by the FRONT NATIONAL on this issue in 1990, with apparent electoral support, forced other parties to reconsider their own positions.

Traditionally France has been a place of refuge for the politically persecuted, but since 1974 stricter controls have been in force to attempt to reduce the numbers of immigrants seeking settlement for this and other causes, especially at times of high unemployment. The *Plan Stoleru* subsidised the repatriation of immigrants from 1977 to 1980, when the *Loi Bonnet* instituted measures against illegal immigration. The measures became more strict during the 1980s. See also: APATRIDES; TRAVAILLEURS ÉTRANGERS

IMMUNITÉ PARLEMENTAIRE
According to *Article 26* of the CONSTITUTION, a DÉPUTÉ or SÉNATEUR cannot be prosecuted for expressing opinions and voting as part of the responsibilities of the role, and especially within parliamentary debates. Except in the case of a FLAGRANT DÉLIT, a member accused of an offence cannot be arrested

during a parliamentary session without the approval of the
ASSEMBLÉE NATIONALE or SÉNAT, as appropriate.

IMPÔT DE SOLIDARITÉ SUR LA FORTUNE
A wealth tax introduced in 1988 on those with a fortune worth
more than 4.13 million francs. The rate of tax is between 0.5
per cent and 1.5 per cent, depending on the size of the fortune,
which includes buildings, shares, money, gold, personal effects
(with certain exceptions), jewels, insurance policies and other
investments. See also: IMPÔT SUR LES GRANDES FORTUNES

IMPÔT LOCAL
A tax raised by a COLLECTIVITÉ LOCALE for local services or
facilities. The range of *impôts locaux* applicable to any one
place varies. See also: TAXE DE BALAYAGE; TAXE D'ENLÈVEMENT
DES ORDURES MÉNAGÈRES; TAXE D'HABITATION; TAXE FONCIÈRE;
TAXE PROFESSIONNELLE

IMPÔT SUR LE REVENU (IR)
The major direct tax payable by French people, payable on the
income received in the previous year. It is calculated on a
household basis, and a taxpayer is allocated a *Quotient familial*
which takes into account family circumstances. Certain
professional costs and other outgoings are allowable against tax,
and certain kinds of income are not taxable, although they
have to be declared in the annual return.

The actual tax payable is graduated according to the taxable
income, ranging from 5 per cent to 56.8 per cent. The stages of
graduation largely depend on the *Quotient familial*. If the
annual tax bill is lower than 400 francs, it is not collected. The
tax is normally payable in three instalments, the first two in
February and May based on the previous year's payments and
adjusted for the third instalment in September, or monthly, if
requested by the taxpayer. Tax bills unpaid on the due date are
increased by 10 per cent. See also: RECOURS GRACIEUX

IMPÔT SUR LES GRANDES FORTUNES
A wealth tax in operation between 1982 and 1986, replaced by
the IMPÔT DE SOLIDARITÉ SUR LA FORTUNE.

INA See: *INSTITUT NATIONAL DE LA COMMUNICATION AUDIOVISUELLE*

INALCO See: *INSTITUT NATIONAL DE LANGUES ET CIVILISATIONS ORIENTALES*

INC See: *INSTITUT NATIONAL DE LA CONSOMMATION*

INCULPÉ
A person who is accused of an offence which is under investigation by a JUGE D'INSTRUCTION. The term has been officially replaced by '*prévenu*'.

INDEMNITÉ
A payment which requires some form of claim, but to which one is entitled because of circumstances or contributions previously made. Examples include: The INDEMNITÉ D'ACCIDENT DE TRAVAIL, which entitles the claimant to free medical treatment, payment by the employer of wages for the day of the accident, daily allowance of half to two-thirds wages for the period when off work, guarantee of re-employment or double redundancy benefits; the INDEMNITÉ JOURNALIÈRE DE MALADIE is payable to an ASSURÉ SOCIAL who receives up to half salary (for up to three years in serious cases) if unable to work because of sickness.

INDICE CGT
An index of the cost of living as it affects the family of the typical working class Parisian. It is calculated monthly on the basis of 15,000 monthly returns in the Paris region. See also: CONFÉDÉRATION GÉNÉRALE DU TRAVAIL

INDICE DES PRIX DE DÉTAIL
An official retail price index, published by the INSTITUT NATIONAL DE LA STATISTIQUE ET DES ÉTUDES ÉCONOMIQUES, based on 160,000 monthly returns from 296 retail outlets throughout France.

INDRE
A DÉPARTEMENT of the CENTRE region, home for 237,505, named after the tributary of the Loire which runs through it, and on which is situated Châteauroux, the CHEF-LIEU (67,090 in the

AGGLOMÉRATION), a centre of the tobacco, engineering, chemicals, textiles, ceramics and food industries. The other large urban area is Issoudun (13,859), a site for metallurgy, printing, fertilizers, leather goods and food industry plants. There is aviation construction in the small town of Argenton-sur-Creuse. One traditional feature of the area is a number of small clothing firms employing women in towns and country areas.

There has been a steady decline in the population of the Indre, in which agriculture has been the mainstay of the economy. Farming is mixed in its character, there being substantial wheat and barley crops, but also significant numbers of goats with associated cheese products.

Tourists are attracted by the numerous local châteaux, including the famous Valençay, and the connections with the writer, George Sand.

In political terms the Indre leant to the Left in the 1980s, François MITTERRAND obtaining a majority proportion of the vote in the 1981 and 1988 ÉLECTIONS PRÉSIDENTIELLES, but the Centre Right controls the CONSEIL GÉNÉRAL.

Code départemental: 36

INDRE-ET-LOIRE

A DÉPARTEMENT of the CENTRE region with a 1990 population of 598,328, named after the two rivers which meet near the Chinon nuclear power station at Avoine. The CHEF-LIEU is Tours (population of the conurbation 270,019), a regional commercial, administrative, tourist and industrial centre whose prosperity was aided by its important place in the railway system. The only other urban area of significant size is Amboise (14,529). The other towns are of medium to small size and are largely local centres which have grown up around their châteaux, of which there are more than 300. The Indre-et-Loire is the central *département* of the Loire valley and as such benefits from the high level of tourist trade.

Vines, maize, barley, wheat and vegetables are major contributors to the agricultural economy, and there is a substantial forestry industry.

In both 1981 and 1988 ÉLECTIONS PRÉSIDENTIELLES, the *Département* voted for MITTERRAND with a substantial majority, whereas its representatives in both parliamentary chambers are drawn from a balance of parties. The CONSEIL GÉNÉRAL is under the control of the Right.

Code départemental: 37

INED See: *INSTITUT NATIONAL D'ÉTUDES DÉMOGRAPHIQUES*

INFANTERIE
The French army's infantry comprises the *Régiments d'infanterie*, *Régiments parachutistes*, *27ème Division alpine* (mountain specialists), and the LÉGION ÉTRANGÈRE. The infantry's nickname is '*la Biffe*' and members of the airforce call them '*les pousse-cailloux*'.

INFRACTION
The committing of an offence. See also: AMENDE; CONTRAVENTION

INGÉNIEUR
A qualified engineer. This requires post-BAC level qualifications, and is higher in status than a TECHNICIEN.

INJONCTION DE PAYER
A writ for payment of unpaid sums in a contract, etc., served through the TRIBUNAL D'INSTANCE.

INP See: *INSTITUT NATIONAL POLYTECHNIQUE*

INRA See: *INSTITUT NATIONAL DE LA RECHERCHE AGRONOMIQUE*

INSCRIPTION SCOLAIRE
In order to register for a child's place in an ÉCOLE MATERNELLE, a parent must produce at the MAIRIE the LIVRET DE FAMILLE, proof of DOMICILE, and a whole range of medical (including vaccination) certificates.

INSÉÉ See: *INSTITUT NATIONAL DE LA STATISTIQUE ET DES ÉTUDES ÉCONOMIQUES*

INSERM See: *INSTITUT NATIONAL DE LA SANTÉ ET DE LA RECHERCHE MÉDICALE*

INSIGNE GRAND INVALIDE CIVIL See: *GRAND INVALIDE CIVIL*

INSIGNE GRAND INVALIDE DE GUERRE See: *GRAND INVALIDE DE GUERRE*

INSPECTEUR D'ACADÉMIE
Since 1983, the main task of the education inspector, based in the ACADÉMIE, usually operating within one DÉPARTEMENT and officially representing the RECTEUR there, is to evaluate the effectiveness of the education system. There is also the task of reporting on the efficiency of individual teachers, the organisation of the BAC, and the deployment and management of the staff in the local ÉCOLES PRIMAIRES. There are nearly 600 *Inspecteurs d'académie* in France. Their role does not extend into higher education.

INSPECTEUR DE L'ENSEIGNEMENT TECHNIQUE (IET)
A specialist education inspector, recruited by CONCOURS from the ranks of experienced teachers of technical education.

INSPECTEUR DE L'ÉDUCATION NATIONALE (IEN)
An education inspector, recruited by CONCOURS from the ranks of serving teachers. There are nearly 1,400 of these inspectors whose main function is to assess INSTITUTEURS, visiting them every few years. They were formerly known as IDEN (*Inspecteurs départementaux de l'éducation nationale*).

INSPECTEUR DÉPARTEMENTAL DE L'ÉDUCATION NATIONALE (IDEN) See: *INSPECTEUR DE L'ÉDUCATION NATIONALE*

INSPECTEUR DES FINANCES
A senior FONCTIONNAIRE within the *Ministère des* FINANCES. There are two grades, the most senior being the 32 *Inspecteurs généraux*, with 108 *Inspecteurs* filling the lower grade. Most are recruited directly from the ÉCOLE NATIONALE D'ADMINISTRATION,

with a maximum of 25 per cent of vacant posts being filled from outside.

The *Inspecteur des finances* has the power to audit or investigate any realm of public finance, including State-owned enterprises. A frequent way of exercising this power is by secondment to a particular agency or industry.

INSPECTEUR DU TRAVAIL
A FONCTIONNAIRE appointed by the *Ministère du* TRAVAIL in order to check that employment legislation or a CONVENTION COLLECTIVE is being carried out. The *Inspecteur du travail* is entitled to visit any place of employment, and to be accompanied on a visit by the DÉLÉGUÉ DU PERSONNEL, who can ask for such a visit. An employer's INFRACTION results in the *Inspecteur's* preparation of a PROCÈS-VERBAL.

INSPECTEUR GÉNÉRAL DE L'ÉDUCATION NATIONALE (IGEN)
A high-ranking education inspector who is concerned with a particular subject area or specialist aspect of school operation. There are about 200 IGEN whose main function is to give advice to the ministry about the overall effectiveness of the system. They define syllabuses, often write text books and chair assessment committees for AGRÉGATION examinations.

INSPECTEUR PÉDAGOGIQUE RÉGIONAL (IPR)
Based in a particular region, the IPR is the local support of the INSPECTEUR GÉNÉRAL DE L'ÉDUCATION NATIONALE, and has as a principal function the assessment of teachers in secondary schools.

INSTITUT CATHOLIQUE DE PARIS
The private sector university with the largest number of approved programmes leading to State qualifications, mainly in the faculty of arts. There are approximately 15,000 registered students, one fifth of whom are foreigners.

INSTITUT DE FRANCE
The academic institution of which the five great ACADÉMIES are a part.

**INSTITUT DE RECHERCHES ET DE COORDINATION
ACOUSTIQUE MUSIQUE (IRCAM)** See: *BOULEZ, PIERRE*

INSTITUT D'ÉTUDES POLITIQUES DE PARIS
The prestigious higher education establishment sometimes
called '*Sciences-Po*' recruiting holders of the BAC who pass a
special entrance examination. About 10 per cent of those who
try, manage to enter by this route. Holders of a LICENCE, MAÎTRISE
or other equivalent qualification can enter the second year of
the three-year course, as can mature applicants with five years'
work experience.

A *diplôme* from this institute is highly regarded. It is also
possible at *Sciences-Po* to work towards CONCOURS for ENA, as
well as CAPES, DEA or DESS qualifications.

INSTITUT FRANÇAIS D'OPINION PUBLIQUE (IFOP)
A private enterprise opinion poll organisation, founded in 1938.

INSTITUT GÉOGRAPHIQUE NATIONAL (IGN)
A map publishing organisation providing a range of maps for
general and tourist use as well as large-scale versions for
specialists.

INSTITUT NATIONAL AGRONOMIQUE See: *ÉCOLE
NATIONALE SUPÉRIEURE AGRONOMIQUE (ENSA)*

**INSTITUT NATIONAL DE LA COMMUNICATION
AUDIOVISUELLE (INA)**
A State-owned enterprise which is a support organisation for
broadcasting services, housing the radio and television
archives, providing training programmes for broadcasting media
professionals, and publishing materials in connection with or
about broadcasts.

INSTITUT NATIONAL DE LA CONSOMMATION (INC)
A State-aided organisation, founded in 1967, providing
information and guidance about consumer affairs, and
publishing CINQUANTE MILLIONS DE CONSOMMATEURS, a monthly
consumer magazine. See also: QUE CHOISIR?

**INSTITUT NATIONAL DE LANGUES ET CIVILISATIONS
ORIENTALES (INALCO)**
A higher education institution in Paris teaching 70 different

languages, with about 9,000 students who enter after obtaining the BAC. Unqualified visitors may attend lectures without having to register, but may not sit examinations. The common name for INALCO is '*Langues-O*'.

INSTITUT NATIONAL DE LA RECHERCHE AGRONOMIQUE (INRA)
A publicly-funded research establishment in Paris which has as its main function the continued improvement and development of the food industry.

INSTITUT NATIONAL DE LA SANTÉ ET DE LA RECHERCHE MÉDICALE (INSERM)
Based in Paris, this is the central research centre for scientific research in public health and medicine.

INSTITUT NATIONAL DE LA STATISTIQUE ET DES ÉTUDES ÉCONOMIQUES (INSEE)
With offices throughout France, INSEE carries out surveys for the information of the ADMINISTRATION and for public information, compiling for instance the INDICE DES PRIX DE DÉTAIL. It is an offence not to give proper information to an INSEE researcher, punishable by an AMENDE.

INSTITUT NATIONAL D'ÉTUDES DÉMOGRAPHIQUES (INED)
A study and research organisation founded in 1945 which publishes a monthly magazine for schools, *Population et sociétés*, reflecting its pluri-disciplinary and internationalist role. See also: SAUVY, ALFRED

INSTITUT NATIONAL POLYTECHNIQUE (INP)
There are three of these institutes – at Grenoble, Nancy and Toulouse – which group together the various locally sited ÉCOLES NATIONALES SUPÉRIEURES D'INGÉNIEURS of specialist disciplines.

INSTITUT PASTEUR
A specialised hospital and huge research organisation founded by Louis Pasteur in 1887 in Paris, and having the status of UTILITÉ PUBLIQUE. The *Institut Pasteur* provides postgraduate training for specialists in research and diagnosis of infectious

diseases and biomedical and biotechnological studies. A recent focus has been on research into AIDS. The funds are partly through State support, partly through commercial contracts and licensing of products, as well as donations. There are now 27 *Instituts Pasteur* worldwide, with about 2,500 staff and 600 permanent research scientists.

INSTITUT RÉGIONAL D'ADMINISTRATION (IRA)

There are five IRA (Bastia, Lille, Lyon, Metz and Nantes) recruiting by CONCOURS experienced employees in the public services (civilian or military) or holders of a DEUG or equivalent. Training is provided for posts as a FONCTIONNAIRE, and salary is paid during the course, which is primarily practical. The final qualification is the *Diplôme d'administration publique* and graduates must work within the ADMINISTRATION for six years or repay earnings gained during their two-year course.

INSTITUT UNIVERSITAIRE DE FORMATION DES MAÎTRES (IUFM)

A teacher training institution, established from 1990 onwards, incorporating the former ÉCOLES NORMALES for primary school teachers and including training courses for secondary school teachers. The two-year training provided follows a common core, with an emphasis on pedagogical skills rather than subject knowledge. Students receive a salary in return for a commitment to teach in a State school.

INSTITUT UNIVERSITAIRE DE TECHNOLOGIE (IUT)

There are 68 IUT providing post-BAC courses towards the DIPLÔME UNIVERSITAIRE DE TECHNOLOGIE with course facilities in over 300 different locations. About 7 per cent of registered university students are working in these IUT on two-year courses which are more general in their nature than those leading to a BREVET DE TECHNICIEN SUPÉRIEUR. Holders of a BTS may transfer to the IUT, and holders of the DUT may transfer to the university. Work experience placement is a compulsory part of the course.

INSTITUTEUR

A teacher in an ÉCOLE PRIMAIRE holding the status of

FONCTIONNAIRE. Since 1990, no new *instituteurs* have been appointed, their replacement being the PROFESSEUR DES ÉCOLES.

An *instituteur* teaches all subjects, with a commitment of 27 hours of classes per week. The basic entry requirement for the CONCOURS for a training course was a BAC + 2 qualification, usually a DEUG, DUT or BTS. Training was given in an ÉCOLE NORMALE.

INTERDICTION DE SÉJOUR
A penal measure which allows a court to impose a ban on residence in a specified area of between two and 10 years for an adult below the age of 65.

INTÉRÊT PUBLIC, D'
The association or activity described thus is recognised as being of benefit to the common good of the country, and usually receives government subsidies. See also: UTILITÉ PUBLIQUE

INTÉRIEUR, MINISTÈRE DE L'
This ministry has the responsibility for maintaining public order and the security of the State and its citizens. The Minister has ultimate control over the POLICE NATIONALE, and is sometimes given the nickname '*le premier flic de France*'. The main arm of the ministry throughout the country is the PRÉFET for each DÉPARTEMENT.

INTERMARCHÉ
A large chain of supermarkets and hypermarkets.

INTERNAT
The boarding annexe of a LYCÉE or similar institution. Because of distance, especially in sparsely populated areas, or in order to attend specialist courses, pupils sometimes board at school on a weekly basis. Usually, the *internat* is supervised by students paying their way through higher education studies. See also: EXTERNE

INTERNEMENT PSYCHIATRIQUE
Most psychiatric patients in hospital are resident through their agreement. Medical and family consent usually has to be given

on entry and after a fortnight. Such patients are free to leave
by request or on medical advice.

Fewer than 4 per cent are in hospital through a *placement
d'office*, to protect themselves or others, by order of a PRÉFET,
or in emergency a MAIRE or COMMISSAIRE DE POLICE. Medical
opinions have to be sought on entry, after 24 hours and after a
fortnight. The order is lifted by ARRÊTÉ PRÉFECTORAL. The
PROCUREUR DE LA RÉPUBLIQUE must be informed, and must visit
the hospital at regular intervals. In case of dispute, the patient,
his or her family or the *Procureur de la République* may appeal
to a JUGE for the order to be reversed.

INTERPELLATION
The process whereby a police officer can demand one's
attendance at a COMMISSARIAT to answer questions. One has
the right to see the official authorisation, but one cannot refuse
a CONVOCATION to go to the police station. Once at the
Commissariat, an *interpellé* has the right to remain silent, and
to refuse to sign a PROCÈS-VERBAL.

INTERRUPTION VOLONTAIRE DE GROSSESSE (IVG)
Abortion of a foetus under 10 weeks has been legal since 1975,
and it has qualified for reimbursement of fees under the SÉCURITÉ
SOCIALE since 1982. If the woman is below the age of 18, the
consent of a person exercising AUTORITÉ PARENTALE or a legal
representative is also required. No hospital is permitted to carry
out abortions if they exceed 25 per cent of all the operations in
that institution.

INTER SERVICE
Telephone information services provided by FRANCE INTER,
covering among others, young people's interests and concerns
(*Inter service jeunes*) and road conditions (*Inter service routes*).

INTIMITÉ
A popular weekly magazine, although with a falling circulation
now of about 350,000.

INVALIDE, CARTE D' See: *CARTE D'INVALIDITÉ*

INVIOLABILITÉ DE DOMICILE See: *DOMICILE*

INVIOLABILITÉ PARLEMENTAIRE See: *IMMUNITÉ PARLEMENTAIRE*

IONESCO, EUGÈNE (1912–   )
A Romanian-born dramatist and painter who spent his childhood in France, and has written in French since his appointment as a journal editor in 1940 in Marseille. Ionesco won international acclaim from 1950 onwards for his plays in which absurd aspects of language are highlighted. Well-known titles include *La Cantatrice chauve*, *La Leçon* and *Le Roi se meurt*.

IPR See: *INSPECTEUR PÉDAGOGIQUE RÉGIONAL*

IPSOS
A private enterprise opinion poll organisation.

IR See: *IMPÔT SUR LE REVENU*

IRA See: *INSTITUT RÉGIONAL D'ADMINISTRATION*

IRCAM See: *BOULEZ, PIERRE*

ISÈRE
A DÉPARTEMENT of the RHÔNE-ALPES region with a population in 1990 of 1.01 million. It is named after the tributary of the Rhône, which flows through the *Département*, and on which stands Grenoble, the CHEF-LIEU, which has a population of 400,141 in its AGGLOMÉRATION, and is a centre for metal engineering and high-tech industries. Other major urban areas are Bourgoin-Jallieu (31,375); Charvieu-Chanvagneux (21,342); La-Tour-du-Pin (11,564); Rives (10,960); Roussillon (27,841); Saint-Marcellin (11,872); Vienne (39,738); and Voiron (36,349). Many of these are industrial centres, typically with textiles, metal industries, pharmaceuticals, electronics, cement works and paper making as sources of employment.

Electricity has been the great strength of the Isère, first hydro-electric, and more recently nuclear. There are a number of such sources in the *Département*.

Forestry, cattle rearing, vines, fruit, cereals, tobacco and nuts are the principal agricultural products.

The winter sports industry is an important part of the local economy, Grenoble having been the centre of the Winter Olympics in 1968, with an appropriate investment in the infrastructure dating from then. There is also a substantial tourist industry in all seasons.

Grenoble and its surroundings have long been considered a highly desirable place to live, and the Isère accordingly attracts many young and ambitious people to live there. It is seen as something of a trendsetter for provincial cities. L'Isle-d'Abeau is a VILLE NOUVELLE a few kilometres south-east of Lyon. MITTERRAND maintained his majority of just over 55 per cent of the vote in the 1981 and 1988 ÉLECTIONS PRÉSIDENTIELLES, and the parliamentary representatives are dominated by the Left. Power on the CONSEIL GÉNÉRAL is however in the hands of the Centre Right, and the RASSEMBLEMENT POUR LA RÉPUBLIQUE became the largest party group in 1992, although the Communists won an additional seat at the same time.

Code départemental: 38

ISSAS See: *DJIBOUTI*

IUFM See: *INSTITUT UNIVERSITAIRE DE FORMATION DES MAÎTRES*

IUT See: *INSTITUT UNIVERSITAIRE DE TECHNOLOGIE*

IVG See: *INTERRUPTION VOLONTAIRE DE GROSSESSE*

JAC See: *MOUVEMENT RURAL DE JEUNESSE CHRÉTIENNE*

J'AI LU
A long-running paperback literature series published by HACHETTE, in which major works of literature are provided in digest form and with introductory criticism.

JANVIER, LE PREMIER
New Year's Day is a FÊTE LÉGALE in France, and has traditionally been the occasion on which presents, known as '*les étrennes*', are exchanged within families.

JARDIN D'ACCLIMATATION
A children's small amusement park and zoo on the western outskirts of the city of Paris.

JARDIN DES PLANTES
A botanical garden, often attached to a scientific institution. The Paris *Jardin des plantes* dates from the seventeenth century, and was laid out as a royal park. It is subject to renovation in the early 1990s.

JE SÈME À TOUT VENT
The slogan of the LAROUSSE publishing empire, emphasising its role of disseminating information.

JEUNESSE AGRICOLE CATHOLIQUE (JAC) See: *MOUVEMENT RURAL DE JEUNESSE CHRÉTIENNE*

JEUNESSE OUVRIÈRE CATHOLIQUE (JOC)
A militant lay Catholic organisation, founded in the 1920s, with an evangelical mission among the younger generation, often critical of conservative Catholicism.

JEUNESSES MUSICALES DE FRANCE (JMF)
A group of 22 regional associations providing concerts and other musical experience for children and young people, as well as support for young performers.

JEUNES TRAVAILLEURS SALARIÉS (JTS) See: *MOUVEMENT RURAL DE JEUNESSE CHRÉTIENNE*

JEUNES VOYAGEURS SERVICE (JVS)
For children aged between four and 14 travelling alone on trains, the SOCIÉTÉ NATIONALE DES CHEMINS DE FER FRANÇAIS provides a hostess service on certain days during school holidays, on reservation and payment of a special fee.

JEU PROVENÇAL See: *BOULE PARISIENNE*

JMF See: *JEUNESSES MUSICALES DE FRANCE*

JO See: *JOURNAL OFFICIEL*

JOBERT, MARLÈNE (1943–)
A television and film actress, whose films include *Tendre Poulet*, *La Zizanie* and *Les Cavaliers de l'orage*.

JOBERT, MICHEL (1921–)
A politician who served in governments of Right and Left in the CINQUIÈME RÉPUBLIQUE. Jobert was the *Directeur de* CABINET for Georges POMPIDOU from 1966 to 1968, and directed the presidential office from 1969 to 1973, becoming *Ministre des* AFFAIRES ÉTRANGÈRES until 1974. He founded the *Mouvement des démocrates*, a pressure group which refuses to accept the logic of a Left and Right division in politics, and worked as *Ministre d'État* for foreign trade from 1981 to 1983. He is often to be seen on television commenting on foreign policy matters.

JOC See: *JEUNESSE OUVRIÈRE CATHOLIQUE*

JOSPIN, LIONEL (1937–)
A Socialist politician who has a loyal following within the PARTI SOCIALISTE. After an academic and administrative career, he became the party's general secretary in 1981 and a DÉPUTÉ. In 1988, he took the post of *Ministre de l'*ÉDUCATION NATIONALE

and pushed through a number of controversial reforms,
including a greater degree of university autonomy. He lost his
post in 1992.

JOUR DE FÊTE See: *FÊTE LÉGALE*

JOUR FÉRIÉ See: *FÊTE LÉGALE*

JOURNAL DU DIMANCHE
A popular tabloid Sunday newspaper, with a circulation of
360,000.

JOURNAL OFFICIEL (JO)
The government's daily gazette, in which all laws and DÉCRETS
are published, as well as information about administrative
measures and official appointments. The JO is available in the
MAIRIE.

JOURS, LES TROIS See: *TROIS JOURS*

JOURS DE FRANCE
A popular weekly magazine founded by Marcel DASSAULT in
1954, of which the circulation is now in serious decline, losing
more than half its sales between 1970 and 1990. It has suffered
severely from the women's magazine published by *Le* FIGARO,
Figaro-Madame.

JOXE, PIERRE (1934–)
Son of Louis Joxe, Pierre Joxe was a Socialist politician and a
minister in DE GAULLE's government. He entered the ASSEMBLÉE
NATIONALE in 1973, and became a member of the European
parliament in 1977. In regional politics, he was *Président* of the
CONSEIL RÉGIONAL for BOURGOGNE from 1979 to 1982. He was
appointed to ministerial posts, becoming *Ministre de l'*INTÉRIEUR
in 1988, and then *Ministre de la* DÉFENSE NATIONALE in Édith
CRESSON's government in 1991, retaining this post under Pierre
BÉRÉGOVOY.

JTS See: *MOUVEMENT RURAL DE JEUNESSE
CHRÉTIENNE*

JUGE

The president or MAGISTRAT DE SIÈGE of any court of law. A *Juge* is appointed by the government, on the recommendation of the GARDE DES SCEAUX after consultation with the CONSEIL SUPÉRIEUR DE LA MAGISTRATURE. Once in post a *Juge* cannot be removed without his or her consent, and is, in theory at least, guaranteed independence by *Article 64* of the CONSTITUTION.

JUGE CONSULAIRE

An unpaid judge who sits in a TRIBUNAL DE COMMERCE, and is elected by the CHAMBRE DE COMMERCE ET DE L'INDUSTRIE.

JUGE DE L'APPLICATION DES PEINES

A MAGISTRAT DE SIÈGE who considers amendments to sentences after a period of imprisonment has begun. It is to the *Juge de l'application des peines* that decisions about reduced sentences for good conduct are referred. He or she also rules on breaches of conditions of suspended sentences, and on breaches of LIBÉRATION CONDITIONNELLE.

JUGE DES AFFAIRES MATRIMONIALES

A MAGISTRAT DE SIÈGE who only deals with divorce cases where there is no dispute, and who rules on custody of children, maintenance allowances, etc.

JUGE DES LOYERS COMMERCIAUX

Usually the *Président* of a TRIBUNAL DE GRANDE INSTANCE, who rules on disputes over commercial rents.

JUGE DES TUTELLES

A MAGISTRAT DE SIÈGE whose function is to act as the judge in the TRIBUNAL D'INSTANCE for cases where rulings are necessary in matters of a child's guardianship.

JUGE D'INSTRUCTION

The examining MAGISTRAT DE SIÈGE with authority from the TRIBUNAL DE GRANDE INSTANCE who investigates a criminal case and assembles evidence, including the possibility of interviewing any suspect and witnesses, reconstructing the scene of the crime. The *Juge d'instruction* can keep a suspect in prison for up to six months in serious cases. The PROCUREUR DE LA

RÉPUBLIQUE can press the *Juge d'instruction* for more speed in proceeding with a case, but the *Juge* does not have to comply. On the basis of the investigations, the *Juge d'instruction* can send an accused to the appropriate court for trial, or declare that there is insufficient evidence. An alternative title for the *Juge d'instruction* is *Magistrat instructeur*.

JUILLET, LE 14 See: *FÊTE NATIONALE*

JUIN, LE 18
In 1940, this was the date on which DE GAULLE made his broadcast from London, calling for those who wanted a free France to rally to him. It was later used as a symbol of his claimed legitimacy to power, in titles such as '*L'Homme du 18 juin*'. Annual commemorations of this date take place in Paris.

JURA
A DÉPARTEMENT of the FRANCHE-COMTÉ region, named after the mountain range which covers much of its area. The population was 248,759 in 1990, which continues the gradual increase since a low of 216,000 immediately after the Second World War. Lons-le-Saunier (AGGLOMÉRATION, 25,189) is the CHEF-LIEU, and the other sizeable urban areas are Champagnole (10,208); Dole, (31,904); and Saint-Claude (13,292).

The industry is small-scale and based on the traditional strengths of optical equipment at Morez, pipe-making (at Saint-Claude), clockmaking, diamond cutting and those connected with the local natural resources – timber, food industry (especially dairy), thermal treatments and wines.

Tourism focuses in particular on the *Département's* sporting facilities – lakes, mountains and plateaux (canoeing, sailing, skiing, flying), as well as its forests and historic sites.

François MITTERRAND'S majority of the vote in 1981 rose slightly in 1988. The Centre Right's control of the CONSEIL GÉNÉRAL was confirmed in the 1992 ÉLECTIONS CANTONALES.

Code départemental: 39

JURÉ
With certain exceptions because of profession, criminal record, or previous service as a juror, any French person between the

age of 23 and 70 who is registered as a voter and is literate in French, can be called to serve on a JURY.

Every year, the MAIRE of each COMMUNE randomly selects names in public from the electoral list after the PRÉFET has issued an ARRÊT in April, which fixes the number of names to be drawn from each *commune* (on the basis of one juror per 1300 inhabitants). The list of names contains three times this number, and is then subject to further selection by a committee of legal personnel and representatives of the CONSEIL GÉNÉRAL, who exclude those who do not qualify. A minimum of 400 *jurés* appear on each DÉPARTEMENT's *Liste annuelle*, with 100 reserves.

At least 30 days before the court sits, the *Président* of the TRIBUNAL DE GRANDE INSTANCE selects at random 35 *jurés* and 10 substitutes, for the *Liste de session*.

A *juré* who does not attend when called, without good reason, is fined an AMENDE.

JURY
In a COUR D'ASSISES, nine JURÉS are called for each criminal case from the 35 on the *Liste de session*. The prosecution may object to four, and the defence to five. Deliberations are secret, and breaching confidentiality can lead to a fine of 10,000 francs and a suspended prison sentence of a month.

JVS See: *JEUNES VOYAGEURS SERVICE*

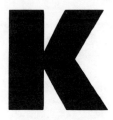

KHÂGNE See: *HYPOKHÂGNE*

KILOMÈTRE ZÉRO
The point outside Notre-Dame cathedral in Paris, from which all distances to other towns and villages are measured.

KLÉBER
A rubber tyre manufacturer with factories in Toul and Troyes. The *Guide Kléber*, a tourist guide was published annually from 1954 to 1982.

KOUCHNER, BERNARD (1939–)
A doctor, the founder of MÉDECINS DU MONDE, who became SECRÉTAIRE D'ÉTAT with the responsibility for humanitarian aid in the 1991 government of Édith CRESSON, and was appointed MINISTRE *de la santé et de l'action humanitaire* in 1992 by Pierre BÉRÉGOVOY. Kouchner was named 'Man of the Year' in 1991 by *Le* POINT.

KRACH
The collapse in investor confidence which provokes an uncontrolled fall in share prices. The last *krach* to affect France was the international crash of October 1987.

KRIVINE, ALAIN (1941–)
A militant Trotskyist who formed a series of left-wing groups in the 1960s and 1970s, and stood in the ÉLECTIONS PRÉSIDENTIELLES of 1969 and 1974, obtaining respectively 2.33 per cent and 2.32 per cent of the first round voting. He remains active as a member of the extreme Left.

LABEL NATIONAL

The names of certain consumer products are controlled by law in order to protect consumers and producers against inauthentic sources. Poultry and cheeses are given a *label national* which determines that their place of origin and quality control are recognised by law. See also: APPELLATION D'ORIGINE CONTRÔLÉE; LABEL RÉGIONAL; NORMES FRANÇAISES

LABEL RÉGIONAL

A certification with legal status guaranteeing the place of origin and the quality of a consumer product. See also: APPELLATION D'ORIGINE CONTRÔLÉE; LABEL NATIONAL; NORMES FRANÇAISES

LACAN, JACQUES (1901–1981)

An influential psychoanalyst who, after mixing in surrealist circles, and developing an interest in linguistics and structuralism, called for a return to the teachings of Freud. In his turn, Lacan became something of a guru and cult figure.

LAFFONT, ROBERT (1916–)

A publisher operating through the traditional bookshop trade and by mail order, with a strong list of reference and general interest titles.

LAGARDE ET MICHARD

In the 1960s the six-volume anthology of extracts from French literature, compiled by André Lagarde and Laurent Michard, sold 100,000 copies annually. The sales continue at about half this rate. The anthology is widely used in secondary schools.

LAGRANGE, LÉO See: *LÉO-LAGRANGE*

LAGUILLER, ARLETTE (1940–)

A militant left-wing politician, a member of LUTTE OUVRIÈRE, who was a candidate in the ÉLECTIONS PRÉSIDENTIELLES in 1974, 1981 and 1988. Her highest proportion of the votes cast was in 1981, when she obtained 2.3 per cent of the vote in the first round.

LAJOINIE, ANDRÉ (1929–   )

A Communist politician, who rose through the ranks of the PARTI COMMUNISTE FRANÇAIS to become its agriculture expert, and was elected DÉPUTÉ for Gannat (ALLIER) in 1978. In 1981, he began a long stint as *Président* of the Communist group in the ASSEMBLÉE NATIONALE, and was the party's official candidate in the 1988 ÉLECTION PRÉSIDENTIELLE, receiving 6.75 per cent of the vote in the first round.

LALONDE, BRICE (1946–   )

A journalist and environmentalist, a prominent figure among the VERTS who entered politics who became a DÉPUTÉ in 1976, stood as a candidate in the ÉLECTION PRÉSIDENTIELLE in 1981 (receiving 3.87 per cent of the vote in the first round), and was appointed SECRÉTAIRE D'ÉTAT *à l'environnement* in 1988, being promoted to *Ministre* by Édith CRESSON in 1991. In 1989, Lalonde broke away from the *Verts*, establishing GÉNÉRATION ÉCOLOGIE.

LAMOUREUX See: *CONCERTS LAMOUREUX*

LANDES

A coastal DÉPARTEMENT in the AQUITAINE region, characterised by the moorland from which it derives its name. The 1990 population was 311,458 (1990) and the CHEF-LIEU is Mont-de-Marsan (35,403). The other sizeable urban area is Dax (35,701).

The natural resources (oil, undergound gas reserves and rock salt) and those exploited by tourism (pine forests, beaches and inland lakes) tend to dominate the local economy. There is a also a considerable military presence, aeronautic engineering and paper-making in the Landes.

Maize, cattle and poultry are principal agricultural products. Specialities are duck liver pâté, asparagus, honey, LABEL NATIONAL *Poulet jaune* and *Armagnac liqueur*.

The Landes is an area which traditionally supports the political Left, and François MITTERRAND obtained comfortable majorities in 1981 and 1988. The Left's absolute majority in the CONSEIL GÉNÉRAL, whose *Président* is Henri EMMANUELLI, was maintained in the 1992 ÉLECTIONS CANTONALES.

Code départemental: 40

LANG, JACK (1939–   )
A lawyer and theatre director who maintained careers in both activities, becoming a member of the CONSEIL DE PARIS in 1977. He was *Ministre de la* CULTURE from 1981 to 1986, and was reappointed in 1988 with extra responsibilities for the BICENTENAIRE and for executing the work entailed in the GRANDS PROJETS of François MITTERRAND. In 1992, as well as retaining these responsibilities, he was appointed MINISTRE D'ÉTAT *de l'*ÉDUCATION NATIONALE. His personal popularity has remained high, regardless of the fortunes of the government. He is also MAIRE of Blois (LOIR-ET-CHER).

LANG, LOI
Introduced in 1982 by Jack LANG, this law makes it illegal to sell a book club edition of a book for less than the price of the original publisher's edition for nine months.

LANGUEDOC-ROUSSILLON
An administrative RÉGION in the south of France, comprising the DÉPARTEMENTS of AUDE, GARD, HÉRAULT, LOZÈRE and PYRÉNÉES-ORIENTALES. The regional capital is Montpellier (Hérault). Important in the Roman period and before, its influence waned as the centre of power moved to Paris, increasingly so after the end of the Middle Ages. The name Languedoc comes from the OCCITAN language, and Roussillon stems from the ancient capital of Rucino, near Perpignan (Pyrénées-Orientales).

Just over two million live in this predominantly rural region, which has been a centre for redevelopment over the period of the CINQUIÈME RÉPUBLIQUE. The Languedoc-Roussillon has received grants to revive its wine-dominated agriculture with modern methods and improved quality production, its tourism with the development of new resorts, and its industrial base with high-technology innovation. One of the effects of such directed planning has been to reverse the population drift, so that young households are moving into the area in search of work. It still provides only one-tenth of the contribution of the ÎLE-DE-FRANCE towards the gross national product, and is well below the national average in income per household.

The CONSEIL RÉGIONAL is balanced between Right and Left wing, and there is a reduction of the traditional power of the Left in the region. In the 1992 ÉLECTIONS RÉGIONALES, the FRONT NATIONAL made important gains, in some areas pushing the PARTI SOCIALISTE into third place, and the VERTS and GÉNÉRATION ÉCOLOGIE made smaller but significant progress.

LANGUES-O See: *INSTITUT NATIONAL DE LANGUES ET CIVILISATIONS ORIENTALES*

LAROUSSE
A large publishing enterprise, founded by Pierre Larousse (1817–1895) who made his reputation through dictionaries and encyclopedias. See also: JE SÈME À TOUT VENT

LAURENT, JACQUES (1919–)
A writer publishing popular fiction under the pseudonym of Cécil Saint-Laurent (e.g. *Caroline chérie*, a low-brow bestseller), historical novels using another pseudonym, Albéric Varenne, and more serious works, including a GONCOURT prize-winner, *Les Bêtises* (1971), essays, including a polemic against SARTRE, *Paul et Jean-Paul*, as well as journalism under his own name.

LAUTERBOURG
This COMMUNE in the DÉPARTEMENT of the BAS-RHIN, on the border with Germany, is the most easterly in France.

LA VILLETTE See: *CENTRE NATIONAL DES INDUSTRIES ET DES TECHNIQUES*

LECANUET, JEAN (1920–)
A centrist politician who was a *Directeur de* CABINET in a number of ministries in the QUATRIÈME RÉPUBLIQUE before becoming a DÉPUTÉ for the SEINE-MARITIME in 1951, serving two terms in this

role and as SÉNATEUR for the same DÉPARTEMENT. Between 1963 and 1965 he was *Président* of the MOUVEMENT RÉPUBLICAIN POPULAIRE and was a candidate in the ÉLECTION PRÉSIDENTIELLE in 1965, coming third with 15.57 per cent of the votes cast. He founded the *Centre démocrate* (later the CENTRE DES DÉMOCRATES SOCIAUX) on the basis of this support, and combined forces with Jean-Jacques SERVAN-SCHREIBER in 1973 in the umbrella organisation of the *Mouvement réformateur*. He held ministerial office under GISCARD D'ESTAING, notably as GARDE DES SCEAUX in 1974 and 1975, and for 10 years (1978–1988) presided over the UNION POUR LA DÉMOCRATIE FRANÇAISE. He has maintained his local power base (MAIRE of Rouen since 1968) and has been active in the European Parliament since 1984.

LECLERC, ÉDOUARD (1926–   )
The founder of the Leclerc chain of retail businesses. His first shop was opened in 1949, and he has continued to expand the business on unusual principles: the shops (hypermarkets, supermarkets, specialist outlets, travel agencies and petrol stations) work on a limited margin, with 25 per cent of pre-tax profits paid to the staff. Leclerc provides a centralised purchasing organisation, but the shops are not obliged to use it. The chain is now expanding into the USA.

LE CLÉZIO, JEAN-MARIE (1940–   )
A novelist who found success early with his winning the PRIX RENAUDOT at the age of 23 with *Le Procès-Verbal*. Le Clézio has been hailed as representative of the post-war generation, and his novels are concerned with a rejection of urban values and the search for nature and nomadic freedom.

LEFÈBVRE, MARCEL (1905–1991)
The former Bishop of Tulle who, in contravention of episcopal and papal authority, established a traditionalist wing of the Catholic church in the 1970s, the *Fraternité sacerdotale de Saint-Pie-X*. His group is virulently anti-Communist, and asserts its right to traditional forms of liturgy, including a Latin mass. He was suspended from his priestly office in 1976, but continued to operate despite this ban.

LÉGION D'HONNEUR

The honours awarded by the State for meritorious achievement, founded by Napoléon in 1802. The PRÉSIDENT DE LA RÉPUBLIQUE is the *Grand Maître* of the order, and its organisation is the responsibility of the *Grand Chancelier* appointed by the *Grand Maître* from among the holders of the *Grand-Croix* for a period of six years. The grades of the *Légion d'honneur* are in descending order of seniority: *Grand-Croix*, *Grand Officier*, *Commandeur*, *Officier*, *Chevalier*. Apart from the *Président de la République* who automatically becomes *Grand Maître*, no person can enter a grade before a period on a lower grade. There is a minimum period of 20 years public service before appointment as a *Chevalier* can be given and other, shorter, qualifying periods before promotion is possible. All members of the order have to propose themselves for the award.

Légionnaires receive an annual token payment, free of tax. A member of the order can be suspended or disqualified if he or she commits a criminal offence or otherwise acts dishonourably. This applies to one or two people per year.

The full dress insignia is a cross with a red ribbon. On less formal occasions, *légionnaires* may wear a small red ribbon in the left lapel.

Until 1962, it was possible for a COMMUNE to be awarded the *Légion d'honneur*, and 64 towns hold the honour as a recognition of their suffering in wartime.

LÉGION ÉTRANGÈRE

The legendary foreign legion, part of the French infantry forces, founded in 1831. Since the Second World War the *Légion étrangère* has taken part in campaigns in Indo-China in the 1950s, and in ALGÉRIE from 1954 to 1962, in Tchad, Zaïre and as part of the UN peace-keeping force in Lebanon.

It numbers about 8,500 men, 60 per cent of whom are not of French nationality. It is estimated that 80 per cent of its members join because of some social or family difficulty. Its disciplinary record is better than the average French army unit. A minimum service term is five years, after six months' probation. It is possible for the *légionnaire* to take an assumed name, but if he does so, he is not permitted to marry, to buy property or a vehicle, or to enact any deed which normally requires a declaration of identity. See also: BOUDIN; CROIX DE GUERRE

LÉGION VIOLETTE See: *ORDRE DES PALMES ACADÉMIQUES*

LÉGISLATIVES See: *ÉLECTIONS LÉGISLATIVES*

LE HAVRE (UNIVERSITÉ)
A relatively small university institution, with faculties of economics, sciences and technology and with 4,000 students.

LEIRIS, MICHEL (1901–1990)
A translator and surrealist poet who continued to publish into his old age. He is famous for his autobiography, *L'Âge d'homme*.

LELOUCH, CLAUDE (1937–)
A popular film director whose films tend to reflect a sentimental and glossy view of life. Among his best known are *Un homme et une femme* (1965) and *Les uns et les autres* (1981).

LÉO-LAGRANGE, FÉDÉRATION
An organisation, named after the first SECRÉTAIRE D'ÉTAT for sports and leisure who held office in 1936, which aims to provide possibilities for community involvement in leisure activities. It runs a number of residential centres for young people.

LÉOTARD, FRANÇOIS (1942–)
An ÉNARQUE who after service as a SOUS-PRÉFET entered centrist politics as MAIRE of Fréjus (VAR) in 1977 and as DÉPUTÉ for the Var in 1978. In 1982 he became *Secrétaire général* of the PARTI RÉPUBLICAIN, and in the following year *Président* of the UNION POUR LA DÉMOCRATIE FRANÇAISE. From 1986 to 1988 he was *Ministre de la* CULTURE.

LEP See: *LIVRET D'ÉPARGNE POPULAIRE; LYCÉE*

LE PEN, JEAN-MARIE (1928–)
A lawyer who was active in student politics in Paris in 1949–1951, became an army officer, serving as a parachutist in Indo-

China, and entered national politics as a DÉPUTÉ in 1956. He temporarily joined the LÉGION ÉTRANGÈRE in ALGÉRIE, resigning his parliamentary seat to do so. In 1963 he took a post as director of a public relations firm, and in 1972 founded the FRONT NATIONAL. He was a candidate in the ÉLECTIONS PRÉSIDENTIELLES in 1974, gaining less than 1 per cent of the vote, and in 1988, with 14.39 per cent. As well as his parliamentary seat, he has taken other elected offices, being a member of the CONSEIL DE PARIS from 1983 and the European Parliament from 1984. In the ÉLECTIONS RÉGIONALES of 1992, he led the *Front national* list in the BOUCHES-DU-RHÔNE, but failed in his attempt to become the *Président* of the CONSEIL RÉGIONAL in PROVENCE-ALPES-CÔTE-D'AZUR.

LEPÉNISTE
A supporter of Jean-Marie LE PEN.

LE ROY-LADURIE, EMMANUEL (1929–   )
An historian who has achieved an international reputation beyond the confines of academic history, in which he specialises in the feudal period, largely for his work *Montaillou, village occitan de 1294 à 1324*.

LEROY-MERLIN
A medium-sized chain of DIY centres which includes among its number the centre with the largest sales area, at Noeux-les-Mines (PAS-DE-CALAIS).

LES 3 SUISSES
A mail-order business which sells goods through a catalogue. It was founded in 1932, and now has 10 million names and addresses on its files.

LÉVI-STRAUSS, CLAUDE (1908–   )
An influential philosopher and anthropologist, who applied the approach of structuralism to his ethnographic work, laying the foundations of structuralism in *Anthropologie structurale* (1958). His most famous work is perhaps *Tristes tropiques* (1955).

LÉVY, BERNARD-HENRI (1948–   )
One of the group of '*nouveaux philosophes*', notable for his

defence of personal liberty and his frequent appearances in the media, where he is known as 'B-HL'. A well-known work is the anti-totalitarian *La Barbarie à visage humain*. In 1991, Lévy published *Les Aventures de la liberté*, a critical view of French fellow-travellers.

LIBÉRATION

A radical daily newspaper, published in Paris, founded in 1973. From modest beginnings, it has gradually built up a circulation of almost 200,000. Since 1988, it has run a Lyon edition as well.

LIBÉRATION CONDITIONNELLE

For those serving prison sentences of less than three years, a JUGE DE L'APPLICATION DES PEINES can permit *Libération conditionnelle* after half the sentence is served, or after two-thirds for a second offence. In the case of longer sentences, the GARDE DES SCEAUX decides on the advice of a local committee on which the *Juge de l'application des peines sits*. Those serving life sentences must serve 15 years before early release can be considered. If the conditions of release are not observed (e.g. regular reporting to the police, compensation payments to victims), the offender can be recalled to prison.

LIBERTÉ D'ALLER ET VENIR

A citizen has the right of access to all public highways, footpaths, beaches, etc. which are held in public ownership and are not subject to specific restrictions.

There are certain rights of access over private property, e.g. in order to carry out repairs, for access to water and fishing rights, and for skiing and climbing.

One has the right to choose one's DOMICILE, except for minors, who must live with their parents, certain officials who have to live within specific COMMUNES, those who are subject to temporary legal arrangements (e.g. after release from DÉTENTION PROVISOIRE, or under LIBÉRATION CONDITIONNELLE).

Vehicle-owners, those liable for SERVICE NATIONAL, and foreigners must notify change of address to the appropriate body. There is no obligation on others to do the same.

LIBERTÉ DE LA PRESSE

The 1881 law on the liberty of the press and the CONSTITUTION guarantee freedom of publication without censorship. A newspaper must carry details of its editor, publisher and printer, and announcements of any judgements against it in tribunals. It must also print any replies from those who claim it has made inaccurate statements about them. Since 1986 the name of the proprietor must also be shown. There is a limit of permitted foreign investment in a newspaper, and a prohibition on financial support from foreign governments. It is illegal to hold control over more than 30 per cent of the national daily press.

LIBERTÉS D'ENTREPRISE See: *AUROUX, LOI*

LICENCE
A higher education diploma awarded after one year's successful study subsequent to the award of a DIPLÔME D'ÉTUDES UNIVERSITAIRES GÉNÉRALES. A *licence* marks the end of the first part of the *Deuxième cycle* of university studies. In 1989, 64,529 *licences* were awarded. See also: MAÎTRISE

LICENCIEMENT
Dismissal from employment must have proper cause, be explained to the employee and COMITÉ D'ENTREPRISE in writing, and follow a strict set of formalities. Redundancy because of the financial state of the enterprise is called *Licenciement économique*. Unless guilty of serious misdemeanour, the person made redundant is entitled to at least one-tenth of a month's salary for each year worked, and if a CONVENTION COLLECTIVE is in operation, usually two months' salary for each year worked.

LIGUE COMMUNISTE RÉVOLUTIONNAIRE
Founded in 1938 by followers of Trotsky, this remains a vocal left-wing organisation, with about 2,500 members. See also: KRIVINE, ALAIN

LIGUE NATIONALE CONTRE LE CANCER
A charitable organisation, founded in 1918, registered as *d'*UTILITÉ PUBLIQUE in 1920, and taking its '*nationale*' title in 1989 when it distributed 172 million francs principally for research and detection.

LIGUE URBAINE ET RURALE
A voluntary organisation, recognised as *d'*UTILITÉ PUBLIQUE since

1970, which acts to protect the countryside and buildings against thoughtless developments instigated by the ADMINISTRATION.

LILLE, UNIVERSITÉ DE

There are three university institutions in Lille, with 56,000 students between them. *Lille I* is officially known as the *Université des sciences et techniques de Lille-Flandres-Artois*, is situated at VILLENEUVE-D'ASCQ (NORD), and has faculties of economics, social sciences, pure, biological, natural and agricultural sciences. *Lille II* (*Université du droit et de la santé*), specialises in medicine, pharmacy, management and law, physical education and sport. *Lille III* is the *Université* Charles-DE-GAULLE.

LIMOGES, UNIVERSITÉ DE

Limoges has a university with 11,000 students, with faculties in medicine, pharmacy, law, economics, humanities, science and arts.

LIMOUSIN

An administrative RÉGION in south central France, comprising the DÉPARTEMENTS of CORRÈZE, CREUSE and HAUTE-VIENNE. The regional capital is Limoges. Much of the region is upland territory, due to its position in the north of the Massif central.

The 1990 population was 722,791, and apart from a small rise in the 1960s and 1970s, there has been a steady reduction in population this century. It is the mainland region with the smallest population, and the lowest contribution to the gross national product, and its mainly agricultural character has meant that it has suffered particularly from the EXODE RURAL.

The Left just held control of the CONSEIL RÉGIONAL in 1992 with the support of the three ecologist members (one GÉNÉRATION ÉCOLOGIE and two VERTS).

LION See: *CODEC*

LIP

A watchmaking firm in Besançon (DOUBS) which was threatened with closure by its Swiss owners in 1973. The workforce refused to accept this decision, took over the business and continued to operate, although later changing to the manufacture of micro-components. The venture was seen as a symbol of workers versus capital, but the operation failed to adapt to changing market conditions which eventually forced its liquidation in 1990. See also: MANUFRANCE; SOCIÉTÉ CO-OPÉRATIVE DE PRODUCTION

LISTE BLOQUÉE
The situation when as part of the SCRUTIN DE LISTE MAJORITAIRE system of voting, it is impossible to cross out any names without the ballot paper becoming invalid.

LISTE ÉLECTORALE
The official list of voters of all those entitled to vote in an ÉLECTION, revised annually by the MAIRIE. Registration is compulsory, and requires proof of identity.

LISTE PANACHÉE
A ballot paper on which a voter can remove names or add those of people who have not declared themselves as candidates.

LIVRE DE POCHE
A book imprint specialising in paperback editions of works that have otherwise appeared in another publisher's edition, or of original non-fiction works. The *Livre de poche* appears in a standard page size, and is the largest single series of pocket-sized paperbacks in France. The term is also used to denote any small paperback.

LIVRET A
A savings account held with a CAISSE D'ÉPARGNE, with a minimum deposit of 10 francs, and a maximum holding of 90,000 francs. It is not permissible for one person to have a *Livret A* account and a *Livret bleu* account with a CRÉDIT MUTUEL. Interest is paid fortnightly at a fixed rate, without deduction of tax, and withdrawals can be made at any *Caisse d'épargne* or post office. The *Livret A* and *Livret bleu* accounts are the most popular non-cheque savings accounts. See also: LIVRET B; LIVRET D'ÉPARGNE POPULAIRE

LIVRET B

A savings account similar to a LIVRET A, but with no maximum holding. The interest rate is fixed, but interest is taxed before payment to the account holder.

LIVRET BLEU See: *LIVRET A*

LIVRET DE FAMILLE

A document provided by the MAIRIE to a couple who are married there, to a single mother when she has her first child, to unmarried parents when they jointly declare their parenthood of a child, or to an adoptive parent. It contains the names of children and their dates and places of birth.

It is used as a convenient form of proof of family links, and has to be produced in order to qualify for certain benefits and reductions. See also: DÉCLARATION DE RECONNAISSANCE D'ENFANT NATUREL

LIVRET D'ÉPARGNE See: *LIVRET A; LIVRET B; LIVRET D'ÉPARGNE-ENTREPRISE; LIVRET D'ÉPARGNE POPULAIRE*

LIVRET D'ÉPARGNE-ENTREPRISE

A fixed-interest tax-free savings account specifically designed to provide investment for one's own business enterprise, available through a bank, a CAISSE D'ÉPARGNE or a MUTUELLE organisation. A minimum amount of 5,000 francs starts the account which must then receive regular further payments of at least 3,600 francs for a period of between two and five years. The maximum holding is 200,000 francs. A fixed interest loan is then available to the account holder to aid the establishment of the enterprise. Only one such account can be held in a tax-paying household.

LIVRET D'ÉPARGNE POPULAIRE (LEP)

A tax-free savings account available to low tax payers, with a minimum first investment of 200 francs, and a maximum holding of 30,000 francs. A LEP can be arranged through a bank, a CAISSE D'ÉPARGNE or a post office, with proof of a low liability to IMPÔT. Interest is earned annually with a bonus for sums left in for more than six months. The rate of interest is at one percentage point higher than a LIVRET A.

LOCATION See: *BAIL; LOGEMENT SOCIAL; LOI MÉHAIGNERIE; LOI MERMAZ*

LOGEMENT SOCIAL
The general term given to publicly-subsidised housing such as HABITATIONS À LOYER MODÉRÉ, IMMEUBLES À LOYER MOYEN, and those covered by the PROGRAMME À LOYER RÉDUIT.

LOI AUROUX See: *AUROUX, LOI*

LOI BONNET See: *IMMIGRATION*

LOI CONSTITUTIONNELLE
Each article of the CONSTITUTION has the status of a *Loi constitutionnelle*, as does any legislative measure which amends or replaces it.

LOI DE 1948
Unusually for modern laws for not being named after the Minister who introduced it, this legislation dating from September 1948 reformed the law concerning the fixing of rentals, and allowed protection for those on low income against unreasonable rises in rent. See also: LOI MÉHAIGNERIE; LOI MERMAZ

LOI DEBRÉ
In 1959, Michel DEBRÉ, then PREMIER MINISTRE, introduced legislation which allowed private schools to receive State subsidies.

LOI DE PROGRAMME
Legislation which is based on plans for the economy.

LOI D'ORIENTATION DE L'ENSEIGNEMENT SUPÉRIEUR See: *LOI FAURE; LOI SAVARY*

LOI FAURE
In 1968, when Edgar FAURE was *Ministre de l'*ÉDUCATION NATIONALE, he made a major reform of higher education, provoked by the student disturbances of that year. The *Loi*

d'orientation de l'enseignement supérieur gave administrative, academic and financial autonomy to higher education institutions. Universities were split into UNITÉS D'ENSEIGNEMENT ET DE RECHERCHE, given elected governing bodies, and allowed to develop their own courses and assessment structures.

LOI HABY See: *HABY, LOI*

LOI LANG See: *LANG, LOI*

LOI MÉHAIGNERIE
The law introduced by Pierre MÉHAIGNERIE in 1986 provides that a cohabiting partner has the right to retain tenancy of rented property after the departure of the named tenant.

LOI MERMAZ
The 1989 law governing the private sector of rented unfurnished accommodation.

LOI ORDINAIRE
Any law passed through the full parliamentary procedure which is not classed as a LOI CONSTITUTIONNELLE or LOI ORGANIQUE.
See also: PROJET DE LOI; PROPOSITION DE LOI

LOI ORGANIQUE
Legislation which gives a precise form to articles of the CONSTITUTION, for example in fixing the number of seats in the ASSEMBLÉE NATIONALE. A *Loi organique* must be submitted to the CONSEIL CONSTITUTIONNEL. No *Loi organique* can be passed without an absolute majority in the *Assemblée nationale*.

LOI QUILLIOT
A measure introduced in 1982 by Roger Quilliot controlling the rents of unfurnished property in the private sector, and replaced by the LOI MÉHAIGNERIE and LOI MERMAZ.

LOI ROYER
A law passed in 1973 (amended in 1987) to restrain the uncontrolled development of out-of-town hypermarkets. As well as establishing for each DÉPARTEMENT a COMMISSION DÉPARTEMENTALE D'URBANISME COMMERCIAL, the *Loi Royer* allowed the local CHAMBRE DE COMMERCE ET DE L'INDUSTRIE to

participate in local commercial planning schemes and to buy small commercial premises in order to promote the advantages of smaller traders.

LOI SAVARY
An education law dating from 1984 which introduced the notion of selection into procedures for entry into university, and into different subsequent stages of study. See also: LOI FAURE

LOI SUR L'ENSEIGNEMENT SUPÉRIEUR See: *LOI SAVARY*

LOIRE
A DÉPARTEMENT of the RHÔNE-ALPES region, named after the Loire river. The population of the Loire was 746,288 in 1990, and the AGGLOMÉRATION of its CHEF-LIEU, Saint-Étienne, was home for 313,338 of these, largely dependent on an industrial economy of textiles, steel, mechanical engineering and electronics. Other urban areas are Montbrison (16,455); Roanne (77,160), especially important for knitwear; Saint-Chamond (81,795); and Saint-Just-Saint-Rambert (43,500). Formerly the coal industry was a major part of the local economy. There are uranium deposits near Saint-Étienne.

Of relatively minor importance is the agricultural sector which is mainly concerned with livestock.

A slight majority for François MITTERRAND in 1981 was retained in 1988. The parliamentary representatives reflect a wide range of political groupings. The CONSEIL GÉNÉRAL is under the control of the Centre Right.

Code départemental: 42

LOIRE-ATLANTIQUE
A DÉPARTEMENT of the PAYS DE LA LOIRE region, situated at the estuary of the River Loire. The Loire-Atlantique has 1,052,109 inhabitants, 492,212 of them living in the Nantes AGGLOMÉRATION. Nantes is a port with major shipbuilding and aeronautical construction, chemicals, rubber, metallurgy, engineering, electronics and food industries. The other centres of population are Châteaubriant (12, 782) and the Saint-Nazaire urban area (131, 511), with a range of heavy industry similar

to that of Nantes as well as terminals for oil and gas pipelines. Because of this reliance on traditional industries, the *Département* was badly hit by unemployment in the 1980s.

Tourism is an important source of economic activity, especially in a range of seaside resorts.

Agriculturally, vineyards, dairy cattle (the *Port-Salut* cheese comes from here), pigs and poultry dominate the scene. Saint-Nazaire has a notable fishing industry.

The area is rather conservative in its political outlook, Saint-Nazaire tending to support the Left and Nantes the Centre. In the ÉLECTIONS PRÉSIDENTIELLES of 1981 and 1988, François MITTERRAND maintained his majority, although the DÉPUTÉS and SÉNATEURS are drawn from a broad range of party groupings. The Centre Right retained control of the CONSEIL GÉNÉRAL in 1992, although there was a small increase in the number of seats held by the PARTI SOCIALISTE.

Code départemental: 44

LOIRET

A DÉPARTEMENT in the CENTRE region, named after the short waterway which flows into the Loire at Orléans, the CHEF-LIEU, home to 243,148 inhabitants. The population of the whole *Département* is 580,601. Orléans is a major railway junction, and has developed industries in food products, aeronautics, engineering, pharmaceuticals, cosmetics, etc., as well as having administrative headquarters of insurance companies at Chécy. The other urban area is the Montargis AGGLOMÉRATION (52,518). There is a nuclear power station at Dampierre on the right bank of the Loire.

Tourism is a significant contributor to the economy, with particular attractions being châteaux at Sully-sur-Loire and Beaugency, Orléans cathedral, a transport museum at Pithiviers and other specialist museums.

Agriculture is relatively less important, but there are crops of maize and some market gardening.

The Loiret favours the political Right, and its parliamentary representatives are mainly from the Right and Centre. In 1981 it voted narrowly for GISCARD D'ESTAING in the ÉLECTION

PRÉSIDENTIELLE, but in 1988 changed its allegiance to François MITTERRAND, who took 51.06 per cent of the vote. The 1992 ÉLECTIONS CANTONALES hardly changed the composition of the Centre Right controlled CONSEIL GÉNÉRAL.

Code départemental: 45

LOIR-ET-CHER

A DÉPARTEMENT of the CENTRE region, with a population of 305,925, named after the two rivers which flow through it, later flowing into the Sarthe and Loire respectively. The CHEF-LIEU is Blois (AGGLOMÉRATION 65,131) with mixed light industry, but primarily known as a tourist centre because of its château and cathedral. The other two urban areas of any size are Romorantin-Lanthenay (17,865), with textiles, printing and precision engineering industries, and Vendôme (22,238) with printing, glove-making and mixed engineering. There is a nuclear power station at Saint-Laurent-des-Eaux on the left bank of the Loire. In the area of Chémery and Soings-en-Sologne, there is major underground gas storage, as part of the national supply network.

The Loir-et-Cher has a large proportion of the *Châteaux de la Loire*, including Blois, Chambord, Cheverny and Vendôme, and is thus a popular tourist destination.

Agricultural activity is dominated by wheat, barley, maize, vineyards and market gardening. It is the leading *département* for asparagus production. There is considerable forestry activity in the Sologne area.

A very narrow majority for François MITTERRAND in the 1981 ÉLECTION PRÉSIDENTIELLE was increased to 54.95 per cent of the vote in 1988. The parliamentary representatives are drawn from the Left and Centre parties. Against the national trend, the PARTI SOCIALISTE made significant gains here in the 1992 ÉLECTIONS CANTONALES, probably because of the popularity of Jack LANG, the MAIRE of Blois, although the Centre Right retained control of the CONSEIL GÉNÉRAL.

Code départemental: 41

LONGCHAMP See: *AUTEUIL; BOIS DE BOULOGNE; GRAND PRIX DE PARIS*

LORRAINE

An administrative RÉGION in the north-east of France, comprising the DÉPARTEMENTS of MEURTHE-ET-MOSELLE, MEUSE, MOSELLE and VOSGES, with frontiers with Belgium, Germany and Luxembourg. The overall population of Lorraine in 1990 was 2.3 million, a figure in gradual decline. Metz (MOSELLE) is the regional capital. The south of the region is mainly agricultural in character, with specialist industrial activity (glassmaking, mineral water, papermaking, etc.). The north is more dependent on traditional heavy industry, and has suffered considerably as the coal and steel industries have been in decline.

Connections with the bordering countries are intricate, and there is much frontier-crossing for employment and other activities. The history of Lorraine has demonstrated the long-term fortunes of French and German power. As well as French, there are Germanic dialects spoken by a small proportion of the population.

The European Community has provided considerable support for the regional economy, in its attempts towards restructuring. The average household income is slightly above the national average.

In the 1992 ÉLECTIONS RÉGIONALES, the PARTI SOCIALISTE lost 11 out of 21 seats, taken by the FRONT NATIONAL and GÉNÉRATION ÉCOLOGIE, and the Centre Right was forced to consider pacts with either of these groups in order to retain effective control of the CONSEIL RÉGIONAL. See also: FRONTALIERS

LOT

A largely rural DÉPARTEMENT in the MIDI-PYRÉNÉES region, named after the principal river which passes through it, a tributary of the Garonne. The Lot has a population of 155,813. The CHEF-LIEU is Cahors (population, 19,735) and the second town is Figeac (9,549). The towns have light industry, but are mainly market centres for the surrounding rural areas.

Tourism is developing as an economic activity, based on prehistoric sites, caves, and medieval villages such as Rocamadour, and castles.

Production of tobacco, wines, dairy products, fruit, truffles, nuts, *foie gras* and some cereals typifies the agriculture of the *Département*. Nevertheless, there is still a drift from the land.

Politically, the Lot traditionally supports the Left, and this is reflected in ÉLECTIONS PRÉSIDENTIELLES and LÉGISLATIVES. A coalition of the PARTI SOCIALISTE and the MOUVEMENT DES RADICAUX DE GAUCHE controls the CONSEIL GÉNÉRAL.

Code départemental: 46

LOTERIE NATIONALE

A weekly lottery which ran in its modern form from 1933 to 1990, with profits going to state finances. (Originally they went to provide aid for ANCIENS COMBATTANTS and victims of rural catastrophes, but the government added the takings to general income from 1945.) Tickets were on sale in 27,000 outlets including DÉBITS DE TABAC, street booths and newsagents, and were bought in graduated portions, the size of the purchase influencing the prize money which could be claimed. The stake ranged from 10 francs to 184 francs in 1989. The draws were held in public, and televised live in later years. Winnings were free of tax. See also: LOTO

LOT-ET-GARONNE

A DÉPARTEMENT of the AQUITAINE region, named after the two rivers which converge at Aiguillon, at the centre of the *Département*. The population is 305,988, of which 60,684 live in the urban area of Agen, the CHEF-LIEU, a major agricultural market centre, and with food industries, chemicals, footwear, textile and pharmaceuticals manufacture. The other urban areas of size are Fumel (13,689) – steel, chemicals, dairy industries; Marmande (23,439) – food industry, furniture, electrical engineering; and Villeneuve-sur-Lot (29,422) – another major market centre for agricultural products.

The Lot-et-Garonne has the highest *départemental* production of *haricots verts*, prunes, hazelnuts and the second for strawberries. Its tobacco production is also significant. Other products are grapes, wines, fruit and vegetables.

Tourists come because of its medieval remains, its Romanesque churches, its lakes and for oddities such as the 1,000 year-old elm tree at Cassignas.

François MITTERRAND gained comfortable majorities in the Lot-et-Garonne in both 1981 and 1988 ÉLECTIONS PRÉSIDENTIELLES, and the parliamentary representatives are drawn from Left and Centre. The Centre Right retained control of the CONSEIL GÉNÉRAL in the 1992 ÉLECTIONS CANTONALES.

Code départemental: 47

LOTO

A game of chance organised on a national scale since 1976, and with a majority holding by the State. There are two games weekly and various ways in which individuals can play on an occasional or subscription basis. There is a one in 57 chance of winning a small prize, and a one in 14 million possibility of winning the top prize. The highest prize on record is 119 million francs. See also: LOTERIE NATIONALE

LOUVRE

The former royal palace in the centre of Paris which is now the home of the *Musée du Louvre*, which has the largest collection of art and antiquities in France. A modernisation plan for the Grand Louvre was completed in 1989, including the *Pyramide du Louvre*, a glass pyramid designed by Ieoh Ming Pei, which leads to the underground entrance halls.

LOYER See: *ALLOCATION LOGEMENT; BAIL; LOGEMENT SOCIAL; LOI DE 1948; LOI MÉHAIGNERIE; LOI MERMAZ*

LOZÈRE

A rural DÉPARTEMENT in the LANGUEDOC-ROUSSILLON region, with a population of 72,814 in 1990, named after Mont-Lozère. The only urban area of any size is Mende, which has 11,286 inhabitants. Saint-Chély-d'Apcher (4,570) has a small ironworks.

The Lozère has the lowest density of population of all *départements*, and the number of inhabitants has continued to fall since a peak of twice the present numbers in the mid-nineteenth century. The rate of decrease has slowed since then, but is still significant. It also benefits from having the lowest recorded rate of crime.

Tourism is based on the *Parc national des Cévennes*, the *Gorges du Tarn*, skiing and medieval remains.

Agriculture is dominated by sheep-raising for cheese products, with some wine produced.

The political character of the Lozère is one of Centre and Right, with GISCARD D'ESTAING in 1981 and Jacques CHIRAC in 1988 receiving substantial majorities in the ÉLECTIONS PRÉSIDENTIELLES, and the two DÉPUTÉS and one SÉNATEUR reflecting the same allegiance. Curiously, a Communist candidate was elected in the ÉLECTIONS CANTONALES in 1992, the first in the *Département* for 16 years, despite the national swing to the Right, and in a CONSEIL GÉNÉRAL in which 21 of the 25 seats are held by the Centre Right.

Code départemental: 48

LUMIÈRE, LOUIS (GRAND PRIX DU CINÉMA FRANÇAIS)

An annual prize for a French film, awarded from 1934 to 1986, named after the younger of the two cinema pioneer brothers.

LUMIÈRE (UNIVERSITÉ)

The official name of the *Université de Lyon II*, which has 22,000 students specialising in social sciences and arts subjects.

LURÇAT, JEAN (1892–1966)

A tapestry artist whose work found great popularity. There are two museums which feature his work, at Angers (MAINE-ET-LOIRE) and Saint-Céré (LOT). His tapestries were woven at AUBUSSON.

LUSTIGER, JEAN-MARIE (1926–   )

Archbishop of Paris since 1981, and cardinal since 1983. A convert to Catholicism from Judaism at the age of 14. He has taken a more traditional stance than his predecessor, François MARTY, and this has helped neutralise to some extent the influence of Marcel LEFÈBVRE.

LUTTE OUVRIÈRE

A militant Trotskyist movement, founded in 1968, which is most active within large firms, but which also participates in party politics by putting up candidates at elections. See also: KRIVINE, ALAIN; LAGUILLER, ARLETTE

LVMH

A holding company with press interests (e.g. MARIE-CLAIRE) as well as its principal activity in luxury goods manufacture and sales, founded on the businesses of Louis VUITTON and *Moët et Hennessy*.

LYCÉE

A secondary school, providing full-time education in preparation for the BACCALAURÉAT. Formerly, a *lycée* selected its pupils at the age of 11, but now it is open to all students after their period in a COLLÈGE, at the age of 15.

Various alternative forms of *lycée* are exemplified below.

A *Lycée agricole* for instance provides courses to the BAC *professionnel* in agricultural sciences. A *Lycée d'enseignement professionnel*, or LEP, provides more specialist courses towards specific *Bac* options, and towards other less advanced vocational qualifications. A *Lycée polyvalent* will tend to have general and vocational courses available. A *Lycée d'enseignement technologique* (formerly '*technique*') specialises in technical courses, and usually does not provide routes to the more traditional *Bac* options. For all these versions in the State system, there are also equivalent private establishments.

In certain *lycées*, there are post-*Bac* courses, especially CLASSES PRÉPARATOIRES and courses leading to BREVET DE TECHNICIEN SUPÉRIEUR level.

The armed services maintain a *Lycée militaire* at La Flèche (SARTHE), familiarly known as the *Prytanée*, which trains future officer cadets. Entry is by CONCOURS. There are also *Lycées militaires* at Aix-en-Provence (BOUCHES-DU-RHÔNE), SAINT-CYR-L'ÉCOLE, a *Lycée naval* at Brest (FINISTÈRE), and two secondary establishments combining the functions of COLLÈGE and *lycée* at Autun (SAÔNE-ET-LOIRE) and the *École des pupilles de l'air* at Montbonnot (ISÈRE). See also: CLASSE DE PREMIÈRE; CLASSE DE SECONDE; CLASSE TERMINALE; INTERNAT

LYON, UNIVERSITÉ DE See: *BERNARD, CLAUDE; LUMIÈRE; MOULIN, JEAN*

LYONNAISE DES EAUX (CLE)

The *Compagnie lyonnaise des eaux* is a large private enterprise whose core activity is in water services.

M6

A private enterprise television channel, transmitting since 1986, and in 1990 reaching 75 per cent of the population. *M6* has a 7.6 per cent share of the audience. It is able to sell advertising space, and has to follow the same restrictions about films as the public sector channels. The principal shareholders are the controlling company of RADIO-TÉLÉVISION LUXEMBOURG and LYONNAISE DES EAUX, each holding 25 per cent of the capital, as well as major banks and finance companies.

MAGAZINE LITTÉRAIRE

A monthly journal of articles and criticism with a circulation of 55,000.

MAGHREB

The group of North African Islamic countries with a Mediterranean coast, and Mauritania, most of which were part of the French empire, and whose relationships with France stem from this connection and with issues concerning migration. See also: BEURS

MAGISTÈRE

A degree awarded after three years of study beyond the level of a DIPLÔME D'ÉTUDES UNIVERSITAIRES GÉNÉRALES or a DIPLÔME UNIVERSITAIRE DE TECHNOLOGIE. The course is at a high level and multi-disciplinary. The first *magistères* were awarded in 1985, and there have been fewer than 100 given each year. See also: MASTÈRE

MAGISTRAT

The general term given to a member of the judiciary or of the State prosecution service. The *Magistrat du parquet* consists of those who perform their task in court in a standing position, e.g. the PROCUREUR DE LA RÉPUBLIQUE, whereas the *Magistrat du siège* comprises the JUGES who give judgements while seated. A *Magistrat instructeur* is also called a JUGE D'INSTRUCTION. See also: CONSEIL SUPÉRIEUR DE LA MAGISTRATURE

MAI, LE PREMIER
A workers' day of demonstrations dating from 1890 and celebrating the demand for the eight-hour day as the norm. The demand was met by law in 1919. It has become traditional to wear a buttonhole of lily of the valley on 1st May, which was given the status of FÊTE LÉGALE in 1947.

MAI 1968
The events of May and June 1968 which combined student unrest, worker dissatisfaction, government uncertainty and a challenge to the status quo of the CINQUIÈME RÉPUBLIQUE, led directly to the RÉFÉRENDUM of 1969 and the resignation of DE GAULLE, as well as reforms in education and a move towards DÉCENTRALISATION. See also: LOI FAURE

MAIF See: *MUTUALITÉ*

MAILLOT JAUNE
The yellow jersey worn by the leading rider in the TOUR DE FRANCE.

MAINE, UNIVERSITÉ DU
The name of the university at Le Mans, with 7,000 students in science, humanities, law, economics and arts.

MAINE-ET-LOIRE
A DÉPARTEMENT of the PAYS DE LA LOIRE region, with a population of 705,869 in 1990, named after the short stretch of water which links the rivers Mayenne and Sarthe to the confluence with the Loire near Angers, the CHEF-LIEU.
   The population of the Angers AGGLOMÉRATION is 206,276, and its main industrial activity is in metallurgy, vehicle components, agricultural machinery, computers, electronics, pharmaceuticals, and *Cointreau* liqueurs. Other large urban areas are Cholet (55,524), a centre for textiles and clothing,

footwear, tyres and electronics, and Saumur (31,612), a centre for producing wine and conserves, precision instruments and a traditional military town. The *Département* is the leading producer of tiles.

The Loire châteaux ensure that tourism is a a major contributor to the local economy.

The agricultural scene in the Maine-et-Loire shows prosperous mixed farming. Principal crops are fruit and vegetables, tobacco and flowers, with a particularly strong place in the production of cultivated mushrooms. Livestock raised are cattle and pigs, with a substantial number of poultry.

The political picture is one of Centre Right strength. GISCARD D'ESTAING obtained a comfortable majority in the 1981 ÉLECTION PRÉSIDENTIELLE, Jacques CHIRAC a much narrower one in 1988. After the 1992 ÉLECTIONS CANTONALES, the Centre Right parties hold 16 of the 20 seats in the CONSEIL GÉNÉRAL.

Code départemental: 49

MAINE-MONTPARNASSE

A quarter of Paris surrounding the railway terminus for passenger services to and from the BRETAGNE and PAYS DE LA LOIRE regions. The Tour Maine-Montparnasse, the highest building in central Paris (210 metres, 58 floors), was opened in 1973.

MAINTIEN DANS LES LIEUX

The entitlement to occupy a rented property by a tenant, or in the case of the divorce, desertion or death of the tenant, by his or her dependants if they were resident in the property at the time. A landlord can repossess a property for his or her own, or family's, occupation, and can remove a tenant after six months' notice if the building is to be demolished, but only if replacement accommodation of at least as high a standard is provided. No person over 70 years old with an income less than 150 per cent of the SMIC can be evicted by a private landlord, without similar replacement accommodation being provided. See also: LOI DE 1948

MAIRE

An official elected by the CONSEIL MUNICIPAL from its members at its first meeting after its election. The *maire* is the chief officer of the COMMUNE, and is responsible for carrying out the decisions of the *Conseil municipal*, signing documents on its behalf. Among other responsibilities are those for the POLICE MUNICIPALE. As a representative of the State, the *maire* is responsible for ÉTAT CIVIL acts, including marriages, supervises local election arrangements, and is called on to participate in other legal or administrative procedures.

The *maire* is paid an annual allowance, depending on the population of the *commune*, ranging from 18,078 francs for the smallest village to 232,943 francs for the *Maire de Paris* (1990 figures).

In larger *communes*, the post of *maire* is occupied as a virtually full-time occupation, although most *maires* have other interests, either political or professional or both. It is often used as a local base for political influence at a national level. See also: ARRÊTÉ MUNICIPAL; CUMUL DES MANDATS; MAIRE-ADJOINT; MAIRIE

MAIRE-ADJOINT
In order to share the workload of a MAIRE, it is possible for a *maire-adjoint* to be elected by the CONSEIL MUNICIPAL. The *maire-adjoint* is given particular responsibilities and receives an annual allowance which is a fixed proportion of that of a *maire*. No more than 30 per cent of the members of the *Conseil municipal* can be *maires-adjoints*. See also: CUMUL DES MANDATS

MAIRE D'ARRONDISSEMENT
In the ARRONDISSEMENTS in Lyon, Marseille and Paris, the *maire d'arrondissement* is elected by the CONSEIL D'ARRONDISSEMENT, a week after the election of the *Maire* of the city. The *maire d'arrondissement* has limited powers, acting as a MAIRE-ADJOINT to the *maire* of the city within the *arrondissement*, but exercising the responsibilities of ÉTAT CIVIL.

MAIRE, EDMOND (1931–)
A prominent union leader from the 1960s to the 1980s, holding the post of *secrétaire général* of the CONFÉDÉRATION FRANÇAISE DÉMOCRATIQUE DU TRAVAIL from 1971 to 1989.

MAIRIE

The centre of the COMMUNE administration, the seat of the CONSEIL MUNICIPAL and of the MAIRE. In some towns, the *Mairie* is called the *Hôtel de Ville*, although this name is sometimes given to the buildings where meetings are held, rather than the offices.

MAISON DE LA CULTURE

An arts centre, established as part of an initiative by André MALRAUX in the 1960s. Eleven centres exist, funded half each by State and COLLECTIVITÉ LOCALE. See also: MAISON DES JEUNES ET DE LA CULTURE

MAISON DE LA RADIO

Also known as *Maison de Radio France*, the headquarters of what was the State broadcasting service, opened in 1962, and hailed as one of the new generation of public buildings in Paris. See also: OFFICE DE LA RADIODIFFUSION ET TÉLÉVISION FRANÇAISE

MAISON DE RETRAITE

A retirement home for the elderly, who can either pay privately for the service, or be funded through the AIDE SOCIALE. Membership of an insurance scheme run by a *Caisse de retraite* guarantees a place in home if required.

MAISON DE SANTÉ

A private enterprise psychiatric hospital.

MAISON DES JEUNES ET DE LA CULTURE (MJC)

One of 1,500 youth centres in a network run by two federations, with almost 700,000 members. The centres are partly funded by COMMUNES, CONSEILS GÉNÉRAUX and by the *Ministère de la jeunesse et des sports*.

MAISON MATERNELLE

In each DÉPARTEMENT, there is a refuge where a woman about to give birth or who has just done so may stay. If she wishes to keep the birth secret, she is entitled to stay over a longer period.

MAÎTRE

The courtesy title of a MAGISTRAT, often abbreviated to *Me* in written form.

MAÎTRE-ASSISTANT
A university teacher who directs demonstrations and practical classes, and provides tutorial help for students following courses to the DIPLÔME D'ÉTUDES UNIVERSITAIRES GÉNÉRALES. AGRÉGÉS or holders of DOCTORATS are eligible to enter the CONCOURS for appointment. The intention of a 1984 ARRÊTÉ was to remove this grade gradually.

MAÎTRE DES CONFÉRENCES
A university teacher who has an obligation to teach and engage in research, and has the official status of *enseignant-chercheur*. A *maître de conférences* gives lectures, supervises practical work, and is recruited by CONCOURS either nationally (by qualifications) or locally, and this process normally requires the candidate to have completed a thesis.

MAÎTRE DES REQUÊTES See: *CONSEIL D'ÉTAT*

MAÎTRISE
A degree awarded after two years study beyond the DIPLÔME D'ÉTUDES UNIVERSITAIRES GÉNÉRALES. About 40 per cent of university students go on to this level of qualification. Among the specialist *maîtrises* available are: MIAGE (*Maîtrise de méthodes informatiques appliquées à la gestion*); MSG (*Maîtrise de sciences de gestion*); and MST (*Maîtrise de sciences et techniques*).

MAJORITÉ
Since 1974 a French person attains full adult rights at the age of 18. Before this date, the age of majority was 21. See also: ÉMANCIPATION

MALLE, LOUIS (1932–)
A film director, who has made films in French and in English. His work is varied in style and approach. Among his best known are *Zazie dans le métro*, *Viva Maria*, and *Au revoir les enfants*.

MALRAUX, ANDRÉ (1901–1976)
A novelist and essayist who established an international reputation with his Goncourt winner in 1933, *La Condition*

humaine, and who wrote extensively about art. He had political adventures in Indo-China in his youth, and fought as a Republican in the Spanish Civil War, inspiring his *L'Espoir* (1937), later as a member of the RÉSISTANCE, and worked closely with DE GAULLE throughout the post-war years, becoming the first *Ministre des affaires culturelles* from 1959 to 1969.

MAMMOUTH
A large chain of hypermarkets, although the *Mammouth* name and logo exists on premises owned and operated by a number of different company groups.

MANCHE
A DÉPARTEMENT of the BASSE-NORMANDIE region, on the coast of the Channel from which it derives its name, with a population in 1990 of 479,630. The CHEF-LIEU is Saint-Lô (AGGLOMÉRATION 26,567), an agricultural market centre and site of a famous stud-farm, and other urban areas are Avranches (14,575); Cherbourg (92,045), a port, with shipbuilding, engineering, telecommunications and nuclear waste industries; Granville (16,860) a port and holiday resort, with metalworks and chemicals; as well as the smallest recognised port, Port Racine near St-Germain-des-Vaux. Fishing is a significant activity in the coastal areas. There is a nuclear power station at Flamanville on the west Cotentin coast. At La Hague, there is treatment of waste nuclear material and production of plutonium.

Agriculture provides beef and dairy cattle, sheep, apples and vegetables, with the highest *départemental* production of carrots. Milk production is one of the highest in France.

Tourism is dominated by the proximity of Mont-Saint-Michel, the cross-channel traffic with Great Britain, and the maritime scenery at the northern end of the Cotentin peninsular.

Politically, the Manche retains an allegiance to the Centre and Right, although in the ÉLECTIONS PRÉSIDENTIELLES, GISCARD D'ESTAING's majority of 59.13 per cent in 1981 was reduced to 50.69 per cent for Jacques CHIRAC in 1988. The Centre Right comfortably retained control of the CONSEIL GÉNÉRAL in 1992.

Code départemental: 50

MANDAT
A political term referring to the period of office of an elected member or official. See also: CUMUL DES MANDATS; SEPTENNAT

MANDAT-CARTE
A money order sent through the postal system to a receiving post office authorising the transfer of funds to a named payee. Sums up to 4,000 francs are paid in cash by the postman on the normal delivery round. See also: MANDAT-LETTRE

MANDAT-LETTRE
A money order, sent by an individual to a recipient who then exchanges it for cash at a post office. See also: MANDAT-CARTE

MANUFRANCE
A former mail-order catalogue firm selling all kinds of hardware, and a manufacturer of bicycles, sewing machines and guns, based in Saint-Étienne, which saved itself from closure by turning into a enterprise partly run by the then Communist CONSEIL MUNICIPAL in the late 1970s, and then as a co-operative venture. It later collapsed. See also: LIP; SOCIÉTÉ CO-OPÉRATIVE DE PRODUCTION

MARABOUT
A publishing imprint in the HACHETTE group, specialising in guide books and literature for children and young people.

MARCHAIS, GEORGES (1920–)
A Communist politician who rose through the ranks of the party to become *Secrétaire général* of the PARTI COMMUNISTE FRANÇAIS in 1972. He entered the ASSEMBLÉE NATIONALE as DÉPUTÉ for the VAL-DE-MARNE in 1973, and has been a member of the European Parliament since 1984. In 1981 he was the Communist candidate in the ÉLECTION PRÉSIDENTIELLE, obtaining 12.24 per cent of the vote in the PREMIER TOUR. He presided over a spectacular decline in the fortunes of the Communist party, and despite attempts to remove him from office and media criticism of his war-time record as a volunteer worker in Germany, he has managed to retain his post.

MARCHÉ À TERME DES INSTRUMENTS FINANCIERS (MATIF)
The futures market, established in Paris in 1986, regulated by Matif SA.

MARCHÉ DES OPTIONS NÉGOCIABLES DE PARIS (MONEP)
The MONEP, established in 1987, is controlled by the CONSEIL DES BOURSES DE VALEURS. Only stockbroking firms which are members of the *Société de Bourse de Paris* are permitted to engage in the traded options market.

MARCHÉ D'INTÉRÊT NATIONAL
A State-controlled agricultural produce market, of sufficient size to be of national significance. They include the markets at Agen (LOT-ET-GARONNE) and RUNGIS.

MARCHÉ RM
A French variant of the financial market, which is falling out of use as international norms are increasingly used. Payment of a deposit only is required at the time of purchase of shares, with full payment (*à règlement mensuel*), within 30 days.

MARÉCHAL DE FRANCE
An honour bestowed on military commanders in wartime, deemed to have made an exceptional contribution to the country's war effort. Since the 1920s it has only been awarded posthumously, and to only four men. The last award was to Pierre Kœnig (1898–1970), 14 years after his death.

MARIAGE CIVIL
Men of 18 years old and women of 15 years old may legally marry in France. Exceptions can be made in special circumstances, but any person under 18 must have parental consent. Normally, three months' notice has to be given, and medical certificates supplied to the MAIRIE of the COMMUNE where the ceremony is to take place. Since 1985 there has been no obligation for a woman to take her husband's name. The ceremony is conducted by the MAIRE or a MAIRE-ADJOINT, is free of charge, but a collection for charity is usually taken.

A religious ceremony does not count as a legal marriage in France. See also: RÉGIME MATRIMONIAL

MARIANNE
A allegorical female representation of the Republic, appearing on public buildings, postage stamps, etc. Marianne wears the BONNET PHRYGIEN, and various models have been used, recently Brigitte Bardot and Catherine DENEUVE. She appears in cartoons as a symbol of the Republic and its principles.

MARIE-CLAIRE
A monthly women's magazine published by the firm of the same name, with a circulation of over 600,000. *Marie-Claire* first appeared in 1937, and now has a series of similar titles in other countries.

MARIE-FRANCE
A monthly women's magazine, with a circulation of over 300,000, published by the German owned Bauer group.

MARIGNY, HÔTEL
A Paris residence owned by the office of the PRÉSIDENT DE LA RÉPUBLIQUE and used to accommodate visiting foreign dignitaries, and also as the location of government press conferences.

MARINE NATIONALE
France has a military naval force of 65,300 (including civilians and support personnel), with commands based at Brest (FINISTÈRE) and Toulon (VAR) for domestic defence, with four other zones in the South Atlantic, Caribbean, Pacific and the Indian Ocean. It includes a nuclear submarine arsenal of five vessels, three of which are constantly at sea, and a conventional fleet. There is a planned reduction in the number of ships by about a fifth by 2000, although a new submarine is to be built.

MARINS-POMPIERS
A branch of the fire and rescue service based in Marseille, where the personnel retain military naval rank. See also: SAPEURS-POMPIERS

MARLY-LE-ROI, PAVILLON DE
A hunting lodge owned by the office of the PRÉSIDENT DE LA RÉPUBLIQUE in the COMMUNE of Marly-le-Roi (YVELINES).

MARNE
A DÉPARTEMENT in the CHAMPAGNE-ARDENNE region, named after the tributary of the Seine,with a population in 1990 of 558,309. The CHEF-LIEU is Châlons-sur-Marne (61,298) and other urban areas are Épernay (34,062); Reims (206,363); and Vitry-le-François (19,920).

The *Département* is dominated by the production of Champagne (four-fifths of which comes from the Épernay and Reims districts), but there is also engineering (car components and small planes at Châlons and Reims), metallurgy and cement making at Vitry, and a variety of food and other light industries. A large military camp is sited at Mourmelon.

Apart from the Champagne vineyards, the agricultural activity is mainly one of cereal production (wheat, barley and maize) beet crops and some dairy cattle.

The Marne changed political allegiance between 1981 and 1988. Having given GISCARD D'ESTAING a vote of 50.39 per cent, it voted for François MITTERRAND by 53.87 per cent. Parliamentary representation is divided between Left and Right, but after the 1992 ÉLECTIONS CANTONALES, the Left had only eight of the 44 seats in the CONSEIL GÉNÉRAL.

Code départemental: 51

MARNE-LA-VALLÉE
One of the VILLES NOUVELLES of the Paris area, comprising 26 COMMUNES, mainly in the DÉPARTEMENT of SEINE-ET-MARNE, but spilling into SEINE-ST-DENIS and VAL-DE-MARNE. It has a population of 120,000, and incorporates the area occupied by Euro-Disneyland.

MARSEILLAISE, LA
A Communist daily newspaper, published in Marseille, with a 1989 circulation of 146,406. See also: HYMNE NATIONAL

MARTINIQUE
A volcanic island DÉPARTEMENT D'OUTRE-MER and RÉGION in the

Caribbean, with a population of 359,579 in 1990. The CHEF-LIEU is Fort-de-France (100,080) and other towns are Lamentin (30,028); la Trinité (11,090); le François (16,925); le Robert (17,713); Rivière Pilote (12,606); Sainte-Marie (18,682); Saint-Joseph (14,036); and Schoelcher (19,825).

The first French settlement was in 1635, and apart from a British occupation in 1759–1762 France has retained control of Martinique since. It became a DOM in 1946.

The economy is based on the export of bananas, rum, petrol and tropical fruits, mainly to France. The biggest trading partner apart from France is the European Community, and the economy is heavily subsidised by France.

There were some autonomist disturbances in the 1980s, and the local *Parti progressiste martiniquais* is the largest group in the CONSEIL RÉGIONAL, although not with a majority. In the 1988 ÉLECTION PRÉSIDENTIELLE, Martinique voters gave the highest level of support received by François MITTERRAND: 70.89 per cent, although the abstentions were also very numerous. All the DÉPUTÉS vote with the Socialists and the two SÉNATEURS come from Socialist and Centre groups.

Code départemental: 972

MARTY, FRANÇOIS (1904–   )
Archbishop of Paris during the late 1960s and 1970s, and cardinal from 1969. A major challenge to his authority came from the movement for worker priests on the Left and from Marcel LEFÈBVRE on the Right. Marty did not wish politics to enter the Church's mission.

MASS
The grouping of *mathématiques appliquées et sciences sociales* which is a popular post-BAC course option leading to a DIPLÔME DES ÉTUDES UNIVERSITAIRES GÉNÉRALES for those who have *Bac* series C, D or E.

MASTÈRE
A qualification given by a GRANDE ÉCOLE after four terms of study following the award of a DIPLÔME D'ÉTUDES APPROFONDIES or an equivalent degree. The *mastère* is not a university degree. See also: MAGISTÈRE

MATERNELLE See: *ALLOCATION 'ASSISTANTE MATERNELLE'; ÉCOLE MATERNELLE*

MATERNITÉ See: *ALLOCATION MATERNITÉ; ASSURANCE MATERNITÉ*

MATIF See: *MARCHÉ À TERME DES INSTRUMENTS FINANCIERS*

MATIGNON, HÔTEL
The eighteenth-century house, sometime the residence of Talleyrand, and later the Austrian Embassy confiscated by the French government during the 1914–1918 war, used since 1936 as the office and residence of the PRÉSIDENT DU CONSEIL and later by the PREMIER MINISTRE.

MATIN, LE
A Paris daily newspaper, founded in 1977, with a circulation of about 90,000, still falling since the peak of 178,000 reached in 1981. It is officially referred to as *Le Matin de Paris*.

MATRA
A group of companies involved in electronics, electrical engineering and armaments, nationalised in 1982 and returned to the private sector in 1988.

MATRICE CADASTRALE
The official land register, giving details of land ownership. An extract from the register is freely available through a MAIRIE.

MAURIAC, FRANÇOIS (1885–1970)
A notable literary figure, who wrote novels, plays and essays, winning the Nobel Prize in 1952. In his later career, he was an influential journalist with *Le* FIGARO and *L'*EXPRESS, strongly supporting DE GAULLE.

MAUROY, PIERRE (1928–)
A technology teacher who became a Socialist politician, rising through the local and national party offices, and being elected to the CONSEIL GÉNÉRAL of the NORD in 1968. He became a DÉPUTÉ in 1973, and in the same year MAIRE of Lille, a position he still holds. In 1974 he became *Président* of the CONSEIL

RÉGIONAL of the NORD-PAS-DE-CALAIS, and five years later a
member of the European Parliament. Mauroy was the first
PREMIER MINISTRE of the François MITTERRAND presidency
(1981–1984). He was *Secrétaire général* of the PARTI SOCIALISTE
from 1988 to 1992, and in 1989 became *Président* of the
COMMUNAUTÉ URBAINE *de Lille*.

MAXICOOP
The name used by the larger supermarkets run by the Co-
opérative movement.

MAYENNE
A mainly rural DÉPARTEMENT in the PAYS DE LA LOIRE region,
named after the river Mayenne which joins the Sarthe near
Angers (MAINE-ET-LOIRE) becoming the Maine at that point. The
population of the *Département* is 278,016. The urban area of
the CHEF-LIEU, Laval houses 56,855 of them. Laval is a centre
for light engineering (telecoms and electronics) and vehicle
components, and the other two urban areas are Château-
Gontier (13,755) – electronics, dairies and cattle market; and
Mayenne town (13,549) – printing and textiles. There is an
important cement works at Saint-Pierre-la-Cour.

The agricultural activity is mainly in dairy and beef cattle,
and there is a specialist industry in breeding racehorses.

Political allegiance is to the Centre and Right, GISCARD
D'ESTAING having obtained a comfortable majority here in 1981,
and Jacques CHIRAC a marginal one in 1988. The Centre Right
has 16 of the 17 seats on the CONSEIL GÉNÉRAL after the 1992
ÉLECTIONS CANTONALES.

Code départemental: 53

MAYOTTE
An island possession in the Indian Ocean, with the status of
COLLECTIVITÉ TERRITORIALE since 1976. Previously Mayotte had
been part of the colony of the Comoro Islands. A majority vote
in Mayotte rejected independence, while the other islands
unilaterally declared independence in 1975. Amidst much
confusion, Mayotte was given its present status as a temporary
measure. A UN vote declared in 1982 that Mayotte should
rejoin the Comoros.

The population was 73,000 in 1988, with 12,026 resident in the largest town, Mamutzu. Ninety-seven per cent of the population are Muslims, and 30 per cent speak French. The economy is based on the production of essences, vanilla, coffee, copra and tropical fruit, mostly exported to France.

The Parliamentary representatives are from centrist groups, and François MITTERRAND received a marginal majority (50.33 per cent) in the 1988 ÉLECTION PRÉSIDENTIELLE.

MÉDAILLE DE LA DÉFENSE NATIONALE
A military decoration, established in 1982, awarded for especially honourable service.

MÉDAILLE DE LA DÉPORTATION ET DE L'INTERNEMENT POUR FAITS DE RÉSISTANCE
A medal issued to all deportees or political internees in the two World Wars.

MÉDAILLE DE LA FAMILLE FRANÇAISE
An award, created in 1920 as an initiative to increase the population after the First World War. Parents with large families are recognised by the award of a medal (bronze, silver or gold, depending on the size of the family), issued by the PRÉFET at the *Fête des* MÈRES.

MÉDAILLE DE LA GENDARMERIE FRANÇAISE
A military decoration awarded to members of the GENDARMERIE NATIONALE and others who have given especially valuable service.

MÉDAILLE DE LA RÉSISTANCE FRANÇAISE
A military decoration awarded between 1943 and 1947 recognising individual deeds and services in the wartime resistance movement. It is overseen by the *Chancellerie of the* ORDRE DE LA LIBÉRATION.

MÉDAILLE DES ÉVADÉS
A military decoration awarded to escapees, both military and civilian, from enemy forces during the First and Second World Wars, when the escape was achieved in dangerous circumstances.

MÉDAILLE DES SERVICES MILITAIRES VOLONTAIRES
A military decoration, awarded since 1975 to personnel who provide service on a voluntary basis, e.g. in recruitment campaigns, training reserves.

MÉDAILLE D'HONNEUR
A medal for honourable service in one's professional life. There are *médailles d'honneur* specific to an organisation (e.g. *Médaille d'honneur de la Police française*) and the more general *Médaille d'honneur du travail*.

MÉDAILLE DU TRAVAIL See: *MÉDAILLE D'HONNEUR*

MÉDAILLE MILITAIRE
A military decoration awarded from 1852 to 1961 to servicemen, and to generals and admirals but not to other officers. The records are organised by the *Grande Chancellerie* of the LÉGION D'HONNEUR. An annual token payment of 30 francs is made to holders of the decoration.

MÉDECIN, JACQUES (1928–   )
The former right-wing MAIRE of Nice (ALPES-MARITIMES), who was regarded as a powerful figure in local politics and a formidable fighter for the city's prestige and influence, until his sudden flight from France to Uruguay in 1990 when irregularities in the public accounts came to light.

MÉDECINS DU MONDE
A charitable organisation established in 1980 to provide medical and humanitarian aid in areas of war and natural calamities. It had a 1990 budget of 150 million francs. See also: KOUCHNER, BERNARD; MÉDECINS SANS FRONTIÈRES

MÉDECINS SANS FRONTIÈRES
A medical charity set up in 1971 with the mission of sending medical teams anywhere in the world to provide relief in disasters, regardless of local bureaucracy. Its working budget in 1990 was 225 million francs. See also: MÉDECINS DU MONDE

MÉDIATEUR DE LA RÉPUBLIQUE
The ombudsman of the ADMINISTRATION or any public service.

The *Médiateur de la République* is appointed for six years by the CONSEIL DES MINISTRES, and has a staff of *délégués départementaux* who can be consulted at the PRÉFECTURE. The powers of the *Médiateur* cover all administrative disputes, but do not extend to legal decisions. Cases for intervention have to be brought through a DÉPUTÉ or SÉNATEUR.

MÉDICIS, PRIX
A literary prize of 4,500 francs, in existence since 1958, awarded annually in November to the writer of a recently published novel or collection of short stories which has an innovative style or approach.

MÉHAIGNERIE, PIERRE (1939–   )
A centrist politician, former minister under Valéry GISCARD D'ESTAING, responsible for the LOI MÉHAIGNERIE, and now leader of the CENTRE DES DÉMOCRATES SOCIAUX, a member organisation of the UNION POUR LA DÉMOCRATIE FRANÇAISE, of which he is a *Vice-Président*. He is a DÉPUTÉ for the ILLE-ET-VILAINE.

MELUN-SÉNART
The smallest VILLE NOUVELLE in the ÎLE-DE-FRANCE region, comprising eight communes in the SEINE-ET-MARNE and two in the ESSONNE. The population is 11,500.

MELVILLE, JEAN-PIERRE (1917–1973)
A film director whose reputation was made as the maker of thriller films. His best known titles are possibly *Le Deuxième Souffle* (1966) and *Le Samouraï* (1967).

MENDÈS FRANCE, PIERRE (1907–1982)
A radical politician whose early career was marked by his being the youngest in several spheres (AVOCAT in 1926, *Docteur en droit* in 1928, DÉPUTÉ in 1932, *Sous-secrétaire d'État* in 1938). He joined DE GAULLE during the Second World War, and was *Ministre de l'économie nationale* in 1944 to 1945. He was a Governor of the International Monetary Fund from 1947 to 1958, PRÉSIDENT DU CONSEIL from June 1954 to February 1955, when he signed the peace treaty for the end of the war in Indo-

China, gave autonomy to Tunisia and rejected the idea of a
common European defence force. During the period 1958–1969
he campaigned against the régime of De Gaulle, and appeared
to support the left-wing attempt to gain power in 1968. He was
the recipient of tributes from François MITTERRAND at the 1981
election result.

MENDÈS FRANCE, UNIVERSITÉ PIERRE
The full title of the *Université de Grenoble II* at the campus in
Saint-Martin-d'Hères, which specialises in law, politics,
economics, humanities, history, history of art, town planning,
arts and management.

MENSUALISATION
Employers must pay their workers at least once a month. The
payment for workers whose pay is calculated on a monthly
basis can be made fortnightly. There is also the possibility for
taxpayers to pay the IMPÔT SUR LE REVENU in monthly instalments.

MERCURE, HÔTELS
A chain of modern hotels, mainly provided for the motorist,
and often situated in suburban areas or on the outskirts of
towns, part of the ACCOR group.

MERCURE DE FRANCE
A literary publishing house, part of the GALLIMARD group.

MÈRES, FÊTE DES
An officially recognised celebration of motherhood, held
annually in May.

MÉRIDIONAL, LE
A Marseille daily newspaper, officially entitled *Le Méridional
– La France*, part of the PROVENÇAL group of newspapers, owned
by HACHETTE, formerly by Gaston DEFFERRE. The circulation
was 70,795 in 1989. There is a Sunday edition with a circulation
of 62,743.

MÉRITE See: *ORDRE NATIONAL DU MÉRITE*

MÉRITE AGRICOLE
The *Ordre du Mérite agricole*, popularly known as '*le poireau*'

is awarded to those who have contributed to agricultural development. At least 15 years of service to farming is required before a person, who must also be at least 30 years old, may qualify for appointment to the rank of *Chevalier*.

MÉRITE MARITIME
The *Ordre du Mérite maritime* works on the same basis as the MÉRITE AGRICOLE.

MÉRITE MILITAIRE
A military order recognising the voluntary work of reservists, awarded between 1957 and 1964.

MERMAZ, LOUIS (1931–)
A teacher, historian and Socialist politician who was *Président de l'*ASSEMBLÉE NATIONALE from 1981 to 1986 and has held various ministerial posts since 1988. He was responsible for the LOI MERMAZ of 1989.

MESSAGERIES
A private enterprise parcels distribution network, specialising in newspaper distribution and mail order sales.The term *'messageries'* is used to describe all such networks rather than one particular company. See also: SERVICE NATIONAL DES MESSAGERIES

MESSIAEN, OLIVIER (1908–1992)
The influential composer whose works express a religious mysticism, and explore his particular theories of composition. Among his best-known works are *Vingt regards sur l'Enfant Jésus*, (1944), and the *Catalogue des oiseaux* (1958). He was organist at *La Trinité* church, Paris, from 1931.

MESSMER, PIERRE (1916–)
A lawyer and linguist who was with the Free French in the desert in the Second World War and after a successful career as a colonial administrator took political office in 1960 as *Ministre des armées*, retaining the post until 1969, taking charge of the TOM in 1971–1972 when he was appointed PREMIER MINISTRE by Georges POMPIDOU. Messmer was first elected in 1968 as a DÉPUTÉ, then in 1970 to the CONSEIL GÉNÉRAL of the

MOSELLE, became MAIRE of Sarrebourg in 1971, and *Président* of the CONSEIL RÉGIONAL of LORRAINE in 1978. He was leader of the RASSEMBLEMENT POUR LA RÉPUBLIQUE in the ASSEMBLÉE NATIONALE from 1986 to 1988, when he left Parliament.

MÉTÉOR
A fully automatic express railway system, planned to open in 1995 on a new MÉTRO line in Paris.

MÉTÉOROLOGIE NATIONALE
The public weather forecasting service, part of the *Ministère des transports*, based in Toulouse (HAUTE-GARONNE).

MÉTRO
A rapid-transit urban railway system, abbreviated from *Chemin de fer métropolitain*. The most famous and most extensive is in Paris, but there are now smaller, modern systems in existence in Lille, Lyon, Marseille, and being developed in Bordeaux (1996) and Toulouse (1993). A light railway or *Métro léger*, named *Orlyval* is due to open in 1992 between Antony (HAUTS-DE-SEINE) and ORLY airport. See also: RÉGIE AUTONOME DES TRANSPORTS PARISIENS; RÉSEAU EXPRESS RÉGIONAL

MÉTROPOLE
This term is used to refer to France as opposed to DOM and TOM.

MÉTROPOLE D'ÉQUILIBRE
Eight cities were thus designated in 1964 as part of the move towards DÉCENTRALISATION, in order to counter-balance the influence of the Paris conurbation. They were Bordeaux (GIRONDE), Lille (NORD), Lyon (RHÔNE), Marseille (BOUCHES-DU-RHÔNE), Nancy (MEURTHE-ET-MOSELLE), Nantes (LOIRE-ATLANTIQUE), Strasbourg (BAS-RHIN) and Toulouse (HAUTE-GARONNE). Four others followed in 1970: Clermont-Ferrand (PUY-DE-DÔME), Dijon (CÔTE-D'OR), Nice (ALPES-MARITIMES) and Rennes (ILLE-ET-VILAINE). The *Métropoles d'équilibre* were often set up alongside new ORGANISATIONS D'ÉTUDES D'AMÉNAGEMENT DES AIRES MÉTROPOLITAINES. See also: TECHNOPOLE

METZ, UNIVERSITÉ DE
The university has 11,000 students following courses in arts,

human, physical and natural sciences, law and languages.

MEURTHE-ET-MOSELLE

A DÉPARTEMENT in the LORRAINE region, named after the
Moselle river, a tributary of the Rhine and its own tributary,
the Meurthe which joins it just north of Nancy, the CHEF-LIEU.
The *Département* had a population of 711,952 in 1990, 11,000
lower than its recorded peak in 1975. The AGGLOMÉRATION of
Nancy has 310,659 inhabitants, and the principal industrial
activity is in engineering and textiles, crystal glass making,
chemicals, footwear and food industries. The other sizeable
towns are Longwy (39,243) – iron and steel industries; Lunéville
(23,626); Neuves-Maisons (15,462); Pont-à-Mousson
(22,657); Toul (22,639); and Villerupt (10,054).

There is a large cement works at Xeuilley, and the largest
conventional power station in France at Pont-à-Mousson. The
dependence on heavy industry has resulted in the *Département's*
severe suffering in the economic recession, especially in the
northern area, where the valleys of the Chiers, Orne and Fensch
have been particularly badly hit.

Agriculture is of less significance than industry. There are
vineyards, barley, fruit orchards and cattle rearing.

Tourism contributes to the local economy: 40,000 hectares of
the *Parc régional de Lorraine* are in the *Département*, the city of
Nancy has medieval and neo-classical buildings including those
in the Place Stanislas, there are châteaux, craft museums, war
cemeteries and remains of the Maginot line.

The political sympathies of the Meurthe-et-Moselle lie
primarily with the Left, although three of the seven DÉPUTÉS come
from the Centre and Right. In the ÉLECTIONS PRÉSIDENTIELLES of
1981 and 1988, François MITTERRAND received comfortable
majorities. Although the Centre Right held control of the
CONSEIL GÉNÉRAL in 1992, the PARTI SOCIALISTE gained a seat,
against the national trend.

Code départemental: 54

MEUSE

A DÉPARTEMENT of the LORRAINE region, with a population of
196,344 in 1990. There has been a gradual decline in population

since the 1960s. Indeed there are seven COMMUNES in the Meuse with no inhabitants at all. In this *Zone rouge*, the PRÉFET appoints MAIRES to administer the areas. The CHEF-LIEU is Bar-le-Duc (18,941 inhabitants in the urban area), with industrial activity in textiles, clothing, woollens, printing, engineering and food products. The only other AGGLOMÉRATION with more than 10,000 inhabitants is Verdun (26,711) where there are engineering, chemicals, printing, dairy, pharmaceuticals and electronics industries.

Other towns, although small, have a range of industrial activity, e.g. Madeleine biscuits at Commercy, cookware and vehicle components at Cousances-les-Forges, optical instruments and spectacles at Ligny-en-Barrois.

Verdun also has legendary status in French history because of its role in the 1914–1918 war. The wartime experiences of the Meuse bring many visitors to the war memorials, museums and cemeteries. Other attractions are the *Parc régional de Lorraine* and relics of Président Poincaré at Nubécourt and Sampigny.

Agricultural activity concentrates on cattle, fruit and barley and forestry.

The political complexion of the Meuse shows support for the Left and the Centre. In the 1981 ÉLECTION PRÉSIDENTIELLE, GISCARD D'ESTAING gained a marginal majority, captured by François MITTERRAND in 1988. The Centre Right reaffirmed its control of the CONSEIL GÉNÉRAL in 1992.

Code départemental: 55

MGEN See: *MUTUALITÉ*

MIAGE See: *MAÎTRISE*

MICHAUX, HENRI (1899–1984)
A Belgian poet and artist who lived a Bohemian existence and was involved with the Surrealists in the 1920s. He took French nationality in the 1950s, continuing to refuse to bow to convention by declining the *Grand Prix national des lettres* in 1965.

MICHELIN
The rubber tyre manufacturer founded by two Michelin

brothers in 1889. The family still controls 40 per cent of the shares. It is now the world's largest tyre producer, having taken over Uniroyal in 1989 and has 18 per cent of the market. In France it employs 37,000 at 24 plants, including five in its home town Clermont-Ferrand (PUY-DE-DÔME).

The firm expanded into the publication of maps and guides and now the *Guide Michelin* is regarded as one of standard hotel and restaurant guides.

MICHELINE
A motorised railcar running on rubber tyres, manufactured by Michelin in the 1930s. The term is often used for any short train running on rural services.

MIDEM
An annual market for records, cassettes and music held in Cannes.

MIDI-LIBRE
The daily newspaper published in Montpellier (HÉRAULT) with a circulation of about 150,000, a drop from its peak in 1983 of 195,000.

MIDI-PYRÉNÉES
The most extensive administrative RÉGION, incorporating the DÉPARTEMENTS of ARIÈGE, AVEYRON, GERS, HAUTE-GARONNE, LOT and TARN-ET-GARONNE. The 1990 population of the region is 2.4 million, and the regional capital is Toulouse.

Agriculture and service industries are the main source of employment, with a concentration of high-tech industry in the Toulouse area. The rural depopulation still continues however, and despite its area the region is relatively sparsely populated. The Midi-Pyrénées contributes 3.4 per cent of the gross national product, and receives support from the European Community for developments in the infrastructure in Ariège and Aveyron.

In the 1992 ÉLECTIONS RÉGIONALES, the Left lost ground to the ecologists and the FRONT NATIONAL. The UNION POUR LA FRANCE holds 38 seats, and the PARTI SOCIALISTE – MOUVEMENT DES RADICAUX DE GAUCHE group has 27 out of a total of 91 in the CONSEIL RÉGIONAL.

MILLER, CLAUDE (1942–   )
A film director who is making a reputation with films such as
L'Effrontée (1985).

MIN See: *MARCHÉ D'INTÉRÊT NATIONAL*

MINEUR See: *AUTORITÉ PARENTALE;*
ÉMANCIPATION; MAJORITÉ

MINISTRE
Under the CONSTITUTION of the CINQUIÈME RÉPUBLIQUE a minister
(correctly, a *Ministre à portefeuille*) is appointed by the PRÉSIDENT
DE LA RÉPUBLIQUE on the advice of the PREMIER MINISTRE, and is
a member of the CONSEIL DES MINISTRES. It is not possible to
retain the positon of DÉPUTÉ as well as that of a minister. See
also: ARRÊTÉ; CABINET; MINISTRE DÉLEGUÉ; MINISTRE D'ÉTAT;
SECRÉTAIRE D'ÉTAT

MINISTRE DÉLÉGUÉ
A junior MINISTRE within a *Ministère*, but more senior than a
SECRÉTAIRE D'ÉTAT, who has responsibility for a particular area
of the department's work. A *Ministre délégué* is a member of
the CONSEIL DES MINISTRES. See also: ARRÊTÉ; CABINET; MINISTRE
D'ÉTAT

MINISTRE D'ÉTAT
A title signifying the enhanced seniority of the politician or the
particular department headed by the MINISTRE. See also: ARRÊTÉ;
CABINET; MINISTRE DÉLÉGUÉ; SECRÉTAIRE D'ÉTAT

MINITEL
A personal computer terminal available in a variety of models
provided by FRANCE-TÉLÉCOM to telephone subscribers,
allowing access through the telephone lines to electronic
enquiry services and the TÉLÉTEL network.

MINITEL ROSE
The use made by MINITEL subscribers of pornographic messages
and information.

MINUTE
A right-wing satirical weekly magazine, with a circulation of

70,000 in 1988. In 1990 it was bought by FRONT NATIONAL
sympathisers.

MIRAGE

A series of military fighter and bomber aeroplanes
manufactured by DASSAULT, sold to the French ARMÉE DE L'AIR
and exported to other countries, including, controversially,
Israel, Iraq, Saudi-Arabia and Libya.

MISSION DE FRANCE

Formed during the Second World War, this organisation within
the Catholic church aims to evangelise those areas, especially in
urban districts, where the church is weak. The priests (about
300 throughout France, most of whom are employed in other
jobs) work in teams and profess a liberal interpretation of
Christianity. The work of the Mission has sometimes brought
it into dispute with the episcopal hierarchy.

MITOYENNETÉ

The shared responsibility for a wall separating two properties.
If there is no evidence that proves otherwise, the law assumes
that *Mitoyenneté* exists.

MITTERRAND, FRANÇOIS (1916–)

A lawyer and journalist who was awarded the CROIX DE GUERRE
in the Second World War, was appointed *Secrétaire général* for
prisoners of war in DE GAULLES's 1944 government, became
DÉPUTÉ for the NIÈVRE from 1946 to 1948, and took a number of
ministerial posts in the QUATRIÈME RÉPUBLIQUE, including
periods as *Ministre de l'*INTÉRIEUR and GARDE DES SCEAUX. He
consolidated his local influence by becoming MAIRE of Château-
Chinon in 1959, SÉNATEUR from 1959 to 1962, and *Président
du* CONSEIL GÉNÉRAL from 1964.

He was the Left's candidate in the ÉLECTION PRÉSIDENTIELLE
of 1965, achieving 44.8 per cent of the vote against De Gaulle
in the second round. When the new PARTI SOCIALISTE was formed
in 1971, Mitterrand was its first *Secrétaire*, and was
influential in drawing up the PROGRAMME COMMUN. He lost in
the second round of the 1974 election to GISCARD D'ESTAING with
49.19 per cent but won in 1981 with 51.76 per cent, thus

becoming the first Socialist PRÉSIDENT DE LA RÉPUBLIQUE in the
CINQUIÈME RÉPUBLIQUE, and was re-elected in 1988 with 54.02
per cent. See also: SOLUTRÉ

MJC See: *MAISONS DES JEUNES ET DE LA CULTURE*

MNOUCHKINE, ARIANE (1939–)
A theatre director who is well-known for her cycles of
Shakespeare plays.

MOBYLETTE
A brand of CYCLOMOTEUR manufactured by *Motobécane*, now
known as MBK. Fifteen million have been sold.

MODES DE PARIS
A monthly fashion magazine, which with its stablemate *Modes
et travaux* has a circulation of one million.

MODIANO, PATRICK (1947–)
A novelist who has caught the popular imagination and is
respected by the critics, winning the *Grand Prix du roman de
l'*ACADÉMIE FRANÇAISE in 1972 for *Les Boulevards de ceinture*,
the *Prix des libraires* in 1976 for *Villa triste*, and the *Prix*
GONCOURT in 1978 for *Rue des boutiques obscures*.

MODULOPASS
A concessionary railcard which allows travel either on specific
routes or through the whole of the railway system, at reduced
rates.

MOLLET, GUY (1905–1975)
A Socialist politician, *Secrétaire général* of the SECTION FRANÇAISE
DE L'INTERNATIONALE OUVRIÈRE from 1946 to 1969, PRÉSIDENT
DU CONSEIL from 1956 to 1957, at the time of the Suez crisis and
the continuing war in ALGÉRIE.

MONDE, LE
A daily newspaper published in Paris during the afternoon
preceding its edition date. It is internationally respected as a
serious, left of Centre commentator on French and world affairs.
Its circulation is 386,000, although election results issues sell over
a million. *Le Monde* is jealous of its editorial independence,

and is wholly-owned by its staff. Monthly and weekly specialist supplements are also published.

MONEP See: *MARCHÉ DES OPTIONS NÉGOCIABLES DE PARIS*

MONNET, JEAN (UNIVERSITÉ)
The university at Saint-Étienne, with 12,000 students in arts, economics, humanities, law, music, sciences and social administration.

MONOPRIX
A chain of popular stores appearing in most towns in France, owned by GALERIES LAFAYETTE.

MONORY, RENÉ (1923–)
A local businessman of the VIENNE and centrist politician, MAIRE of Loudun from 1959, who became SÉNATEUR in 1968, and was appointed to Ministerial posts in 1977–1978 and as *Ministre de l'*ÉDUCATION NATIONALE in 1986–1988. In 1985 he became *Président du* CONSEIL RÉGIONAL of POITOU-CHARENTES. See also: PLAN MONORY

MONSIEUR MEUBLE
A chain of furniture stores run by a co-operative.

MONTAGNE, LA
A daily newspaper, published in Clermont-Ferrand (PUY-DE-DÔME) with a circulation of 250,000 and a Sunday edition selling slightly more, dominating press sales in the Massif central.

MONTAIGNE, MICHEL DE (UNIVERSITÉ) See: *BORDEAUX, UNIVERSITÉS DE*

MONTAND, YVES (1921–1991)
A singer and film actor who was also active in humanitarian political causes. Early in his life he was an admirer of the Communists, but later became an outspoken anti-Stalinist. Among his well-known roles were performances in COSTA-GAVRAS's *L'Aveu* and *État de siège*, and Claude BERRI's *Jean de Florette* and *Manon des sources*.

MONT-BLANC See: *HAUTE-SAVOIE*

MONT DE PIÉTÉ
A popular name for a pawnbroker, now known officially as
CRÉDIT MUNICIPAL.

MONTHERLANT, HENRY DE (1896–1972)
A novelist, poet and playwright who was fascinated by bullfighting and travel, but who in post-war years gradually lost
his sight and lived a solitary life until committing suicide. A
cycle of novels written in the late 1930s, *Les Jeunes Filles*, is
entirely about men. His plays are noted for the theme of heroic
grandeur such as in *La Reine morte* (1942) and *Le Cardinal
d'Espagne* (1960).

MONTPELLIER, UNIVERSITÉS DE
There are three university institutions in Montpellier
(HÉRAULT): *Montpellier I* is the largest, with 18,000 students
following law, social science, economics, management,
medicine, pharmacy and biology courses; *Montpellier II*, or
the *Université des sciences et techniques du Languedoc*, with
11,000 students; and *Montpellier III*, or the *Université Paul-
Valéry*, with 15,000 students in the fields of arts, languages,
humanities and economics. The original medical faculty is the
oldest in the world, tracing its foundation to 1021.

MONUMENT HISTORIQUE
A listed building, structure or archaeological site which receives
State aid and protection, managed on a regional basis by the
Ministère de la CULTURE. See also: IMMEUBLE CLASSÉ

MOREAU, JEANNE (1928–   )
A film actress who has appeared in a wide range of French
films, among them François TRUFFAUT's *Jules et Jim* and *La
Mariée était en noir*, and Louis MALLE's *Viva Maria*.

MORBIHAN
A DÉPARTEMENT in the BRETAGNE region, taking a BRETON name
meaning 'small sea'. The population in 1990 was 619,754, and
the CHEF-LIEU, Vannes, where there are wireworks, food-
processing and plastics industries, is home to 45,576. The other

urban areas of size are Auray (14,313); Hennebont (19,165); Locmiquélic-Port-Louis (12,774); Lorient (107,088); and Pontivy (13,140). Food-processing is the most widespread industrial activity, with shipbuilding and fishing at Lorient (which ranks as the second fishing port in France, as well as having oyster beds). Kaolin is a major natural resource.

The farming is mainly in small units, with a concentration on market gardening, pigs, dairy cattle and poultry. The Morbihan is the country's lead producer of turkeys, and ninth in milk production.

The *Département* is rich in pre-historic sites (e.g. Carnac) and the coastline and natural harbours make this a popular tourist destination. The inhabitants have to cope with the lowest life expectancy in France for men (67.3 years) and fifth lowest for women (77.4 years).

Politically, the Morbihan is by tradition dominated by the Right, although François MITTERRAND received 52.99 per cent of the poll in the ÉLECTION PRÉSIDENTIELLE in 1988. The FRONT NATIONAL has considerable support here, possibly through local loyalty to Jean-Marie LE PEN who comes from the Morbihan. The results of the 1992 ÉLECTIONS CANTONALES meant that the Centre Right have 36 out of 42 seats in the CONSEIL GÉNÉRAL.

Code départemental: 56

MOSELLE

A DÉPARTEMENT of the LORRAINE region, named after the tributary of the Rhine which flows through it, with a population of 1,011,261 in 1990. The CHEF-LIEU is Metz (AGGLOMÉRATION 193,117) with engineering, vehicle parts (CITROËN), breweries and an inland port. The other main conurbations are Carling-l'Hôpital (10,094), Creutzwald (18,849), Forbach (97,847), Hagondage (66,929), Saint-Avold (26,962), Sarrebourg (16,464), Sarreguemines (25,593) and Thionville (132,386).

The Moselle has over half the iron ore resources in France, almost half the coal, (although mining has virtually stopped), and accounts for about a quarter of the country's steel production. About half Lorraine's steelworkers are employed at one plant, at Florange, near Thionville. Much of this industrial concentration is in the Moselle valley, which is also the site of cotton mills. There is a large cement works at Héming.

Agriculture is accordingly less important, although some cereals (primarily barley) are grown, and there is some rearing of cattle and sheep.

Women residents in the Moselle have the second lowest life expectancy in France: 77.1 years. At Cattenom towards the border with Luxembourg, there is a nuclear power station. Tourist attractions include the *Parc régional de Lorraine* and the Maginot line museum at Gravelotte.

The traditional political allegiance has been to support the Centre, and the Parliamentary representation demonstrates a balance of opinions. A marginal majority for GISCARD D'ESTAING in the 1981 ÉLECTION PRÉSIDENTIELLE was turned into a comfortable margin for François MITTERRAND in 1988. The Centre Right, however, control the CONSEIL GÉNÉRAL.

Code départemental: 57

MOTION DE CENSURE

A motion in the ASSEMBLÉE NATIONALE which must be signed by 10 per cent of the DÉPUTÉS if it is to be debated. Only votes for the motion are counted. If these amount to a majority of *députés*, the PREMIER MINISTRE must present the resignation of the government to the PRÉSIDENT DE LA RÉPUBLIQUE. If the motion is defeated, the signatories are not permitted to table another *Motion de censure* in the same parliamentary session.

MOULIN, JEAN (UNIVERSITÉ)

The official title of the *Université de Lyon-III*, after the local and national RÉSISTANCE leader, which has 15,000 students studying law, management, languages, arts and humanities.

MOULINEX

A manufacturer of household electrical appliances, with 13 factories in France and an annual turnover of six billion francs. Eighty per cent of this is generated abroad.

MOUSTAKI, GEORGES (1934–   )
A singer, composer and actor who combines the *chansonnier* style with a night-club sophistication.

MOUVEMENT DES RADICAUX DE GAUCHE (MRG)
A political grouping founded in 1972 which has about 10,000 local councillors as members.

MOUVEMENT RÉPUBLICAIN POPULAIRE (MRP)
A political group of the Centre Right, founded in 1945, and influential during the QUATRIÈME RÉPUBLIQUE. Its power waned when DE GAULLE took office and established the CINQUIÈME RÉPUBLIQUE. See also: LECANUET, JEAN

MOUVEMENT RURAL DE JEUNESSE CHRÉTIENNE
A Catholic youth movement, incorporating the *Jeunesse agricole catholique* (JAC), with a wide membership in rural areas. The JAC is composed of young farming families and trainees, the JTS (*Jeunesse travailleurs salariés*) of apprentices, employees and unemployed farm workers, and the *Groupe école* is aimed at school children and students.

MR BRICOLAGE
A chain of DIY centres, run on a co-operative basis.

MRG See: *MOUVEMENT DES RADICAUX DE GAUCHE*

MRJC See: *MOUVEMENT RURAL DE JEUNESSE CHRÉTIENNE*

MRP See: *MOUVEMENT RÉPUBLICAIN POPULAIRE*

MSG See: *MAÎTRISE*

MST See: *MAÎTRISE*

MUSÉE NATIONAL
A museum directly under the control of the *Ministre de la* CULTURE.

MUTILÉ DE GUERRE See: *CARTE D'INVALIDITÉ*

MUTUALITÉ
A movement of organisations which exist to benefit and support

their own members. The most common form of *Mutualité* is in the field of insurance, in which a *Mutuelle* has no shareholders apart from its member customers.

Two examples are the MAIF (*Mutuelle assurance des instituteurs de France*) and the MGEN (*Mutuelle générale de l'éducation nationale*), which originated as insurance companies for those working in the education system, but have now diversified into providing a wider range of services for their members. See also: ASSURANCE AUTO OBLIGATOIRE

MUTUELLES DU MANS ASSURANCES
The popular name for the *Groupe des mutuelles générales françaises*, formerly a State-owned insurance company, sold to its members in 1987. See also: MUTUALITÉ

NANCY, UNIVERSITÉ DE
The two universities at Nancy have about 33,000 students between them. *Nancy-I* provides courses in medicine, pharmacy, biology, mathematics, physical sciences, physical education and sport; *Nancy-II* in law, economics, politics, humanities, arts and languages. See also: INSTITUT NATIONAL POLYTECHNIQUE

NANTES, UNIVERSITÉ DE
There are 26,000 students at this institution which has faculties of medicine, pharmacy, law, politics, humanities, science, mathematics and arts.

NAP See: *NEUILLY-AUTEUIL-PASSY*

NATHAN
A publisher and maker of board games, now part of the PRESSES DE LA CITÉ group.

NATIONALISATION
There have been two major nationalisation programmes since the Second World War. In 1945, the coal mining industry, AIR FRANCE, the BANQUE DE FRANCE, electricity and gas companies, RENAULT and major banks and insurance companies were taken over by the State. In 1982, major steel firms and manufacturers were nationalised, more banks and finance companies, and ELF-AQUITAINE. See also: NI-NI; PRIVATISATION

NATIONALITÉ
French nationality is held automatically by all those who are born in France (including DOM and TOM), either of French parents or if the child is unable to claim the nationality of the parents. If only one of the child's parents is French, the child can decline French nationality in the six months before the

eighteenth birthday. If different nationality can be proved, any person can at any age apply to lose French nationality. In any of the above cases, except where both parents are French, the CODE *de la nationalité* allows the government to object to the final confirmation of nationality in the year preceding the eighteenth birthday.

After six months of marriage to a French person, the partner can formally become French by declaration to the TRIBUNAL D'INSTANCE. An adult resident in France for five years can apply for naturalisation, which is granted after investigation taking about 18 months by the *Ministère des affaires sociales*. Normally, a naturalised French person cannot hold elected public office for ten years, and may not become a FONCTIONNAIRE for five years. Committing a serious offence or DÉLIT results in withdrawal of nationality from a naturalised French person. See also: DÉGRADATION CIVIQUE; ÉTAT CIVIL; IMMIGRÉS; SERVICE NATIONAL

NAVARRE, YVES (1940–)
A prolific novelist and playwright who won the *Prix* GONCOURT in 1980 for *Le Jardin d'acclimatation*.

NAVETTE PARLEMENTAIRE
The process by which texts of new laws move between ASSEMBLÉE NATIONALE and SÉNAT, if there are amendments made by the Sénat.

NÉGOCIATION OBLIGATOIRE
A law of 1982 requires employers to renegotiate rates of pay and conditions of employment with their workforce annually. Every five years there must be negotiations about grading.

NEUILLY-AUTEUIL-PASSY (NAP)
A nickname to indicate the upper bourgeois lifestyle ascribed to these fashionable quarters of west Paris and HAUTS-DE-SEINE.

NICE, UNIVERSITÉ DE
Based at SOPHIA-ANTIPOLIS, the university provides courses in medicine, law, economics, sciences, arts, humanities, information technology and management, and has 22,000 students.

NICE-MATIN

A daily newspaper published in Nice with a circulation of over 250,000, and a Sunday edition selling marginally fewer. It sells throughout the ALPES-MARITIMES and neighbouring DÉPARTEMENTS, including those in CORSE.

NIÈVRE

A mainly rural DÉPARTEMENT of the BOURGOGNE region, named after the tributary of the Loire which joins it at the CHEF-LIEU, Nevers, an urban area with a population of 58,915, a quarter of the whole *Département's* population of 233,278. The only other towns of any size are Cosne-sur-Loire (13,184) and Decize (9,057), where there is a tyre factory. Industrial activity is largely light engineering, although there is a steelworks at Imphy, with specialist businesses, e.g. the stockbreeding Herd-Book headquarters for Charolais cattle at Nevers, the racing car trials grounds at Magny-Cours. There are deposits of coal at la Machine and kaolin at Saint-Pierre-le-Moûtier.

The *Département* is a major producer of fine wines, having 587 APPELLATION D'ORIGINE CONTRÔLÉE labels at Pouilly-sur-Loire and 60 VDQS growths. Agriculture concentrates on beef cattle, and sheep-rearing. The upland area of the Morvan has a forestry industry.

Tourism is important, and the proximity to Paris and Lyon means that a large number of second homes are found in the Nièvre.

Château-Chinon has the distinction of being the home political base of François MITTERRAND. The Nièvre has shown a loyalty to the broader socialist cause in its selection of DÉPUTÉS and SÉNATEURS. The proportions of the vote for Mitterrand in the 1981 and 1988 ÉLECTIONS PRÉSIDENTIELLES were among the highest recorded: 62.91 per cent and 63.96 per cent respectively. In the 1992 ÉLECTIONS CANTONALES, the Socialists narrowly retained their control of the CONSEIL GÉNÉRAL, including among their number Pierre BÉRÉGOVOY who became PREMIER MINISTRE the following week.

Code départmental: 58

NI-NI

The nickname given to the policy of Michel ROCARD's

government in not finalising a nationalisation or privatisation plan.

NOËL See: *FÊTE LÉGALE*

NOIR, MICHEL (1944–)
The MAIRE of Lyon who rose in the ranks of the RASSEMBLEMENT POUR LA RÉPUBLIQUE to become an influential figure, and his resignation from the party in 1990 has been interpreted as the strategy of a possible future challenger to Jacques CHIRAC.

NOIRET, PHILIPPE (1930–)
A prominent film actor whose career has included roles in Bertrand TAVERNIER's *L'Horloger de Saint-Paul* and Louis MALLE's *Zazie dans le métro*.

NON-INSCRIT
An independent politician, a candidate for elected office without a party affiliation, is described thus.

NON-LIEU
If a JUGE D'INSTRUCTION decides that there is insufficient evidence to commit the INCULPÉ to trial, an *Ordonnance de non-lieu* is issued, which effectively is the end of the investigation.

NORD
A largely urban DÉPARTEMENT of the NORD-PAS-DE-CALAIS region, the most northerly in France, and the most heavily populated, with 2,531,855 inhabitants. The CHEF-LIEU is Lille, the fourth city of France, with 950,265 inhabitants in the AGGLOMÉRATION which abuts the frontier with Belgium. Other major urban areas are Armentières (57,738); Aulnoye-Aymeries (20,802); Cambrai (47,719); Douai (160,343); Dunkerque (190,879); Hazebrouck (20,567); Maubeuge (102,772); Saint-Amand-les-Eaux (19,979); and Valenciennes (336,481).

This is a highly industrialised *Département*, with textiles, coal mining and iron and steel industries the traditional basis of the local economy. There is also a considerably diversified range of other enterprises, including machine-tools, automobile and railway manufacturing, chemicals, brewing, mail order distribution, paints, soap making and food processing. No coal has been mined since 1990.

Dunkerque is a major container and ferry port, and there is a nuclear power station on the coast at Gravelines.
Valenciennes is an important terminal in the national networks of gas and oil pipelines.

The agricultural activity is relatively less important, but there is market gardening and wheat and barley crops, and pigs and cattle are bred in significant numbers.

The Nord has the lowest life expectancy of any *Département* for women (76.4 years), and the third lowest for men (67.6 years). It suffers the third highest rate of crime in the country.

The Nord has traditionally been a bastion of the Left, but recent years have seen the FRONT NATIONAL make strong advances here. In the ÉLECTIONS PRÉSIDENTIELLES in 1981 and 1988, François MITTERRAND gained comfortable majorities, and most of the DÉPUTÉS come from the Socialist group, with a few Communists. In the 1992 ÉLECTIONS CANTONALES, the Nord fell to the Centre Right, with the RASSEMBLEMENT POUR LA RÉPUBLIQUE making the largest gains. The Socialists remain the largest single group on the CONSEIL GÉNÉRAL, but the Left can call on only 38 out of the 79 seats.

Code départemental: 59 See also: VILLENEUVE-D'ASCQ

NORD-ÉCLAIR
A daily newspaper, published in Roubaix (NORD) by the *Publiprint-Régions* group, with a circulation of 56,000, a drop since the mid-1980s. Another of their dailies is *Nord-Matin*, which appears in Lille, and has increased its circulation to 99,000 over the same period.

NORD-MATIN See: *NORD-ÉCLAIR*

NORD-PAS-DE-CALAIS
An administrative RÉGION comprising two DÉPARTEMENTS, the NORD and PAS-DE-CALAIS, with 3.96 million inhabitants. The regional capital is Lille. The Nord-Pas-de-Calais is predominantly urbanised and the basis of the economy is the industry which has grown on the coalfield (where coal

production has stopped) and the cross-channel traffic through the ports of Boulogne, Calais and Dunkerque. The proximity to Belgium, and the forthcoming opening of the Channel Tunnel place the region in a strong position for international trade.

Its agricultural activity provides high proportions of France's salad vegetables, potatoes and other vegetables, it lands one quarter of the fish in France, and has three-quarters of the country's mail-order business. It is the major producing region for textiles, and the food-processing industry is very important.

The European Community has helped fund changes in the infrastructure necessitated by the decline of the coal and steel industries.

The traditional leading position of the Left was lost in the 1992 ÉLECTIONS RÉGIONALES, in which the FRONT NATIONAL, GÉNÉRATION ÉCOLOGIE and the VERTS all made considerable gains.

NORMANDIE See: *BASSE-NORMANDIE; HAUTE-NORMANDIE*

NORMES FRANÇAISES (NF)
A legally recognised guarantee of quality. In order to obtain an NF approval, the product has to be investigated by the *Association française de normalisation*, who require the manufacturer to honour guarantees in the case of consumer complaint. See also: ÉTIQUETAGE

NOTAIRE
A qualified lawyer who is entitled to practise by advising clients, carrying out formalities concerning ACTES and contracts, especially regarding property. A *notaire* is appointed by the GARDE DES SCEAUX but acts as a self-employed professional or as a partner in a practice, which is restricted for some business to the geographical territory of the local COUR D'APPEL.

NOTRE TEMPS
A monthly magazine for retired people published by BAYARD-PRESSE with a circulation of 1.15 million.

NOURISSIER, FRANÇOIS (1927–   )
A novelist and critic, with a regular column in *Le Figaro-*

magazine, winner of the *Prix* FÉMINA in 1970 for *La Crève*, who has been *Secrétaire général* of the ACADÉMIE GONCOURT since 1977.

NOUS DEUX
A weekly women's magazine, with a circulation in 1989 of 565,000, which shows a fall from its peak in 1960 of 1.3 million.

NOUVEL ÉCONOMISTE, LE
A weekly economic journal with a circulation of 100,000.

NOUVEL, JEAN (1945–)
An architect with the reputation of being something of an outlaw, who since the 1970s has fought against the narrow school of official architecture. In 1979 he organised a campaign against plans for the development of *Les Halles* in Paris. Among his works are the *Institut du monde arabe*, LOGEMENT SOCIAL at Saint-Ouen (SEINE-SAINT-DENIS), the centre thermal at Perpignan (PYRÉNÉES-ORIENTALES) and the reconstruction of the OPÉRA DE LYON. He has proposed a 400 metres tower block for *La* DÉFENSE.

NOUVELLE-CALÉDONIE
A group of Pacific islands forming a TERRITOIRE D'OUTRE-MER, with a population of 164,173. The TOM has been a French possession since 1853. An independence movement has been active since the 1960s, and violent incidents occurred in the 1980s. The *Front de libération nationale kanak et socialiste* (FLNKS) was formed in 1984 to press for independence. After a period of direct rule from Paris, a new constitutional arrangement took effect in 1989, and a referendum on the question of independence is due in 1998.

In the 1988 ÉLECTION PRÉSIDENTIELLE of 1988, François MITTERRAND received only 9.7 per cent of the votes cast. All the parliamentary representatives in Paris are from the RASSEMBLEMENT POUR LA RÉPUBLIQUE. See also: PISANI, EDGARD

NOUVELLE RÉPUBLIQUE, LA
A daily newspaper published in Tours (INDRE-ET-LOIRE), with a circulation of 269,000 sold widely throughout the CENTRE and POITOU-CHARENTES regions.

NOUVELLE REVUE FRANÇAISE (NRF)
A publishing imprint used by GALLIMARD for serious new literature. In the years before the Second World War, NRF published many works which have become classics.

NOUVELLES GALERIES
A chain of department stores, controlled by GALERIES LAFAYETTE since 1991. The group also controls the BAZAR DE L'HÔTEL DE VILLE.

NOUVEL OBSERVATEUR, LE
A radical weekly news magazine, popular among intellectuals, with a circulation of 403,000 in 1989.

NOVEMBRE, LE ONZE See: *FÊTE LÉGALE*

NOVOTEL
A chain of hotels, catering for the business market, owned by ACCOR.

NRF See: *NOUVELLE REVUE FRANÇAISE*

NRJ See: *RADIO LIBRE*

NUMÉRO MINÉRALOGIQUE
The *code départemental* which is used on the *plaque d'*IMMATRICULATION of vehicles, as the first numbers in the CODE POSTAL and as an abbreviation in many other circumstances.

NUMÉRO VERT
A business telephone number which can be called free of charge. All calls are charged to the receiving subscriber.

OAS See: *ORGANISATION DE L'ARMÉE SECRÈTE*

OBJET CONTRE REMBOURSEMENT See: *ENVOI CONTRE REMBOURSEMENT*

OBJET EN INSTANCE
A letter or parcel retained in a post office because it cannot be delivered, for want of a signature or payment.

OBSÈQUES NATIONALES
The state funeral ceremony provided for those whose contribution to the nation warrants it, according to the decision of the government. The family of the deceased can decline the opportunity, as did those of DE GAULLE and Georges POMPIDOU. *Obsèques solennelles* are less elaborate.

OCCITAN
The language, formerly current in the southern half of the country, in the area thus known as *Langue d'Oc*, but which since medieval times has steadily lost prestige and currency to French. It is estimated that there are now four million speakers of the different dialects, in which vocabulary and pronunciation vary greatly.

In the education system, *Occitan* has the status of a regional language and can be learnt in schools in the ACADÉMIES of Aix, Bordeaux, Clermont-Ferrand, Limoges, Montpellier, Nice and Toulouse. 10,647 pupils were following courses in 1987. The universities at Avignon, Aix, Montpellier and Toulouse also provide courses. See also: OCCITANIE

OCCITANIE
The movement which has gathered more popular support in recent years to promote the position of OCCITAN language and

culture. There are various organisations of different political persuasions proclaiming similar aims. In the 1980s there were a number of mass demonstrations in southern cities.

OCCUPATION
The period from 1940 to 1944 when there was a German occupation of the northern half of France, and the entire Atlantic coastal zone. See also: VICHY

OCÉANE
The AUTOROUTE A11 between Paris and Nantes (LOIRE-ATLANTIQUE), managed by COFIROUTE.

OCKRENT, CHRISTINE (1944–   )
A broadcaster who became prominent in her role as presenter of the evening news programme on *Antenne 2* (now FRANCE 2).

ODÉON See: *THÉÂTRE NATIONAL DE L'ODÉON*

OFFENSE AU PRÉSIDENT
It is a DÉLIT for the press to publish insults against the serving PRÉSIDENT DE LA RÉPUBLIQUE and for anyone to behave insultingly towards him or her.

OFFICE CHRÉTIEN DES PERSONNES HANDICAPÉES ET INADAPTÉES
A charity with 32,000 members working on behalf of the disabled.

OFFICE DE LA JUSTIFICATION DE LA DIFFUSION (OJD)
A non-profit making ASSOCIATION giving independent assessments of newspaper and magazine circulation, financed by its members which are mainly press organisations and advertising companies.

OFFICE DE LA RADIODIFFUSION ET TÉLÉVISION FRANÇAISE (ORTF)
The State broadcasting organisation set up in 1964 to oversee all aspects of radio and TV programmes, with its governing body appointed by the CONSEIL DES MINISTRES. It retained its monopoly after a reform in 1972 which gave more autonomy to the programme-makers, but was replaced in 1974 by separate

bodies for programme making, transmission, etc. See also:
COMMISSION NATIONALE DE LA COMMUNICATION ET DES LIBERTÉS;
CONSEIL SUPÉRIEUR DE L'AUDIOVISUEL; HAUTE AUTORITÉ DE LA
COMMUNICATION AUDIOVISUELLE; MAISON DE LA RADIO

OFFICE FRANÇAIS DE PROTECTION DES RÉFUGIÉS ET APATRIDES (OFPRA)
A State department which has the responsibility for political
refugees and stateless persons, and which also carries out the
administration of their requests for residence.

OFFICE NATIONAL DES FORÊTS (ONF)
A State-owned enterprise which manages the publicly owned
forest areas, in conjunction with COLLECTIVITÉS LOCALES, in
France and the DOM.

OFFICE NATIONAL D'INFORMATION SUR LES ENSEIGNEMENTS ET LES PROFESSIONS (ONISEP)
The national careers and education guidance service run by the
*Ministère de l'*ÉDUCATION NATIONALE, with centres in every
DÉPARTEMENT and a CONSEILLER D'ORIENTATION available in each
LYCÉE and a network of CENTRES D'INFORMATION ET D'ORIENTATION.
Information services are provided for parents as well as for
pupils, and a wide range of publications is available.

OFFICE PUBLIC D'AMÉNAGEMENT ET DE CONSTRUCTION (OPAC)
The national department which oversees the management and
construction of HABITATIONS À LOYER MODÉRÉ. See also:
LOGEMENT SOCIAL

OFFICIEL DES SPECTACLES
A weekly listings magazine giving details of Paris events and
entertainments, with a circulation of 186,000.

OFFICIER DE LA POLICE JUDICIAIRE See: *POLICE JUDICIAIRE*

OFFICIER DE PAIX
A senior uniformed police officer with responsibility over the
work of GARDIENS DE LA PAIX.

OFPRA See: *OFFICE FRANÇAIS DE PROTECTION DES RÉFUGIÉS ET APATRIDES*

OISE

A DÉPARTEMENT of the PICARDIE region, named after the tributary of the Seine which runs through it, with a 1990 population of 725,575. This figure shows a steep increase since the 1982 census of 661,6781. The CHEF-LIEU is Beauvais (AGGLOMÉRATION 55,817), a centre for the manufacture of carpets, tractors and brushes, as well as chemical and engineering industries, and the site of a famous Gothic cathedral. Other towns in the Oise are Chantilly (28,128), a centre for horse-breeding and racing; Compiègne (62,778), with engineering, chemicals, glass and rubber industries; Creil (82,505) – steel-making and a dormitory town for Paris; Crépy-en-Valois (13,222); Liancourt (10,638); Méru (11,928); Noyon (15,660); Pont-Sainte-Maxence (12,718) – ceramic works; and Senlis (14,432), an engineering town and site of another Gothic cathedral.

The agricultural activity is less important and is predominantly that of cereal production, there being significant crops of wheat and considerable market gardening and milk production.

The Oise is very much influenced by Paris, and much of the continuing population growth can be ascribed to an increase in daily commuting to the capital from the south of the *Département*. Tourism is largely directed at historic sites such as the armistice railway carriage at Rethondes, and the Beauvais and Senlis cathedrals, but there is also an ASTÉRIX theme park at Plailly.

Politically, the Oise gave François MITTERRAND comfortable majorities in both 1981 and 1988 ÉLECTIONS PRÉSIDENTIELLES. The DÉPUTÉS and SÉNATEURS are relatively evenly divided between Left and Right. The Centre Right further tightened its grip over the CONSEIL GÉNÉRAL in 1992, with the RASSEMBLEMENT POUR LA RÉPUBLIQUE as the largest party group.

Code départemental: 60

OJD See: *OFFICE DE LA JUSTIFICATION DE LA DIFFUSION*

OK!
Formerly known as *OK âge tendre*, this is a teenage magazine dealing with the world of pop music and fashion, with a weekly circulation of 212,000.

OKAPI
A children's magazine published by BAYARD-PRESSE, with a fortnightly circulation of 130,000.

OLDENBOURG, ZOÉ (1916–   )
A prolific writer and novelist of Russian origin, well known for *La Pierre angulaire*, the *Prix* FÉMINA winner of 1953 and *Le Bûcher de Montségur* (1959).

OLYMPIA
The Paris theatre which is often used for pop music concerts and spectacular shows. A performance at the Olympia is considered to be the peak of achievement. Its full name *Olympia-Bruno-Coquatrix* commemorates the impresario who owned it.

OMNIBUS
A railway train which stops at all stations on its route.

ONF See: *OFFICE NATIONAL DES FORÊTS; ORCHESTRE NATIONAL DE FRANCE*

ONISEP See: *OFFICE NATIONAL D'INFORMATION SUR LES ENSEIGNEMENTS ET LES PROFESSIONS*

OPAC See: *OFFICE PUBLIC D'AMÉNAGEMENT ET DE CONSTRUCTION*

OPCVM See: *ORGANISME DE PLACEMENT COLLECTIF EN VALEURS MOBILIÈRES*

OPÉRA DE LA BASTILLE
A new opera house opened in Paris in 1990 to mark the BICENTENAIRE, after much controversy over its design, cost and artistic policy.

OPÉRA DE LYON
An performing company with an international reputation.

Recent musical directors have included the British John Eliot Gardner. The present holder of the post is Kent Nagano. See also: NOUVEL, JEAN

OPÉRA DE PARIS
The only opera and ballet company in France which has the status of THÉÂTRE NATIONAL. It has performed in its present premises, the *Palais* GARNIER, since 1875, and also uses the *Salle Favart*, as well as performing on tour. The *Opéra de Paris* runs two training schools, the *École d'art lyrique* and the *École de danse*.

OPPOSITION
The group of parties or political groups who do not form the governing majority, and which claim to offer an alternative. There is no official opposition in France. See also: ALTERNANCE; OUVERTURE

ORCHESTRE COLONNE
A symphony orchestra, founded in 1873 and first directed by Édouard Colonne, performing at the *Théâtre du Châtelet* in Paris.

ORCHESTRE DE PARIS
The current name of the symphony orchestra established in 1828 by the *Société des concerts du Conservatoire*, and now based at the *Salle* PLEYEL. The orchestra has had a series of internationally renowned musical directors, and is well known throughout the world through recordings.

ORCHESTRE LAMOUREUX See: *CONCERTS LAMOUREUX*

ORCHESTRE NATIONAL DE FRANCE (ONF)
A symphony orchestra formed in 1934, based in Paris.

ORCHESTRE PASDELOUP See: *CONCERTS PASDELOUP*

ORDONNANCE
An order with legal status issued by DÉCRET by the government after authority has been agreed by the ASSEMBLÉE NATIONALE and SÉNAT, replacing the normal process of making a new law.

Such powers are used in extraordinary circumstances and only for limited periods. Each *Ordonnance* has to be signed by the PRÉSIDENT DE LA RÉPUBLIQUE and published when it becomes immediately effective, but loses its validity if not formally approved by the parliament within a fixed time limit.

ORDONNANCE PÉNALE
The JUGE in a TRIBUNAL DE POLICE can make a decision on the basis of the documentary evidence, without the defendant being present. If found guilty, the offender has 30 days to comply with the punishment (usually an AMENDE FORFAITAIRE) or can ask for a hearing in the normal way.

ORDRE DE LA LIBÉRATION See: *COMPAGNON DE LA LIBÉRATION*

ORDRE DU MÉRITE MILITAIRE See: *MÉRITE MILITAIRE*

ORDRE DES ARTS ET LETTRES
An order of those whose achievements in artistic and literary fields have been judged to be worthy of the award of (in increasing seniority) *Chevalier*, *Officier* or *Commandant*. 300 appointments to the rank of *Chevalier* are made annually.

ORDRE DES PALMES ACADÉMIQUES
A similar, although more numerous, order to the ORDRE DES ARTS ET LETTRES, for those working in the ÉDUCATION NATIONALE.

ORDRE NATIONAL DU MÉRITE
An honourable order, founded in 1963, similar to the LÉGION D'HONNEUR, and administered by the same office.

OREAM See: *ORGANISATION D'ÉTUDE D'AMÉNAGEMENT DES AIRES MÉTROPOLITAINES*

ORGANISATION DE L'ARMÉE SECRÈTE (OAS)
The right-wing terrorist organisation, active in 1961 and 1962 against DE GAULLE and his sympathisers, and against Algerians in an unsuccessful attempt to retain French control over ALGÉRIE. They made a number of assassination attempts against De Gaulle. See also: PETIT-CLAMART

ORGANISATION DE SECOURS See: *PLAN ORSEC*

ORGANISATION D'ÉTUDE D'AMÉNAGEMENT DES AIRES MÉTROPOLITAINES (OREAM)
As part of the DÉCENTRALISATION policy, a number of OREAM were established in order to provide a structure for economic development in provincial areas, outside the confines of a major city. See also: MÉTROPOLE D'ÉQUILIBRE; TECHNOPOLE

ORGANISME DE PLACEMENT COLLECTIF EN VALEURS MOBILIÈRES (OPCVM) See: *FONDS COMMUN DE CRÉANCES; SOCIÉTÉ D'INVESTISSEMENT À CAPITAL VARIABLE*

ORIENTATION SCOLAIRE
The guidance process given to pupils and their parents in choosing appropriate options when changing from one stage of education to the next. See also: CONSEILLER D'ORIENTATION; OFFICE NATIONAL D'INFORMATION SUR LES ENSEIGNEMENTS ET LES PROFESSIONS

ORLÉANS, HENRI D' (1908–   ) See: *COMTE DE PARIS*

ORLÉANS, UNIVERSITÉ DE
A university with 12,000 students following courses in arts, sciences, humanities, law and economics.

ORLY
A COMMUNE in the VAL-DE-MARNE, south of Paris, famous for its international airport. Completed in 1961 it was the first airport in the world purpose-built for large passenger aircraft. Traffic dropped after the opening of the new airport at ROISSY in 1973, but by 1979 had returned to its previous level.

ORLYVAL See: *MÉTRO*

ORMESSON, COMTE JEAN D' (1925–   )
A best-selling novelist, who achieved success with *La Gloire de l'empire* (1971) and *Au plaisir de Dieu* (1974), a kind of autobiographical tale of an aristocratic family. A member of the ACADÉMIE FRANÇAISE since 1973, and editor of *Le* FIGARO from 1974 to 1977, D'Ormesson continues to write a humorous

column in the weekly *Figaro-magazine*, and often appears on radio and television as an intellectual of the Right.

ORNE

A mainly rural DÉPARTEMENT of the BASSE-NORMANDIE region, with a population of 293,183 in 1990, named after the river which rises in the *Département* and flows to the sea past Caen (CALVADOS). The CHEF-LIEU is Alençon (39,176 in the AGGLOMÉRATION), and other towns of size are Argentan (16,413); Flers (24,357); and l'Aigle (12,663). There is light industry in some urban areas, including significant food-processing.

The main feature of farming in the Orne is the dairy and beef cattle herds, and there is considerable horse-breeding, especially the local *Percheron* breed. Specialist food products are *Camembert* cheese, cider and calvados.

Forest areas, the *Parc régional de Normandie*, châteaux, craft and liberation museums make the Orne attractive to tourists.

François MITTERRAND took 45.02 per cent of the vote in the 1981 ÉLECTION PRÉSIDENTIELLE and achieved a marginal majority in 1988. The Parliamentary representatives demonstrate a balance of political allegiance between Left, Right and Centre. The Centre Right's control of the CONSEIL GÉNÉRAL was reaffirmed in 1992.

Code départemental: 61

ORSAY, MUSÉE D'

A fine art museum in the former *Gare d'Orsay* railway terminus in Paris, with three million visitors annually. The exhibits include the Impressionist collection previously held in the *Musée du jeu de paume*.

ORSEC See: *PLAN ORSEC*

ORTF See: *OFFICE DE LA RADIODIFFUSION ET TÉLÉVISION FRANÇAISE*

ORTHOGRAPHE, RÉFORME DE L'

A proposal from the ACADÉMIE FRANÇAISE attempting to simplify the rules of French spelling was subject to some derision in the press in 1991.

OS See: *OUVRIER SPÉCIALISÉ*

OUEST-FRANCE
The daily newspaper with the largest circulation in France. Its headquarters are in Rennes (ILLE-ET-VILAINE) but it has numerous editions in other western towns and cities. The 1989 circulation was 786,000.

OUTRE-MER See: *COLLECTIVITÉ TERRITORIALE; DÉPARTEMENT D'OUTRE-MER; TERRITOIRE D'OUTRE-MER*

OUVERTURE
The attempt to broaden the base of government within the groupings of the Left and Centre which took place in the ROCARD government of 1988. It thus included members of the MOUVEMENT DES RADICAUX DE GAUCHE and the UNION POUR LA DÉMOCRATIE FRANÇAISE, retaining a majority from the PARTI SOCIALISTE.

OUVRIER SPÉCIALISÉ (OS)
Rather a misnomer, as this term refers to a semi-skilled or unskilled worker, who is likely to be involved in low-grade, repetitive work.

PACA See: *PROVENCE-ALPES-CÔTE-D'AZUR*

PACIFIQUE, UNIVERSITÉ FRANÇAISE DU
A university in Papeete, Tahiti (POLYNÉSIE FRANÇAISE) which has faculties of law and science.

PACTE See: *PROJET D'ACTIVITÉS ÉDUCATIVES ET CULTURELLES*

PAE See: *PROJET D'ACTIONS ÉDUCATIVES*

PAF See: *PAYSAGE AUDIOVISUEL FRANÇAIS; POLICE DE L'AIR ET DES FRONTIÈRES*

PAIEMENT PAR CHÈQUE See: *CHÈQUE SANS PROVISION*

PALAIS BOURBON
The eighteenth-century Paris residence on the left bank of the Seine, built for one of Louis XIV's daughters, which is now the home of the ASSEMBLÉE NATIONALE.

PALAIS DE L'ÉLYSÉE See: *ÉLYSÉE, PALAIS DE L'*

PALAIS DES CONGRÈS
The largest auditorium in Paris is in this conference centre which can also be used as a concert hall, theatre, etc.

PALAIS DU LUXEMBOURG
The home of the SÉNAT, in the *Jardin du Luxembourg* in Paris. The palace was built in the seventeenth century as a residence for *Marie de Médicis*. Since the Revolution it has had a variety of public uses, including a prison, the seat of the *Directoire* in 1795, the government headquarters in 1848, a hospital, the PRÉFECTURE of the Seine in 1871, a museum, the

Luftwaffe regional HQ, the venue for the 1946 Peace Conference, as well as periods in similar roles to its present one.

PALAIS GARNIER
The main opera house of the OPÉRA DE PARIS, designed by Charles Garnier in 1862.

PALAIS OMNISPORTS PARIS-BERCY
An indoor arena, seating 17,000 spectators, in the south-east district of Paris, used for all kinds of sports and musical events. See also: BERCY

PALAIS ROYAL
The seventeenth-century palace of Cardinal Richelieu, left to Louis XIII on his death, and which later became the site of popular promenades, shops, cafés and sideshows. The *Théâtre du Palais Royal* dates from the eighteenth century and continues the tradition of presenting comedies. See also: COMÉDIE FRANÇAISE; CONSEIL D'ÉTAT

PALMES ACADÉMIQUES See: *ORDRE DES PALMES ACADÉMIQUES*

PANHARD
A French armaments manufacturer, which was previously a renowned name in motor car production.

PANTHÉON
A domed former church of Paris's patron saint, Geneviève, designed in the mid-eighteenth century by Soufflot which became a civil monument during the Revolution. The *Panthéon* commemorates the great historical personalities of republican France, some of whose tombs are found there.

PANTHÉON-ASSAS (UNIVERSITÉ)
The official name of the *Université de Paris-II*, specialising in law, social sciences and economics. It has 20,000 students.

PANTHÉON-SORBONNE (UNIVERSITÉ)
The ceremonial title of the largest of the 13 public universities

in Paris, *Paris-I*, which has 34,000 students in economics, humanities, languages, law and politics.

PAOLI, PASCAL (UNIVERSITÉ) See: *CORSE, UNIVERSITÉ DE*

PAP See: *PRÊT POUR L'ACCESSION À LA PROPRIÉTÉ*

PAPIER TIMBRÉ
A legal form on which duty has been paid and which is thus suitable for use in registering legally binding transactions and various ACTES.

PÂQUES
The religious festival of Easter is not in itself a FÊTE LÉGALE, but the next day, *le lundi de Pâques*, is. There is nowadays no Easter break for schools or other educational establishments apart from this, unless Easter coincides with the *Vacances de printemps*.

PARC DES PRINCES
The open-air sports stadium in the AUTEUIL area of Paris, with seats for almost 50,000, where the largest sporting events usually take place.

PARC NATIONAL
There are seven national parks in France, including one in GUYANE. The designated areas have restrictions about constructions and building developments, and regulated facilities for tourists.

PARENTS See: *ALLOCATIONS; AUTORITÉ PARENTALE; CONSEIL DE CLASSE; CONSEIL D'ÉCOLE; FÉDÉRATION DES PARENTS D'ÉLÈVES DE L'ENSEIGNEMENT PUBLIC; UNION NATIONALE DES ASSOCIATIONS DE PARENTS D'ÉLÈVES DE L'ENSEIGNEMENT LIBRE*

PARI MUTUEL URBAIN (PMU)
A network of off-course horse-race betting offices, established in 1930, closely regulated by the *Ministère de l'*AGRICULTURE, often in DÉBITS DE TABAC. Bets are placed by buying fixed price

tickets which predict winners or finishing positions of runners. The most popular form is the *Tiercé* which requires the player to predict the first three places.

PARIBAS
A banking and finance group, previously the *Banque de Paris et des Pays-Bas*, which was nationalised in 1982 and re-privatised in 1987. Its assets place it in fourth position in France's banking industry.

PARIS
Paris has the status of a DÉPARTEMENT in the ÎLE-DE-FRANCE region. It is also a COMMUNE with its own MAIRE and the elected body is the CONSEIL DE PARIS. Because of its unique position as the largest city and as the capital, other unusual arrangements apply for its government. For instance since 1800, the security of the city has the responsibility of a unique PRÉFET DE POLICE.

The 1990 population of Paris was 2.154 million. This figure shows the first indication of a change in the population since 1954 when it was 2.85 million. The decline has been as a result of movement to the suburbs, and of the urban renewal programmes which have reduced the density of habitation. Perhaps more than in other countries, the place of Paris as the country's capital city has been especially dominant, and policies of regionalisation and DÉCENTRALISATION have been put in place in order to compensate for this. These measures have on the whole had only a marginal effect on business and commerce.

In both the ÉLECTIONS PRÉSIDENTIELLES of 1981 and 1988, Paris voted for the right-wing candidate, GISCARD D'ESTAING receiving 53.56 per cent, and Jacques CHIRAC 54.67 per cent. Parliamentary and *Conseil de Paris* elected members are more evenly balanced.

Code départemental: 75   See also: ARRONDISSEMENT; AXES ROUGES; CONCESSIONS DE PARIS; MAIRE D'ARRONDISSEMENT; MÉTRO; RÉGIE AUTONOME DES TRANSPORTS PARISIENS; RÉSEAU EXPRESS RÉGIONAL

PARIS, UNIVERSITÉS DE
The LOI FAURE split higher education into 13 universities in Paris

and its BANLIEUE. The only one referred to only by number is *Paris-VII*, which has 28,000 students in sciences, arts, medicine and humanities. See: CURIE, PIERRE ET MARIE; DESCARTES, RENÉ; PANTHÉON-ASSAS; PANTHÉON-SORBONNE; PARIS-DAUPHINE; PARIS-NANTERRE; PARIS-NORD; PARIS-SORBONNE; PARIS-SUD; PARIS-VAL-DE-MARNE; SORBONNE-NOUVELLE; VINCENNES-SAINT-DENIS

PARIS-CÂBLE
A joint public and private company which provides cable television to subscribers in Paris, and aims to cover the whole of the capital by 1993.

PARIS-DAUPHINE, UNIVERSITÉ DE
The official name for the *Université de Paris-IX*, with 6,500 students following courses in management, information technology, applied mathematics and economics.

PARISCOPE
A weekly entertainments listing magazine, with a regular readership of 180,000.

PARISIEN, LE
Also known as *Le Parisien libéré*, reflecting its first appearance in 1944, the daily newspaper with the largest circulation (405,000) in the Paris area, with local suburban editions. A prolonged labour dispute about new technology in the mid-1970s seriously affected circulation, but *Le Parisien* can still be said to be Paris's local daily.

PARIS-MATCH
A weekly magazine which established a high reputation for photo-journalism in the 1950s and 1960s. It lost circulation as television took over that role, and now tends to deal largely in stories about celebrities. Its circulation is now 875,000, about half its sale during its peak years. See also: FILIPACCHI

PARIS-NANTERRE, UNIVERSITÉ DE
Situated in the western BANLIEUE at Nanterre (HAUTS-DE-SEINE), this university is also known as *Paris-X*, although it is administratively in the ACADÉMIE of Versailles (YVELINES). There are 32,000 students studying economics, law, arts, humanities,

technology, sport and physical education. It was at Nanterre in 1968 where Daniel COHN-BENDIT and his group of student activists sparked off the events of that year, leading eventually to the LOI FAURE.

PARIS-NORD, UNIVERSITÉ DE

The *Université de Paris-XIII*, in Villetaneuse (SEINE-SAINT-DENIS) in the northern BANLIEUE, part of the ACADÉMIE of Créteil (VAL-DE-MARNE). The 16,000 students are in faculties of arts, sciences, law, humanities and medicine.

PARIS-NORMANDIE

A daily newspaper, published in Rouen, despite its connection with the capital in its title, with a circulation in 1989 of 117,500, which shows a steady decline. Its main market is HAUTE-NORMANDIE.

PARIS-SORBONNE, UNIVERSITÉ DE

The *Université de Paris-IV*, with 25,000 students of languages, civilisation, literature and arts.

PARIS-SUD, UNIVERSITÉ DE

A scientific university, also known as *Paris-XI*, with 27,000 students on a site at Orsay (ESSONNE).

PARIS-TURF

A daily sports newspaper, with a concentration on horse-racing, with a circulation of 127,000.

PARIS-VAL-DE-MARNE, UNIVERSITÉ DE

A multi-campus university based on Créteil (VAL-DE-MARNE) in the south-east BANLIEUE with 20,000 students, also known as *Paris-XII*.

PARIS-VINCENNES, UNIVERSITÉ DE See: *VINCENNES-SAINT-DENIS*

PARLEMENT See: *ASSEMBLÉE NATIONALE; SÉNAT*

PARLEMENTAIRES See: *DÉPUTÉ; SÉNATEUR*

PARLY II

One of the earliest greenfield shopping centres, established in 1969 at le Chesnay (YVELINES).

PARQUET See: *MAGISTRAT*

PART-DIEU, LA
A commercial urban renewal development in Lyon, on the site
of a former barracks, which includes the largest retail sales
area outside the Paris area, but also offices, housing and a
station for the TRAIN À GRANDE VITESSE (TGV).

PARTI COMMUNISTE FRANÇAIS (PCF)
A political grouping of declining importance, the PCF was the
largest single party organisation in French politics for many
years. Its origins are in the *Section française de l'internationale
communiste* (SFIC) founded in 1920. In recent years, it has
maintained loyalty to the USSR communist position, which has
lost it much sympathy among the electorate, and among many
intellectuals, especially after Soviet action in Hungary (1956)
and Czechoslovakia (1968). Through its Labour wing in the
CONFÉDÉRATION FRANÇAISE DU TRAVAIL, it took a conciliatory role
in 1968 and influenced strongly the *Accords de* GRENELLE.

In 1981, there were four Communist ministers in the MAUROY
government. The PCF leader since 1972 has been Georges
MARCHAIS. Its share of voting in 1988 was 6.78 per cent in the
ÉLECTION PRÉSIDENTIELLE and 11.32 per cent in the ÉLECTIONS
LÉGISLATIVES. In the immediate post-war years, it had been
consistently receiving about a quarter of the vote. The ranks of
PCF DÉPUTÉS has fallen steadily, too. There were 86 in 1978,
but only 26 in number 10 years later. The overall vote for the
party's lists in the ÉLECTIONS RÉGIONALES in 1992 was 8 per cent,
just over half of the proportion achieved by the FRONT
NATIONAL. See also: CEINTURE ROUGE; COLONEL-FABIEN, PLACE DU;
FITERMAN, CHARLES; HUMANITÉ; LAJOINIE, ANDRÉ; MARSEILLAISE;
PROGRAMME COMMUN; UNION DE LA GAUCHE

PARTI RADICAL SOCIALISTE
The popular name of the *Parti républicain radical et radical-
socialiste*, established in 1901, and thus the oldest of the
present political parties. It was a loose grouping of notables
before the Second World War, and provided a number of
PRÉSIDENTS DU CONSEIL in the QUATRIÈME RÉPUBLIQUE. In the

CINQUIÈME RÉPUBLIQUE, it has had a marginal influence only, except as a Centrist pressure-group within the UNION POUR LA DÉMOCRATIE FRANÇAISE. It has three DÉPUTÉS and 17 SÉNATEURS.

PARTI RÉPUBLICAIN (PR)
Founded in 1977 as a support organisation for Valéry GISCARD D'ESTAING, largely from his *Républicains indépendants*, this is a Centre Right political group with liberal ideals, dominated in the 1980s by François LÉOTARD. It claims 185,000 members and has 30 DÉPUTÉS. The *Parti républicain* forms part of the UNION POUR LA DÉMOCRATIE FRANÇAISE.

PARTI RÉPUBLICAIN RADICAL ET RADICAL-SOCIALISTE See: *PARTI RADICAL SOCIALISTE*

PARTI SOCIALISTE (PS)
The successor to the SFIO (*Section française de l'internationale ouvrière*) after the Communists split off in 1920 to form what later became the PARTI COMMUNISTE FRANÇAIS. The current name was adopted in 1969 and François MITTERRAND became first secretary in 1971. A PROGRAMME COMMUN with the Communists followed in 1972, and the PS gradually became the leading left-wing party in France.

After Mitterrand's victory in the 1981 ÉLECTION PRÉSIDENTIELLE, the PS formed the majority of the government until 1986 and again from 1988. However, Mitterrand has been at pains to distance himself from party issues, and the influence the party has had on policies has sometimes been limited. There are various groupings or *Clubs de réflexion* within the party which debate issues.

There are 187,000 members, and in the 1988 Parliament 258 DÉPUTÉS and 67 SÉNATEURS. In addition there were over 1,000 PS members of CONSEILS GÉNÉRAUX, although this number was severely reduced in the 1992 ÉLECTIONS CANTONALES. See also: CENTRE D'ÉTUDES, DE RECHERCHES ET D'ÉDUCATION SOCIALISTES; CHEVÈNEMENT, JEAN-PIERRE; FABIUS, LAURENT; JOSPIN, LIONEL; MAUROY, PIERRE

PARTI SOCIALISTE UNIFIÉ (PSU)
A splinter group from the former SFIO (*Section française de*

l'internationale ouvrière) formed in 1960. It had more radical policies than the PARTI SOCIALISTE, and having developed an ecologically focussed stance, merged with the *Nouvelle Gauche* in 1990 to form *Alternative rouge et verte*. See also: ROCARD, MICHEL

PARTICIPATION
A shibboleth of the late 1960s, when employees and students called for a greater influence in the way institutions were run. The call for more '*Participation*' underlay many of the grievances which came to the surface in 1968. The '*Participation*' idea was sometimes called the Yugoslav model.

PASCAL, BLAISE (UNIVERSITÉ) See: *CLERMONT-FERRAND, UNIVERSITÉ DE*

PAS-DE-CALAIS
A DÉPARTEMENT of the NORD-PAS-DE-CALAIS region, with a population of 1,433,203 in 1990, named after the sea passage known in English as the Straits of Dover. The CHEF-LIEU is Arras (AGGLOMÉRATION 79,607), an industrial centre with engineering, metalworks, cement-making, food-processing, textiles and chemicals, and other urban areas are Aire-sur-la-Lys (10,571); Berck (19,693); Béthune (244,719), with rubber, motor vehicles, plastics, clothing, chemicals and precision industries; Boulogne-sur-Mer (95,930), mainland Europe's busiest fishing port, with steelworks, cross-channel ferry traffic and food-processing; Calais (101,768), the largest French port, and third largest in the world, with chemicals, machine tools, electrical engineering, lace-making, toys, clothing and synthetic fibre industries; Étaples (23,412); Isbergues (12,726); Lens (323,174), with chemicals, metallurgy, clothing, vehicle parts, luggage and food-processing industries; Marquise (12,678); Oignies (16,660), where the last coal mine of the region closed down; and Saint-Omer (53,062), with packaging, crystal, clothing, telecommunications industries.

Although industrial activity dominates the *Département*, the Pas-de-Calais is an important production area for barley, flax, tobacco, fresh vegetables and for beet-crops, it produces half of France's coffee chicory, and is high in the ranks for pig production. Its fishing industry provides three-quarters of the national herring, whiting, coley and cod catch.

The holiday resorts of the coast such as Berck and le Touquet (where there is an annual motor-cycle rally on the dunes), the range of Gothic architecture in historic town centres, and the marinas at Calais, Boulogne and Étaples all help to make this an area of interest to tourists. The French terminal for the Channel Tunnel is at Sangatte.

For residents, life is harder. The life expectancy for men is only 67.3 years, the lowest in France, and for women it is 76.5 years, the second lowest.

The political strength has been traditionally on the Left. François MITTERRAND had comfortable majorities here in both the 1981 and 1988 ÉLECTIONS PRÉSIDENTIELLES, and the Left dominates the parliamentary representation. The PARTI SOCIALISTE and the PARTI COMMUNISTE FRANÇAIS retain a reduced majority within the CONSEIL GÉNÉRAL in the 1992 ÉLECTIONS CANTONALES.

Code départemental: 62

PASQUA, CHARLES (1927–   )
A right-wing politician who was *Ministre de l'*INTÉRIEUR from 1986 to1988 and is now the leader of the RASSEMBLEMENT POUR LA RÉPUBLIQUE in the SÉNAT in which he sits as SÉNATEUR for the HAUTS-DE-SEINE. He is also *Président* of that *département's* CONSEIL GÉNÉRAL.

PASSY See: *NEUILLY-AUTEUIL-PASSY*

PASTEUR, LOUIS (UNIVERSITÉ)
The official name of *Université de Strasbourg-I* which has 16,000 students in medicine, pharmacy, science, mathematics, economics and geography. See also: INSTITUT PASTEUR

PAT See: *PRIME D'AMÉNAGEMENT DU TERRITOIRE*

PATHÉ
The second largest group of cinemas in France, based on the same firm which introduced newsreels into cinemas in 1898. See also: CARTE PATHÉ CINÉMA; PATHÉ-MARCONI

PATHÉ-MARCONI
A sound-recording enterprise founded in 1886 by the *Pathé* brothers, and absorbed into the British EMI group in 1936. See also: PATHÉ

PATRONAT See: *CONSEIL NATIONAL DU PATRONAT FRANÇAIS*

PAU ET DES PAYS DE L'ADOUR, UNIVERSITÉ DE
A university with 11,000 students following courses in arts, economics, humanities, law and sciences.

PAYSAGE AUDIOVISUEL FRANÇAIS (PAF)
A generic term used by François MITTERRAND in his plans for broadcasting to denote the mixed economy for television and radio services, as opposed to the State monopoly or commercial 'free for all'. See also: CONSEIL SUPÉRIEUR DE L'AUDIOVISUEL

PAYS BASQUE
The area in the PYRÉNÉES-ATLANTIQUES, known by Basque nationalists as *Euzkadi nord*, which is the French part of the home territory of the Basque people. There are a number of Basque political organisations, which in the late 1980s gained up to 10 per cent of the vote in local elections. In the late 1970s, there were a number of violent nationalist incidents. See also: BASQUE

PAYS DE L'ADOUR, UNIVERSITÉ DU See: *PAU*

PAYS DE LA LOIRE
An administrative RÉGION comprising the DÉPARTEMENTS of LOIRE-ATLANTIQUE, MAINE-ET-LOIRE, MAYENNE, SARTHE and VENDÉE, with a combined population of 3.06 million, and administered from the regional capital, Nantes. The region is heterogeneous in character, and has perhaps found a regional identity difficult to establish, as it has been created almost for administrative convenience.

Its CONSEIL RÉGIONAL has a majority of members from Centre Right groups, the Left suffering severe losses in the 1992 ÉLECTIONS RÉGIONALES, to the advantage of the FRONT NATIONAL, GÉNÉRATION ÉCOLOGIE and VERTS.

PAYS QUINT
A tiny area on the border with Spain, administered through the treaty of Bayonne (1856), where French inhabitants have special privileges concerning their land despite the territory being in Spain.

PAYSAN
Traditionally the term used to denote a peasant farmer, whose land ownership would be small, and who lived in a simple manner, although this sometimes masked considerable prosperity. The word is also used to describe a person of rural background, even if little residence in the country actually applies to that person. Thus, many French people who live in cities come from families with close connections with a rural pays, and are proud of their paysan background.

PAZ See: *PLAN D'AMÉNAGEMENT DE ZONE*

PC See: *PRÊT CONVENTIONNÉ*

PCEM See: *PREMIER CYCLE D'ÉTUDES MÉDICALES*

PCF See: *PARTI COMMUNISTE FRANÇAIS*

PCV See: *PERCEVOIR, À*

PDG See: *PRÉSIDENT-DIRECTEUR-GÉNÉRAL*

PÉAGE See: *AUTOROUTE*

PÉCHINEY-UGINE-KUHLMANN
Usually known simply as *Péchiney*, this is a giant industrial group of companies with interests in aluminium production and that of other non-ferrous metals. *Péchiney* was nationalised in 1982 with the State holding 82 per cent of the control.

PEGC See: *PROFESSEUR D'ENSEIGNEMENT GÉNÉRAL DE COLLÈGE*

PEINE DE MORT
The death penalty was abolished in France in 1981. Before then, it had been used rarely (less frequently than once a year), and

the method of execution was the guillotine. The FRONT NATIONAL has called for its reinstatement.

PEL See: *PLAN D'ÉPARGNE-LOGEMENT; PRÊT D'ÉPARGNE-LOGEMENT*

PÈLERINAGE
There are a number of Christian shrines in France, where pilgrimages regularly occur. Some have an international renown, e.g. Lourdes (HAUTES-PYRÉNÉES), which receives well over five million visitors a year. Others have festivals dating back to the Middle Ages, e.g. Rocamadour (LOT) which attracts one million visitors annually.

PELOTE BASQUE
A ball game dating back to the fifteenth century, which exists in a number of varieties. Players are in teams of up to three (depending on the variant) and use wooden bats, gloves or extended gloves made from leather and wicker to catch and volley the ball.

PENSION ALIMENTAIRE
The maintenance payment provided after a divorce for the divorced spouse and children, and also for a child recognised by its natural parents who are not married, normally index-linked to the INDICE DES PRIX DE DÉTAIL. The *Pension alimentaire* for children is continued after re-marriage of the adult recipient.

PENSION D'INVALIDITÉ See: *ASSURANCE INVALIDITÉ*

PENSION DE RETRAITE
Normally, provided sufficient contributions have been made, it is possible to receive a SÉCURITÉ SOCIALE retirement pension from the age of 60. All members of the scheme can draw the pension from 65, or if they are unable to work through certified disability.

Women are entitled to benefits higher than their contributions would warrant if they have looked after children full-time. All parents of more than three children receive a 10 per cent higher pension payment.

In 1991, the minimum annual *Pension de retraite* was 34,276 francs, and the maximum possible 65,320 francs.

PENSION DE REVERSION
The surviving spouse of a deceased pensioner is entitled to just over half the pension payable, provided that the marriage is at least two years old at the time of death, the survivor is at least 55 years old, and that other income is less than the SALAIRE MINIMUM INTERPROFESSIONNEL DE CROISSANCE.

PENTECÔTE See: *FÊTE LÉGALE*

PEP See: *PLAN D'ÉPARGNE POPULAIRE*

PERCEVOIR, À (PCV)
A reversed charge telephone call, only available for international calls.

PÉRIODE BLANCHE
The regular peak period for travel on rail and air services, normally from midday Friday until midday Saturday, and from Sunday afternoon to midday Monday, and certain FÊTES LÉGALES. See also: CARRÉ JEUNE; CARTE KIWI; PÉRIODE BLEUE; PÉRIODE ROUGE

PÉRIODE BLEUE
The off-peak periods for travelling on rail and air services, virtually at all times except those in PÉRIODE BLANCHE. See also: CARRÉ JEUNE; CARTE COUPLE; CARTE D'INVALIDITÉ; CARTE JEUNE SNCF; CARTE KIWI; CARTE VERMEIL; PÉRIODE ROUGE

PÉRIODE ROUGE
On a few peak days in the year, notably at the beginning and end of August, or around major holiday dates, this classification is given to high peak periods for rail and air travel, and no concessions are valid. See also: PÉRIODE BLANCHE; PÉRIODE BLEUE

PÉRIPHÉRIQUE
An abbreviation for the ring road of a major city, and especially for the *boulevard Périphérique*, the 35 kilometre express ring

road which surrounds Paris and carries one million vehicles a day.

PERMIS DE CHASSE

It is illegal to hunt without a licence, which is issued to those above 16 years of age on payment of a fee, and if successful in an examination. The licence is permanent but has to be renewed annually. Failure to carry a licence while hunting is punishable by a small AMENDE FORFAITAIRE, and hunting without a licence carries a fine of between 3,000 and 6,000 francs. See also: DROIT DE CHASSE

PERMIS DE CONDUIRE

A driving licence issued to a driver over 18 years of age who has passed the two-part qualifying test. The first part is a theoretical test of 40 questions based on slide photographs testing knowledge of the CODE DE LA ROUTE. Thirty-five correct answers are required to pass this part, which can be taken at 16 years of age if a motorcycle or car licence is required. The second part is a practical test in traffic, accompanied by an examiner, and has to be taken within two years of the first stage. The kind of vehicle in which a successful candidate takes this test determines the level for which a licence is issued.

Licences issued in 1992 and afterwards include a points total which is subject to deductions if driving offences are committed (three for the most serious, one for lighting offences, etc). Six months will be necessary between the removal of the last point and ability to drive again. Three years driving free of any offences will result in the initial points total being restored, and there are possibilities for regaining lost points if a driver follows a two-day course in accident prevention. See also: AUTO-ÉCOLE; CONDUITE ACCOMPAGNÉE

PERMIS DE CONSTRUIRE

All building construction needs permission before any work is started. An application is sent to the MAIRIE and permission is granted either by the MAIRE or the PRÉFET, and is valid for up to two years. See also: PLAN D'OCCUPATION DES SOLS

PERMIS DE DÉTENTION D'ARMES AU FEU

Apart from hunting guns, possession of firearms requires the owner to have a permit issued by the local COMMISSARIAT or GENDARMERIE NATIONALE.

PERMIS DE PÊCHE

The only fishing allowed in fresh waters in the DOMAINE PUBLIC is through current membership of an *Association agréée de pêche et de pisciculture*, of which there exist 4,200, covering the whole of French rivers, canals and lakes. Membership costs 150 francs annually and there is an additional *Taxe piscicole* costing 117 francs for most amateur anglers. There are various concessions available for those not able to pay the full rate.

PERNOD-RICARD

A major producer of wines and spirits including the two brands incorporated in the name.

PERPIGNAN, UNIVERSITÉ DE

A small university by French standards, with 4,500 students in humanities, sciences and social sciences.

PERQUISITION

The legal search of premises or vehicle (when it is often called *fouille d'un véhicule*) carried out by an officer of the POLICE JUDICIAIRE. In the case of a CRIME or a FLAGRANT DÉLIT, the permission of the owner is not required. In other enquiries, such permission is normally required, although this provision can be disregarded if terrorist activity is suspected, or in the case of a COMMISSION ROGATOIRE. There are special procedures for conducting searches where professional confidentiality may be compromised (e.g. in the case of a doctor).

With certain exceptions, a *Perquisition* cannot be authorised between the hours of 21.00 and 06.00.

PERRIER

A mineral water bottling company which controls the production at a number of sources, including the well-known Perrier source in Vergèze (GARD), Contrexéville (VOSGES) and Vichy (ALLIER).

In 1990, all sales of Perrier were stopped for a few weeks while a slight imbalance in the natural ingredients affected the source.

PÉTAIN, PHILIPPE (1856–1951)
A professional soldier who attained the status of national hero in his role of defending Verdun in the First World War, and who led the VICHY government from 1940 to 1944, pursuing a right-wing, anti-Jewish policy which effectively served the interests of the Nazi occupiers of the rest of France. Pétain was condemned to death after the end of the war, but his sentence was commuted to life imprisonment. He died in captivity.

PÉTANQUE
A variety of the BOULE group of games, played with metal bowls.

PETIT-CLAMART
In the BANLIEUE of VAL-DE-MARNE, le Petit-Clamart has its place in history as the site of a spectacularly unsuccessful attempt to assassinate DE GAULLE in 1962. See also: ORGANISATION DE L'ARMÉE SECRÈTE

PETITE CEINTURE
The ring road which surrounds Paris and connects all the *portes* which mark the major road entry points at the city limits. The RÉGIE AUTONOME DES TRANSPORTS PARISIENS operates a circular bus service along the route, known as *la Petite Ceinture*. See also: PÉRIPHÉRIQUE

PETITE COURONNE
The ring of COMMUNES which surround Paris, bordering on the city limits. See also: CEINTURE ROUGE; GRANDE COURONNE

PETITES ET MOYENNES ENTREPRISES (PME) See: *CONFÉDÉRATION GÉNÉRALE DES PETITES ET MOYENNES ENTREPRISES*

PETITES ET MOYENNES INDUSTRIES (PMI) See: *CONFÉDÉRATION GÉNÉRALE DES PETITES ET MOYENNES ENTREPRISES*

PETITE VÉNERIE
A classification within the hunting fraternity, denoting hunts for hares with packs of beagles and other small dogs.

PEUGEOT

The largest private enterprise vehicle manufacturer in France, still partly owned by the family descendants of Robert Peugeot who founded the firm in 1896. Peugeot now owns CITROËN, as well as the former American Chrysler operation in Europe, functioning under the Talbot brand.

The main works is at Sochaux (DOUBS), virtually a company town, and there is another large plant at Mulhouse (HAUT-RHIN).

PEYREFITTE, ALAIN (1925–   )

An ÉNARQUE writer, ACADÉMICIEN, former diplomat and politician, who took various ministerial posts in governments of the CINQUIÈME RÉPUBLIQUE, under DE GAULLE, Georges POMPIDOU and Valéry GISCARD D'ESTAING. His final post as minister was as GARDE DES SCEAUX from 1977 to 1981.

PEYREFITTE, ROGER (1907–   )

A diplomat and writer, educated at SCIENCES-PO, who won the *Prix* RENAUDOT in 1944 for *Les Amitiés particulières*, a novel on a homosexual theme, made into a film in 1964. He has written many witty and satririical novels, and fought a long fight against his dismissal from the diplomatic service in 1945, with success only in 1978. *Alexandre le Grand* is a trilogy completed in 1980.

PHARMACIE D'OFFICINE

An officially licenced private enterprise pharmacy. Licences are issued by the PRÉFET at a ratio depending on the size of the urban population. Staffing must comply with a ratio expressed as a proportion of the business's turnover.

PHÉNIX

A nuclear breeder reactor commissioned in 1973 at Marcoule (GARD), but non-operational for most of its life to date.

PHILO

The tag given to the LYCÉE stream who followed what came to be known as the BAC A, because of its inclusion of a philosophy course as a major element. It was previously considered the peak of intellectual achievement in secondary schools, but in recent years has lost prestige to *Bac C*.

PHOSPHORE
A monthly magazine for students at the LYCÉE stage of education, published by BAYARD-PRESSE, with a circulation of 100,000.

PIAF, ÉDITH (1915–1963)
The legendary music-hall singer who personified the mythical Parisian woman, and who endeared herself to the public because of her tempestuous private life.

PIALAT, MAURICE (1925–)
A television and film director whose work concentrates on close social observation, including films such as *Passe ton bac d'abord* (1979) and *Police* (1985).

PICARDIE
An administrative RÉGION, comprising the DÉPARTEMENTS of AISNE, OISE and SOMME, with a combined population in 1990 of 1.8 million. The regional capital is Amiens (SOMME).

The region was able to make use of the DÉCENTRALISATION policy in order to free it a little from the heavy influence of nearby Paris. There was initially considerable rejuvenation of the industrial and agricultural infrastructure which provided some counter-balance to the declining fortunes of the textile sector. The population levels have been stable.

Picardie is perhaps best-known internationally for its role in the First World War. Much of its territory was devastated during the trench warfare.

All major party groups suffered losses in the 1992 ÉLECTIONS RÉGIONALES, but especially the PARTI SOCIALISTE, to the benefit of the FRONT NATIONAL, GÉNÉRATION ÉCOLOGIE and VERTS. Control remained in the hands of the Centre Right.

PICARDIE, UNIVERSITÉ DE
The official name of the university at Amiens where 16,000 students follow courses in arts, economics, humanities, law, medicine, pharmacy, politics and science.

PIC DU MIDI
The mountain in the HAUTES-PYRÉNÉES which is also the site of the highest-placed television transmitter in France.

PIÈCE OFFICIELLE
An official document which can be used as a certificate or supporting evidence.

PIED-NOIR
A French person of European descent who returned to live in France at the independence of ALGÉRIE.

PIGALLE
The district of Paris, south of Montmartre, which is noted for its night-life and rather dubious reputation. It used to be a district of artists.

PILOTE
An influential cartoon magazine which appeared from 1959 to 1989, published by *Dargaud*, in which, among others, ASTÉRIX received its first edition.

PINAY, ANTOINE (1891–   )
A former minister and PRÉSIDENT DU CONSEIL (1952–1953) of the QUATRIÈME RÉPUBLIQUE and *Ministre des* FINANCES ET DE L'ÉCONOMIE under DE GAULLE in 1958 of 1960, who filled the post of MÉDIATEUR from 1973 to 1974.

PIN'S
The fashion of collecting series of badges burst upon France after the 1987 international tennis tournament at the *Stade* ROLAND-GARROS, when the sponsors used it as a means of publicity. Over 200 million were produced in 1991.

PISANI, EDGARD (1918–   )
A former administrator (including terms as PRÉFET) who entered politics as a SÉNATEUR for the HAUTE-MARNE in 1954. He held ministerial posts in DE GAULLES's administration (notably as *Ministre de l'*AGRICULTURE 1961–1966) and was elected again to the SÉNAT in 1974 as a Socialist. In the 1980s he was called on to perform various special tasks, including taking charge of

NOUVELLE-CALÉDONIE, and from 1986 as a *Chargé de mission* for the PRÉSIDENT DE LA RÉPUBLIQUE.

PISTON, CENTRALE See: *ÉCOLE CENTRALE DES ARTS ET MÉTIERS*

PIVOT, BERNARD (1935–   )
An author and television presenter, famous for his role in the success of the TV arts programme *Apostrophes* and later the ANTENNE 2 Saturday evening series *Bouillon de culture*.

PJ See: *POLICE JUDICIAIRE*

PLAFOND LÉGAL DE DENSITÉ (PLD)
The maximum level of density of new building in any particular area, set by the local COMMUNE. Developers wishing to exceed this maximum have to pay to the *commune* a sum equal to the price of the land which would have to be bought to keep the density no higher than the ceiling. This can be waived in the case of multi-storey buildings, or in a ZONE D'AMÉNAGEMENT CONCERTÉ.

PLAINTE
A legal process of complaint, possible if one claims to have suffered a wrongdoing, and taking the form of a formal letter to the PROCUREUR DE LA RÉPUBLIQUE, or to a senior JUGE D'INSTRUCTION or by making a personal declaration to a HUISSIER for consideration by a TRIBUNAL DE POLICE or a TRIBUNAL CORRECTIONNEL.

PLAN
The national economic planning instrument, formally approved by parliament, and lasting usually four or five years. A senior FONCTIONNAIRE, the *Commissaire au plan* has the responsibility of drawing up the plan in negotiations with various sectors of the ADMINISTRATION. Jean Monnet was the first holder of this post and the first *Plan* lasted from 1947 to 1953. See also: PLAN, 10ème

PLAN, 10ème
The PLAN referring to 1989–1992 has two main objectives: to

provide a strategy for national economic growth, and to consolidate the position of France within the European Community.

The means identified for achieving these aims are developments in education and training (including a commitment to 80 per cent of the year-group at BACCALAURÉAT level by the year 2000); improved competitiveness, with an increasing share of resources devoted to research and development; social improvements, especially for pensioners and families, and taxation based on a wider spectrum of incomes; infra-structural support for economically or socially weaker areas; and greater efficiency in public services. See also: PLAN ÉTAT-RÉGIONS

PLAN 'ARMÉES 2000'
The strategic plan for modernising the administration and organisation of the French armed forces in the last decade of the twentieth century.

PLANCHON, ROGER (1931–)
A theatre director who was instrumental in establishing the reputation of the THÉATRE NATIONAL POPULAIRE in Villeurbanne (RHÔNE).

PLAN D'AMÉNAGEMENT DE ZONE (PAZ)
In a ZONE D'AMÉNAGEMENT CONCERTÉ, if a PLAN D'OCCUPATION DES SOLS is not fully observed or not in operation, a PAZ is drawn up to replace it.

PLAN D'ÉPARGNE-LOGEMENT (PEL)
A tax-free fixed-interest savings scheme available through a bank, with a bonus provided by the State after five years. After five years, a loan for buying or developing property for the residence of the borrower can be obtained, repayable over a period up to 15 years. See also: COMPTE ÉPARGNE-LOGEMENT

PLAN D'ÉPARGNE POPULAIRE (PEP)
A savings scheme providing funds for retirement, available from a bank, post office, a CAISSE D'ÉPARGNE or an insurance company. If funds are not withdrawn during the first eight years,

interest is tax-free, and a bonus is paid. The maximum holding is 600,000 francs for an individual, double for a couple. The bonus is credited annually at the rate of 25 per cent of the investments in that year, up to a maximum bonus of 1,500 francs per year. See also: PLAN D'ÉPARGNE RETRAITE

PLAN D'ÉPARGNE-RETRAITE (PER)
A pension scheme for salaried workers, in which the funds must be invested in shares, SICAV or endowment assurance policies. The scheme provides a lump sum or annuity benefit. See also: PLAN DE'ÉPARGNE POPULAIRE

PLAN D'OCCUPATION DES SOLS (POS)
Drawn up by the COMMUNE in consultation with DÉPARTEMENT, RÉGION, CHAMBRE DE COMMERCE ET DE L'INDUSTRIE and other representative bodies where appropriate, the POS gives a general plan of land use and building development strategies for the area, and is a public document. Normally building developments should not contravene the POS. See also: PERMIS DE CONSTRUIRE; PLAN D'AMÉNAGEMENT DE ZONE

PLAN ÉTAT-RÉGION
The procedure in which RÉGIONS make joint commitments for spending in conjunction with the State, in the consultative process of drawing up the PLAN.

PLAN MONORY
An educational reform, enacted by the *Ministre de l'*ÉDUCATION NATIONALE, René Monory in 1986. This provided regulations for a standard pattern of the week in a LYCÉE, with revised specifications for course content towards the BACCALAURÉAT, a reduction in the length of mid-term school holidays and changes in certain teachers' contractual obligations, notably the replacement of the grade of PROFESSEUR D'ENSEIGNEMENT GÉNÉRAL DES COLLÈGES by the PROFESSEUR CERTIFIÉ.

PLAN ORSEC RAD
An emergency plan for co-ordinating evacuation and treatment of sufferers in the case of a radiation disaster.

PLAN ORSEC TOX
An emergency plan for co-ordinating evacuation and treatment
for sufferers in the case of a pollution disaster.

PLATEAU D'ALBION
The site in the VAUCLUSE of a major nuclear weapons firing-
range.

PLD See: *PLAFOND LÉGAL DE DENSITÉ*

PLÉIADE, BIBLIOTHÈQUE DE LA
A prestigious edition of classic literary works published by
GALLIMARD.

PLEINS POUVOIRS See: *ARTICLE 16*

PLEYEL, SALLE
The principal concert hall in Paris, seating 2,300 in the
auditorium.

PLI NON-URGENT
A postal item which is charged at a lower rate, and subject to
a lower priority in the sorting and delivery process.

PLON
A Paris general publisher, part of the PRESSES DE LA CITÉ group.

PLR See: *PROGRAMME À LOYER RÉDUIT*

PLUS-VALUE
A category of tax which is paid on capital gains.

PLUTON
A land-based nuclear missile, deployed since 1974, and from
1992 being replaced by the Hadès missile.

PM See: *POLICE MILITAIRE; PRÉPARATION
MILITAIRE*

PME See: *CONFÉDÉRATION GÉNÉRALE DES PETITES
ET MOYENNES ENTREPRISES*

PMI See: *CONFÉDÉRATION GÉNÉRALE DES PETITES
ET MOYENNES ENTREPRISES*

PMU See: *PARI MUTUEL URBAIN*

PNEUMATIQUE
The system of pneumatic tubes interconnecting Paris post
offices which provided a fast letter delivery service, but which
ceased operation in 1984.

PODIUM-HIT
A monthly pop-culture magazine with a circulation of over
200,000.

POHER, ALAIN (1909–   )
A politician of the Centre who has had a distinguished career
as *Président du* SÉNAT since 1968. Trained as an engineer and
lawyer, Poher spent five years as a SÉNATEUR in the QUATRIÈME
RÉPUBLIQUE, was President of the European Commission in
1955–1957 and has been a member of the European Parliament
since 1958. In his capacity as *Président du Sénat*, Poher was
interim PRÉSIDENT DE LA RÉPUBLIQUE after DE GAULLE's
resignation, and after POMPIDOU's death.

POINT, LE
A Centre Right weekly news magazine, with the majority of
the shares owned by GAUMONT. Its 1990 circulation was
265,000.

POINTE DE CORSEN
The most westerly point in France, at the tip of the Breton
peninsular in the FINISTÈRE.

POIREAU
The popular term for the ORDRE DU MÉRITE AGRICOLE.

POITIERS, UNIVERSITÉ DE
24,000 students follow courses in arts, economics, geography,
history, languages, law, medicine, pharmacy, physical
sciences, social sciences, sport and physical education at this
university.

POITOU-CHARENTES
The administrative RÉGION comprising the DÉPARTEMENTS of
CHARENTE, CHARENTE-MARITIME, DEUX-SÈVRES and VIENNE, and

with a population in 1990 of 1.59 million. The regional capital is Poitiers (VIENNE).

Traditionally known as a region producing high quality food and drink, Poitou-Charentes was an example in the 1980s of how traditional provincial values were changing. Prominent politicians from the region, e.g. Édith CRESSON (MAIRE of Châtellerault – VIENNE, and René MONORY – *Président* of that DÉPARTEMENT'S CONSEIL GÉNÉRAL), were able to influence decisions to bring high-tech industries into the region, and it was one of the first areas to develop a regional identity within the framework of DÉCENTRALISATION.

The region's agricultural base remains strong, with a substantial food-processing industry.

Poitou-Charentes has a particular place in the religious make-up of France. Poitiers was the most northerly point of the Islamic Saracens' campaign in the eighth century, and more recently the region has become a centre for Calvinist Protestants.

In the 1992 ÉLECTIONS RÉGIONALES, the region followed the national trend of electing representatives of the FRONT NATIONAL, GÉNÉRATION ÉCOLOGIE and the VERTS, largely at the expense of the PARTI SOCIALISTE, with the traditional Centre Right retaining overall control.

POLICE DE L'AIR ET DES FRONTIÈRES (PAF)

The section of the POLICE NATIONALE which has the responsibility for guarding frontiers (land, airports and seaports), carrying out government immigration policy and control, supervising civil aviation activity, and investigating aviation and rail accidents.

POLICE JUDICIAIRE (PJ)

The POLICE NATIONALE and GENDARMERIE NATIONALE sections concerned with preventing and investigating organised crime, administered in regional divisions, under the supervision of the PROCUREUR DE LA RÉPUBLIQUE. See also: DIRECTION CENTRALE DE LA POLICE JUDICIAIRE

POLICE MILITAIRE (PM)

A section of the GENDARMERIE NATIONALE which deals with

policing matters concerning military establishments and personnel.

POLICE MUNICIPALE

Towns may run their local police force, sometimes under the direction of seconded officers of the POLICE NATIONALE, to carry out minor or routine policing operations. See also: GARDE CHAMPÊTRE

POLICE NATIONALE

The *Direction générale de la Police nationale* is responsible to the *Ministre de l'*INTÉRIEUR. Police officers are FONCTIONNAIRES and are therefore recruited by CONCOURS to posts as, in descending order of seniority, COMMISSAIRE DE POLICE, INSPECTEUR DE POLICE, OFFICIER DE PAIX and GARDIEN DE LA PAIX.

In towns of more than 10,000 inhabitants the force is called the *Police urbaine*, and in all towns, a supplementary force, responsible to the MAIRE, is the POLICE MUNICIPALE. Equivalent policing in rural areas is the responsibility of the GENDARMERIE NATIONALE which is not part of the *Police nationale*.

The principal sections of the *Police nationale* are the COMPAGNIES RÉPUBLICAINES DE SÉCURITÉ, *Direction centrale des Polices urbaines*, DIRECTION DE LA SURVEILLANCE DU TERRITOIRE, *Inspection générale de la Police nationale* (a supervisory and monitoring body), POLICE JUDICIAIRE, POLICE DE L'AIR ET DES FRONTIÈRES and RENSEIGNEMENTS GÉNÉRAUX. See also: SERVICE NATIONAL

POLICE URBAINE See: *POLICE NATIONALE*

POLYNÉSIE FRANÇAISE

A group of 130 islands and atolls in the Pacific Ocean where there has been a French presence since the mid-eighteeenth century, including the archipelago formerly known as the Friendly Islands. One of the largest islands in *Polynésie française* is Tahiti. Another island is Mururoa, used in recent years for nuclear testing. The population in 1988 was 194,600. The CHEF-LIEU, Papeete has 23,555 inhabitants, and other urban areas are Faaa (24,048) and Pirae (13,366), all of which are on Tahiti.

The territory has the status of a TERRITOIRE D'OUTRE-MER, and since 1977 has had internal autonomy, with an *Assemblée territoriale* as its local parliament, and with a *Président du gouvernement*. The political parties of France are represented locally, as well as movements of local concern only. In 1991, the RASSEMBLEMENT POUR LA RÉPUBLIQUE won 18 of the 41 seats in the *Assemblée territoriale*.

The local economy is based on fishing, tropical fruits and coconut oil, and the Mururoa experimental station has brought its own influence to the territory. Tourism, especially from the USA and France, has become a major element in the economy.

POLYTECHNIQUE See: *ÉCOLE POLYTECHNIQUE*

POMME D'API
One of a series of children's monthly magazine titles, published by BAYARD-PRESSE, with a circulation of 150,850.

POMPES FUNÈBRES
Funeral arrangements can be provided by the COMMUNE as a monopoly, if it so wishes, or by private enterprise. In all cases, the rates chargeable are fixed by the *commune* for the provision of basic services (coffin, hearse, driver and pall-bearers), and for a range of burial services. Additional requirements have prices for which the competitive market operates. The services provided by the *commune* have to be paid for the day before the funeral.

A *commune* has to provide a place of burial for anyone who was resident in the *commune* at the time of death, anyone who died there regardless of place of residence, and anyone with a family plot in the municipal cemetery. With the permission of the PRÉFET, a body can also be buried on private property situated at least 35 metres outside a built-up area.

POMPIDOU, GEORGES (1911–1974)
A graduate of the ÉCOLE NORMALE SUPÉRIEURE, who joined DE GAULLE's administration in 1945 after a career as a teacher. He maintained his career as a FONCTIONNAIRE and later as a banker with the Rothschild group, all the while working with De Gaulle (at the end of the QUATRIÈME RÉPUBLIQUE becoming his *Directeur*

de CABINET). In 1962 he was appointed PREMIER MINISTRE, played an important role in containing the events of MAI 1968, for which he was promptly dismissed. On De Gaulle's resignation, he was elected PRÉSIDENT DE LA RÉPUBLIQUE in 1969 in his first ever election for public office. He was later struck by an illness which was never publicly clarified in his lifetime, and died in office. See also: BEAUBOURG; FONDATION CLAUDE POMPIDOU

PONIATOWSKI, MICHEL (1922–   )
An ÉNARQUE of Polish aristocratic ancestry (he holds the title of Prince), a historian and writer on social issues, who played a leading role in the RÉPUBLICAINS INDÉPENDANTS, both in the party organisation, and as a minister in Valéry GISCARD D'ESTAING'S government. Having been *Directeur de* CABINET for Giscard d'Estaing from 1959 to 1962, he was *Ministre de la santé* in 1973–1974 and then MINISTRE D'ÉTAT *de l'*INTÉRIEUR until 1977, when he took a post as personal Ambassador for the PRÉSIDENT DE LA RÉPUBLIQUE.

PONTS ET CHAUSSÉES See: *ÉCOLE NATONALE DES PONTS ET CHAUSSÉES*

PORTE-PAROLE DU GOUVERNEMENT
A minister who takes responsibility for overseeing announcements of government policy and relations with the mass media.

PORTES DE PARIS
The main exit and entry points for the city area, based on the access points through the 1870 fortifications, linked by the PETITE CEINTURE, and sometimes terminal points for the MÉTRO lines.

POS See: *PLAN D'OCCUPATION DES SOLS*

POSTE
The State monopoly postal service, running post offices, collection and delivery services, and a range of financial services. The initials PTT are still in common use, based on the unified *Postes, télégraphes et téléphones* organisation set up in the nineteenth century. The title officially changed in 1959 to *Postes*

et télécommunications. The *Poste* was established as an independent State-owned business in 1991. See also: CODE POSTAL; COMPTE-CHÈQUES POSTAL; COURRIER D'ENTREPRISE À DISTRIBUTION EXCEPTIONNELLE; PLI NON-URGENT

POSTE, TÉLÉCOMMUNICATIONS ET ESPACE (MINISTÈRE DE LA) (PTE)
The ministry which oversees the postal and telecommunications networks. See also: FRANCE TÉLÉCOM; POSTE

POSTÉCLAIR
The facsimile service provided by FRANCE-TÉLÉCOM.

POTIN, FÉLIX See: *FÉLIX POTIN*

POUJADE, PIERRE (1920–)
The leader of the *Union de défense des commerçants et artisans*, otherwise known as the *Mouvement Poujade*, which was active and politically influential in the 1950s, as a right-wing parliamentary grouping. Since the mid-1970s its influence has been more as a support organisation for the self-employed.

POUPONNIÈRE SOCIALE
A day nursery for children of three years of age and younger.

POURBOIRE
Tips cannot be required, and charges for service must be identified and included in the bill presented. In some places, tipping is forbidden.

POURVOI EN CASSATION
A referral of a legal case by one or more parties in the case to the COUR DE CASSATION.

POUVOIR LIBÉRATOIRE DES PIÈCES
Currently valid coins may be offered in payment up to a certain maximum quantity. Beyond that figure, they may legally be refused. Thus, it is possible to refuse more than 50 coins of one franc, five and ten francs (if all of the same value) if offered at one time, or more than ten francs if paid wholly in half franc coins; five francs if paid in 20, 10 or five centimes coins, and

one franc if paid in one or two centime coins. See also: COURS
LÉGAL

POUVOIRS SPÉCIAUX See: *ARTICLE 16*

PR See: *PARTI RÉPUBLICAIN*

PRATS-DE-MOLLO
The most southerly point in France is the mountain of la Bague
de Bordeillat, near Prats-de-Mollo (PYRÉNÉES-ORIENTALES).

PRÉFECTURE
The administrative headquarters of the DÉPARTEMENT, and seat
of the PRÉFET. *Préfecture* is also used as an alternative term for
the CHEF-LIEU of the *département*.

PRÉFECTURE DE POLICE DE PARIS See: *PRÉFET DE
POLICE DE PARIS*

PRÉFET
The senior government official and representative of State
power in each DÉPARTEMENT, appointed by a DÉCRET of the
PRÉSIDENT DE LA RÉPUBLIQUE, usually after a period of service as
a SOUS-PRÉFET. He or she (the first woman *Préfet* being Yvette
Chassagne, appointed to the LOIR-ET-CHER in 1981) is responsible
for executing government decisions and for co-ordinating the
State ADMINISTRATION. See also: COMMISSAIRE DE LA RÉPUBLIQUE;
PRÉFET DE RÉGION

PRÉFET DE POLICE DE PARIS
In addition to the PRÉFET of Paris, there is a senior official
responsible for POLICE NATIONALE and POLICE MUNICIPALE in the
city, appointed by the *Ministre de l'*INTÉRIEUR. He has a brief
over fire, rescue and civil defence matters which extends to the
HAUTS-DE-SEINE, SEINE-SAINT-DENIS and VAL-DE-MARNE.

PRÉFET DE RÉGION
The government official who has the responsibility for ensuring
that government policy for economic development is enacted
in the administrative RÉGION. He or she acts as government
representative in dealings with the CONSEIL RÉGIONAL, as well
as co-ordinating all civil service activities in the region.

He or she is appointed by the CONSEIL DES MINISTRES and is responsible to the PREMIER MINISTRE. If the DÉPARTEMENT of the regional capital is also the CHEF-LIEU of a RÉGION MILITAIRE, the title of *Commissaire de la République de zone de défense* is also held. See also: CONFÉRENCE ADMINISTRATIVE RÉGIONALE; PRÉFET

PRÉLÈVEMENT LIBÉRATOIRE
A payment of tax directly deducted from interest-bearing investments, which can be advantageous for a person subject to the IMPÔT SUR LE REVENU who is liable to a high rate of tax.

PREMIER CYCLE
The first two-year stage of higher education studies, leading normally to the award of a DIPLÔME D'ÉTUDES UNIVERSITAIRES GÉNÉRALES.

PREMIER MINISTRE
The post created as part of the CONSTITUTION of the CINQUIÈME RÉPUBLIQUE for the head of the government. The *Premier Ministre* is appointed by the PRÉSIDENT DE LA RÉPUBLIQUE and forms a government of ministers whom he or she recommends to the *Président* for appointment.

He or she has the responsibility for the overall management of government affairs, and can delegate certain powers to ministers, issue DÉCRETS, preside over the CONSEIL DES MINISTRES if invited to do so by the *Président de la République*, and defends the government in the ASSEMBLÉE NATIONALE. The *Premier Ministre* must be consulted by the *Président de la République* before the taking of PLEINS POUVOIRS.

The first woman *Premier Ministre* was Édith CRESSON, appointed in 1991. See also: CHAMPS-SUR-MARNE; MATIGNON; PRÉSIDENT DU CONSEIL

PREMIER TOUR
The first round of voting in an ÉLECTION, held on a Sunday. If no candidate receives more than 50 per cent of the votes, a second round is held a fortnight later, the candidates with the smallest number of votes being eliminated. See also: SCRUTIN DE LISTE MAJORITAIRE

PRÉPARATION MILITAIRE (PM)

Voluntary military training for those aged at least 17, with parents' consent, which permits special benefits in completing SERVICE MILITAIRE, with, for instance, for those who do very well, entry into officer training courses as part of the *Service militaire*.

PRESCRIPTION

The period of validity during which a right can be exercised, or proceedings after a criminal offence can be taken.

PRÉSIDENT DE LA RÉPUBLIQUE

Under the CONSTITUTION of the CINQUIÈME RÉPUBLIQUE, the *Président de la République* is elected for seven years as Head of State. Since 1965, the election has been by universal suffrage, whereas before this the *Président de la République* was elected by an electoral college.

The *Président de la République* appoints the PREMIER MINISTRE and the CONSEIL DES MINISTRES, which he or she chairs, is the head of the armed forces, signs LOIS, DÉCRETS and ORDONNANCES. He or she is guardian of the Constitution and refers to the CONSEIL CONSTITUTIONNEL in cases of difficulty. Similarly the *Président de la République* has the responsibility of ensuring the independence of the MAGISTRATS. He or she is able to dissolve the ASSEMBLÉE NATIONALE, can consult the population by RÉFÉRENDUM and can rule by PLEINS POUVOIRS in certain situations.

It has been a feature of the *Cinquième République* that the *Président de la République* has taken overall charge of foreign policy. See also: DE GAULLE; ÉLECTION PRÉSIDENTIELLE; ÉLYSÉE; GISCARD D'ESTAING; MITTERRAND; POMPIDOU

PRÉSIDENT-DIRECTEUR GÉNÉRAL (PDG)

The chairman and chief executive of a large business.

PRÉSIDENT DU CONSEIL

The title of the equivalent of the PREMIER MINISTRE in the QUATRIÈME RÉPUBLIQUE, in which it was a much weaker post than that of its replacement.

PRÉSIDENT D'UNIVERSITÉ
The vice-chancellor of a university. See also: RECTEUR
D'ACADÉMIE

PRESSES DE LA CITÉ
A major publishing group with imprints such as BORDAS and
PLON, and part owner of FRANCE-LOISIRS, operating as a subsidiary
of the HAVAS organisation.

PRESSES UNIVERSITAIRES DE FRANCE (PUF)
A Paris-based publisher of academic and informative books,
including the QUE SAIS-JE? series.

PRESTATION COMPENSATOIRE
A divorced person (unless the divorce is entirely the fault of
that person) can claim a special allowance if the divorce causes
severe financial difficulties, and this can be charged to the other
partner. See also: PENSION ALIMENTAIRE

PRESTATION FAMILIALE See: *ALLOCATION; PRIME DE DÉMÉNAGEMENT*

PRÊT CONVENTIONNÉ (PC)
A loan for purchase of new property, or for building or
rebuilding a house, provided that the rebuilding conforms to
current regulations concerning minimum standards.

The loan is granted by a bank, a CAISSE D'ÉPARGNE, the CRÉDIT
AGRICOLE or CRÉDIT FONCIER DE FRANCE, for periods up to 20 years,
depending on the purpose of the loan, and for sums up to 90
per cent of the cost of the work, subject to regional maxima.
The rate of interest is about 10 per cent, and varies according
to lender and size of loan. It is permissible to borrow on a
Prêt conventionné simultaneously with another kind of loan. A
borrower of a PC may be entitled to the AIDE PERSONNALISÉE AU
LOGEMENT. See also: COMPTE ÉPARGNE-LOGEMENT; PLAN ÉPARGNE-
LOGEMENT; PRÊT POUR ACCESSION À LA PROPRIÉTÉ; PRÊT 1 POUR CENT
PATRONAL

PRÊT D'ÉPARGNE-LOGEMENT (PEL) See: *COMPTE ÉPARGNE-LOGEMENT; PLAN D'ÉPARGNE-LOGEMENT*

PRÊT POUR ACCESSION À LA PROPRIÉTÉ (PAP)

Sometimes called the *Prêt aidé pour accession à la propriété*, this is a fixed or variable interest loan for the purchase of a home and for work to improve older homes to current standards, granted over 15, 18 or 20 years by a *Société de crédit immobilier* HLM or the CRÉDIT FONCIER DE FRANCE, up to maximum sums depending on geographical location, number of incomes and family size. If the variable rate of interest is paid, it increases over the period of the loan. A borrower of a PAP may be entitled to the AIDE PERSONNALISÉE AU LOGEMENT. See also: COMPTE ÉPARGNE-LOGEMENT; HABITATION À LOYER MODÉRÉ; PLAN ÉPARGNE-LOGEMENT; PRÊT CONVENTIONNÉ; PRÊT 1 POUR CENT PATRONAL

PRÊT 1 POUR CENT PATRONAL

If an enterprise has at least 10 employees, it is possible for the employer to grant loans to them for the purchase or improvement of a home, up to a possible 15 per cent of the total purchase price or 60 per cent of improvements, and subject to certain maximum sums, depending on the employee's circumstances. See also: COMPTE ÉPARGNE-LOGEMENT; PLAN ÉPARGNE-LOGEMENT; PRÊT CONVENTIONNÉ; PRÊT POUR ACCESSION À LA PROPRIÉTÉ

PRÉVENTION ROUTIÈRE

The public road safety organisation.

PRÉVENU See: *INCULPÉ*

PRÉVERT, JACQUES (1900–1977)

A popular poet and screen writer who was strongly influenced by the Surrealist movement. He is perhaps most famous for his 1945 collection *Paroles*, some of which have been set to music, and his screenplay for *Quai des Brumes*, a film by Marcel Carné in 1937. In 1975, he and his brother Pierre, a film director, won the *Grand Prix national du cinéma*.

PRIME À L'AMÉLIORATION DE L'HABITAT (PAH)

This grant of up to 20 per cent of the cost of improvement works to an occupied residence can be paid to the owner or occupier, and up to 50 per cent if this includes adaptations for a disabled person. Normally the recipient has to retain occupancy for 10 years or repay the grant. The grant is subject to certain maximum sums and is paid through the MAIRIE.

PRIME À L'AMÉNAGEMENT DU TERRITOIRE See: *ZONE À RÉGIME PRÉFÉRENTIEL*

PRIME DE DÉMÉNAGEMENT
A grant awarded to families with at least three young children if moving residence within two years of the birth of the youngest, and if they qualify for the AIDE PERSONNALISÉE AU LOGEMENT or ALLOCATION LOGEMENT.

PRIME DE DÉVELOPPEMENT RÉGIONAL (PDR)
A government grant paid to an enterprise which expands its activity outside the Paris area. The amount of grant payable is related to the number of jobs created by the new development.

PRINTEMPS
A major retailing group of companies, based on the Paris department store founded in 1865. There are now 17 *Printemps* stores and 47 others connected with the chain, and the group also controls EUROMARCHÉ, PRISUNIC and other retail chains.

PRIORITÉ À DROITE
The rule of driving priority is that unless there are indications otherwise, a driver should give way to a vehicle approaching from the right. On a roundabout, however, the rule is to give way to traffic approaching from the left.

PRIORITÉ D'EMPLOI AUX HANDICAPÉS ET MUTILÉS
An employer with more than 10 workers must offer at least 10 per cent of the posts vacant to disabled or war-wounded personnel, or pay an annual penalty.

PRISUNIC
A chain of retail department stores aimed at the lower end of the market, owned by the PRINTEMPS group.

PRIVATISATION
The policy of the government headed by Jacques CHIRAC from 1986 to 1988, despite some opposition from François

MITTERRAND, was to return to the private sector the banks and some other businesses which had been nationalised in 1945 and 1982. The policy was designed to take effect over a period of five years, and certain State-owned businesses were named as being privatisable.

PRIX D'AMÉRIQUE
An annual trotting horse-race is run at Vincennes in January for this prize, created in 1920, which in 1991 was worth 3.5 million francs.

PRIX DE DIANE
An annual horse-race run at Chantilly in June over a distance of 2.1 kilometres, for a prize of 1.4 million francs. The *Prix de Diane* has existed since 1843.

PRIX DE L'ARC DE TRIOMPHE
A prestigious annual flat race for three year old horses run since 1920 at LONGCHAMP on the first Sunday in October. The prize is five million francs.

PRIX DE NOVEMBRE
A literary prize established in 1989, with a value of 20,000 francs, sponsored by *Cassegrain*, a stationery firm, and considered to be independent of publishers' influence.

PRIX DU MAIRE See: *CONCOURS 'LE PRIX DU MAIRE'*

PRIX FÉMINA See: *FÉMINA, PRIX*

PRIX GONCOURT See: *ACADÉMIE GONCOURT*

PRIX LOUIS-DELLUC
An annual prize for a French film, awarded in December, and named after the first specialist film critic in France who also founded CINÉ CLUBS.

PRIX RENAUDOT See: *RENAUDOT, PRIX*

PROCÈS-VERBAL
A written legal statement alleging facts which can be used in criminal proceedings.

PROCURATION
A proxy vote available in certain circumstances to ÉLECTEURS absent from their COMMUNE on voting day, or those who are unable to visit a polling station because of disability or infirmity.

'*Procuration*' is also the power of attorney giving authorisation, for example, to draw money from another person's account.

In rare instances, it is also possible to enact marriage '*par procuration*'.

PROCUREUR
The public prosecuting AVOCAT appointed by the GARDE DES SCEAUX, and part of the PARQUET. Depending on the importance of the court, there can be one or more *Procureur-général* and sometimes a *Procureur-adjoint*. In the TRIBUNAL DE GRANDE INSTANCE, the role is undertaken by the *Procureur de la République*.

PROFESSEUR
The generic title for a qualified teacher in secondary or higher education, or musical education at any level. Until the introduction of the title PROFESSEUR DES ÉCOLES, this would not have referred in any way to teachers in primary schools.

PROFESSEUR AGRÉGÉ
A holder of the AGRÉGATION, teaching in secondary (usually a LYCÉE) or higher education, who is contracted for 15–17 hours of teaching a week.

PROFESSEUR CERTIFIÉ See: *CERTIFICAT D'APTITUDE AU PROFESSORAT DE L'ENSEIGNEMENT DU SECOND DEGRÉ.*

PROFESSEUR D'ENSEIGNEMENT GÉNÉRAL DES COLLÈGES (PEGC) See: *CERTIFICAT D'APTITUDE AU PROFESSORAT D'ENSEIGNEMENT GÉNÉRAL AU COLLÈGE*

PROFESSEUR DES ÉCOLES See: *INSTITUTEUR*

PROGRAMME À LOYER RÉDUIT (PLR)
A similar, but less expensive version of the LOGEMENT SOCIAL provided by the HABITATION À LOYER MODÉRÉ.

PROGRAMME COMMUN
The joint electoral platform agreed by the PARTI COMMUNISTE FRANÇAIS and the PARTI SOCIALISTE in order to improve their chances of taking power in the 1970s. It included a 40 hour week, price controls, nationalisation of key sectors of the economy, a decentralised secular education system, a reduction in the legal power of the State, a commitment of the government to the programme, and a disarmament and world peace initiative. See also: UNION DE LA GAUCHE

PROGRÈS, LE
The principal daily newspaper published in Lyon with a circulation in 1989 of 355,000, and 342,000 for the Sunday edition. *Le Progrès* was bought by Robert HERSANT in 1985 and now forms part of his *Groupe du Progrès-Dauphiné*.

PROJET CACQUOT
An 10-year engineering project in the Baie du Mont-Saint-Michel to harness the power of the tides to generate electricity.

PROJET D'ACTIONS ÉDUCATIVES (PAE)
An additional funding in an ÉCOLE MATERNELLE and an ÉCOLE PRIMAIRE to overcome social and cultural inequality, usually used to provide an improved environment, or extra library or arts facilities.

PROJET D'ACTIVITÉS ÉDUCATIVES ET CULTURELLES (PACTE)
A local curriculum project run in a school through the initiative of a teacher, and supplementing the nationally agreed programme.

PROJET DE LOI
A proposal for legislation placed before the ASSEMBLÉE NATIONALE in the name of the PREMIER MINISTRE thus signifying that it is a government initiative. See also: PROPOSITION DE LOI

PROMENADE DES ANGLAIS
The seven kilometre seafront in Nice, made fashionable by rich English tourists in the late nineteenth century.

PROMESSE DE VENTE AVEC DÉDIT See: *PROMESSE DE VENTE SYNALLAGMATIQUE*

PROMESSE DE VENTE FERME See: *PROMESSE UNILATÉRALE DE VENTE*

PROMESSE DE VENTE SYNALLAGMATIQUE
Also known as a *Compromis de vente*, or a *Promesse de vente avec dédit*, this is a contract of sale and purchase of a property subject to certain conditions being successfully completed, validated by the payment of a deposit by the purchaser. The deposit is forfeited if the purchaser withdraws, and 200 per cent of the deposit is returned to the purchaser if the vendor withdraws. See also: PROMESSE UNILATÉRALE DE VENTE

PROMESSE UNILATÉRALE DE VENTE
Also called a *Promesse de vente ferme*, this is a contract of sale and purchase of a property, subject to the payment of a deposit (usually 10 per cent of the price) by the purchaser and with the possibility of a period during which both parties may reconsider their decision. If the purchaser withdraws, the deposit is forfeited. Once the agreed period is passed, the contract is binding. See also: PROMESSE DE VENTE SYNALLAGMATIQUE

PROMODÈS
A retailing group controlling chains of supermarkets and hypermarkets under the CONTINENT, CHAMPION, CODEC, SHOPI and other names.

PROPOSITION DE LOI
A proposal for legislation introduced for debate in the ASSEMBLÉE NATIONALE by a DÉPUTÉ as opposed to a member of the government. See also: PROJET DE LOI

PROTECTION CIVILE
The national organisation of civil defence is the responsibility of the *Ministre de l'*INTÉRIEUR through the *Direction de la sécurité civile*. There is a special fleet of helicopters at strategic points, and specialists in bomb disposal, rescue and mass evacuation available to the service. In each DÉPARTEMENT, the PRÉFET has the power to co-ordinate operations.

PROTECTION DE LA ROUTE See: *PRÉVENTION ROUTIÈRE*

PROTECTION SOCIALE See: *SÉCURITÉ SOCIALE*

PROTESTANTISME
The principal organisation representing the various Protestant churches in France is the *Fédération protestante de France*, founded in 1904. It is a national body speaking for 15 different groupings, the largest of which is the ÉGLISE RÉFORMÉE DE FRANCE.

PROVENÇAL See: *OCCITAN*

PROVENÇAL, LE
A daily newspaper, published in Marseille, with a circulation of 159,000 in 1989, and a Sunday edition of 165,000. *Le Provençal* is part of the HACHETTE group.

PROVENCE-ALPES-CÔTE-D'AZUR (PACA)
The administrative RÉGION of the south-east, comprising the DÉPARTEMENTS of ALPES-DE-HAUTE-PROVENCE, ALPES-MARITIMES, BOUCHES-DU-RHÔNE, HAUTES-ALPES, VAR and VAUCLUSE. The overall population, growing rapidly, is 4.25 million, and the regional capital is Marseille.

There is relatively little industry, and service activities account for the major part of the economy. Individual incomes are higher than average for the country, although this is heavily weighted in favour of the ALPES-MARITIMES. The PACA is notable for the rivalry of its two major cities, Marseille and Nice, which tends to reflect this imbalance in prosperity, and the political differences between their representatives have often dominated the development of the region.

In the 1992 ÉLECTIONS RÉGIONALES, the PACA was widely expected to show significant gains for the FRONT NATIONAL, and Jean-Marie LE PEN led its list in the Alpes-Maritimes. In the event, the FN did well in Nice, but the relative success of the *Majorité présidentielle* list led by Bernard TAPIE was the national surprise, and although the FN more than doubled the number of *Conseillers régionaux* to 34, the Centre Right retained its overall control.

PROVENCE, UNIVERSITÉ DE See: *AIX-MARSEILLE*

PROVINCE
Any part of France which is outside the immediate environs of
Paris. Because of the unusually dominant position of Paris,
this division has been more marked than in some countries, and
this perceived distance still remains in many ways. The term '*en
province*' is considered by many to be derogatory and is being
replaced in media talk by '*en régions*'.

PROVISEUR
The head of a LYCÉE, a full time administrator who has
performed service as a PROFESSEUR AGRÉGÉ, and has succeeded
in the recruitment CONCOURS.

PRUD'HOMME See: *CONSEIL DE PRUD'HOMMES*

PRYTANÉE NATIONAL MILITAIRE DE LA FLÈCHE See:
LYCÉE

PS See: *PARTI SOCIALISTE*

PSU See: *PARTI SOCIALISTE UNIFIÉ*

PTE See: *POSTE, TÉLÉCOMMUNICATIONS, ESPACE
(MINISTÈRE DE LA)*

PTT See: *POSTE*

PUBLICIS
The most profitable advertising agency in France.

PUBLICITÉ
Advertising is permitted on public and private television except
for illegal articles: tobacco, pharmaceutical products, certain
financial services, all drinks with an alcohol content of more
than 1 per cent, books, cinema films and the press. There are
certain regulations about the amount of advertising – in general,
six minutes per hour is the average maximum permitted.

PUBLICITÉ MENSONGÈRE
Misleading or untruthful advertising is illegal, and action can
be taken by the DIRECTION DÉPARTEMENTALE DE LA CONCURRENCE

ET DE LA CONSOMMATION ET DE LA RÉPRESSION DES FRAUDES against offenders.

PUF See: *PRESSES UNIVERSITAIRES DE FRANCE*

PUPILLE DE L'ÉTAT
Formerly termed *Pupille de la nation*, a child who has been taken into care by the AIDE SOCIALE. Children of soldiers killed in action are often in this category.

PUY-DE-DÔME
A DÉPARTEMENT of the AUVERGNE region, with a 1990 population of 598,213, named after the volcanic mountain just south of the CHEF-LIEU, Clermont-Ferrand (AGGLOMÉRATION, 254,416). Clermont-Ferrand is the headquarters of MICHELIN and its rubber industries (although the work-force is being reduced), has the BANQUE DE FRANCE's printing works, engineering, bio-tech, electronics, food-processing, cycles and clothing industries among its sources of employment. Other urban areas are Issoire (13,559), an aluminium and metal construction centre; Riom (25,110), with tobacco and pharmaceuticals; and Thiers (16,688), the cutlery capital of France, but with other metal industries, plastics and clothing. There is a steelworks at les Ancizes, in an otherwise rural setting.

The Puy-de-Dôme has a considerable number of thermal springs which attract both tourists and those seeking thermal treatment. Volvic is a well-known mineral water source. Other tourist attractions include the *Parc régional des volcans d'Auvergne*, a large number of lakes and a rich geological variety, and a remarkable number of cheeses.

The parliamentary representatives of the Puy-de-Dôme are predominantly Socialist. In the ÉLECTIONS PRÉSIDENTIELLES, François MITTERRAND's slight majority of 1981 was increased in 1988 to 54.87 per cent in 1988. However in 1992, the CONSEIL GÉNÉRAL fell to the Centre Right, with the UNION POUR LA DÉMOCRATIE FRANÇAISE making the largest gains.

Code départemental: 63

PYRAMIDE DU LOUVRE See: *LOUVRE*

PYRÉNÉES-ATLANTIQUES

A DÉPARTEMENT in the AQUITAINE region, formerly known as
Basses-Pyrénées, on the border with Spain and on the Atlantic
coast, with a population of 578,475 in 1990, and including the
French PAYS BASQUE. The CHEF-LIEU is Pau (134,625 in the urban
area, with natural gas and oil industries, engineering, dairy and
footwear). The other AGGLOMÉRATIONS are Bayonne (124,135),
a port with aviation, chemicals and engineering works; Biarritz
(28,742), a major tourist resort; Hendaye (11,578); Mourenx
(11,102) – textiles and cosmetics; Oloron-Sainte-Marie (15,842)
– aviation industry, wood, leather and confectionery; Orthez
(10,15) – textiles, paper and footwear; and Saint-Jean-de-Luz
(24,978) – fishing port, food-processing and seaside resort. A
huge subterranean natural gas resource is exploited at Lacq,
feeding into the national network, and a oil pipeline between
Lacq and Bayonne.

The main agricultural products are wines, maize, and ewes'
milk.

There are a number of tourist resorts, both on the coast and
inland at various spa towns.

The DÉPUTÉS and SÉNATEURS for the Pyrénées-Atlantiques
come from a broad range of party groupings. In 1981, Valéry
GISCARD D'ESTAING gained a small majority in the ÉLECTION
PRÉSIDENTIELLE and François MITTERRAND took a similarly
marginal majority in 1988. In the 1992 ÉLECTIONS CANTONALES,
the Centre Right maintained its overall control of the CONSEIL
GÉNÉRAL.

Code départemental: 64

PYRÉNÉES-ORIENTALES

A mainly rural DÉPARTEMENT of the LANGUEDOC-ROUSSILLON
region, on the Mediterranean coast and on the border with
Spain. The population in 1990 was 363,793, including a
substantial majority who speak Catalan as well as French. The
CHEF-LIEU, Perpignan, with 137,915 inhabitants in its urban area,
is a major market for wine, fruit and vegetables, with toy and
hat-making industries. There is no other town with a population
above 10,000.

Main agricultural products are wines and apéritifs (including *Byrrh*, *Banyuls*, *Corbières* and *Rivesaltes*), fruit (the Pyrénées-Orientales is the second largest producer of apricots in France), honey and vegetables.

Tourism is an important economic factor, and the *Département* has the advantage of sun, the COMMUNE of Eus receiving the most hours of sun (2,644 hours per year) in the country, skiing resorts, spa towns, marinas, a rich heritage of abbeys and Romanesque churches, and mountain and coastal lakes.

Unemployment has been running at an uncomfortably high rate in recent years.

A comfortable majority in the 1981 ÉLECTION PRÉSIDENTIELLE for François MITTERRAND was reduced to a more marginal figure in 1988. The parliamentary representation shows a balance between Left and Right, but the CONSEIL GÉNÉRAL is controlled by the Centre Right, a slight swing towards the Left being recorded in the 1992 ÉLECTIONS CANTONALES.

Code départemental: 66

QUAI CONTI
The address of the ACADÉMIE FRANÇAISE.

QUAI D'ORSAY
The address of the *Ministère des* AFFAIRES ÉTRANGÈRES.

QUARTIER LATIN
The area in central Paris on the left bank of the Seine which is
the heart of the university quarter and therefore a centre of
student activity.

QUART MONDE
A charitable organisation established in 1957 to support people
in difficulties. It has family centres, retraining establishments,
libraries, support services for learning called *Clubs de savoir*,
and now acts through 200 local committees.

QUATRIÈME RÉPUBLIQUE
The régime established by the Constitution of 1946, which lasted
until 1958. Its history was marked a by a series of weak
governments, partly due to the ASSEMBLÉE NATIONALE's relatively
powerful role as opposed to that of the PRÉSIDENT DU CONSEIL,
and partly because of the large number of disparate party
groupings. This executive weakness made it difficult to deal
with colonial difficulties and the war in ALGÉRIE.

QUE CHOISIR?
A monthly consumer magazine with a circulation of 212,000,
running comparative tests of products, and published by the
Union fédérale des consommateurs, an independent
organisation which has always criticised the State support
given to its rival publication, CINQUANTE MILLIONS DE
CONSOMMATEURS. A connected publication is *Que Choisir?
Santé*.

QUELLE
A mail-order catalogue enterprise founded in 1965, distributing about four million of its catalogues to customers from its base in Orléans (LOIRET).

QUENEAU, RAYMOND (1903–1976)
A novelist and poet, highly influenced by the Surrealists, best-known for his best-seller *Zazie dans le métro* (1959) but also for his innovative approach to poetry, exemplified by *Cent mille milliards de poèmes* (1961). Queneau was also a translator of American novels, working for GALLIMARD.

QUE SAIS-JE?
A paperback imprint of PRESSES UNIVERSITAIRES DE FRANCE in a standard format of 128 page books which aim to give the reader a brief authoritative summary of a subject. There have been more than 60 million sales since the start of the series in 1941.

QUID
An annual compendium of facts, published since 1963, by LAFFONT, and now a kind of institution. *Quid* includes material on all subjects, but focuses in detail on France.

QUILLIOT, LOI See: *LOI QUILLIOT*

QUINZAINE
A fortnight, but also half a month, starting on the first or sixteenth day of a month.

QUOTIDIEN DE PARIS, LE
As its name suggests, a daily newspaper published in Paris. *Le Quotidien de Paris* was founded in 1974, but suffered an interruption in production for 17 months in 1978–1979. Its circulation in 1989 was 80,000 and its deficit was mounting.

QUOTIENT ÉLECTORAL
In an ÉLECTION using the proportional representation system, a calculation of the number of votes cast divided by the number of seats available gives the *Quotient électoral*, which is the minimum number of votes necessary for a seat to be gained.
See also: SCRUTIN DE LISTE À LA REPRÉSENTATION PROPORTIONELLE

QUOTIENT FAMILIAL See: *IMPÔT SUR LE REVENU*

RABANNE, PACO (1934–)
A Spanish-born fashion designer who settled in France in 1965, and whose collections include the use of plastics, metals and highly coloured materials.

RABELAIS, FRANÇOIS (UNIVERSITÉ)
The official title of the university at Tours with arts, economics, languages, law, management, medicine, pharmacy, and science courses, taking 21,000 students. The university forms part of the ACADÉMIE of Orléans-Tours.

RACING CLUB DE FRANCE
A sports club with 20,000 members, with a foundation dating back to 1882, originally based in the BOIS DE BOULOGNE, with a wide range of facilities in the Paris area. The international stadium at Colombes (HAUTS-DE-SEINE) is one of the premises owned and managed by the club.

RADAR
A chain of retail stores, mainly supermarkets carrying the *Radar* name, but also a number of MONOPRIX stores are within the group's ownership, and it owns *Dames de France*, the women's fashion chain.

RADIO ADOUR NAVARRE See: *RADIO-TÉLÉ LUXEMBOURG*

RADIO BLEUE
A radio service of RADIO FRANCE, broadcasting 14 hours per day with programmes aimed at the over 50 age group, with a diet mainly composed of French songs.

RADIOCOM 2000
The national mobile telephone network operated by FRANCE TÉLÉCOM.

RADIO FRANCE

The State-owned radio broadcasting company, with its headquarters at the MAISON DE LA RADIO. Its income comes principally from the REDEVANCE, with a small amount from advertising revenue. The national stations are RADIO BLEUE, FIP, FRANCE CULTURE, FRANCE INFO, FRANCE INTER and FRANCE MUSIQUE, of which *France Inter* has the largest audience. There are also 47 local radio stations.

RADIO FRANCE INTERNATIONALE (RFI)

The State-owned radio service, now split from RADIO FRANCE, broadcasting throughout the world in 14 languages. It is estimated that the audience is 80 million.

RADIO LIBRE

Any radio station independent of RADIO FRANCE. It has only been legal for such stations to broadcast from French territory since 1981, although some had been operating as pirate stations before that. Advertising has been permitted since 1984. Since 1986 national networks of *radios libres* have been possible, whereas only purely local stations were previously authorised. By 1989, there were 1,800 radios libres in France, some being national networks, and others tiny operations.

The *radio libre* with the largest audience is NRJ, which started in an Paris attic bedroom in 1982 and now has 150 stations and 9.9 per cent of the radio audience.

RADIO MONTE-CARLO (RMC)

A RADIO PÉRIPHÉRIQUE, 83 per cent of which is owned by the French State through SOFIRAD, with the rest being owned by the Monte-Carlo authorities. Its French service broadcasts on long wave from a transmitter in ALPES-DE-HAUTE-PROVENCE and there are FM services to urban areas in the southern half of the country, Reims and Paris.

RADIO PÉRIPHÉRIQUE

Any radio broadcasting organisation which is independent of RADIO FRANCE, and of which the capital and the administration is located outside French territory. See also: EUROPE 1; RADIO-TÉLÉ LUXEMBOURG; RADIO MONTE-CARLO; SUD-RADIO

RADIO SONORE
A subsidiary of the SOCIÉTE NATIONALE DE RADIO ET DE TÉLÉVISION POUR L'OUTRE-MER making and broadcasting radio programmes to the DOM and TOM. Except for the transmitters serving MAYOTTE and WALLIS-ET-FUTUNA, the service also relays FRANCE INTER.

RADIO-SORBONNE
An educational radio service, relaying university lectures and other programmes for distance learning students following LICENCE and AGRÉGATION courses.

RADIO-TÉLÉ LUXEMBOURG (RTL)
The broadcasting network owned by the private *Compagnie luxembourgeoise de télédiffusion*, and operating since 1931 on radio, and 1955 on television. The present concession ends in 1995. The principal services are in German and French, and an English language service ceased operation in 1991. RTL's French language radio service is provided on long wave from Luxembourg (therefore, a RADIO PÉRIPHÉRIQUE) and with local FM transmitters in France. The French language television service is directed to eastern France and Belgium. The company has a major holding in M6.

RADIO TÉLÉVISION BELGE DE LA COMMUNAUTÉ FRANÇAISE (RTBF)
The French language service provided by the Belgian national broadcasting organisation, available to viewers and listeners in north-east France.

RADIO-TÉLÉVISION SUISSE-ROMANDE
The French language service broadcast from Lausanne, Switzerland.

RAINBOW WARRIOR
A boat owned by the Greenpeace movement which was the object of a failed sinking operation conducted by French secret agents in New Zealand in 1985, while on manoeuvres to obstruct French nuclear testing in POLYNÉSIE FRANÇAISE, provoking protests from the New Zealand Government. Revelations of the French

Government's role in the affair led to the resignation of Charles HERNU.

RALLYE
A medium-sized chain of hypermarkets.

RAMBOUILLET, CHÂTEAU DE
One of the residences available to the PRÉSIDENT DE LA RÉPUBLIQUE, usually used for international conferences.

RASSEMBLEMENT POUR LA RÉPUBLIQUE (RPR)
A right-wing party group formed in 1976 to continue the tradition of the followers of DE GAULLE, and recalling the original name of his 1947 support group, the *Rassemblement du peuple français*. Its antecedents under the CINQUIÈME RÉPUBLIQUE were: the UNR, *Union pour la Nouvelle République* (1958–1962); the UNR–UDT, *Union pour la Nouvelle République – Union démocratique du travail* (1962–1967); the UD-V, *Union des démocrates pour la Cinquième République* (1967–1968); the UDR, *Union pour la défense de la République*, renamed in 1971 the *Union des démocrates pour la République* (1968–1976). The frequency of name changes (seven names in 30 years) reflects both De Gaulle's own scorn for party organisation, the group's domination by one man, and their need to reaffirm their concern for particular issues of the moment.

The RPR was established as a support party for Jacques CHIRAC who retains his position as its leader. He has tried to loosen the ties with the Gaullist tradition and worked to set up a strong party structure. Rifts began to show in 1990 as the younger generation of politicians voiced dissatisfaction with Chirac's hold on power. See also: ACTION OUVRIÈRE ET PROFESSIONNELLE; COHABITATION; NOIR, MICHEL; UNION POUR LA FRANCE

RATP See: *RÉGIE AUTONOME DES TRANSPORTS PARISIENS*

RÉAGE, PAULINE
The pseudonym of the otherwise anonymous author of the erotic novel *Histoire d'O*.

RECENSEMENT
The national census occurring at intervals of six, seven, eight or nine years. The last three censuses were in 1975, 1982 and 1990. The census is conducted by the INSTITUT NATIONAL DE LA STATISTIQUE ET DES ÉTUDES ÉCONOMIQUES. See also: SERVICE NATIONAL

RÉCEPTION D'UNE MAISON NEUVE
The handing-over ceremony of a new house to its owner by the builder, supported by a PROCÈS-VERBAL which is taken as evidence of agreement or includes details of defects noted by the purchaser. Guarantees date from the date of the *Réception d'une maison neuve*, and last for 10 years (minor repairs being free of charge for one year).

RÉCLUSION À PERPÉTUITÉ
Life imprisonment of which a minimum period from 15 years must be served before LIBÉRATION CONDITIONNELLE can be considered. No prisoner will normally serve more than 30 years.

RECOURS GRACIEUX
An appeal made to the tax authorities asking for sympathy in dealing with one's case, if payment is difficult because of severe financial problems. A *recours gracieux* is only possible if the demand for tax is not disputed.

RECTEUR D'ACADÉMIE
The administrative head of the ÉDUCATION NATIONALE in a particular ACADÉMIE, through whom the Ministry will direct its measures. The *académie's* headquarters are thus known as the *rectorat*. A *recteur* is usually a political appointment.

RECTORAT See: *RECTEUR D'ACADÉMIE*

REDEVANCE TÉLÉVISION
The annual television receiving licence, payable for each residence, regardless of the number of sets owned. The fee depends on whether a monochrome or colour set is used, and if a video-recorder is available. Old people and certain groups of disabled, provided that their income is lower than the basic taxable level, are excused payment.

The licence fee is distributed to the State-owned programme companies according to a formula based on the size of their audience and the quality of their programmes, as decided by a committee appointed by the PREMIER MINISTRE.

REDOUBLEMENT
The repetition of a school year, theoretically abolished in secondary schools in 1984. It used to be a feature of the system that transfer to the next year was dependent on a satisfactory level of achievement. *Redoublement* is still possible in the primary schools, and just under 5 per cent of pupils repeated a year in 1989–1990.

REDOUTE, LA
The largest mail-order catalogue firm, serving 10 million customers from its headquarters in Roubaix (NORD), and now with branch shops. It has a range of 30 specialist catalogues, as well as its general list. The original business was a woollen firm on the site of a former military redoubt, hence its name.

RÉFÉRENDUM
Under *Article 11* of the CONSTITUTION, the PRÉSIDENT DE LA RÉPUBLIQUE has the power to carry out a referendum of ÉLECTEURS on a question concerning the organisation of the State or a matter which might change its nature. This power is infrequently invoked, although DE GAULLE used it as a direct appeal to the electorate.

Referenda have been called on eight occasions since 1958: in that year, on the Constitution itself; in 1961 on self-determination for ALGÉRIE; in 1962 on the ÉVIAN agreement; in the same year, on ÉLECTION PRÉSIDENTIELLE by universal suffrage; in 1969, on regionalisation; in 1972, on the enlarging of the European Community; in 1988 on the revised status for NOUVELLE-CALÉDONIE; and in 1992, on the Maastricht treaty.

RÉFUGIÉ POLITIQUE See: *APATRIDES; OFFICE FRANÇAIS DE PROTECTION DES RÉFUGIÉS ET APATRIDES*

RÉGIE

A State-owned authority which controls an industry or public service. Thus, RENAULT is a *régie*.

RÉGIE AUTONOME DES TRANSPORTS PARISIENS (RATP)

The Paris public transport authority, set up in 1948, owner and operator of the MÉTRO, RÉSEAU EXPRESS RÉGIONAL and buses in the city of Paris and the RÉSEAU DE BANLIEUE, with a role in co-ordinating the Paris area services of the SOCIÉTÉ NATIONALE DES CHEMINS DE FER FRANÇAIS. A new tramway starts operation in 1992 under the RATP between Saint-Denis and Bobigny (SEINE-SAINT-DENIS). See also: CARTE ORANGE; MÉTÉOR; ORLYVAL

RÉGIME MATRIMONIAL

There are five basic formats for a marriage agreement under French law. The *Régime de la communauté d'acquêts* gives common ownership only of possessions acquired after the marriage, and is the standard arrangement, assumed to be the case if another *régime* is not chosen.

The *Régime de la communauté de meubles et d'acquêts* allows both parties to retain their individual ownership of previously held property, and of any buildings given to him or her during the marriage.

The *Régime de la communauté universelle* means that all possessions are common to both parties, whereas the opposite is true of the *Régime de la séparation des biens*. No common ownership during the marriage is also a feature of the *Régime de participation aux acquêts*, but at the end of the marriage, each partner has a right to half of the other's belongings. See also: MARIAGE CIVIL

RÉGION

A geographical grouping of DÉPARTEMENTS (or in the case of a DOM, sometimes a single *département*) which is an administrative unit of growing importance. Each *Région* has a PRÉFET DE RÉGION, and a CONSEIL RÉGIONAL. In addition to strategic economic planning for its area, the *Conseil régional* also has the responsibility for the provision of LYCÉES, training and apprenticeships. See also: COMMISSION DE DÉVELOPPEMENT ÉCONOMIQUE RÉGIONAL; CONSEIL ÉCONOMIQUE ET SOCIAL RÉGIONAL; DÉCENTRALISATION

RÉGION AÉRIENNE
A territorial division of military airspace, due to be replaced by the RÉGION MILITAIRE DE DÉFENSE.

RÉGION MARITIME
The naval geographical division, due to be replaced by the RÉGION MILITAIRE DE DÉFENSE.

RÉGION MILITAIRE
The territorial division of France for operations by the ARMÉE DE TERRE, due to be replaced by the RÉGION MILITAIRE DE DÉFENSE.

RÉGION MILITAIRE DE DÉFENSE (RMD)
A territorial division of France, common to all the armed services, envisaged under the PLAN 'ARMÉES 2000'.

RÉGION PARISIENNE
No longer an administrative RÉGION, the *Région parisienne* is now the term used for the area which is most heavily influenced by Paris, but not necessarily conforming to any other exact boundaries. In its more precise sense the *Région parisienne* was the official term from 1961 to 1976 for the district now covered by the ÎLE-DE-FRANCE region.

RÉGLEMENTATION DE SÉJOUR See: *CARTE DE RÉSIDENT: CARTE DE SÉJOUR; IMMIGRATION; INTERDICTION DE SÉJOUR*

RÉGLEMENTATION DE TRAVAIL
Immigrants who are seeking work but do not hold nationality of a member-state of the European Community are supposed to obtain a work permit before entering France. There are special concessions for those with Algerian nationality. The employer must check these papers, and register the details of a foreign worker's employment for inspection by the ADMINISTRATION. See also: CARTE DE RÉSIDENT; CARTE DE SÉJOUR; IMMIGRATION

REIMS CHAMPAGNE-ARDENNE, UNIVERSITÉ DE
20,000 students attend this university which offers courses in arts, economics, humanities, law, medicine, pharmacy and science.

RELATIONS AVEC LE PARLEMENT
There is normally a MINISTRE with this sole responsibility, who takes charge of ensuring the smooth management of the government's legislative programme in Parliament.

RENAUDOT, PRIX
An annual literary prize (the full name of which is the *Prix Théophraste-Renaudot*, taking the name of a seventeenth-century newspaper proprietor) awarded to the author of a French novel published within the previous 12 months. The prize is a lunch given to the winner on the day of the following year's award. The original idea in 1925 was to redress the misjudgements allegedly made by the ACADÉMIE GONCOURT, and for this reason the date is always the same as that of the *Prix Goncourt*.

RENAULT
The State-owned motor vehicle manufacturer, and the largest in France, founded by Louis Renault in 1898. Its main production is at Flins (YVELINES) and Le Havre (SEINE-MARITIME), while its original plant at Billancourt (HAUTS-DE-SEINE) a former stronghold of the CONFÉDÉRATION GÉNÉRALE DU TRAVAIL, is due to close in 1992.

RENNES, UNIVERSITÉ DE
One of the two universities in Rennes is *Rennes-I*, situated at Villejean to the west of the city, where courses are provided in economics, humanities, law and management to 24,000 students. See also: HAUTE-BRETAGNE, UNIVERSITÉ DE

RENSEIGNEMENTS GÉNÉRAUX (RG)
The section of the POLICE NATIONALE which gathers intelligence on political groups and foreigners, especially with a view to preventing threats to public order. The RG also monitor betting and gaming activity.

RENTE VIAGÈRE
A loan paid as a taxable annuity until the death of the borrower on the security of the residence, available to anyone who owns a property, but really of interest only to the older generation. The property passes to the lender on the borrower's death. Depending on the agreement between the parties, the *Rente viagère* payable rises in accordance with an inflation index, and any dispute about this rise can be referred to the TRIBUNAL D'INSTANCE.

RENTRÉE
The period in September each year when the holidays finish and normal economic and academic life begins again.

REPOS OBLIGATOIRE
If Sunday is a working day in any business, the employer is obliged to allow workers a day off each week. The assumption is that normally there will be no work on a Sunday.

RÉPUBLICAIN LORRAIN, LE
A daily newspaper, published in Metz, with a circulation in 1989 of 193,000 in LORRAINE.

RÉPUBLICAINS INDÉPENDANTS
The political party founded by Valéry GISCARD D'ESTAING in 1966, absorbed into the PARTI RÉPUBLICAIN in 1977.

RÉPUBLIQUE DU CENTRE, LA
A daily newspaper, published in Orléans, with a circulation in 1989 of 64,500, selling mainly in the LOIRET.

RER See: *RÉSEAU EXPRESS RÉGIONAL*

RÉSEAU DE BANLIEUE
The public transport network in the Paris suburbs, under the control of the RÉGIE AUTONOME DES TRANSPORTS PARISIENS.

RÉSEAU EXPRESS RÉGIONAL (RER)
The rapid-transit rail network in the Paris area, constructed from the 1960s as a strategic part of the plans for the development of the region. It is linked to the MÉTRO and is operated by the RÉGIE AUTONOME DES TRANSPORT PARISIENS and the SOCIÉTÉ

NATIONALE DES CHEMINS DE FER FRANÇAIS. At its centre is the largest underground station in the world at CHÂTELET-les-Halles.

RÉSEAU FERROVIAIRE
The national railway network, operated by the SOCIÉTÉ NATIONALE DES CHEMINS DE FER FRANÇAIS.

RÉSEAU NUMÉRIQUE À INTÉGRATION DE SERVICE (RNIS)
A digital communications system based on the telephone service, allowing phone, fax and computer connections to be made through one integrated line. The service started in Paris in 1988 under the *Numéris* name.

RÉSEAU ROUTIER
The national road network, including in descending order of strategic importance, roads classified as AUTOROUTE, ROUTE NATIONALE, CHEMIN DÉPARTEMENTAL, CHEMIN COMMUNAL, CHEMIN RURAL.

RÉSEAU URBAIN
The bus network within a city. In Paris, it is operated by the RÉGIE AUTONOME DES TRANSPORTS PARISIENS.

RÉSIDENCE SECONDAIRE
Almost three million second homes exist in France, two-thirds of them in rural areas, the rest by the sea. They can be financed, if new, by a COMPTE ÉPARGNE-LOGEMENT or a PLAN ÉPARGNE-LOGEMENT.

RÉSISTANCE
The movements set up to resist the German occupation and the VICHY régime in the Second World War. Eventually a co-ordinating organisation, the *Conseil national de la Résistance* was established under the leadership of Jean MOULIN. Other major groupings included the Communist FTP (*Francs-tireurs partisans*) and the FFI (*Forces françaises de l'intérieur*), both of which are also known as *maquis*. See also: DE GAULLE

RESNAIS, ALAIN (1922–)
A film director of the New Wave, famous for *Hiroshima mon*

amour (1959) and *L'Année dernière à Marienbad* (1961). After falling out of popularity, Resnais had success in the 1980s with films such as *L'Amour à mort* (1984) and *Mélo* (1986).

RESTAURANTS DU CŒUR
A charitable organisation which serves meals to the poor, mainly in the winter, founded by COLUCHE in 1985.

RESTAURANTS, RÉGLEMENTATION DES
Prices must be displayed in a restaurant with any imposed service charge specified. It must be made clear on the menu if the price includes drink, and if so, it must specify the quantity and nature. Except in a self-service restaurant, it is against regulations to impose a cover charge or for bread. Water must be supplied free of charge on request.

RETRAITE
The normal retirement age for men and women is 60, although in some public organisations, it is possible to retire with full benefits at 55. See also: AIDE SOCIALE; ALLOCATION AUX MÈRES DE FAMILLE; ALLOCATION AUX VIEUX TRAVAILLEURS SALARIÉS; ALLOCATION SPÉCIALE VIEILLESSE; CARTE ÉMERAUDE; CARTE VERMEIL; PENSION DE RETRAITE

RÉUNION
An island DÉPARTEMENT D'OUTRE-MER and RÉGION in the Indian Ocean, with a population 1990 of 597,823. The CHEF-LIEU is Saint-Denis (121,299) and other large towns are Saint-Paul (71,669); Saint-Pierre (58,846); le Tampon (47,593); Saint-Louis (37,420); Saint-André (35,049); and Saint-Benoît (26,187).

The name comes from a decision by the Revolutionary Convention to commemorate the meeting of the *Marseillais* and the *Gardes nationaux* for the attack on the *Palais des Tuileries* in 1792, but since then it has also been called *Île Bonaparte* or *Île Bourbon,* depending on the ruling regime. It has been a French possession since 1642. There are a number of smaller island dependencies.

The economy depends largely on metropolitan France. Agricultural products are sugar cane, fruit, rum, molasses, essences, vanilla, tobacco and maize. Tourism is an increasing contributor to the economy.

Réunion was severely hit by cyclones in 1980, 1986 and 1989. There is a growing separatist movement, largely channelled through the broadcasts of Radio-Free-DOM.

François MITTERRAND gained more than 60 per cent of the votes in the 1988 ÉLECTION PRESIDENTIELLE, but in parliament, the DÉPUTÉS and SÉNATEURS are mainly from the opposition parties. The Right retained its hold over the CONSEIL GÉNÉRAL in the 1992 ÉLECTIONS CANTONALES, but gains were made by the *Parti communiste réunionnais*.

Code départemental: 974

RÉUNION, UNIVERSITÉ DE LA
There are 4,400 students at this university in Saint-Denis-de-la-Réunion, following courses in arts, economics, humanities, law, politics and sciences.

REVEL, JEAN-FRANÇOIS (1924–   )
A journalist and essayist who has written analyses of totalitarianism, including *Ni Marx ni Jésus* (1970), and *La Tentation totalitaire* (1976).

REVENU MINIMUM D'INSERTION (RMI)
An allowance, making up the difference between actual income and a notional basic figure (in 1991 the monthly basic figure was 2,163 francs), intended to support opportunities for retraining and rehabilitation for the disadvantaged. It is available to adults above 25 years of age who have a low income and are not following a course of study. The *Revenu minimum d'insertion* can be used to help the recipient attend, for example, adult literacy classes, or life-skills courses, and also gives the right to full SÉCURITÉ SOCIALE benefits and to an ALLOCATION LOGEMENT. Each application is negotiated individually, and is dealt with usually by a charitable organisation or the local social services support system. The RMI was introduced in 1988, with the intention to end in 1992.

RFI See: *RADIO FRANCE INTERNATIONALE*

RFO See: *SOCIÉTÉ NATIONALE DE RADIO ET DE TÉLÉVISION POUR L'OUTRE-MER*

RG See: *RENSEIGNEMENTS GÉNÉRAUX*

RHÔNE

A DÉPARTEMENT of the RHÔNE-ALPES region, named after the river
which passes through it, with a population of 1.5 million in 1990,
1.21 million of them living in the AGGLOMÉRATION of Lyon, the
CHEF-LIEU. Lyon is France's second city, with a strategic role in the
commerce and administration of the country, with enormous
industrial developments concentrating traditionally on textiles and
chemicals, but also important for the motor industry, engineering,
electronics, metal and glass industries, an international trade fair and
a world-renowned cancer research establishment. Feyzin has a
complex of oil refineries and gas terminals, and Villeurbanne is a
centre for chemicals and commercial vehicle construction. Other
towns outside the Lyon urban area are Anse (17,762); l'Arbresle
(12,625); Tarare (10,720); Vaulx-en-Vélin (44,174); and
Villefranche-sur-Saône (48,223).

Agricultural activity focuses on *Beaujolais* wine production,
tobacco, fruit (especially cherries), cattle, pigs and poultry.

In politics, the Rhône is dominated by the Lyon conurbation.
Its parliamentary representation is drawn from a wide range
of political colours whereas its CONSEIL GÉNÉRAL and the
COMMUNAUTÉ URBAINE of Lyon (COURLY) have been Centre
Right controlled for some years. In the 1981 ÉLECTION
PRÉSIDENTIELLE, François MITTERRAND had a marginal majority,
but this was lost to Jacques CHIRAC in 1988.

Code départemental: 69

RHÔNE-ALPES

The administrative RÉGION incorporating the DÉPARTEMENTS of
AIN, ARDÈCHE, DRÔME, HAUTE-SAVOIE, ISÈRE, LOIRE, RHÔNE and
SAVOIE. The regional capital is Lyon, and the region is home to
5.35 million, the second most highly populated. About 10 per
cent of these are immigrants and their families.

The region is geographically and culturally diverse, including
the declining heavy industries of the LOIRE, the intensely
industrialised Lyon area and the Alps, heavily dependent on
tourism, as well as the high-tech industries of the Grenoble area.

One particular feature of the region is the strength of the PETITES ET MOYENNES INDUSTRIES, and they employ a higher proportion of workers than the national average.

In the 1992 ÉLECTIONS RÉGIONALES, voters in this region followed the national trend of supporting candidates from the FRONT NATIONAL, GÉNÉRATION ÉCOLOGIE and VERTS lists in sufficient numbers to destabilise the control of the Centre Right.

RHÔNE-POULENC
The largest French chemicals manufacturing group of companies, including companies producing pharmaceuticals, plastics, agro-chemicals, etc. Most of the turnover is accounted for by export. *Rhône-Poulenc* was nationalised in 1982, and the State retains over 90 per cent of the control.

RICARD See: *PERNOD-RICARD*

RINALDI, ANGELO (1940–)
A novelist whose *La Maison des Atlantes* won the *Prix* FÉMINA in 1971.

RIVETTE, JACQUES (1928–)
A film director in the New Wave, who came into prominence because of the attack made on his *La Religieuse* (1966) by traditional Catholic groups.

RMC See: *RADIO MONTE-CARLO*

RMD See: *RÉGION MILITAIRE DE DÉFENSE*

RMI See: *REVENU MINIMUM D'INSERTION*

RNIS See: *RÉSEAU NUMÉRIQUE À INTÉGRATION DE SERVICE*

ROBBE-GRILLET, ALAIN (1922–)
The literary critic and novelist, who became the theorist of the '*nouveau roman*' movement in the 1950s, but who in later years has written in a more conventional style. His best known works include the novels *Les Gommes* (1953) and *Le Voyeur* (1955) and the essay *Pour un nouveau roman* (1963).

ROBERT, DICTIONNAIRE
One of the major French language dictionaries. The 2,000 page *Petit Robert* (first published in 1967) has high sales and is an authoritative dictionary. The full version is the GRAND ROBERT. The *Robert* firm has collaborated with the British publisher Collins to produce a range of bi-lingual dictionaries.

ROCARD, MICHEL (1930–   )
An ÉNARQUE who entered the ADMINISTRATION and became a specialist in the national budget before entering politics. He was *Secrétaire général* of the PARTI SOCIALISTE UNIFIÉ from 1967 to 1973, standing as its candidate in the ÉLECTION PRÉSIDENTIELLE in 1969, gaining 3.61 per cent of the vote in the PREMIER TOUR, but becoming a DÉPUTÉ in the same year. Joining the PARTI SOCIALISTE in 1974, he held ministerial posts from 1981, resigning as *Ministre de l'*AGRICULTURE in 1985. In 1988–1991 he was PREMIER MINISTRE, and has been seen as a potential candidate for the Socialists in a forthcoming presidential contest. See also: OUVERTURE

ROCHER, YVES
A mail-order and direct sales chain of franchise shops selling naturally based cosmetics and beauty products, with 30 per cent of the capital held by its eponymous founder.

ROHMER, ÉRIC (1920–   )
A former teacher who became a film director, classed within the New Wave, well known for his *Ma nuit chez Maud* (1969), and later series of films such as the 1980s *Comédies et proverbes*. His films are about various manifestations of love.

ROISSY
The newest Paris airport, Charles DE GAULLE, which opened in 1974, with a third phase due to open in 1995 is situated in the COMMUNE of Roissy-en-France (SEINE-ET-MARNE).

ROLAND-GARROS
A complex of tennis courts in the BOIS DE BOULOGNE, opened in 1928, named after an aviator and tennis player who had died in 1918, and since its opening the site of the Paris International Championship.

ROMAN À L'EAU DE ROSE
A light romantic novel, normally intended for female readers.
The genre sells millions of copies each year.

ROMILLY, JACQUELINE DE (1913–   )
A Classical scholar, translator and teacher of Greek, the second
woman to be elected to the ACADÉMIE FRANÇAISE (in 1988).

ROND-POINT
The name used by hypermarkets owned by the Co-operative
movement.

ROSSI, TINO (1907–1983)
A Corsican crooner, very popular for well over three decades,
who also acted in films, achieving an everlasting success in
Petit Papa Noël.

ROSSIF, FRÉDÉRIC (1922–1990)
A television film maker renowned for his *La Fête des animaux*
and the series of major documentaries entitled *Cinq colonnes
à la une*. His film *Mourir à Madrid* was suppressed, so as not
to displease Spain's General Franco. A native of Montenegro,
Rossif was educated in Rome and joined the LÉGION ÉTRANGÈRE
and the Free French forces in Africa in 1941 before settling in
France.

ROTHSCHILD
The famous *Banque Rothschild* was one of the banks
nationalised in 1982. Another branch of the family owns the
Mouton Rothschild château in the Bordeaux wine region.

ROUEN, UNIVERSITÉ DE
There are 20,000 students on the campus at Mont-Saint-Aignan
follow courses in arts, economics, humanities, law, medicine,
pharmacy and science.

ROUTE DÉPARTEMENTALE
A main road with its number preceded by a *D* within its
DÉPARTEMENT, and therefore considered to be a major part of the
district road network. Some *routes départementales* are not
designed for fast traffic. See also: AUTOROUTE; ROUTE NATIONALE

ROUTE NATIONALE
A major road, part of the strategic national network, and
usually classified for '*grande circulation*'. The road's number
has the prefix *N*, which it retains for the whole of its length.
See also: AUTOROUTE; ROUTE DÉPARTEMENTALE

ROY, JULES (1907–)
A prolific novelist and essayist. His novel *La Vallée heureuse*
won the *Prix* RENAUDOT in 1946, and he has written a series
of novels set in ALGÉRIE.

ROYER, JEAN (1920–)
A former INSTITUTEUR and PROFESSEUR who entered politics, and
became DÉPUTÉ for the INDRE-ET-LOIRE in 1958, and MAIRE of
Tours in 1959, holding these posts ever since. After ministerial
posts in 1973 and 1974, Royer resigned from the government,
and was a candiate in the 1974 ÉLECTION PRÉSIDENTIELLE, polling
2.64 per cent of the votes in the first round. See also: LOI ROYER

RPR See: *RASSEMBLEMENT POUR LA RÉPUBLIQUE*

RTBF See: *RADIO-TÉLÉVISION BELGE DE LA
COMMUNAUTÉ FRANÇAISE*

RTL See: *RADIO-TÉLÉVISION LUXEMBOURG*

RUNGIS
The COMMUNE in the southern BANLIEUE of Paris (VAL-DE-MARNE)
which is the home of the new wholesale market for fresh food,
the largest such establishment in the world. The market moved
from *Les Halles* in central Paris in 1969, and is the premier
MARCHÉ D'INTÉRÊT NATIONAL.

SA See: *SOCIÉTÉ ANONYME*

SABATIER, PAUL (UNIVERSITÉ)
The official name of the *Université Toulouse III*, which
specialises in arts, economics, information technology,
languages, management, medicine, pharmacy, science, and has
26,000 students.

SABATIER, ROBERT (1923–)
A poet, essayist and novelist, whose work often takes the theme
of the inter-war years.

SACEM See: *SOCIÉTÉ DES AUTEURS, COMPOSITEURS
ET ÉDITEURS DE MUSIQUE*

SACILOR See: *USINOR*

SAFER See: *SOCIÉTÉ D'AMÉNAGEMENT FONCIER ET
D'ÉTABLISSEMENT RURAL*

SAGAN, FRANÇOISE (1935–)
A novelist who had early success with *Bonjour tristesse* (1954)
and then *Un Certain Sourire*. She was seen as the symbolic
emancipated woman, and has continued to write novels, plays
and memoirs.

SAINT-AMAND-MONTROND
A COMMUNE in the CHER which claims to be the centre of France.
The exact spot is marked by a tower. See also: BRUÈRES-
ALLICHAMPS; CHAZEMAIS; VESDUN

SAINT-CYR
The town of Saint-Cyr-l'École (YVELINES) is so called because

of the officer training school which was sited there from 1808 to 1944. See also: ÉCOLE MILITAIRE

SAINT-ÉTIENNE, UNIVERSITÉ DE See: *MONNET, JEAN (UNIVERSITÉ)*

SAINT-GERMAIN-DES-PRÉS
As well as being an ancient abbey and the oldest church in Paris, *Saint-Germain-des-Prés* has given its name to its local district which was the cradle of existentialism and other intellectual movements. See also: GRÉCO, JULIETTE; SARTRE, JEAN-PAUL

SAINT-GOBAIN
The largest glass maker in France, nationalised in 1982, and privatised again in 1986. It employs almost 90,000.

SAINT-JOHN PERSE (1887–1975)
The pseudonym of Alexis Saint-Léger Léger, a poet from a family of planters in GUADELOUPE, who won the Nobel prize for literature in 1960. It was only after a career as a senior FONCTIONNAIRE and diplomat that he published his poetry, the first appearing in 1941 when as a refugee, he became the librarian of the Library of Congress in Washington. He returned to France in 1946. His famous collections include *Anabase* (1924), *Exil* (1942) and *Amers* (1957).

SAINT-LAURENT, YVES (1936–   )
A fashion designer who had early success with his designs published in *Vogue* at the age of 17. On Christian Dior's death in 1957, he became artistic director of that house, and later set up his own business. He has been influential in establishing fashions followed by others.

SAINT-LAZARE
The Gare Saint-Lazare is the railway terminal in Paris for the lines serving Normandy and the north-west BANLIEUE.

SAINT-NOM-LA-BRETÈCHE
A private golf course at la Tuilerie-Bignon (YVELINES), and the venue for the French open championship.

SAINT-QUENTIN-EN-YVELINES
The national golf centre opened in 1990 in this COMMUNE in the YVELINES.

SAINT-PIERRE-ET-MIQUELON
A former DÉPARTEMENT D'OUTRE-MER and now a COLLECTIVITÉ TERRITORIALE in the North Atlantic, about 25 kilometres off the coast of Newfoundland. The total population in 1990 of the eight islands which form the archipelago was 6,392. Saint-Pierre-et-Miquelon had its first French settlement in 1604, but has sometimes been held by the British.

The economy is almost entirely based on the fishing industry, with exports mainly to USA, France, Canada and Portugal. There is a developing tourist activity.

Saint-Pierre-et-Miquelon sends one DÉPUTÉ and one SÉNATEUR to Paris, has a local CONSEIL GÉNÉRAL, and in 1988 supported Jacques CHIRAC who obtained 56.21 per cent of the vote, in the ÉLECTION PRÉSIDENTIELLE.

Code territorial: 975

SAINT-VÉRAN
The COMMUNE with the highest altitude in the whole of Europe. Saint-Véran is in the HAUTES-ALPES. The village's highest point at ground level is 2,042 metres (2,071 at the top of the church tower).

SAISIE
Legal seizure of property by a HUISSIER in order to settle outstanding debts.

SALACROU, ARMAND (1899–1989)
A dramatist and member of the ACADÉMIE GONCOURT whose plays include *Atlas Hôtel, La Terre est ronde* (1938) and *Boulevard Durand* (1960).

SALAIRE MINIMUM INTERPROFESSIONNEL DE CROISSANCE (SMIC)
The basic minimum wage, below which it is illegal to set an adult rate, introduced in 1970. The rate identified is that for one hour's work, and the calculation is indexed to the cost of

living as published by the INSTITUT NATIONAL DE LA STATISTIQUE ET DES ÉTUDES ÉCONOMIQUES. Any increase is payable from 1 July, the decision being formally made by DÉCRET. See also: SALAIRE MINIMUM INTERPROFESSIONNEL GARANTI (SMIG)

SALAIRE MINIMUM INTERPROFESSIONNEL GARANTI (SMIG)

A basic minimum wage, index-linked to the cost of a notional shopping basket of goods, in operation from 1950. The indexing was ineffective and for most purposes the SMIG was replaced by the SALAIRE MINIMUM INTERPROFESSIONNEL DE CROISSANCE in 1970.

SALLE GAVEAU See: *GAVEAU*

SALLE PLEYEL See: *PLEYEL*

SALUT

Formerly known as *Salut les copains*, a fortnightly magazine for teenagers, especially featuring the world of pop music. Its original success in 1962 was the beginning of the FILIPACCHI group's fortunes. Its present circulation has fallen, with 140,000 recorded in 1989, compared with 742,000 in 1972.

SAMARITAINE, LA

A major Paris department store, founded in 1870.

SANTÉ, LA

A prison, dating from the late nineteenth century, situated in southern Paris.

SAÔNE-ET-LOIRE

A DÉPARTEMENT in the BOURGOGNE region, named after the two rivers which pass through it, and with a population in 1990 of 559,413, a reduction from its recorded peak in 1982 of 571,852. The CHEF-LIEU is Mâcon (urban area 45,004), with printing, chemicals, engineering, clothing, food-processing and timber industries, and a major wine market, and other large towns are Autun (17,906), a centre for metallurgy, textiles, clothing, household equipment; Chalon-sur-Saône (77,498); Digoin (13,114), with sanitary ware and pottery industries; the

COMMUNAUTÉ URBAINE of le Creusot (40,903) and Montceau-les-Mines (47,283), with a steelworks and engineering, rubber goods, coal, electronics, textiles and clothing industries. There is a stainless steel plant and uranium extraction at Gueugnon.

Tourists are attracted by the *Musée Lamartine* at Mâcon, the photographic museum and watersports at Chalon, the abbey at Cluny and other ancient churches, prehistoric remains, a number of lakes, the *Parc régional du Morvan* and the spa of Bourbon-Lancy. A number of residents of the Lyon area have a RÉSIDENCE SECONDAIRE in the *Département*.

In agriculture, the Saône-et-Loire is a major centre for cattle and sheep rearing and has a substantial wine production.

The political allegiance of the area tends to be with the Centre Left, and in both the 1981 and 1988 ÉLECTIONS PRÉSIDENTIELLES, François MITTERRAND had a comfortable majority. The Centre Right, however, controls the CONSEIL GÉNÉRAL, and the 1992 ÉLECTIONS CANTONALES did not make a significant change.

Code départemental: 71   See also: SOLUTRÉ

SAPEURS-POMPIERS
The national fire and rescue service is provided by professionals and volunteers, in the approximate ratio of 1:10. Since 1982, they have been organised on a *départemental* basis, previously having been more dependent on the *Ministère de l'*INTÉRIEUR. In Paris and its adjacent DÉPARTEMENTS, the fire and rescue service is provided by a military force, the *Brigade de sapeurs-pompiers de Paris*, part of the ARMÉE DE TERRE. See also: MARINS-POMPIERS

SAPRITCH, ALICE (1916–1990)
An actress and humourist, who became something of a Paris character, and who seemed equally at home in serious parts or on television advertisements.

SARCELLES
A COMMUNE in the VAL D'OISE which was rapidly developed in the post-war years as a dormitory town for Paris, and has been used as a symbol of the social crisis which arose in new suburban areas which were devoid of a sense of community and roots for the inhabitants.

SARL See: *SOCIÉTÉ ANONYME*

SARRAUTE, NATHALIE (1900–   )
A novelist and playwright of Russian birth, one of the leaders of the *Nouveau Roman* movement who has returned to a more orthodox style in recent years. Her first novel was *Tropismes* (1939) and others have included *Portrait d'un inconnu* (1949) and *Enfance* (1983).

SARRE
Now one of the Länder of Germany, Sarre was a territory under French administration from 1945 to 1955, when its population voted by plebiscite to return to Germany.

SARTRE, JEAN-PAUL (1905–1980)
The writer and philosopher who dominated the French intellectual scene after the Second World War. His novels, plays and philosophical writing expound the theory of existentialism, of which he is the best known proponent. Sartre was a teacher in several prestigious LYCÉES before leaving the profession in 1945. His life with Simone de BEAUVOIR was also a well-documented feature of the Paris literary scene.

SARTHE
A DÉPARTEMENT in the PAYS DE LA LOIRE region, with a 1990 population of 513,614, named after the tributary of the Loire on which its CHEF-LIEU, le Mans stands. Le Mans, with motor (especially RENAULT), aviation, agricultural equipment, electronics, clothing, tobacco, insurance and dairy industries, as well as being the site of the international 24-hour motor race, has 189,070 inhabitants in its AGGLOMÉRATION. Other urban areas are la Ferté-Bernard (11,269), which has metallurgy, electronics and agricultural foodstuff industries; La Flèche (14,953), a centre for electrical engineering, printing, packing, aluminium, and the PRYTANÉE MILITAIRE; and Sablé-sur-Sarthe (12,178), with similar employment to la Ferté-Bernard.

The Sarthe is an important area for dairy cattle and poultry, with some significant wheat and maize production.

Parliamentary representation shows a balance of Left and Right. In the ÉLECTIONS PRÉSIDENTIELLES, François MITTERRAND'S slender majority in 1981 was considerably strengthened in 1988. Nevertheless, in the 1992 ÉLECTIONS CANTONALES, the Centre Right reasserted its control over the CONSEIL GÉNÉRAL.

Code départemental: 72

SATOLAS

The fast growing regional and international airport for the RHÔNE-ALPES region, situated east of Lyon.

SAUGEAIS

A curious anomaly of history allows the continued existence of the *République de Saugeais*, a territory comprising 12 COMMUNES within the DOUBS and about 2,000 inhabitants, which has its own presidency, recognised for certain functions, as well as its own flag. The origin is the privilege of the local *Abbaye de Montbenoît*.

SAUTET, CLAUDE (1924–   )

A film director who has taken as a theme the developments within a family and between couples. His best-known titles are perhaps *Vincent, François, Paul et les autres* (1974) and *Un mauvais fils* (1980).

SAUVY, ALFRED (1902–1990)

A statistician and economist of great influence. Educated at the ÉCOLE POLYTECHNIQUE, he was the founding director of the INSTITUT NATIONAL D'ÉTUDES DÉMOGRAPHIQUES. Among his many works are *Richesse et population* (1943), *De Malthus à Mao-Tsé-Toung* (1958) and *La France ridée* (1979).

SAVARY, ALAIN (1918–1988)

A former governor of SAINT-PIERRE-ET-MIQUELON and administrator who entered politics and became secretary of the PARTI SOCIALISTE from 1969 to 1971. He was the first *Ministre de l'*ÉDUCATION NATIONALE of the MITTERRAND presidency, resigning in 1984 because of the withdrawal of the PROJET DE LOI aimed at reform of private schools, in the face of enormous opposition. See also: LOI SAVARY

SAVOIE

A mountainous DÉPARTEMENT in the RHÔNE-ALPES region, with

a population of 305,118 in 1990, part of the former kingdom which became part of France in 1860. The CHEF-LIEU is Chambéry (urban area 102,548), a commercial centre and also with metallurgy, chemical, food-processing and glass industries, and the other major towns are Aix-les-Bains (35,472), the largest thermal spa in France, also with boilermaking and electronics industries; Albertville (26,513) – clothing industry and centre of the 1992 Winter Olympics; and Saint-Jean-de-Maurienne (10,263) – where PÉCHINEY has its largest aluminium plant. There is a steelworks at Ugine, and another at Moutiers, which, like most settlements are rather small, befitting the Alpine situation.

The principal growth industry is tourism, largely connected with winter sports, but also comprising year round visitors.

Because of the terrain, agriculture is less important, but there is significant cheese production.

The DÉPUTÉS and SÉNATEURS for the Savoie are drawn from Left and Right. In both the1981 and 1988 ÉLECTIONS PRÉSIDENTIELLES, François MITTERRAND gained a tiny majority of the vote. There were some exchanges of seats in the 1992 ÉLECTIONS CANTONALES between Right and Left, but overall the power in the CONSEIL GÉNÉRAL remained in the control of the Centre Right.

Code départemental: 73

SAVOIE, UNIVERSITÉ DE
There are 7,000 students at this university in Chambéry, following courses in arts, humanities, law, science and social sciences.

SCEAUX, GARDE DES See: *GARDE DES SCEAUX*

SCHAEFFER, PIERRE (1910–   )
A composer who was one of the first exponents of *Musique concrète*.

SCHÉMA DIRECTEUR D'AMÉNAGEMENT ET D'URBANISME (SDAU)
A local structure plan set up as one of the provisions of the LOI ROYER.

SCHTROUMPF
A group of cartoon characters first appearing in Belgium in 1958. A theme park, 'Big Bang Schtroumpfs', was opened in 1989 in Hagondage (MOSELLE).

SCHUMAN, ROBERT (UNIVERSITÉ) See: *STRASBOURG, UNIVERSITÉS DE*

SCIENCE ET VIE
A monthly popular science magazine, with a circulation of 357,000.

SCIENCES-PO See: *INSTITUT D'ÉTUDES POLITIQUES DE PARIS*

SCOP See: *SOCIÉTÉ CO-OPÉRATIVE OUVRIÈRE DE PRODUCTION*

SCOUTS DE FRANCE
The Catholic scouting organisation, with about 110,000 members in over 1,500 local troops. See also: ÉCLAIREUSES ET ÉCLAIREURS DE FRANCE; GUIDES DE FRANCE

SCPI See: *SOCIÉTÉ CIVILE DE PLACEMENT IMMOBILIER*

SCRUTIN
The descriptions below indicate the forms of election more generally available in contemporary France. Sometimes, the title of a particular format might vary slightly from those given here.

SCRUTIN À MODE MIXTE
A voting system for the election of the CONSEIL MUNICIPAL in COMMUNES with fewer than 3,500 inhabitants, incorporating elements of the SCRUTIN DE LISTE MAJORITAIRE and the SCRUTIN DE LISTE À LA REPRÉSENTATION PROPORTIONELLE, and involving two rounds of voting. In the first round, a list of candidates which obtains more than 50 per cent of the votes cast will be allocated half the seats available, with the other half distributed to the other parties' lists in proportion to their share of the vote. If there is no absolute majority on the first round, a second round is held, but lists which received fewer than 10 per cent of the

votes in the first round are eliminated. In the second round, the list receiving the largest number of votes is allocated half the seats.

SCRUTIN DE LISTE À LA REPRÉSENTATION PROPORTIONNELLE
The method of voting used in elections of SÉNATEURS if the DÉPARTEMENT has five or more of them, and in elections for the CONSEIL RÉGIONAL. It was also used in the 1986 ÉLECTIONS LÉGISLATIVES.

Once the votes are cast, the QUOTIENT ÉLECTORAL is calculated, and seats allocated accordingly, starting at the top of a list of candidates.

SCRUTIN DE LISTE MAJORITAIRE
The method of voting used in elections for SÉNATEURS where there are fewer than five seats for a DÉPARTEMENT. Parties or groups present lists of candidates up to the number of seats vacant. Electors cast votes for a list. If one list receives more than half the votes, it wins all the seats. If no absolute majority is won, a second round may be held, where it is not necessary to obtain more than 50 per cent of the votes to be elected.

SCRUTIN MAJORITAIRE See: *SCRUTIN DE LISTE MAJORITAIRE; SCRUTIN UNINOMINAL MAJORITAIRE*

SCRUTIN PROPORTIONNEL See: *SCRUTIN DE LISTE À LA REPRÉSENTATION PROPORTIONNELLE*

SCRUTIN UNINOMINAL MAJORITAIRE
The method of voting used for the ÉLECTIONS PRÉSIDENTIELLES and ÉLECTIONS CANTONALES, or where in an election for the CONSEIL GÉNÉRAL, one candidate is elected per CANTON.

Voters make a choice for an individual candidate. If one person receives more than 50 per cent of the votes on the first round, he or she is elected. If not, a second round is held, and the person with the highest number of votes is elected.

SDAU See: *SCHÉMA DIRECTEUR D'AMÉNAGEMENT ET D'URBANISME*

SDECE See: *SERVICE DE DOCUMENTATION EXTÉRIEURE ET DE CONTRE-ESPIONNAGE*

SEB
An electrical manufacturing group, specialising in small household equipment, and incorporating the *Calor*, *Rowenta*, *Seb* and *Tefal* brand names.

SECAM
An acronym based on the formula '*Séquentiel couleur à mémoire*', the system of colour television pictures used by the French broadcasting services.

SECONDE See: *CLASSE DE SECONDE*

SECOURS POPULAIRE FRANÇAIS (SPF)
A major charitable organisation linked to the PARTI COMMUNISTE FRANÇAIS, founded in 1946, with the UTILITÉ PUBLIQUE status, and with over 700,000 members. The SPF provides meals for the poor, holidays for those unable to afford them, and has a number of international projects.

SECOURS VIAGER
A tax-free benefit paid to the surviving spouse of a deceased recipient of the ALLOCATION AUX VIEUX TRAVAILLEURS SALARIÉS, provided that he or she is older than 55, and has been married to the deceased for at least two years. The benefit is of equal value to the *Allocation aux vieux travailleurs salariés*.

SECRET DE LA CORRESPONDANCE
It is an offence, punishable by a prison sentence of between three months and five years, to open confidential correspondence before the addressee has received it. However, postal officials are permitted to open envelopes if they suspect that regulations have been breached, and prison officers have the right to open prisoners' mail, except for that to and from lawyers.

SECRET PROFESSIONNEL
Professional confidentiality may be breached in cases where injustice might otherwise occur, or in the interests of the State.

Those with financial information are obliged to disclose this to tax authorities.

SECTEUR FRANÇAIS DE BERLIN
As part of the peace settlement after the Second World War, French troops, as members of the Allied occupying forces, had a right of presence in a sector of West Berlin.

SECTION D'ÉDUCATION SPÉCIALISÉE (SES)
Established as part of the *Loi* HABY, the SES provide education for children with serious learning difficulties, for whom the TRONC COMMUN does not apply.

SECTION DE TECHNICIENS SUPÉRIEURS (STS)
A specialist section of a LYCÉE D'ENSEIGNEMENT PROFESSIONNEL which provides training courses towards the BREVET DE TECHNICIEN SUPÉRIEUR, a BAC + 3 qualification.

SECTION FRANÇAISE DE L'INTERNATIONALE OUVRIÈRE (SFIO) See: *PARTI COMMUNISTE FRANÇAIS; PARTI SOCIALISTE*

SECRÉTAIRE D'ÉTAT
A junior ministerial post with specific responsibilities, usually reporting to a MINISTRE or a MINISTRE D'ÉTAT. A *secrétaire d'État* does not in normal circumstances attend a meeting of the CONSEIL DES MINISTRES.

SÉCU See: *SÉCURITÉ SOCIAL*

SÉCURITÉ CIVILE See: *PROTECTION CIVILE*

SÉCURITÉ SOCIALE
The national system of social security has existed since 1938. It is now divided into *régimes* or classifications of membership. Its governing bodies, the *Caisse nationale* and *Caisses régionales* have equal representation of employers' and workers' organisations, and the medical profession and the MUTUALITÉ movement are represented in the organisation. The *Sécurité sociale* absorbs one of the highest proportions of the gross national product in Europe, and its influence extends to benefits for maternity, childhood, unemployment, old age

pensions, sickness, housing and other areas. See also: AIDE SOCIALE; ALLOCATIONS; ASSURANCES; RETRAITE

SEGHERS, PIERRE (1906–1987)

A poet of Dutch ancestry who set up his own publishing business, mainly to publish the works of other poets. Seghers published *La Résistance et ses poètes* and *Anthologie des poètes maudits du XXème siècle*, and left his business to Robert LAFFONT.

SÉGUÉLA, JACQUES (1934–   )

A publicist who was responsible for the successful 1981 campaign of François MITTERRAND, under the slogan *La Force tranquille*.

SÉGUY, GEORGES (1927–   )

A printing worker and electrician who became the railway workers' leader in the CONFÉDÉRATION GÉNÉRALE DU TRAVAIL in 1961, and the *Secrétaire général* of the whole union from 1967 to 1982.

SEINE

The former DÉPARTEMENT which was largely made up of PARIS, before the administrative reorganisation of the RÉGION PARISIENNE in 1964. It was the previous user of the *code départemental* 75.

SEINE-ET-MARNE

The largest of the DÉPARTEMENTS of the ÎLE-DE-FRANCE region in area, but the one with the lowest population (1.97 million in 1990) named after the two rivers which pass through it.

The Seine-et-Marne has a mix of outer BANLIEUE on Paris's eastern extremity and rural landscapes with small country market towns. The CHEF-LIEU is Melun (92,433 in the AGGLOMÉRATION), with engineering, aviation, chemicals and foodstuffs industries. Other large centres of population are Champagne-sur-Seine (22,536); Champs-sur-Marne (21,611); Chelles (45,365); Combs-la-Ville (19,974); Coulommiers (20,338); Esbly (19,290); Fontainebleau (35,706); Lagny-sur-Marne (46,147); Meaux (63,006); Montereau-Faut-Yonne (26,035); Nemours (18,962); Ozoir-la-Ferrière (19,031); Pontault-Combault (26,804); Roissy (18,688); Savigny-le-

Temple (18,520); Torcy (18,681); and Villeparisis (18,790).

Two VILLES NOUVELLES are partly in the *Département*: MARNE-LA-VALLÉE and MELUN-SÉNART.

Industrial activity is exemplified by food-processing in Coulommiers and Villenoy, printing in Nanteuil-les-Meaux, glassmaking at Nemours and optics at Provins. There is a small steelworks at Montereau-Faut-Yonne.

Wheat and maize are cultivated in significant quantities, with some barley.

François MITTERRAND held on to his small 1981 majority here in the 1988 ÉLECTION PRÉSIDENTIELLE. Parliamentary representatives are drawn from a wide range of party groups. The Centre Right strengthened its control of the CONSEIL GÉNÉRAL in 1992, with 31 out of 42 seats.

Code départemental: 77

SEINE-ET-OISE

A former DÉPARTEMENT, which disappeared in 1964 as part of the reorganisation of the RÉGION PARISIENNE. It was split into ESSONNE, VAL-D'OISE and YVELINES, and was the previous holder of the *code départemental* 78.

SEINE-MARITIME

The coastal DÉPARTEMENT in the HAUTE-NORMANDIE region, including the mouth of the Seine river near le Havre. The overall population of the Seine-Maritime was 1.22 million in 1990. The CHEF-LIEU, Rouen, accounts for 379,879 of these in its urban area, and has employment in chemicals, papermaking, metallurgy, textiles, oil refining, electronics industries and in its activities as a port (it is the largest European port in its handling of cereals, and the world leader in exports of flour and phosphates). Other major centres of population are Barentin (19,499); Dieppe (41,812), a cross-channel ferry and fishing port, with shipbuilding, food-processing and metallurgy; Elbeuf (51,083) with textiles, plastics and a RENAULT plant; Eu (20,506); Fécamp (23,096), a centre for the canned and frozen fish trade, and home of Bénédictine liqueur; le Havre, the second French port in terms of traffic, with motor, engineering, cement, oil and petrochemical industries; and Yvetot (13,972).

There are nuclear power stations on the coast at Paluel and Penly.

The *Département* makes a significant contribution to French agriculture, principally in beef and dairy cattle.

Tourism is a major contributor to the local economy, with attractions ranging from seaside resorts, châteaux, abbeys and historic houses, and coastal scenery to connections with Victor Hugo at Villequier, Jeanne d'Arc, Corneille and Flaubert at Rouen.

In 1981 and 1988, François MITTERRAND was well supported in the ÉLECTIONS PRÉSIDENTIELLES, gaining more than 60 per cent of the vote in 1988. Most DÉPUTÉS elected in 1988 were Socialists, whereas SÉNATEURS come from a wider range of parties. The Centre Right retained its control of the CONSEIL GÉNÉRAL in the 1992 ÉLECTIONS CANTONALES.

Code départemental: 76

SEINE-SAINT-DENIS

An almost entirely urban and predominantly industrial DÉPARTEMENT in the ÎLE-DE-FRANCE region, in the northern BANLIEUE of Paris, with a population of 1.38 million in 1990. The CHEF-LIEU is Bobigny (44,659) and other large COMMUNES are Aubervilliers (67,557); Aulnay-sous-Bois (82,314); Bagnolet (32,600); Bondy (46,666); Clichy-sous-Bois (28,150); Drancy (60,707); Épinay-sur-Seine (48,714); Gagny (36,064); la Courneuve (34,139); Le Blanc-Mesnil (46,956); Les Lilas (20,118); Livry-Gargan (35.406); Montfermeil (25,556); Montreuil (94,754); Neuilly-sur-Marne (31,461); Noisy-le-Grand (54,032); Noisy-le-Sec (54,032); Pantin (47,303); Pierrefitte-sur-Seine (23.822); Romainville (23,563); Rosny-sous-Bois (37,489); Saint-Denis (89,988); Saint-Ouen (42,343); Sevran (48,478); Stains (34,879); Tremblay-en-France (31,385); Villemoble (26,863); and Villepinte (30,303).

In almost every case, major industrial firms have plants in these communes, ranging, for example, from ALSTHOM at La Courneuve, to CITROËN at Aulnay-sous-Bois and SAINT-GOBAIN at Aubervilliers.

Other features of the *Département* are the tourist attraction of Saint-Denis, where the royal basilica of France is situated. Drancy was the site of the infamous transit camp for deportees from 1940 to 1944.

Politically the Seine-Saint-Denis is a traditional fief of the Left. In the 1981 and 1988 ÉLECTIONS PRÉSIDENTIELLES, François MITTERRAND gained good majorities, with Georges MARCHAIS receiving the highest proportion in the PREMIER TOUR in 1981. Socialists and Communists dominate the numbers of parliamentary representatives, and the CONSEIL GÉNÉRAL is one of only two in the country in which the PARTI COMMUNISTE FRANÇAIS is the largest group.

Code départemental: 93

SEITA See: *SOCIÉTÉ NATIONALE D'EXPLOITATION INDUSTRIELLE DES TABACS ET ALLUMETTES*

SÉLECTION DU READER'S DIGEST
Despite the tautology in the title, the French edition of the Reader's Digest, normally called *Sélection*, sells 1.1 million copies monthly, by far the largest sales for a monthly publication.

SEM See: *SOCIÉTÉ D'ÉCONOMIE MIXTE*

SEMAINE LÉGALE
The normal working week is considered to be 39 hours long, spread over five or six days, with employees being entitled to 125 per cent of normal rates for 40–47 hours, and 150 per cent beyond that.

SEMEUSE
One of the manifestations of MARIANNE is the symbolic sower, seen on postage stamps, coins and in other effigies.

SEMPÉ, JEAN-JACQUES (1932–)
A cartoonist, known by his surname only, who is widely published in collections as well as in newspapers and magazines. Sempé's characteristic style is a gentle mocking of urban life.

SÉNAT
The upper house of parliament, which meets in the PALAIS DU

LUXEMBOURG in Paris, is composed of 321 SÉNATEURS, 296 drawn from metropolitan France, eight from DÉPARTEMENTS D'OUTRE-MER, three from TERRITOIRES D'OUTRE-MER, one from MAYOTTE, one from SAINT-PIERRE-ET-MIQUELON, and 12 representing French nationals overseas. Roughly a third of the *sénateurs* are elected every three years for a nine-year term. Elections are by electoral colleges on a *départemental* level. In metropolitan France, this means that for each DÉPARTEMENT, the DÉPUTÉS, members of the CONSEIL GÉNÉRAL and delegated representatives of each CONSEIL MUNICIPAL elect the *sénateurs*. One *sénateur* is elected for the first 154,000 of the *département's* population, with another seat available for each additional 250,000 inhabitants.

Its role is to vote laws and the State budget, to introduce a PROPOSITION DE LOI, to modify the text of PROJETS DE LOI before they are returned for a second reading in the ASSEMBLÉE NATIONALE, and for its members to participate in COMMISSIONS MIXTES PARITAIRES to resolve differences between the two houses.

The *Président du Sénat* is elected by the *sénateurs* from within their numbers to serve for three years. The *Président du Sénat* since 1968 has been Alain POHER. This office is second only in rank to that of the PRÉSIDENT DE LA RÉPUBLIQUE, and indeed its holder acts as *Président de la République intérimaire* if the head of State is incapacitated. See also: NAVETTE PARLEMENTAIRE; SCRUTIN DE LISTE À LA REPRÉSENTATION PROPORTIONNELLE; SCRUTIN DE LISTE MAJORITAIRE

SÉNATEUR
A member of the SÉNAT, who must be at least 35 years old. The other minimum conditions for election are the same as those for DÉPUTÉS. See also: CUMUL DES MANDATS

SENNEP (1894–1982)
Known by his surname, a famous satirical cartoonist whose work appeared in *Le* FIGARO from 1945 to 1967.

SÉPARATION DE CORPS
The legal separation of a married couple.

SEPT, LA
Actually an acronym of *Société d'édition de programmes de*

télévision, a programme maker and broadcaster established in 1986, and transmitting on *France-Régions* 3 (now FRANCE 3) from 1987, and later on TDF 1. *La Sept* also transmits programmes by cable to other European countries.

SEPTENNAT
The seven-year term of office of the PRÉSIDENT DE LA RÉPUBLIQUE, specified by the CONSTITUTION of the CINQUIÈME RÉPUBLIQUE.

SERVAN-SCHREIBER, JEAN-JACQUES (1924–)
A journalist, founder of *l'*EXPRESS, and politician of the Centre, whose book *Le Défi américain* (1967) was influential in setting out the centrists' view of the need for dynamic economic modernization. He now lives in the USA.

SERVICE DE DOCUMENTATION EXTÉRIEURE ET DE CONTRE-ESPIONNAGE (SDECE)
The government foreign intelligence gathering and counter-espionnage service, which is restricted to operations outside France, and is responsible to the *Ministère de la justice*. There were accusations of covert operations within France in the 1970s and 1980s, especially in relation to monitoring tax returns and infiltrating Communist organisations. See also: DIRECTION DE LA SURVEILLANCE DU TERRITOIRE; DIRECTION GÉNÉRALE DE LA SÉCURITÉ EXTÉRIEURE; RENSEIGNEMENTS GÉNÉRAUX

SERVICE MILITAIRE See: *SERVICE NATIONAL*

SERVICE NATIONAL
All French males between the ages of 18 and 35 are liable to be called up for national service. Since 1991, the period of service is of 10 months duration. About 70 per cent of those liable are in fact called up. Since 1970, it has been possible for women to serve as well, but few do so. Most conscripts serve in one of the armed services, including the GENDARMERIE NATIONALE, but it is also possible to serve in the POLICE NATIONALE, or in voluntary service abroad for a period of 16 months.

Certain excepted categories are excused service, e.g. PUPILLES DE L'ÉTAT, owners of businesses, those of double nationality, residents abroad, and many are rejected for medical reasons.

Full-time students can delay their service beyond the normal call-up age of 19, depending on their progress in their studies.

Conscientious objectors have to serve two years in support roles in public service specified by the *Ministère des affaires sociales et de la solidarité nationale*. In 1988, about 4,500 were registered as conscientious objectors. See also: TROIS JOURS

SES See: *SECTION D'ÉDUCATION SPÉCIALISÉE*

SEUIL, LE
A general publisher and distributor for other publishers, based in Paris.

SEYRIG, DELPHINE (1932–1990)
An actress and film star who developed a dreamy, ethereal style in her film roles. Two of her films are *L'Année dernière à Marienbad* and *Le Charme discret de la bourgeoisie*.

SFP See: *SOCIÉTÉ FRANÇAISE DE PRODUCTION ET DE CRÉATION AUDIOVISUELLE*

SGEN See: *SYNDICAT GÉNÉRAL DE L'ÉDUCATION NATIONALE*

SICAV See: *SOCIÉTÉ D'INVESTISSEMENT À CAPITAL VARIABLE*

SICOMI See: *SOCIÉTÉ IMMOBILIÈRE POUR LE COMMERCE ET L'INDUSTRIE*

SIEGEL, MAURICE (1919–1985)
A journalist who worked for many newspapers and RTL before taking control of EUROPE 1 and boosting the fortunes of the station. He later was the founder of the weekly magazine VENDREDI, SAMEDI, DIMANCHE, known commonly as VSD.

SIFFRE, MICHEL (1939–   )
A geologist and potholer whose caving exploits are well known and documented in books and films he has made. In 1972, he spent 205 days underground in Texas.

SIGNORET, SIMONE (1921–1985)
An actress and film star, who was also a militant member of

the PARTI COMMUNISTE FRANÇAIS. She made over 50 films, among which are *Les Enfants du paradis*, *La Ronde*, and *Room at the Top*, for which she won an Oscar in 1959 despite having been a victim of McCarthyism earlier in the decade. Her second husband was Yves MONTAND, with whom she made a number of films.

SII See: *SOCIÉTÉ IMMOBILIÈRE D'INVESTISSEMENT*

SIMON, CLAUDE (1913–)
A Nobel prize winning novelist (he won in 1985) and distinguished photographer, whose 1960 book, *La Routes des Flandres*, is a major example of the '*nouveau roman*'. His first novel was *Le Tricheur* (1946), and others include *L'Herbe* (1958) and *L'Acacia* (1989).

SIMONIN, ALBERT (1905–1981)
After a series of different jobs, Simonin became well-known as a writer with the 1953 publication of *Touchez pas au grisbi*, a novel written largely in underworld slang, which was made into a successful film. *Le Petit Simonin illustré* is an amusing slang dictionary.

SIVOM See: *SYNDICAT INTERCOMMUNAL À VOCATION MULTIPLE*

SIVU See: *SYNDICAT INTERCOMMUNAL À VOCATION UNIQUE*

SIXIÈME, CLASSE DE See: *CYCLE D'OBSERVATION*

SMIC See: *SALAIRE MINIMUM INTERPROFESSIONIEL DE CROISSANCE*

SMICARD
An employee who earns the SMIC.

SMIG See: *SALAIRE MINIMUM INTERPROFESSIONNEL GARANTI*

SNALC See: *SYNDICAT NATIONAL DES LYCÉES ET COLLÈGES*

SNCF See: *SOCIÉTÉ NATIONALE DES CHEMINS DE FER FRANÇAIS*

SNECMA See: *SOCIÉTÉ NATIONALE D'ÉTUDES ET DE CONSTRUCTION DE MOTEURS D'AVIONS*

SNES See: *SYNDICAT NATIONAL DES ENSEIGNANTS DU SECOND DEGRÉ*

SNESup See: *SYNDICAT NATIONAL DE L'ENSEIGNEMENT SUPÉRIEUR*

SNIAS See: *AÉROSPATIALE*

SOBOUL, ALBERT (1914–1982)
A history professor at PARIS-SORBONNE and renowned historian of the French Revolution. A member of the RÉSISTANCE, Soboul was a life-long member of the PARTI COMMUNISTE FRANÇAIS.

SOCHAUX See: *DOUBS; PEUGEOT*

SOCIALISME ET RÉPUBLIQUE
A left-wing pressure group within the PARTI SOCIALISTE, one of whose leaders is Jean-Pierre CHEVÈNEMENT. It is the replacement of the CENTRE D'ÉTUDES, DE RECHERCHE ET D'ÉDUCATION SOCIALISTES.

SOCIÉTÉ ANONYME (SA or SARL)
The abbreviated form of *Société anonyme à responsabilité limitée*, which indicates in full the status of limited company.

SOCIÉTÉ CIVILE DE PLACEMENT IMMOBILIER (SCPI)
This is a generic term for a company which has the sole purpose of owning and managing rented accommodation. An SCPI is not permitted to develop properties for sale. It is excused company tax, and is not quoted on the BOURSE. An SCPI is generally a subsidiary operation of a bank or a finance company.

SOCIÉTÉ CO-OPÉRATIVE OUVRIÈRE DE PRODUCTION (SCOP)
The full title of a co-operative manufacturer, of which there were almost 1,000 in 1982. Some SCOP were formed through

employee buyouts of existing businesses. See also: LIP; MANUFRANCE

SOCIÉTÉ D'AMÉNAGEMENT FONCIER ET D'ÉTABLISSEMENT RURAL (SAFER)

A SAFER is a funding organisation which allows small farmers or those wishing to maintain the rural infrastructure to finance projects, by buying land and reselling it within five years to those who will carry out the projects. There are 27 SAFER in metropolitan France.

SOCIÉTÉ D'ÉCONOMIE MIXTE (SEM)

A company which is jointly financed by state and private capital.

SOCIÉTÉ DE FINANCEMENT DES INDUSTRIES CINÉMATOGRAPHIQUES (SOFICA)

These were introduced in 1985. Taxpayers are allowed to reduce their liability to the IMPÔT SUR LE REVENU by making contributions to a SOFICA, which must finance French language films which do not contravene certain restrictions of character and taste.

SOCIÉTÉ DES AUTEURS, COMPOSITEURS ET ÉDITEURS DE MUSIQUE (SACEM)

The organisation which protects the interests of its members, by collecting and distributing performance and recording rights payments, founded in 1851. SACEM also acts as a support for retired members in need, and has a more public role as the promoter of performances throughout France. See also: GRAND PRIX DE LA SACEM

SOCIÉTÉ D'INVESTISSEMENT À CAPITAL VARIABLE (SICAV)

A unit trust fund of shares, open to private investors. No more than 5 per cent of the fund can be placed in the shares of any one firm. It is possible to link a SICAV to a life assurance policy.

SOCIÉTÉ EUROPÉENNE DE PROGRAMMES DE TÉLÉVISION See: *SEPT*

SOCIÉTÉ FINANCIÈRE DE RADIODIFFUSION (SOFIRAD)

The State-owned holding company which owns shares in

broadcasting services other than those directly controlled by the State. Thus 93 per cent of RADIO MONTE-CARLO is owned by SOFIRAD. The PRÉSIDENT-DIRECTEUR-GÉNÉRAL is appointed by the CONSEIL DES MINISTRES.

SOCIÉTÉ FRANÇAISE D'ENQUÊTES PAR SONDAGE (SOFRES)

A private enterprise market research and polling company, in existence since 1962.

SOCIÉTÉ FRANÇAISE DE PRODUCTION ET DE CRÉATION AUDIOVISUELLE (SFP)

A State-owned television programme maker, able to sell its productions on the open market since 1982. In effect almost its entire output is used by the State-owned channels.

SOCIÉTÉ GÉNÉRALE

The fourth largest bank in France, founded in 1864, nationalised in 1946, and privatised again in 1987. It has 2,000 branches and 3.6 million account holding customers. An attempt to buy back for the State more than the 20 per cent of the capital retained in 1987 failed in 1988, and caused a government scandal with accusations of dishonest dealings.

SOCIÉTÉ IMMOBILIÈRE D'INVESTISSEMENT (SII)

A company receiving investments which are used for the construction and letting of residential and commercial property. The first SII was established in 1958.

SOCIÉTÉ IMMOBILIÈRE POUR LE COMMERCE ET L'INDUSTRIE (SICOMI)

An investment company permitted to own and rent commercial or residential property. There are 60 SICOMIs.

SOCIÉTÉ NATIONALE DE RADIO ET DE TÉLÉVISION POUR L'OUTRE-MER (RFO)

The State-owned company which operates in the DOM and TOM. With certain exceptions, the normal provision is a local radio station and FRANCE INTER, as well as FRANCE 2, broadcasts.

SOCIÉTÉ NATIONALE DES CHEMINS DE FER FRANÇAIS (SNCF)

The nationalised railway company, formed in 1937 from the

amalgamation of the private enterprise systems. A contractual arrangement with the State ensures a planned investment programme and guarantees of a subsidy for socially necessary services. A small amount of finance is also raised through private sources. See also: RÉSEAU EXPRESS RÉGIONAL; SERVICE NATIONAL DES MESSAGERIES; TRAIN À GRANDE VITESSE

SOCIÉTÉ NATIONALE DES INDUSTRIES AÉRONAUTIQUES ET SPATIALES (SNIAS) See: *AÉROSPATIALE*

SOCIÉTÉ NATIONALE D'ÉTUDES ET DE CONSTRUCTION DE MOTEURS D'AVIONS (SNECMA)
The aero-engine manufacturer, nationalised as an amalgamation of other firms in 1945, with its headquarters at Corbeil (ESSONNE), and with most of its plants in the southern BANLIEUE of Paris. SNECMA employs almost 28,000.

SOCIÉTÉ NATIONALE D'EXPLOITATION INDUSTRIELLE DES TABACS ET ALLUMETTES (SEITA)
The nationalised concern which holds the monopoly of all tobacco production and imports in France, controlling sales and distribution through DÉBITS DE TABAC. The ban on tobacco advertising on broadcast media seems to have had little effect on consumption, which has remained virtually steady at around 100,000 tons annually in the 1980s. From 1993, all tobacco advertising is illegal.

SOCIÉTÉ POUR L'EXPANSION DES VENTES DE PRODUITS AGRICOLES ET ALIMENTAIRES (SOPEXA)
A marketing organisation which represents the interests of growers in publicising and promoting French food and drink.

SODIMA See: *COOPÉRATIVE AGRICOLE*

SOFICA See: *SOCIÉTÉ DE FINANCEMENT DES INDUSTRIES CINÉMATOGRAPHIQUES*

SOFIRAD See: *SOCIÉTÉ FINANCIÈRE DE RADIODIFFUSION*

SOFRES See: *SOCIÉTÉ FRANÇAISE D'ENQUÊTES PAR SONDAGE*

SOISSON, JEAN-PIERRE (1934–   )
An ÉNARQUE and senior FONCTIONNAIRE who entered politics in 1968, and became MAIRE of Auxerre in 1971. Soisson took a leading role in the RÉPUBLICAINS INDÉPENDANTS, held various ministerial posts in the government of GISCARD D'ESTAING and was *Secrétaire général* of the PARTI RÉPUBLICAIN from 1977 to 1978. In the 1988 OUVERTURE, he was appointed *Ministre du travail*, and in 1991 *Ministre de la fonction publique*.

SOLDAT INCONNU
The tomb of the unknown soldier from the First World War lies under the *Arc de Triomphe*, in Paris. A similar tomb of a soldier killed in the Indo-Chinese War of the 1950s is in the national cemetery at Notre-Dame-de-Lorette (PAS-DE-CALAIS). See also: CÉRÉMONIAL DU SOUVENIR; SOUVENIR FRANÇAIS

SOLEX
A best-selling brand of CYLOMOTEUR, which ceased production in 1988. The *Solex* and *Motobécane* firms were taken over by the Japanese company Yamaha in 1986.

SOLIDARITÉ NATIONALE
One of the early themes of the MITTERRAND presidency from 1981, reflected in a *Ministère de la solidarité, de la santé, et de la protection sociale*, and an ALLOCATION SOLIDARITÉ.

SOLLERS, PHILIPPE (1936–   )
A novelist, winner of the *Prix* MÉDICIS in 1961, who was also influential in the theory of criticism expounded in TEL QUEL.

SOLUTRÉ
A prehistoric site in the SAÔNE-ET-LOIRE which has taken on a political flavour in recent years as the objective of an annual walk by François MITTERRAND.

SOMME
A DÉPARTEMENT in the PICARDIE region, named after its principal river, the site of a major military campaign in the First World

War. The population of the Somme in 1990 was 547,825, and of these, 154,498 lived in the AGGLOMÉRATION of Amiens, the CHEF-LIEU, a centre for textiles, metallurgy, chemicals, food-processing and rubber tyres. Other urban areas are Abbeville (26,405) – sugar-processing, textiles and metallurgy; Albert (10,010) – dairy industry, machine-tools and engineering; and Péronne (10,988) – textiles and food-processing. The same pattern of industry is repeated on a smaller in the minor centres of population.

The main agricultural activity is in sugar beet, potatoes, wheat and barley production, with some dairy cattle, pigs and poultry.

The Somme is the *département* with the fifth lowest life expectancy for women.

The political make-up of the Somme shows general support for the Left, with François MITTERRAND receiving majorities in the 1981 and 1988 ÉLECTIONS PRÉSIDENTIELLES. The Centre Right, however, controls the CONSEIL GÉNÉRAL, although there was a slight swing to the Left in the 1992 ÉLECTIONS CANTONALES.

Code départemental: 80

SOPEXA See: *SOCIÉTÉ POUR L'EXPANSION DES VENTES DES PRODUITS AGRICOLES ALIMENTAIRES*

SOPHIA-ANTIPOLIS
A high-tech commercial and industrial development at Valbonne (ALPES-MARITIMES), within the Cannes-Grasse-Antibes conurbation, promoted since 1969 with a particular focus on information technology and electronics industries. Sophia-Antipolis is the centre of a group of TECHNOPOLES in the south-east, and is a model for similar planned developments elsewhere.

SORBONNE
The ancient centre of the original Paris university. The term is loosely used to indicate the prestigious centre of literary and philosophical studies, but more strictly refers only to certain establishments in the Paris university structure. See also: PARIS, UNIVERSITÉ DE

SORBONNE-NOUVELLE (UNIVERSITÉ)
The official name of Paris III university with faculties of modern

languages, literature and civilisation. It has 17,000 students.

SOS AMITIÉ
A charity which aims to provide help for those suffering from depression and in despair. It runs a telephone help-line service.

SOUS LES DRAPEAUX See: *SERVICE MILITAIRE*

SOUS-PRÉFECTURE
The administrative offices of a SOUS-PRÉFET, situated in the main town of an ARRONDISSEMENT. The town itself is also called the *sous-préfecture*.

SOUS-PRÉFET
The FONCTIONNAIRE, responsible to and with delegated powers from the PRÉFET, based in a SOUS-PRÉFECTURE, and with powers within the ARRONDISSEMENT.

SOUSTELLE, JACQUES (1912–1990)
An ÉNARQUE (having been admitted at the early age of 17) who became an anthropologist and an expert on ancient Mexican civilisations, and a Gaullist politician, who was one of the first to join DE GAULLE in 1940. He was the governor general in ALGÉRIE from 1955, a Minister in De Gaulle's administration from 1958, but sided against his former leader over the Algerian question. After a period of exile he returned to France in 1968 and was elected to the ACADÉMIE FRANÇAISE in 1982.

SOUVENIR FRANÇAIS, LE
An association with 300,000 members, dedicated to the maintenance of war memorials and tombs of military and other personnel who were killed in action. See also: CÉRÉMONIAL DU SOUVENIR; SOLDAT INCONNU

SPF See: *SECOURS POPULAIRE FRANÇAIS*

SPIROU
A weekly cartoon magazine, dating from 1936, and with a circulation in 1987 of 33,000.

STATION VERTE DE VACANCES
A rural inland holiday resort which conforms to certain minimum standards of provision and is registered as a member of the *Fédération française des stations vertes de vacances et villages de neige*.

STENDHAL (UNIVERSITÉ)
The title of the *Université de Grenoble-III* on the Saint-Martin-d'Hères campus, with 6,000 students following courses in communications, languages and literature.

STS See: *SECTION DE TECHNICIENS SUPÉRIEURS*

STOCK
A Paris publishing house, now an imprint within the HACHETTE group.

STRASBOURG, UNIVERSITÉS DE
Apart from the *Université Louis*-PASTEUR, there are two universities in the city, *Strasbourg-II* with 12,000 students in arts, history, humanities, social sciences, theology, physical education and sport, and *Strasbourg-III* (*Université Robert Schuman*) with 8,000 students following courses in journalism, law, politics, social sciences and technology.

SUBVENTION POUR LA LUTTE CONTRE L'INSALUBRITÉ
A grant payable to improve the conditions of a dwelling to proper standards. The owner has to have been occupying the premises for two years, and must continue to live there for fifteen years, or the grant has to be repaid. See also: PRIME À L'AMÉLIORATION DE L'HABITAT

SUD-RADIO
A RADIO PÉRIPHÉRIQUE broadcasting from ANDORRE between 1962 (formerly *Radio Andorre*) and 1981, when it was allowed to use transmitters in France at Muret (HAUTE-GARONNE). SOFIRAD sold its controlling interest in 1987, since when it has operated as a RADIO LIBRE over the regions of AQUITAINE, LANGUEDOC-ROUSSILLON and MIDI-PYRÉNÉES.

SUD-OUEST
A daily newspaper, published in Bordeaux, with a circulation

of 376,000 in 1989. The Sunday edition sells 295,000. The paper dominates the market in AQUITAINE.

SUEZ, BANQUE
The *Banque de l'Indochine et de Suez*, one of the 36 banks nationalised in 1981–1982, was sold back to the private sector in 1987.

SULITZER, PAUL-LOUP (1946–   )
A financial consultant who has also written international best-selling novels such as *Money* (1980), *Cash* (the winner of the 1981 *Prix du livre d'été)* and *Le Roi vert*.

SUPÉLEC See: *ÉCOLE CENTRALE*

SUPÉRETTE
A small self-service store, usually a food supermarket, with a sales floor of between 120 and 400 square metres.

SUPPLÉANT
In a Parliamentary election using the SCRUTIN DE LISTE MAJORITAIRE, a reserve candidate is elected at the same time to be the replacement of a sitting DÉPUTÉ in the case of death, membership of the government or absence on government service for more than six months. The *Suppléant* is normally the unelected candidate with the highest number of votes from the same list. This system obviates the need for by-elections.

   A *Suppléant* who takes the seat of a member of the government cannot stand against that person in the following election.

SUPOPTIC See: *ÉCOLE CENTRALE*

SURENCHÈRE
Within 10 days of the date of house or building sale by auction, it is possible to make a new offer through an AVOCAT of 10 per cent above the agreed sale price. The auction is held again, starting at the new offer price which is binding if no further offer is received. The process is only possible once. See also: VENTE AUX ENCHÈRES

SYNDICAT DE COMMUNES
A joint grouping of neighbouring COMMUNES to provide a range of services more efficiently or economically. See also: COMMUNAUTÉ URBAINE; SYNDICAT INTERCOMMUNAL À VOCATION MULTIPLE; SYNDICAT INTERCOMMUNAL À VOCATION UNIQUE

SYNDICAT D'INITIATIVE
A local tourist information service, funded by municipal authorities and local businesses.

SYNDICAT GÉNÉRAL DE L'ÉDUCATION NATIONALE (SGEN)
A union for teachers and researchers from all aspects of education, allied to the CONFÉDÉRATION FRANÇAISE DÉMOCRATIQUE DU TRAVAIL.

SYNDICAT INTERCOMMUNAL À VOCATION MULTIPLE (SIVOM)
There are almost 2,000 SIVOM linking neighbouring COMMUNES for the joint provision of a range of services. See also: SYNDICAT DE COMMUNES; SYNDICAT INTERCOMMUNAL À VOCATION UNIQUE

SYNDICAT INTERCOMMUNAL À VOCATION UNIQUE (SIVU)
About 12,000 SIVU exist in France, whereby groups of COMMUNES have collaborated to provide jointly a particular service. The largest number of SIVU (about 3,500) concern provision of water supplies, and another large number arrange the educational responsibilities of *communes* on a joint basis. See also: SYNDICAT DE COMMUNES; SYNDICAT INTERCOMMUNAL À VOCATION MULTIPLE

SYNDICAT MIXTE
A consortium of COLLECTIVITÉS LOCALES of different status and other public bodies, formed in order to manage specific developments of common interest.

SYNDICAT NATIONAL DE L'ENSEIGNEMENT SUPÉRIEUR (SNESup)
A vocal and influential union of 5,000 teachers in higher education.

SYNDICAT NATIONAL DES ENSEIGNANTS DU SECOND DEGRÉ CLASSIQUE, MODERNE ET TECHNIQUE (SNES)
A union of 70,000 teachers in COLLÈGES and LYCÉES.

SYNDICAT NATIONAL DES LYCÉES ET COLLÈGES (SNALC)
One of the oldest unions for teachers (founded in 1905), reflecting moderate opinion among its 12,500 members in secondary schools.

SYSTÈME D
A monthly DIY magazine with a circulation of 161,000, in print since 1924.

SYSTÈME U
A co-operative chain of about 1,300 foodstores with the brandnames *Unico*, *Super U*, *Hyper U* and *Marché U*.

TAAF See: *TERRES AUSTRALES ET ANTARCTIQUES FRANÇAISES*

TABAC See: *DÉBIT DE TABAC*

TACHELLA, JEAN-CHARLES (1925–)
A film director who has achieved commercial success with films such as *Cousin, cousine* (1975) and *Escalier C* (1985).

TAPIE, BERNARD (1943–)
A millionaire Socialist politician (DÉPUTÉ for the BOUCHES-DU-RHÔNE in the 1988 elections), who owns the ADIDAS business and also the Marseille football team O M Marseille. In 1991–1992 he presented himself as the leader of the PARTI SOCIALISTE'S fight in the PROVENCE-ALPES-CÔTE-D'AZUR region against the rising power of the FRONT NATIONAL, and was successful in leading a list in the ÉLECTIONS RÉGIONALES. He was appointed *Ministre des villes* in Pierre BÉRÉGOVOY'S government, but resigned after a few weeks, accused of financial wrongdoing.

TARIF EJP
An abbreviation of *Tarif effacement jour de pointe*, this is a special electricity rate which, in return for a very high rate of payment for a nominated 22 days in peak use months, gives the benefits of a reduced rate for the whole of the rest of the year.

TARN
A DÉPARTEMENT in the MIDI-PYRÉNÉES region, named after its principal river, with a 1990 population of 342,741. There was a major leap in population in the early 1970s. The CHEF-LIEU is Albi (urban area, 62,182), an agricultural market centre with industrial activity in steelmaking, synthetic fabrics, glassmaking and power (coal and electricity). Other towns are Carmaux

(17,307), a coal-mining town, with chemicals, textiles and plastics industries; Castres (46,481) – engineering, machine-tools, quarrying, textiles, clothing, furniture and pharmaceuticals; Gaillac (11,742) – plastics and wines; Graulhet (13,523) – leather goods, sizes and gelatines; and Mazamet (25,484) – fell- mongering, leather treatments, wood industries, toys and chemicals.

The agricultural activity of the Tarn includes rearing sheep and veal calves, vineyards, maize and bee-keeping, with a substantial forestry element. The medieval heritage (e.g. the town of Cordes, the churches and art works at Albi, the connections with the Cathars in Lavaur) attracts a good number of tourists.

Women living in the Tarn have the fifth highest life expectancy in France at 79.9 years.

In the 1980s, the political strength in the *Département* was that of the PARTI SOCIALISTE. They provided most of the parliamentary representatives, and François MITTERRAND managed to maintain a 55 per cent majority in both the 1981 and 1988 ÉLECTIONS PRÉSIDENTIELLES. In the ELECTIONS CANTONALES of 1992, the Left retained 25 of its 26 seats in the Conseil, as in the CONSEIL GÉNÉRAL of 43 seats.

Code départemental: 81

TARN-ET-GARONNE

A mainly rural DÉPARTEMENT of the MIDI-PYRÉNÉES region, in which the two rivers of its name meet, with a population in 1990 of 200,220. The CHEF-LIEU, Montauban, is home to 51,224 and is a centre for fruit, vegetable and poultry distribution, as well as having furniture, lighting, hi-fi and footwear industries. The other large towns are Castelsarrasin (11,317), with a metal foundry; and Moissac (11,971), which has a rubber works.

Fruit and vegetables are the principal products of the Tarn-et-Garonne farmers, and there is also wheat, maize and geese for *pâté de foie gras*.

In politics, the Tarn-et-Garonne behaves almost exactly as its neighbour, the TARN, although the Centre Right gained seats in the 1992 ÉLECTIONS CANTONALES, but not enough to dislodge the control of the Left.

Code départemental: 82

TAT See: *TRANSPORT AÉRIEN RÉGIONAL*

TATI, JACQUES (1908–1982)
The film director and comic actor who made legendary films such as *Les Vacances de Monsieur Hulot* (1953) and *Trafic* (1971). His films take a wryly critical look at modern urban life.

TAVERNIER, BERTRAND (1941–)
A film director whose first feature, *L'Horloger de Saint-Paul* (1973) was an instant success and typifies his portrayal of provincial France, seen again in films such as *Un Dimanche à la campagne* (1985). Tavernier has also made a number of films with historical themes, such as *Que la fête commence* (1975), set in the eighteenth century. His *La Guerre sans nom* (1992) was a controversial treatment of witnesses to the Algerian War.

TAXE À LA VALEUR AJOUTÉE See: *TAXE SUR LA VALEUR AJOUTÉE*

TAXE D'APPRENTISSAGE
A tax of 0.5 per cent of the total payroll levied on industries and businesses in order to support training schemes. Firms can specify that a proportion of their payment is directed to a particular training institution (e.g. a LYCÉE *d'enseignement technologique*, or a CENTRE DE FORMATION D'APPRENTIS). At least a fifth of the sum paid must support apprenticeship schemes.

TAXE DE BALAYAGE
A local tax payable by residents of Paris to the CONSEIL DE PARIS, calculated on the size of the frontage on the public footpath.

TAXE D'ENLÈVEMENT DES ORDURES MÉNAGÈRES
A local tax payable by all those liable to the TAXE FONCIÈRE except for factories and properties occupied by the ADMINISTRATION, and calculated in the same way, to pay for refuse collection services.

TAXE DÉPARTEMENTALE SUR LES REVENUS (TDR)
This local income tax measure was proposed by Socialist DÉPUTÉS in 1992 as a partial reform for the TAXE D'HABITATION, but it was not favoured by Pierre BÉRÉGOVOY.

TAXE DE SÉJOUR
A COMMUNE can raise income from its local hotels by charging a tax on visitors.

TAXE D'HABITATION
A local tax providing roughly a quarter of the locally raised income of the COLLECTIVITÉS LOCALES, based on the value of the property (as fixed in 1980) occupied on 1 January in any year. The rate of tax payable varies between COMMUNES. The sum payable can be reduced using similar calculations as those used for the IMPÔT SUR LE REVENU. Those above the age of 60, and widows and widowers of any age, if not liable to the *Impôt sur le revenu*, are not required to pay the *Taxe d'habitation*. See also: TAXE DÉPARTEMENTALE SUR LES REVENUS

TAXE DIFFÉRENTIELLE SUR LES VÉHICULES À MOTEUR See: *VIGNETTE*

TAXE FONCIÈRE
About half the locally raised income of the COLLECTIVITÉS LOCALES comes from this local tax, payable by property owners. It cannot be passed on to tenants. The unit of calculation for flats and houses is the value calculated for the TAXE D'HABITATION. The *Taxe foncière sur les propriétés bâties* is subject to reductions for those with low incomes and for certain other categories, and is not payable by those above 75 years of age without taxable income.

The *Taxe foncière sur les propriétés non bâties* is payable on undeveloped land, and is based on land values calculated by official valuers. An owner is excused tax for 30 years on newly planted woodland.

TAXE LOCALE DE L'ÉQUIPEMENT (TLE)
A local tax payable in a COMMUNE with more than 10,000 inhabitants, levied on the builders and management companies of housing developments at the rate of between 1 and 5 per cent of the value of the property.

TAXE PROFESSIONNELLE
A local tax on members of the professions who earn fees rather than salaries. The amount payable is calculated on the basis on the value of the premises occupied, together with a notional value of the enterprise's material belongings.

The *Taxe professionnelle* provides roughly half the locally raised income of the COLLECTIVITÉS LOCALES.

TAXE SUR LA VALEUR AJOUTÉE (TVA)
The first TVA was introduced in 1954, and its imposition made more widespread from 1968. It put on a national basis the tax payable on purchases which was previously subject to local variation. Certain activities are exempt (e.g. daily press, health and medical services, insurance brokers) and the rate payable varies according to the nature of the product or service. The standard rate was 18.6 per cent, and there were lower rates (5.5 per cent) and higher rates (22 per cent) applicable in 1991.

TAXE SUR LES SALAIRES
An employer not subject to the TAXE SUR LA VALEUR AJOUTÉE must make an annual declaration of the amount payable in wages and salaries to the work force, and has to pay a tax of 4.25 per cent and upwards of this sum.

TDR See: *TAXE DÉPARTEMENTALE SUR LES REVENUS*

TECHNICIEN
A qualified person who has received a certificate of at least the level of *Brevet professionnel* which is at a higher level than the BREVET D'ÉTUDES PROFESSIONNELLES. See also: INGÉNIEUR

TECHNOPOLE
A designated high technology centre which acts as a focus for scientific research and development with a direct effect on the local industrial and economic environment.

TÉLÉ 7 JOURS
The leading weekly broadcasting and entertainments listings magazine, published by HACHETTE and selling three million per week. This is the highest selling of all weekly French magazines.

Télé 7 jours sponsors an annual award of the *7 D'Or de Télé 7 jours* prizes in recognition of achievement in French television.

TÉLÉACHAT
The system of shopping via TÉLÉTEL or in telephone response to televised adverts.

TÉLÉCARTE
A plastic card available in 50 or 120 units for use in public telephone kiosks, most of which have been converted to this system and do not accept coins. The *Télécarte* is also used as a medium for advertising revenue for FRANCE-TÉLÉCOM, and special issues are now in existence, giving rise to a thriving collectors' market.

TÉLÉCOM See: *FRANCE TÉLÉCOM*

TÉLÉGRAMME DE BREST, LE
Despite its name, this daily newspaper is published in Morlaix (FINISTÈRE) and has a circulation of 184,000.

TÉLÉ MAGAZINE
A weekly listings magazine with a circulation of 375,000.

TÉLÉPOCHE
A weekly broadcasting and entertainments listings magazine with a 1989 circulation of 1.73 million.

TÉLÉRAMA
A weekly television magazine with a circulation of 515,000 in 1990.

TÉLÉTEL
A computerised information network available to all telephone subscribers who have a MINITEL terminal available. The initial *Télétel* service was intended to replace the paper telephone directories, for which *Minitel* terminals were provided free of charge to any user who requested one. The network has since developed into an enormous range of public and commercial services with varying rates for access.

TÉLÉVISION FRANÇAISE 1 (TF1)

The original French television channel, formerly controlled strictly by the State in every respect. State control gradually diminished and since 1987, TF1 has been a private company. Its operating licence requires it to transmit for an average of 14 hours daily, and its programmes must include at least 50 per cent which are of French origin.

TEL QUEL

A literary review founded in 1960 by Philippe SOLLERS to promote the idea of literary structuralism.

TERMINALE, CLASSE

The final year before the BACCALAURÉAT, and therefore normally consisting of students aged 17–18. The final year for other qualifications is also called the *Classe terminale*. See also: LYCÉE

TERRES AUSTRALES ET ANTARCTIQUES FRANÇAISES (TAAF)

A TERRITOIRE D'OUTRE-MER south of the Antarctic Circle, comprising the *Terre Adélie* and four island group territories, the Îles Amsterdam, Crozet, Kerguelen and Saint-Paul. The last of these is uninhabited, and the residents of the other areas are scientific and support staff in research stations.

TERRITOIRE DE BELFORT

A DÉPARTEMENT in the FRANCHE-COMTÉ region, with a population of 134,097, more than 50 per cent of whom (74,443) live in the urban area of Belfort, the CHEF-LIEU and a railway engineering centre, with new industries in computers and gas turbines. Delle (11,166) has engineering industries.

The *Département* was given its status in recognition of its historic defence against the Prussians in 1871. It has the meteorological distinction of having France's wettest spot at Lepuix on the southern slopes of the *Ballon d'Alsace*, where the rainfall is 24 centimetres a year.

In both the 1981 and 1988 ÉLECTIONS PRÉSIDENTIELLES, the *Département's* electors supported François MITTERRAND, and their three parliamentary representatives come from the PARTI

SOCIALISTE. The Centre Right narrowly overtook the socialists in the 1992 ÉLECTIONS RÉGIONALES.

Code départemental: 90   See also: CHEVÈNEMENT, JEAN-PIERRE

TERRITOIRE D'OUTRE-MER (TOM)
An overseas territory, constitutionally part of the Republic. The citizens have French nationality. The *Assemblée territoriale* and *Conseil du gouvernement* are elected local bodies. In comparison with a DÉPARTEMENT D'OUTRE-MER, a TOM has greater autonomy but its citizens do not directly elect representatives for the ASSEMBLÉE NATIONALE or SÉNAT. See also: MAYOTTE; NOUVELLE-CALÉDONIE; POLYNÉSIE FRANÇAISE; TERRES AUSTRALES ET ANTARCTIQUES FRANÇAISES; WALLIS-ET-FUTUNA

TESSIER, CARMEN (1911–1980)
A journalist and gossip-writer in FRANCE-SOIR and a number of other newspapers, who was both fashionable and popular. Her column *Les Propos de la commère* had the reputation of being read by *concierges* and ministers.

TF1 See: *TÉLÉVISION FRANÇAISE 1*

TGB See: *TRÈS GRANDE BIBLIOTHÈQUE*

TGV See: *TRAIN À GRANDE VITESSE*

THÉÂTRE DE L'EST PARISIEN
Formerly in public ownership, now owned by a company controlled by its founder, Guy Rétoré, and subsidised by the *Ministère de la* CULTURE.

THÉÂTRE DE BOULEVARD
The generic term for the commercial theatres of Paris which provide a diet principally of light entertainment.

THÉÂTRE FRANÇAIS
The eighteenth-century building in Paris which houses the *Salle Richelieu* used by the COMÉDIE-FRANÇAISE.

THÉÂTRE MARIGNY
A large theatre in Paris which has had a varied life since its

opening in 1850, having been an opera house and music hall before its present role as a house for serious theatre.

THÉÂTRE MUSICAL DE PARIS
Formerly known as the *Théâtre du Châtelet*, it was the home of a circus until its renovation as a venue for subsidised operas and musical performances in 1980.

THÉÂTRE NATIONAL DE CHAILLOT (TNC)
Formerly the home of the THÉÂTRE NATIONAL POPULAIRE, this theatre in Paris became a separate subsidised organisation in 1972, with the special function of promoting contemporary plays. See also: CHAILLOT; VITEZ, ANTOINE

THÉÂTRE NATIONAL DE L'ODÉON
A Paris theatre company based in an eighteenth-century building with two houses, occupied by students in the MAI 1968 events, and seen then as a symbol of artistic rebellion against the status quo. Its principal function is to perform contemporary works, but it also hosts performances by the COMÉDIE-FRANÇAISE. See also: BARRAULT, JEAN-LOUIS

THÉÂTRE NATIONAL DE L'OPÉRA See: *OPÉRA DE PARIS*

THÉÂTRE NATIONAL DE STRASBOURG
A subsidised drama company based in Strasbourg who also tour in France and abroad. The *Théâtre national de Strasbourg* is based on the former *Centre dramatique de l'Est*, founded in 1946. See also: CENTRE DRAMATIQUE NATIONAL

THÉÂTRE NATIONAL POPULAIRE (TNP)
This private theatre company was founded by Jean VILAR in 1930 in Paris, using the *Palais de* CHAILLOT, and developed a world-wide reputation for its productions of classic and modern works. In 1972, it transferred to Villeurbanne in the Lyon BANLIEUE (RHÔNE) where it continues to receive public subsidies.

THOMAS, PASCAL (1945–)
A film director who has achieved commercial success with films such as *Les Zozos* (1972) and *Le Chaud Lapin*.

THOMSON
An electronics and electrical equipment group of companies, nationalised in 1982.

TIERCÉ See: *PARI MUTUEL URBAIN*

TIERCE OPPOSITION
After a case heard in the TRIBUNAL D'INSTANCE or the TRIBUNAL DE GRANDE INSTANCE, a third party affected by the court's decision who might not have been present can appeal against the decision.

TIMBRE AMENDE
The purchase of a *Timbre amende* in a DÉBIT DE TABAC for the appropriate amount satisfies the requirement of an AMENDE FORFAITAIRE.

TIMBRE FISCAL
An excise stamp can be bought in a DÉBIT DE TABAC for passports or for a CARTE NATIONALE D'IDENTITÉ.

TIMBRE-TAXE
A postage due stamp or mark which indicates the amount of excess to be paid by the recipient.

TINTIN
The cartoon hero invented by the Belgian artist Hergé, the pseudonym of Georges Rémi (1907–1983). The pseudonym relates to his initials in reverse order. The first Tintin story appeared in 1929. The books have been published in more than 40 languages and by 1988 accounted for sales of 130 million copies (85 million of which were in French).

TIR AU BEURSAULT
A French variant of archery, practised particularly in PICARDIE, in which two targets facing each other are used, arrows being shot at each one in turn.

TITRE-RESTAURANT
A voucher which can be exchanged for part of the price of a restaurant meal on working days at participating restaurants.

Employees can receive a *Titre-restaurant* as part of their benefits. Its redemption value in 1990 was 32 francs.

TITULAIRE See: *AGENT TITULAIRE*

TIXIER-VIGNANCOUR, JEAN-LOUIS (1907–1989)
A prominent AVOCAT and Right-wing politician who was a candidate in the ÉLECTION PRÉSIDENTIELLE in 1965, gaining 5.19 per cent of the votes in the PREMIER TOUR.

TOM See: *TERRITOIRE D'OUTRE-MER*

TOTAL – COMPAGNIE FRANÇAISE DES PÉTROLES (CFP)
An oil and petroleum group founded in 1924 to exploit French interests in the Persian oil fields, with a minority holding by the State. It now operates in 75 countries with over 500 subsidiary companies, controls 25 per cent of the oil refining industry in France and 20 per cent of petrol sales.

TOUBON, JACQUES (1941–   )
A politician who had a career within public service following his training at the ÉCOLE NATIONALE D'ADMINISTRATION and then became a leading party worker for the RASSEMBLEMENT POUR LA RÉPUBLIQUE, taking the post of *Secrétaire général* between 1984 and 1988. He has been MAIRE-ADJOINT of Paris since 1983, and a Paris DÉPUTÉ since 1981.

TOULON ET DU VAR, UNIVERSITÉ DE
A small university, by French standards, with 4,000 students following courses in economics, law, science and technology. The campus is at la Garde (VAR).

TOULOUSE, UNIVERSITÉ DE
As well as the *Université Paul-SABATIER*, there are *Toulouse-I*, with 16,000 students mainly in social sciences, with other faculties of information technology, languages, law and mathematics, and *Toulouse-II* (*Toulouse le Mirail*) with 20,000 students almost all of whom follow arts courses.

TOUR D'ARGENT
A renowned Paris restaurant which specialises in *canard au sang*.

TOUR DE FRANCE
The annual cycle race, perhaps the most prestigious in the world, which was founded in 1903. A different series of stages is designed each year, but the finish is always in Paris around 14 July along the *avenue des* CHAMPS-ÉLYSÉES.

TOUR EIFFEL
The *Tour Eiffel* was built for the 1889 *Exposition de Paris*, the competition for the design being won by Gustave Eiffel (1832–1923) a bridge-builder and engineer. It rapidly became known as the symbol of modern Paris, and was protected from demolition in 1913 because of its important role as a radio transmitter. With television aerials, its height is now 320 metres. It is owned by the Paris city authorities, and as one of the CONCESSIONS DE PARIS, is currently operated by the *Société nouvelle d'exploitation de la Tour Eiffel*, the majority of whose capital is owned by the city.

TOUR MAINE-MONTPARNASSE
A high-rise (210 metres) office and commercial development built as part of the modernisation of the Montparnasse quarter of Paris in 1973.

TOURAINE AIR TRANSPORT (TAT) See: *TRANSPORT AÉRIEN TRANSRÉGIONAL*

TOURNIER, MICHEL (1924–)
A novelist whose reputation lies in his ability to recreate the magic of myth and legend. Among his best-selling books are *Vendredi ou les limbes du Pacifique* (1967), based on the Robinson Crusoe story, and *Gaspar, Melchior et Balthazar* (1980). He won the *Prix* GONCOURT in 1970 with *Le Roi des Aulnes*.

TOUSSAINT
All Saints' Day, 1 November, is a FÊTE LÉGALE, when by tradition, French people flock to cemeteries to lay chrysanthemums on their family graves. Normally, schools have a week's break at this time.

TOUVIER, PAUL (1916–)
A leader of the *Milice française* in Lyon during the VICHY régime

who was protected after the war by right-wing Catholic
organisations. He was seized by police in 1989 from inside a
Nice monastery, released on bail in 1991 and the resulting
decision of a NON-LIEU in response to accusations of crimes
against humanity led to much controversy in 1992.

TRAIN À GRANDE VITESSE (TGV)

The new generation electric railway train for which special track
has been built on some routes, and which reaches speeds of
up to 270 kilometres per hour. The first TGV service, between
Paris and Lyon, started in 1981, and by 1991, 48 cities were
connected by TGV services. A TGV service is planned in Texas.

TRANSPORT AÉRIEN TRANSRÉGIONAL (TAT)

A private enterprise airline based in Tours (INDRE-ET-LOIRE) on
the former *Touraine Air Transport*. By absorbing a number of
other small provincial airlines, TAT has become a major
regional force in air traffic, and operates on behalf of AIR
FRANCE in 30 countries, and its aircraft now carry the title 'TAT
European Airlines'.

TRAVAIL À DOMICILE

Workers at home are entitled to receive at least the SALAIRE
MINIMUM INTERPROFESSIONNEL DE CROISSANCE, and must register
for SÉCURITÉ SOCIALE in the normal way. The 1986 estimate was
that there were 42,000 working at home, with 33,600 of these
being women.

TRAVAIL À TEMPS PARTIEL

Part-time employees have the same rights as full-time workers.
If full-time posts become available in the business, existing part-
timers must be given priority in opportunities for applying. In
1988, about 12 per cent of the workforce was composed of
part-timers.

TRAVAIL DE NUIT

It is illegal for those below the age of 18 to work in industry
between the hours of 2200 and 0600. Until 1987 a similar
restriction applied to women.

TRAVAIL DOMINICAL

Paid Sunday work, which affects 20 per cent of the working

population on at least one occasion a year. The position of shop hours on a Sunday is unclear, the law stating they should be closed except in case of social need.

TRAVAIL TEMPORAIRE
Contracts for temporary posts must be drawn up to set a maximum of six or twelve months' service, and can be renewed only once. Those employed for a holiday job must, with certain exceptions, be at least 16 years old, cannot be required to do more than eight hours a day or 39 hours a week. There are specific regulations concerning seasonal work for young people.

TRAVAILLEURS ÉTRANGERS
The 1990 estimate of foreign workers in France was 1.7 million (including 500,000 women). The figure has remained around 1.5 million since 1975. See also: IMMIGRATION

TRENET, CHARLES (1913–   )
A popular singer, nicknamed '*le fou chantant*', whose record of *La Mer* was a worldwide success in the 1950s.

TRENTE GLORIEUSES, LES
The 30-year period after the Second World War in which economic recovery and development was maintained at an ever-expanding rate, interrupted only by the oil crisis of the 1970s.

TRÈS GRANDE BIBLIOTHÈQUE (TGB)
Officially known as the *Bibliothèque de France*, one of the controversial GRANDS PROJETS of François MITTERRAND, the TGB is a new complex built at BERCY for opening in 1996 to house the main collections of the BIBLIOTHÈQUE NATIONALE. The design by Dominique Perrault is remarkable for the four glass towers at each corner of the site.

TRÉSOR PUBLIC
The financial accounting arm of the State, with a network of local offices.

TRÉSORIER-PAYEUR GÉNÉRAL
The senior State finance officer in a RÉGION, who must be

consulted by the PRÉFET on strategic matters with financial implications.

TRIBUNAL ADMINISTRATIF

A tribunal of appeal against decisions of the ADMINISTRATION. If representations to the appropriate office have had no effect, an aggrieved citizen can bring cases to the tribunal which relate to any specific decision which affects him or her, including taxation cases. The tribunal is composed of ÉNARQUES who consider written evidence and notify the interested parties of their ruling by post. It is possible to appeal against their ruling to the CONSEIL D'ÉTAT. See also: MÉDIATEUR

TRIBUNAL CORRECTIONNEL

The criminal court which deals with DÉLITS. Cases are brought by the JUGE D'INSTRUCTION, the PROCUREUR or by the victim of the offence if evidence is such not to require investigation. Normally three JUGES hear the case, but if the offence is relatively minor, e.g. issuing unauthorised cheques, a single judge can sit.

The trial is in public, with the state being represented by the *Procureur*. Sentences can range up to 20 years in prison.

TRIBUNAL DE COMMERCE

The part-time judges are elected from among business personnel by their peers, who are either members of a CHAMBRE DE COMMERCE ET DE L'INDUSTRIE or senior managers and proprietors of enterprises. The *Tribunal de commerce* hears cases of disputes between businesses, commercial malpractice, breach of contract, etc. It can fine a guilty party up to 13,000 francs, and if the fine is higher, it is subject to appeal in the COUR D'APPEL.

TRIBUNAL DE GRANDE INSTANCE

The civil court which deals with cases more complicated than can be settled in the TRIBUNAL D'INSTANCE. Three JUGES sit in public session, and the *Président du tribunal* can act alone in case of emergency. Family cases are held in private. An AVOCAT is necessary for each party in a case heard in this court. See also: TIERCE OPPOSITION

TRIBUNAL D'INSTANCE
A civil court for dealing with relatively simple cases, concerning possession of goods and property, PENSIONS ALIMENTAIRES, care over children and disabled adults, small claims disputes.

One JUGE presides over this court, and proceedings are kept as informal as possible. More complicated cases are heard by the TRIBUNAL DE GRANDE INSTANCE. See also: TIERCE OPPOSITION; TRIBUNAL DES BAUX RURAUX

TRIBUNAL DE POLICE
The criminal court which deals with INFRACTIONS. The State is represented by the PROCUREUR DE LA RÉPUBLIQUE, or in very minor cases a COMMISSAIRE DE POLICE. An AVOCAT can represent a defendant but it is not obligatory. A procedure which does not require the presence of the defendant is the ORDONNANCE PÉNALE. It is possible to appeal against a sentence of six days or more in prison, or a fine above 160 francs.

TRIBUNAL DE PRUD'HOMMES See: *CONSEIL DE PRUD'HOMMES*

TRIBUNAL DES BAUX RURAUX
A civil court including landowners and farmers, presided over by a JUGE from the TRIBUNAL D'INSTANCE to rule on disputes about agricultural land tenancies.

TRIBUNAL DES CONFLITS
An administrative court which rules on difficulties arising from contradictory statutes which place the ADMINISTRATION and the law in conflict. It has 10 members elected from the CONSEIL D'ÉTAT and the COUR DE CASSATION, and is chaired by the GARDE DES SCEAUX.

TRIBUNAL PARITAIRE See: *TRIBUNAL DES BAUX RURAUX*

TRIBUNAL POUR ENFANTS
A JUGE *des enfants* is chosen for three years from among the judges in a TRIBUNAL DE GRANDE INSTANCE to deal with cases brought against minors. The *Juge* is assisted by voluntary assessors when considering DÉLITS. More serious offences, if the

defendant is 16 or 17, are heard in the COUR D'ASSISES *des Mineurs*.

The proceedings are in private, and no press account may appear. An AVOCAT must be present for the defence.

TRICOLORE
The Revolutionary emblem created for the *Garde nationale de Paris* in 1789 and adopted in the form of a national flag in 1790. The present version with three equal vertical stripes of blue, white and red was fixed by the 1946 Constitution of the QUATRIÈME RÉPUBLIQUE.

TRIGANO, GILBERT (1920–)
A former anarchist who became a Trotskyist and eventually a Socialist who was one of the co-founders of the CLUB MED, and is now its *Président*. As a popular and dynamic apostle of leisure, he was called upon to be a special adviser to François MITTERRAND in the early 1980s.

TRIMESTRE
A financial quarter period, or a school or university term.

TROISIÈME ÂGE, UNIVERSITÉS DU
A network of higher education institutions which provide low-cost courses for retired people, without the need for entry qualifications. The first was opened in 1973 in Toulouse.

TROISGROS
An internationally-renowned restaurant in Roanne (LOIRE), named after its founding owner Jean Troisgros (1926–1983).

TROIS JOURS
Despite its name, a period of one or two days in which selection procedures for SERVICE NATIONAL are carried out from among those called up. Conscripts attend one of 10 centres for medical and aptitude tests. Those who do not attend are considered fit for service.

TROIS QUARTIERS
A well-known Paris department store opened in 1930 which closed in 1990.

TROIS SUISSES, LES
The second largest mail-order catalogue firm in France, with 12 million catalogues distributed annually.

TRONC COMMUN
As part of the policy to give all secondary school pupils a partly common curriculum, a common core has been steadily increasing in COLLÈGES and LYCÉES. It now accounts for most of the *collège* curriculum and a substantial part of that in the *Classe de* SECONDE.

TROYAT, HENRI (1911–   )
A Russian-born successful novelist, biographer and playwright who has often entered the best-seller lists while sometimes suffering critical attacks. An early novel, *L'Araignée* (1938), won the *Prix* GONCOURT. Other works include *Tant que la terre durera* and *Viou*. Troyat has been a member of the ACADÉMIE FRANÇAISE since 1959.

TRUFFAUT, FRANÇOIS (1932–1984)
A film director in the New Wave who made a mark because of the semi-autobiographical nature of his Antoine Doinel cycle, including *Les 400 coups* (1959), in which he used one actor, Jean-Pierre Léaud, for the principal role in the whole series. He is also well known for his love of the cinema as an activity, e.g. *La Nuit américaine* (1973).

TURBOTRAIN
A gas turbine passenger train used on medium length main lines, mainly cross-country, from 1970. An early plan for the TRAIN À GRANDE VITESSE was based on the same principle, but was abandoned in favour of electricity.

TUTELLE
Legal guardianship, in which a JUGE from the TRIBUNAL DE GRANDE INSTANCE is appointed *Juge des tutelles*, and has a monitoring responsibility over guardianships in the area. The *Conseil de famille* (four to six members of the child's family or family friends) can be consulted in the designation of a *Tuteur* from outside their number. The *Tuteur's* actions are monitored by a *Subrogé tuteur*, who is a member of the *Conseil de famille*.

TVA See: *TAXE SUR LA VALEUR AJOUTÉE*

UAP See: *UNION DES ASSURANCES DE PARIS*

UAT See: *UNION AÉROMARITIME DE TRANSPORT*

UDERZO, ALBERT (1927–)
A popular cartoonist responsible for much of the work in PILOTE, as well as ASTÉRIX (jointly with GOSCINNY) and *Lucky Luke*, a cowboy series.

UDF See: *UNION POUR LA DÉMOCRATIE FRANÇAISE*

UER See: *UNITÉ D'ENSEIGNEMENT ET DE RECHERCHE*

UFR See: *UNITÉ DE FORMATION ET DE RECHERCHE*

UGINE
A subsidiary firm of USINOR-SACILOR, based on the steelworks at Ugine (SAVOIE).

UNAPEI See: *UNION NATIONALE D'ASSOCIATIONS DE PARENTS D'ENFANTS INADAPTÉS*

UNAPEL See: *UNION NATIONALE DES ASSOCIATIONS DES PARENTS D'ÉLÈVES DE L'ENSEIGNEMENT LIBRE*

UNEF See: *UNION NATIONALE DES ÉTUDIANTS DE FRANCE*

UNICO See: *SYSTÈME U*

UNION, L'
The daily newspaper published in Reims (MARNE) with a 1989 circulation of 110,000 in the CHAMPAGNE-ARDENNE region. This is a drop from the 1970 peak of 152,000.

UNION AÉROMARITIME DE TRANSPORT (UAT)
One of the founding companies which merged in 1963 to form UTA (UNION DES TRANSPORTS AÉRIENS).

UNION DE LA GAUCHE
The alliance of opposition parties formed in 1972 to establish the PROGRAMME COMMUN for implementation when the Left gained power. It was dissolved in 1984.

UNION DES ASSURANCES DE PARIS (UAP)
A group of nationalised insurance firms reorganised in 1968 in one commercial entity.

UNION DES TRANSPORTS AÉRIENS (UTA)
A passenger and cargo airline formed in 1963 by the merger of UNION AÉROMARITIME DE TRANSPORT and *Transports aériens internationaux* (TAI) and since 1990 with AIR FRANCE as majority shareholder. UTA operates between France and the Middle and Far East, Africa, the Pacific and the West coast of the USA.

UNION DU RASSEMBLEMENT ET DU CENTRE See: *UNION POUR LA DÉMOCRATIE FRANÇAISE*

UNION FÉDÉRALE DES CONSOMMATEURS See: *QUE CHOISIR?*

UNION FRANÇAISE
The name given to French territories in the former Empire during the QUATRIÈME RÉPUBLIQUE. See also: COMMUNAUTÉ FRANÇAISE

UNION NATIONALE DES ASSOCIATIONS DE PARENTS D'ENFANTS INADAPTÉS (UNAPEI)
A pressure group with over 60,000 members representing the interests of disabled children and their families.

UNION NATIONALE DES ASSOCIATIONS DES PARENTS D'ÉLÈVES DE L'ENSEIGNEMENT LIBRE (UNAPEL)
A vocal pressure group standing for the interests of pupils in private schools and their families. It claims over 800,000 family members. See also: FÉDÉRATION DES CONSEILS DE PARENTS D'ÉLÈVES DES ÉCOLES PUBLIQUES

UNION NATIONALE DES ÉTUDIANTS DE FRANCE (UNEF)
The largest students' union grouping, split in 1971 between
various factions reflecting different left-wing stances. There
are five recognised groupings within the UNEF *Indépendante
et démocratique*, and a separate organisation for UNEF
Solidarité étudiante.

UNION POUR LA DÉMOCRATIE FRANÇAISE (UDF)
A political party grouping of the Centre Right, established in
1978 and incorporating the CENTRE DES DÉMOCRATES SOCIAUX,
PARTI RADICAL SOCIALISTE, PARTI RÉPUBLICAIN, and the *Parti
social-démocrate*. Jean LECANUET was its founding leader and it
supported Valéry GISCARD D'ESTAING in the 1981 ÉLECTION
PRÉSIDENTIELLE, Simone VEIL in the 1979 and 1984 and Giscard
in the 1989 European elections. Its 1988 Presidential candidate
was Raymond BARRE.
    In the ÉLECTIONS LÉGISLATIVES of 1988, it formed the electoral
pact with the RASSEMBLEMENT POUR LA RÉPUBLIQUE of the *Union
du rassemblement et du centre*, and in 1992 for the ÉLECTIONS
RÉGIONALES, the *Union pour la France*.

UNION POUR LA FRANCE (UPF) See: *UNION POUR LA
DÉMOCRATIE FRANÇAISE*

UNITÉ DE FORMATION ET DE RECHERCHE (UFR)
These may retain the name of *Faculté* or *Département* in some
cases, but the UFR is the officially recognised term for the basic
unit of university organisation. They can be organised on the
basis of a phase of study (e.g. UFR *de premier cycle*) or by
discipline (e.g. UFR *de lettres*). Each UFR is managed by an
elected *Conseil* of up to 40 members, who must include
representatives from outside its membership, and the *Conseil*
elects its director.

UNITÉ D'ENSEIGNEMENT ET DE RECHERCHE (UER)
See: *LOI FAURE*

UNITÉ URBAINE
A group of residential properties with a population of at least
20,000, in one or more COMMUNES.

UNIVERSITÉ
A term sometimes used in the singular to denote the whole of the university sector of higher education. This use derives from the monolithic view of the highest layer of the State system, and reflects a similar use of *l'école, le collège* and *le lycée,* emphasising the perceived similarity between establishments.

UNIVERSITÉ CATHOLIQUE DE L'OUEST
About 8,000 students follow courses in arts, education, linguistics, psychology, and theology for state diplomas as well as on other courses at this UNIVERSITÉ LIBRE at Angers (MAINE-ET-LOIRE).

UNIVERSITÉ CATHOLIQUE DE LYON
There are 7,000 students in this UNIVERSITÉ LIBRE which provides courses in arts, law, philosophy, science and theology.

UNIVERSITÉ DU TROISIÈME ÂGE See: *TROISIÈME ÂGE*

UNIVERSITÉ LIBRE
A privately funded university institution. It is possible for courses to be validated by State qualifications, and seven institutions have some of their courses certificated in this way. The State remains the only body which can award degrees. The principal *Universités libres* are Catholic organisations. See also: FÉDÉRATION UNIVERSITAIRE ET POLYTECHNIQUE; INSTITUT CATHOLIQUE DE PARIS; UNIVERSITÉ CATHOLIQUE DE L'OUEST; UNIVERSITÉ CATHOLIQUE DE LYON

UPF See: *UNION POUR LA FRANCE*

URBA, AFFAIRE
A scandal of embarrassment to the government in the late 1980s, when it was found that the *Urba-Technic* property development firm had been used as an illicit source of funds for a large number of PARTI SOCIALISTE election expenses, and fraudulent invoices had been produced. The affair is sometimes referred to as the *Affaire des fausses factures*.

USINE DE LA RANCE
The largest tidal power station in the world, completed in 1966 at the mouth of the Rance river (ILLE-ET-VILAINE).

USINOR-SACILOR
The State-owned (since 1981) steel manufacturer, the third European producer of steel, and accounting for 80 per cent of French production. The group has been formed as a process of gradual amalgamations of firms in what became a loss-making industry. The final merger of *Usinor-Sacilor* took place in 1987.

USUFRUIT
The right of tenancy or lease of goods held by an existing tenant or beneficiary of a will, but without ownership being transferred.

UTILITÉ PUBLIQUE
An organisation such as an ASSOCIATION or a charity can be recognised as of *utilité publique* if it fulfils a function of benefit to the community. An organisation recognised of *utilité publique* benefits from taxation privileges, but also has restrictions on the use of its funds.

VADIM, ROGER (1928–   )
A film director who is renowned for having discovered Brigitte Bardot. His many films include *Et Dieu créa la Femme* (1956) in which Bardot achieved stardom, *Surprise-partie* (1983) and *Le Repos du guerrier.*

VAL-DE-MARNE
A mainly urban DÉPARTEMENT in the ÎLE-DE-FRANCE region, named after the basin of the river Marne, forming the south-eastern BANLIEUE of Paris, with a total population of 1.21 million in 1990. The CHEF-LIEU is Créteil (82,088), which has the largest purpose-built regional shopping centre in Europe, and other COMMUNES with large populations are: Alfortville (36,119), with an enormous gas works; Arcueil (20,334) – electronics and telecommunications; Cachan (24,666); Champigny-sur-Marne (74,486) – metalworks; Choisy-le-Roi (34,068), with a RENAULT factory and the site of the major Paris sewage works; Fontenay-sous-Bois (51,868); FRESNES (26,959); Ivry-sur-Seine (53,619), with the world's largest refuse incineration plant, and oil refineries; l'Haÿ-les-Roses (29,746); le Perreux-sur-Marne (28,477); Maisons-Alfort (53,375); Nogent-sur-Marne (25,248); ORLY (21,646); Saint-Maur-des-Fossés (77,206); Sucy-en-Brie (25,839); Thiais (27,515); Villejuif (48,405); Villeneuve-le-Roi (20,325); Villeneuve-Saint-Georges (26,952), which has the most modern railway marshalling yard in Europe; Villiers-sur-Marne (22,740); Vincennes (42,267); and Vitry-sur-Seine (82,400), with power stations, chemicals, pharmaceuticals and metal industries.

Apart from this industrial base which also extends to food-processing and distribution, the Val-de-Marne also produces a wide range of cut flowers and other horticultural stock, and

Boissy-Saint-Léger is the world centre for new varieties of orchid.

The *Département* was formed as part of the 1964 reorganisation of the RÉGION PARISIENNE. It has maintained a left-wing stance in politics, with many communes being dominated by the PARTI COMMUNISTE FRANÇAIS, and this was confirmed in the 1992 ÉLECTIONS CANTONALES. In both the 1981 and 1988 ÉLECTIONS PRÉSIDENTIELLES, François MITTERRAND had a comfortable majority.

Code départemental: 94   See also: RUNGIS

VAL-D'OISE

A DÉPARTEMENT in the ÎLE-DE-FRANCE, comprising the outer north-west BANLIEUE of Paris and an agricultural belt, taking its name from the Oise river which flows through it, just before its confluence with the Seine. The population of the *Département* was 1.04 million in 1990. Pontoise (27,150) is the CHEF-LIEU, and other large urban areas are Argenteuil (93,096) – chemicals, engineering and market-gardening; Beaumont-sur-Oise (28,482); Bezons (25,680); Cergy (48,226); Cergy-Pontoise (139,121), a VILLE NOUVELLE; Eaubonne (22,153); Ermont (27,947); Fosses (18,409); Franconville (33,802); Garges-lès-Gonesse (42,144); Gonesse (23,152); Goussainville (28,324; Herblay (22,135); Montmorency (20,920); Sannois (25,229); SARCELLES (56,833); Taverny (25,151); and Villiers-le-Bel (26,110). Most of these places are dormitory towns for Paris workers, and there are a number of smaller settlements in the rural part of the *Département*, such as Magny-en-Vexin.

The agricultural activity is mainly in the production of cereals, beet and potatoes, market gardening and mushrooms. There are considerable tourist attractions, such as forests, lakes and archaeological sites.

The *Département* was formed as part of the Paris region reorganisation in 1964. In both the 1981 and 1988 ÉLECTIONS PRÉSIDENTIELLES, the voters of the Val-d'Oise gave a comfortable majority to François MITTERRAND, and Left-wing groups dominate the parliamentary representation. The CONSEIL GÉNÉRAL is controlled by Centre Right groups, and this was confirmed in the 1992 ÉLECTIONS CANTONALES.

Code départemental: 95

VALENCIENNES ET DU HAINAUT-CAMBRÉSIS, UNIVERSITÉ DE

There are almost 8,000 students at this university in Valenciennes (NORD) in the Lille ACADÉMIE, following courses in arts, humanities and sciences.

VANEL, CHARLES (1892–1989)

An actor who appeared in films from 1912 (*Jim Crow*) to 1987 (*Les Saisons du plaisir*)! A classic performance was with Yves MONTAND in *Le Salaire de la peur*.

VAR

A DÉPARTEMENT of the PROVENCE-ALPES-CÔTE-D'AZUR region, with a population in 1990 of 814,731 and a Mediterranean coastline. The name derives from the river which now, because of boundary changes in 1860, does not actually flow through the *Département*. The CHEF-LIEU is Toulon (urban area 437,493), a naval and commercial port, with metal industries, munitions manufacturing, publishing, pharmaceuticals, and a major trade in horticultural produce. Other centres of population are Brignoles (11,239), with a bauxite works; Draguignan (34,186), an administrative centre; Fréjus-Saint-Raphaël (73,489); le Lavandou (10,295); Roquebrune-sur-Argens (10,389); and Sainte-Maxime (12,992), the last four being coastal resorts. A famous smaller resort is Saint-Tropez.

The principal agricultural production is of fruit and vegetables, with a major element being the *Côtes de Provence* wine. Goats are also kept. The forest resources of the Var are of major significance, and the area is prone to summer forest fires.

Apart from the coastal resorts, tourists have a wealth of Roman remains to attract them, as well as the dramatic inland scenery of the gorges, lakes and falls.

In the 1981 ÉLECTION PRÉSIDENTIELLE, Valéry GISCARD D'ESTAING received a small majority, and in 1988, Jacques CHIRAC a comfortable one. This support for the Right is reflected in the Var's representation in parliament, and in the CONSEIL GÉNÉRAL elected in 1992.

Code départemental: 83

VARDA, AGNÈS (1928–   )
A film director whose work was internationally noticed in 1962 with *Cléo de 5 à 7*, and she has used the same style of documentary drama in later films such as *Sans toit ni loi* (1985). *Jacquot de Nantes* (1992) is inspired by her love for Jacques DEMY.

VARENNE, RUE DE
The street of the residence of the PREMIER MINISTRE, the *Hôtel* MATIGNON.

VASARÉLY, VICTOR (1908–   )
An artist, born in Hungary, who works in painting, sculpture and tapestry, a member of the Kinetic Art movement. The museum of his work in the village of Gordes (VAUCLUSE) is a popular destination for visitors.

VAT See: *VOLONTAIRES DE L'AIDE TECHNIQUE*

VAUCLUSE
A DÉPARTEMENT of the PROVENCE-ALPES-CÔTE-D'AZUR region, with a population in 1990 of 467,075, named after the *Plateau du Vaucluse*, which itself incorporates the PLATEAU D'ALBION. The CHEF-LIEU is Avignon (AGGLOMÉRATION 145,147) – paper-making, filters, chemicals, science industries, metallurgy, food-processing, textiles and packaging, the site of the FESTIVAL D'AVIGNON, and a MARCHÉ D'INTÉRÊT NATIONAL. Other urban areas include Apt (14,381), with a candied fruit industry; Bollène (13,907), with a hydro-electric power station, furniture, brick-making and nuclear fuels; CARPENTRAS (40,673) – fireworks and spices, food-processing and a MIN; Cavaillon (31,193), with a MIN specialising in fruit; l'Isle-sur-la-Sorgue (15,564); Orange (26,964) – insulation materials, footwear; and Pertuis (15,791). Other centres of industry are the largest tomato cannery in France at Camaret-sur-Aigues and the cardboard factories at Valréas, this last-mentioned town being in a enclave, totally surrounded by the DRÔME.
   Wine is an important product of the Vaucluse, including *Châteauneuf-du-Pape* and *Côtes-du-Rhône*. The principal agricultural activity however is in fruit production, with goats, truffles, and lavender as features of the upland areas. Forestry

too makes a significant contribution to the local economy.

Tourism is an important source of income, both because of natural features and the historic cities of Avignon, Orange and Vaison-la-Romaine.

François MITTERRAND's comfortable majority in the 1981 ÉLECTION PRÉSIDENTIELLE was reduced to a marginal 50.34 per cent in 1988. Three Left-wing and one Right-wing DÉPUTÉS and two Right-wing SÉNATEURS represent the *Département* in parliament. The previously Left-wing CONSEIL GÉNÉRAL was replaced by a more finely balanced council in 1992.

Code départemental: 84

VAULX-EN-VELIN

A COMMUNE in the RHÔNE, in Greater Lyon, Vaulx-en-Velin achieved national prominence in 1990 when riots broke out among young unemployed groups. The disturbances were interpreted by media and the authorities as a protest over the difficulties experienced by underprivileged, mainly immigrant, communities.

VAUTRIN, JEAN (1933–)

A novelist whose *Un grand pas vers le bon Dieu* won the *Prix* GONCOURT in 1989.

VD See: *ENVOI EN VALEUR DÉCLARÉE*

VDQS See: *VIN DÉLIMITÉ DE QUALITÉ SUPÉRIEURE*

VEIL, SIMONE (1927–)

A survivor of Nazi deportation, and a senior legal administrator in the *Ministère de la justice* who entered politics through national office in her profession, having been appointed *Secrétaire général* of the CONSEIL SUPÉRIEUR DE LA MAGISTRATURE in 1970. She held ministerial office under Valéry GISCARD D'ESTAING, and turned her attention to European affairs from 1979, when she was elected to the European Parliament, and as its president from 1979 to 1982. Since 1984, she has led the Liberal and Democrat group in the European Parliament.

VÉLIZY 2

An enormous 1970s shopping development on a greenfield site in the COMMUNE of Vélizy-Villacoublay (YVELINES).

VÉLOMOTEUR See: *CYCLOMOTEUR*

VENDÉE

A DÉPARTEMENT on the Atlantic coast in the PAYS DE LA LOIRE region, taking the name of the historic territory of which it is part. The CHEF-LIEU is la-Roche-sur-Yon, which is home to 45,219 of the *Département's* 509,293 inhabitants (in 1990) and has household equipment, clothing, chemicals, tyre and food industries. Other urban areas are Challans (14,203), with poultry farming and boat-building; Fontenay-le-Comte (16,246) – ball-bearings manufacture, plywood fabrication, tobacco and mechanical engineering; les Herbiers (13,413) – textiles, clothing, footwear, boats and small cars; les Sables-d'Olonne (35,352) – fishing, commercial and yachting port, shipbuilding and food-processing; and Saint-Gilles-Croix-de-Vie (16,614) – shipbuilding. Food-processing and associated activities also occur in smaller centres of population.

Mixed farming predominates in the rural areas, with cattle, pigs, fruit-growing as well as oysterbeds and fishing on the coast.

Tourism is important, too, with a steady trade not only at the coast, but also on the major islands, the Île d'Yeu and, connected by a road causeway and a bridge, the Île de Noirmoutier. The *Département* is rich in religious buildings and in museums.

The Vendée was the *Département* with the second highest proportion of votes for Valéry GISCARD D'ESTAING in the 1981 ÉLECTION PRÉSIDENTIELLE (60.38 per cent) and in 1988, Jacques CHIRAC had a comfortable lead (53.92 per cent). This strength of the Centre Right is reflected in parliamentary representatives, and composition of the CONSEIL GÉNÉRAL, before and after 1992.

Code départemental: 85

VENDREDI, SAMEDI, DIMANCHE (VSD)

A weekly popular news and leisure magazine, founded by Maurice SIEGEL, with a mix of analysis and general features, with a circulation of 280,000.

VENTE À CRÉDIT
The customer has the right of withdrawal from a credit agreement within seven days of signing. The total cost of the credit has to be clearly stated in the agreement. Interest-free credit is available from certain retailers, but they are not allowed to advertise this outside their premises, and a discount for a full payment must be offered.

VENTE AU DÉBALLAGE See: *VENTE EN SOLDES*

VENTE AUX ENCHÈRES
A sale by auction requires the services of a NOTAIRE, and the auction is held traditionally for the duration of a lighted candle. See also: SURENCHÈRE

VENTE AVEC PRIMES
Inducement to purchase, in the form of free gifts or bonuses, is forbidden by law unless their value is less than 7 per cent of the product sold (for goods up to 500 francs in price) or 30 francs plus 1 per cent of the product sold if it is more expensive than 500 francs. Special offers of reduced rates for bulk, etc., are not prohibited.

VENTE EN SOLDES
The advertising of reduced price sales must make it clear if all goods are included, or just a selection. The pre-sale price must be shown on the goods. The customer's rights to have faulty goods replaced are not invalidated by notices claiming not to allow exchanges or refunds.

VENTE EN VIAGER
The sale of a residence in return for a life annuity and, if the vendor occupies the property, the right to remain in it until death. See also: RENTE VIAGÈRE

VENTE FORCÉE
Inertia selling whereby a customer is required to pay for or return unsolicited goods is illegal in France.

VENTE JUDICIAIRE
A sale of property coming from a bankrupt or liquidated

concern. The AVOCAT acting for the liquidators requests a *Vente judiciaire* which then operates as a VENTE AUX ENCHÈRES.

VENTE PAR ADJUDICATION DEVANT NOTAIRE
A VENTE AUX ENCHÈRES for a group of properties coming onto the market through the offices of a NOTAIRE.

VENTE PAR CORRESPONDANCE (VPC)
It is estimated that 50 per cent of French households use mail-order for buying goods. The main suppliers are: *La* BLANCHE PORTE; CAMIF; QUELLE; *La* REDOUTE; Yves ROCHER; and *Les* TROIS SUISSES.

VENTURA, LINO (1919–1987)
A popular film actor of Italian origin, who first performed in *Touchez pas au grisbi*, based on SIMONIN's novel, and established himself in the roles of romantic tough guy. A classic television performance can be seen in *Un taxi pour Tobrouk*.

VERCORS (1902–1991)
The pseudonym of Jean Bruller, an engraver and member of the RÉSISTANCE, who became a writer best known for his short work, *Le Silence de la mer* (1942), which deals with the German occupation in the Second World War.

VERDUN See: *MEUSE; VOIE SACRÉE*

VERSAILLES, UNIVERSITÉ DE
A small university by French standards with 3,000 students, established in 1991 at SAINT-QUENTIN-EN-YVELINES initially with courses only to DEUG level.

VERTS, LES
The Green Party formed in 1984. Before then, ecologist groups had participated in elections and in 1981 Brice LALONDE obtained more than one million votes in the ÉLECTION PRÉSIDENTIELLE. The 1988 candidate was Antoine WAECHTER, who obtained a similar result. As part of the OUVERTURE, Lalonde became MINISTRE DÉLÉGUÉ *à l'environnement*.

In 1989, there was considerable success for the party in municipal and European elections, but 1990 saw a split between

Lalonde and Waechter, the former establishing GÉNÉRATION ÉCOLOGIE. The effect was to reduce substantially the vote for *les Verts* in the 1992 ÉLECTIONS CANTONALES and RÉGIONALES. Nevertheless, 105 seats were gained in CONSEILS RÉGIONAUX.

VESDUN
A village in the CHER, one of those with a claim to be the geographical centre of France if one does not include CORSE in the calculation. See also: BRUÈRES-ALLICHAMPS; CHAZEMAIS; SAINT-AMAND-MONTROND

VEUVE-CLICQUOT, PRIX
An annual award for the French businesswoman of the year, funded by the champagne producer.

VIAGER See: *RENTE VIAGÈRE; VENTE EN VIAGER*

VIANSSON-PONTÉ, PIERRE (1920–1979)
A journalist on newspapers of the RÉSISTANCE and later on *Le MONDE*, for which he headed the political staff, and also a chronicler of Gaullism.

VICHY
The Right-wing government at Vichy (ALLIER) between 1940 and 1944 was headed by Philippe PÉTAIN, and collaborated with the Third Reich in Germany especially in its anti-Jewish policies, ostensibly in an attempt to protect the part of France occupied by German forces. Mention of the Republic was removed from official references. The motto *Liberté, égalité, fraternité* was replaced by *Travail, famille, patrie*, and the name adopted by the régime was *État français*. See also: RÉSISTANCE

VIDÉOPOSTE
A TÉLÉTEL service for the holder of a COMPTE-CHÈQUES POSTAL, allowing access to the account details and to savings accounts, and permitting certain transactions to be carried out from the MINITEL terminal.

VIE, LA
A weekly Catholic magazine with a circulation of 265,000, a reduction on its peak in the late 1950s of 477,000.

VIENNE

A DÉPARTEMENT of the POITOU-CHARENTES region, with a 1990 population of 380,181, named after the tributary of the Loire which passes through it. The CHEF-LIEU is Poitiers (105,279), with mechanical engineering, electronics, aviation construction, pneumatic gauges, chemicals, and an old university centre. The other urban area is Châtellerault (34,678), with engineering and electronics, paper-making, footwear and food-processing. Smaller settlements have some minor industrial activity.

The agricultural activity of the Vienne is mixed. Wheat, wine, sheep, fruit and market-gardening are its main features.

The principal tourist attractions are the large number of ancient churches, and FUTUROSCOPE, just north of Poitiers.

The *Département* is attractive to those who desire a long life. Women have the longest life expectancy for the whole of France (80.2 years), and men the second-longest (72.8 years), after the neighbouring DEUX-SÈVRES.

The parliamentary representation for the Vienne shows a balance of Left and Right, with François MITTERRAND raising the level of his 1981 majority here in the 1988 ÉLECTION PRÉSIDENTIELLE. The Centre Right, however, consolidated their control of the CONSEIL RÉGIONAL in the 1992 ÉLECTIONS CANTONALES, in which Édith CRESSON, although for a few more days PREMIER MINISTRE, had to enter the second round of voting to retain her seat.

Code départemental: 86

VIGNETTE

A tax on vehicles payable on initial registration and then annually in November until the vehicle is 25 years old. The amount payable varies according to the DÉPARTEMENT, the age of the vehicle and the size of its engine, the funds collected going to the *département*. Vehicles over five years old are charged at half the full rate. A vehicle has to be registered in the *département* of the owner's DOMICILE. A disc proving payment is displayed in the windscreen. The *vignette* does not apply to motorcycles. Heavy goods vehicles are charged special rates through the DOUANE and not the *département*. See also: IMMATRICULATION, PLAQUE D'

VILAR, JEAN (1912–1971)
An influential theatre director, the founder of the FESTIVAL D'AVIGNON and the director of the THÉÂTRE NATIONAL POPULAIRE from 1951 to 1963. Vilar was instrumental in opening the repertoire of French theatre to a wider range of foreign plays.

VILLAGES VACANCES FAMILLES (VVF)
An ASSOCIATION providing relatively low cost holiday centres for families, often based on self-catering or communal meals. There are a number of other organisations, including *associations* or trade unions which operate such ventures largely on a non-commercial basis.

VILLENEUVE D'ASCQ
A VILLE NOUVELLE set up in 1970 in the Lille AGGLOMÉRATION (NORD) with a 1990 population of 65,320.

VILLES NOUVELLES
New towns set up from the 1960s in an attempt to combat unplanned urban sprawl and to boost the infrastructure to support new forms of employment. Among these were small communities allied to industrial developments at Bagnoles-sur-Cèze-lès-Marcoule (GARD), and Mourenx (PYRÉNÉES-ATLANTIQUES). The planned expansion of an existing town such as le Mirail in the Toulouse AGGLOMÉRATION (GARONNE) was another development.

In the Paris area, five *Villes nouvelles* were established, now at varying stages of growth: Cergy-Pontoise (VAL-D'OISE), Évry (ESSONNE), Marne-la-Vallée (mainly in SEINE-ET-MARNE), Melun-Sénart (SEINE-ET-MARNE) and Saint-Quentin-en-Yvelines (YVELINES). See also: VILLENEUVE D'ASCQ

VILLIERS, GÉRARD (1929–   )
A popular writer of spy stories in a series entitled *La série SAS*.

VILLOT, JEAN (1905–1979)
A Roman Catholic prelate, archbishop of Lyon in the mid 1960s and later and adviser to Pope Paul VI before becoming Vatican Secretary of State.

VINCENOT, HENRI (1912–1985)
A writer of fiction based on his native BOURGOGNE, including a

best-seller *La Billebande* (1978) and *Les Étoiles de Compostelle* (1982).

VIN DÉLIMITÉ DE QUALITÉ SUPÉRIEURE (VDQS)

A wine which has passed strict controls of quality and is guaranteed to come from a particular area. All wines which have an APPELLATION D'ORIGINE CONTRÔLÉE are VDQS wines, but the reverse does not necessarily apply.

VINCENNES-SAINT-DENIS, UNIVERSITÉ DE

The *Université de Paris-XIII*, formerly known as *Paris-Vincennes*, situated at Saint-Denis (SEINE-SAINT-DENIS), with 22,000 students following courses in humanities with science and technology. It pioneered new teaching approaches, and is still the only university in France which accepts students without BACCALAURÉAT qualifications, provided they have three years of work experience or are mothers of young children.

VINGT-QUATRE HEURES DU MANS

The annual motor race which has been contested since 1923 on ordinary roads and a special track at le Mans (SARTHE).

VITEZ, ANTOINE (1930–1990)

A theatre director who ran the THÉÂTRE NATIONAL DE CHAILLOT, was successful in avant-garde and unorthodox productions, and put his personal stamp on his interpretations of the classical repertoire.

VOIE SACRÉE

The road from Bar-le-Duc to Verdun (MEUSE), which was kept open in the 1916 battle to maintain the French defence of Verdun.

VOIX DU NORD, LA

A daily newspaper, published in Lille (NORD), with a circulation in 1989 of 372,000 and a dominant position in the NORD-PAS-DE-CALAIS region.

VOLKOFF, VLADIMIR (1932–   )

A writer of rather complex spy novels, including *Le Retournement* (1979) and *Les Hommes du Tsar* (1988).

VOLONTAIRES DE L'AIDE TECHNIQUE (VAT) See:
SERVICE NATIONAL

VOLONTAIRES DU SERVICE NATIONAL (VSN)
By opting for a longer period of SERVICE NATIONAL than the
minimum, volunteers (up to a maximum of 25,000 a year) can
benefit from enhanced payment and privileges. The engagement
can be from 16 to 24 months.

VOSGES
A DÉPARTEMENT in the LORRAINE region, named after the
mountain range which is its principal geographical feature,
with a 1990 population of 386,324. This is a fall from the 1975
figure of 397,957, and the Vosges never recovered its 1911
peak of 433,914. The CHEF-LIEU is Épinal (urban area 50,895),
with textiles and clothing industries. Other centres of
population are Gérardmer (10,366), a mountain resort; la
Bresse (13,084), a winter sports centre; le Thillot (13,875) –
tanning industry; Remiremont (18,721) – textiles and
metallurgy; Saint-Dié (27,461) – textiles, metallurgy and
electrical engineering; and Thaon-les-Vosges (11,231), another
textiles centre. Smaller centres depend on the substantial forestry
industry, especially furniture, musical instruments. The Vosges,
however, has the afforested area most seriously damaged by air
pollution in the whole of France.

Tourism, sometimes connected with spas, is another
important part of the local economy. Contrexéville and Vittel
are noted mineral water sources.

Male residents have the sixth shortest life expectancy in the
country: 68.8 years.

The Vosges is one area which changed its presidential vote
between 1981 and 1988, Valéry GISCARD D'ESTAING receiving 50.16
per cent of the votes in 1981, but François MITTERRAND taking
a majority of 54.77 per cent in 1988. In the 1992 ÉLECTIONS
CANTONALES, the Right made gains and comfortably controls the
CONSEIL GÉNÉRAL.

Code départemental: 88

VOTE DE CONFIANCE
The government can ask the ASSEMBLÉE NATIONALE to give it a

vote of confidence by attaching particular importance to a specified PROJET DE LOI. If no MOTION DE CENSURE successfully follows within 24 hours, it is considered that the DÉPUTÉS have asserted their confidence in the government. No government has lost a vote of confidence in the CINQUIÈME RÉPUBLIQUE.

VOTE PAR PROCURATION
An elector can appoint a proxy to cast a vote on his or her behalf if for any reason, it is not possible to reach the polling station. The formalities have to be completed in advance, in the presence of a MAGISTRAT or an officer of the POLICE JUDICIAIRE.

VSD See: *VENDREDI, SAMEDI, DIMANCHE*

VSN See: *VOLONTAIRES DU SERVICE NATIONAL*

VUITTON, LOUIS
A manufacturer of fashionable baggage since 1854, a member of the *Comité* COLBERT, and now part of the LVMH group.

WAECHTER, ANTOINE (1949–　)
The leader of *Les* VERTS, and one of their members in the
European Parliament since 1989. Waechter was a candidate in
the 1988 ÉLECTION PRÉSIDENTIELLE, polling 3.01 per cent of the
vote in the first round.

WALLIS-ET-FUTUNA
An island TERRITOIRE D'OUTRE-MER in the South Pacific, with a
population of 13,705. The two main archipelagos take their
name from the principal volcanic islands Wallis and Futuna,
and have been under French control since 1887, although
occupied by the USA from 1942 to 1946. Previously a
protectorate, Wallis-et-Futuna took TOM status in 1961. The
local administration combines the normal TOM provision of a
Conseil territorial and an *Assemblée territoriale* with the
traditional control exercised by local chieftains and royalty.
  The economy is largely based on agriculture, with
predominant products being bananas, tropical fruits and pigs.
Agreements with Japan and Korea exist to allow fishing rights
within 200 miles.

WALINE, MARCEL (1900–1982)
An expert in financial and constitutional law who wrote many
legal treatises including *Traité de science et de législation
financière* (1951), taught in the law faculty in Paris and from
1971 was a member of the CONSEIL CONSTITUTIONNEL.

WEIL, ANDRÉ (1906–　)
A mathematician of international renown, a specialist in
algebraic geometry whose main book is *Basic Number Theory*.
Weil has lived in the USA since 1958.

WEISS, LOUISE (1893–1983)
A writer and politician from an upper-class Jewish-Protestant background who passed the AGRÉGATION at the age of 21, became a nurse during the First World War and founded the political review *L'Europe nouvelle* in 1918. She travelled widely, wrote novels and other books, often emphasising the European theme. In later life she was a member of the European Parliament.

WINCKLER, PAUL (1898–1982)
A press publisher whose main interest was in BANDES DESSINÉES. From 1929 he co-operated with Walt Disney, and published *Le Journal de Mickey* from 1934. At one period he was the owner of FRANCE-SOIR.

X

A nickname for the ÉCOLE POLYTECHNIQUE or for its students and former students.

XENAKIS, IANNIS (1922–   )

A Greek-born composer of electronic music, in which computer-produced sound is interwoven with that made by traditional instruments. A pupil of MESSIAEN, Xenakis has composed avant-garde works such as *Diamorphoses* (1958) and *Nuits* (1967).

YACINE, KATEB (1929–1989)

A French and Algerian writer of journalism, novels, poetry and plays, fluent in French and Arabic. His best known novel is Nedjina (1956). In 1987 Yacine was awarded the *Grand Prix national des lettres*. He remained a staunch supporter of Stalin.

YONNE

A DÉPARTEMENT in the BOURGOGNE region, named after the tributary of the SEINE which runs through it, and with a 1990 population of 323,026. The CHEF-LIEU is Auxerre (urban area 42,005), which has a wide range of light industry, including wood trades, metal processing, engineering, machine-tools, electrical construction, book production and clothing. Other centres of population, each given here with examples of their different industries include Migennes (13,321) – boilermaking, industrial sheet metals, signalling equipment, safety equipment, electronics, plastic packaging and food-processing; Sens (33,621) – engineering, smelting, boilermaking, transport equipment, flour-milling, camping equipment and printing. Other smaller towns have the same rich diversity of industrial activity.

Maize, barley, wheat and sugar beet are the principal agricultural crops. Wine is also produced (including *Chablis*) and dairy and beef cattle and forestry also contribute to the economy.

The tourist industry is quite important, and its attractions include a number of châteaux, prehistoric remains, the *Parc régional du Morvan*, lakes, canals and rivers, as well as the basilica at Vézelay, a place of pilgrimage.

A marginal majority in the Yonne for François MITTERRAND in the 1981 ÉLECTION PRÉSIDENTIELLE was slightly increased in

1988, whereas the parliamentary representation shows a balance between Left and Right. In the 1992 ÉLECTIONS CANTONALES, there was hardly any change in the Centre Right's control of the CONSEIL RÉGIONAL, with Socialists and Communists retaining their strength in their own traditional areas of support.

Code départemental: 89

YOURCENAR, MARGUERITE (1903–1987)

The anagrammatic pseudonym of Marguerite de Crayencour, a novelist who became a naturalised American in 1947, but took French nationality again in 1979 in order to become the first woman to enter the ACADÉMIE FRANÇAISE. Her *L'Œuvre au noir* won the *Prix* FÉMINA in 1968, and her best-seller is *Les Mémoires d'Hadrien* (1951). She also published poetry, including *La Nouvelle Eurydice* (1931). In 1977 she was awarded the *Grand Prix de littérature de l'Académie française.*

YVELINES

A DÉPARTEMENT of the ÎLE-DE-FRANCE region, formed in 1964, partly composed of the western outer suburbs of Greater Paris, partly the industrialised Seine valley and partly the remains of the ancient forest area, from which the *Département* derives its name. The 1990 population of the Yvelines was 1.3 million. The CHEF-LIEU is Versailles (87,789), with light industries but mainly important for administrative reasons, and the site of the royal palace. Other major centres of population are Conflans-Sainte-Honorine (31,467) – river-boat building; Élancourt (22,584); Houilles (29,650); la-Celle-Saint-Cloud (22,834); le Chesnay (29,542); Maisons-Laffitte (22,168); Mantes-la-Jolie (189,103) – cementworks, cooperative distribution of cereals, rubber, aeronautics, motor industry, (including the RENAULT factory at Flins) and a railway freight centre; Montigny-le-Bretonneux (31,687); Plaisir (25,877); Poissy (36,745), with PEUGEOT car works; Rambouillet (24,443); Saint-Germain-en-Laye (39,926); SAINT-QUENTIN-EN-YVELINES, a VILLE NOUVELLE (120,559); Sartrouville (50,329); Trappes (30,878); and Vélizy-Villacoublay (20,725). Many of these COMMUNES are dormitory areas for Paris. There is a steelworks at Bonnières-sur-Seine.

Fruit, vegetables and cereals are important agricultural products.

Because of the position of Versailles, the Yvelines contains a number of other residences having royal or aristocratic connections, and these are now major attractions for tourists.

The political make-up of the Yvelines reflects the variety of its population, with representatives in the ASSEMBLÉE NATIONALE, SÉNAT, CONSEIL GÉNÉRAL and CONSEIL RÉGIONAL coming from a wide range of party groupings. In the 1992 ÉLECTIONS CANTONALES, the Centre Right retained its control over the *Département*. In the 1981 ÉLECTION PRÉSIDENTIELLE, Valéry GISCARD D'ESTAING received a marginal majority, increased slightly by Jacques CHIRAC in 1988.

Code départemental: 78

ZAC See: *ZONE D'AMÉNAGEMENT CONCERTÉ*

ZAD See: *ZONE D'AMÉNAGEMENT DIFFÉRÉ*

ZEHRFUSS, BERNARD (1911–   )
An architect whose reputation was made by his designs for
major public buildings in Paris such as the *Palais de
l'UNESCO*, the CENTRE NATIONAL DES INDUSTRIES ET DES
TECHNIQUES, and the PALAIS OMNISPORTS PARIS-BERCY.

ZEP See: *ZONE D'ENVIRONNEMENT PROTÉGÉ*

ZIDI, CLAUDE (1934–   )
A film director whose amusing and popular films are often seen
on French television, among them, *L'Aile ou la cuisse* (1976),
Les Ripoux (1984) and *Ripoux contre Ripoux* (1990).

ZIF See: *ZONE D'INTERVENTION FONCIÈRE*

ZONE À RÉGIME PRÉFÉRENTIEL
An area designated for industrial redevelopment. Businesses
which set up plants in the zones, thereby creating jobs are
given special tax advantages, grants (such as the *Prime
d'aménagement du territoire*) and other support. See also:
DÉLÉGATION À L'AMÉNAGEMENT DU TERRITOIRE ET À L'ACTION
RÉGIONALE; ZONE FRANCHE

ZONE À URBANISER EN PRIORITÉ (ZUP)
A development zone in an AGGLOMÉRATION which includes
residential, commercial and industrial projects planned at the
instigation of a COLLECTIVITÉ LOCALE. The ZUP scheme has been
replaced by the ZONE D'AMÉNAGEMENT CONCERTÉ.

ZONE BLEUE
A controlled parking area in a town. The *Zone bleue* in Paris lasted from 1957 to 1981.

ZONE D'AMÉNAGEMENT CONCERTÉ (ZAC)
A similar scheme to the ZONE À URBANISER EN PRIORITÉ which it replaced. Development within the ZAC has to be consistent with its overall plan, which can be wholly developed by a public authority or in collaboration with private interests. It is also possible for a private individual or business to have a contract for the development.

ZONE D'AMÉNAGEMENT DIFFÉRÉ (ZAD)
A designated area within a town in which for a period up to 14 years, the public authorities have priority rights of purchase when premises or land become available.

ZONE D'ENVIRONNEMENT PROTÉGÉ (ZEP)
A measure in force between 1977 and 1983, replaced by the PLAN D'OCCUPATION DES SOLS, and which was designed to ensure the conservation of rural buildings and landscape from new development.

ZONE DE PEUPLEMENT INDUSTRIEL OU URBAIN (ZPIU)
A classification of COMMUNES which are either entirely urbanised or partly so. Ninety per cent of the population live in a ZPIU.

ZONE D'INTERVENTION FONCIÈRE (ZIF)
An area in a COMMUNE of more than 10,000 inhabitants wherein the COLLECTIVITÉ LOCALE had priority rights of purchase at market price of land to provide public green spaces, a LOGEMENT SOCIAL, or for some other beneficial purpose. The ZIF arrangements have been replaced by the *Droit de préemption urbaine* (DPU).

ZONE FRANC
The world monetary zone where the Franc is regarded as the principal measure. It comprises France, the DOM and TOM, MAYOTTE, Monaco, and the countries of the COMMUNAUTÉ FINANCIÈRE AFRICAINE.

ZONE FRANCHE

An area which has been exempted from the payment of certain taxes. These can be to allow for the circumstances of FRONTALIERS, or to encourage industrial or commercial development (e.g. the reductions in TAXE PROFESSIONNELLE in a ZONE À RÉGIME PRÉFÉRENTIEL).

ZONE ROUGE See: *MEUSE*

ZPIU See: *ZONE DE PEUPLEMENT INDUSTRIEL OU URBAIN*

ZUP See: *ZONE À URBANISER EN PRIORITÉ*

Bibliography

There is a wide range of material available on modern France, from annual statistical publications to more personal views on various aspects of the country. This select list gives details of some of the works consulted in compiling this dictionary and which would be worthy of further study for more detailed treatment of the topics.

I have excluded from the list the daily press and news periodicals, because the range is so vast. Publications regularly updated on an annual or more occasional basis are often an excellent point of reference, however.

The most comprehensive publication, although restricted in the amount of detail it can provide on any one topic, is the invaluable Fremy, D. and Fremy, M. (eds) *Quid*, which appears annually, published by Robert Laffont. It even warrants an entry of its own in the dictionary.

Also appearing on a regular basis are:

Masurel, E. *L'Année dans 'Le monde'* (Folio)
Raphanel, S. and Vert, B. *Le Guide des formalités* (Prat/ Europa)
Verdie, M. (ed). *L'État de la France et de ses habitants* (La Découverte)

Modern and Contemporary France, the quarterly journal of the Association for the Study of Modern and Contemporary France (from 1993, published by Longman) is available by subscription and in academic libraries.

Books on specific areas are listed below:

Ardagh, J. *France Today* (Penguin, 1988)

Buss, R. *The French Through Their Films* (Batsford, 1988)

Cox, C. *A Pocket Dictionary of Contemporary France* (Berg, 1988)

Dang, R (ed). *Guide des métiers de l'enseignement* (Hachette, 1991)

De Gunten, R., Martin, A. and Niogret, M. *Les Institutions de la France* (Nathan, 1988)

Fell, M. and Bossuyt, D. *Guide du citoyen aujourd'hui* (Hachette, 1988)

Flower, J. E. (ed.) *France Today*, 7th edn (rev.) (Hodder & Stoughton, 1993)

Froment, R. and Lerat, R. *La France* (three volumes, Bréal, 1989)

Hanley, D. L., Kerr, A. P. and Waites N. H. *Contemporary France – Politics and Society Since 1945* (Routledge & Kegan Paul, 1984)

Howorth, J. and Ross, G. (eds). *Contemporary France* (three volumes, Pinter, 1987, 1988, 1989)

Labrune, G. *La Géographie de la France* (Nathan, 1988)

Lewis, H. D. *The French Education System* (Croom Helm, 1985)

McCarthy, P. (ed). *The French Socialists in Power 1981–1986* (Greenwood Press, 1987)

Mantoux, T. *BCBG – Le Guide du bon chic bon genre* (Hermé, 1985)

Mazey, S. and Newman, M. (eds). *Mitterrand's France* (Croom Helm, 1987)

Michaud, G. and Kimmel, A. *Le Nouveau Guide France* (Hachette, 1990)

Monnerie, A. (ed). *En France aujourd'hui: idées, arts, spectacles* (Clé international, 1987)

Union fédérale des consommateurs, *Guide des démarches administratives* (1990)

Wright, V. *The Government and Politics of France* (Hutchinson, 1989)